Brief contents

T0334061

Contents

***Introduction to Financial and Management Accounting,*
First Edition**

Publisher: Annabel Ainscow

List Manager: Jenny Grene

Marketing Manager: Sophie Clarke

Senior Content Project Manager: Phillipa Davidson-Blake

Manufacturing Manager: Eyvett Davis

Typesetter: SPi GLobal

Cover Design: Infuze

Cover Image: ©iStock.com/alenchi

© 2019, Cengage Learning EMEA

ALL RIGHTS RESERVED. No part of this work covered by the copyright herein may be reproduced or distributed in any form or by any means, except as permitted by U.S. copyright law, without the prior written permission of the copyright owner.

For product information and technology assistance, contact us at **emea.info@cengage.com**

For permission to use material from this text or product and for permission queries, email **emea.permissions@cengage.com**

British Library Cataloguing-in-Publication Data

A catalogue record for this book is available from the British Library.

ISBN: 978-1-4737-6434-7

Cengage Learning, EMEA
Cheriton House, North Way
Andover, Hampshire, SP10 5BE
United Kingdom

Cengage Learning is a leading provider of customized learning solutions with employees residing in nearly 40 different countries and sales in more than 125 countries around the world. Find your local representative at: **www.cengage.co.uk**.

Cengage Learning products are represented in Canada by Nelson Education, Ltd.

For your course and learning solutions, visit **www.cengage.co.uk**.

Purchase any of our products at your local college store or at our preferred online store **www.cengagebrain.com**.

ed in the United Kingdom by Ashford Colour Press
Number: 01   Print Year: 2019

INTRODUCTION TO FINANCIAL AND MANAGEMENT ACCOUNTI

FIRST EDITION

Cengage EMEA

 CENGAGE

Australia • Brazil • Mexico • Singapore • United Kingdom • United States

Preface

Introduction to Financial Accounting

Every business in the world, be it large or small, uses the same system of bookkeeping. An accountant in India will record transactions in exactly the same way as an accountant in Edinburgh. This is the universal application of financial accounting and anyone who becomes skilled in its application will be able to prepare and understand a set of accounts.

Financial Accounting can be a complex subject. At one level it is bound by all sorts of rules and legal requirements which instruct the accountants in how they must prepare a set of financial statements of, say, a large multi-national company. At a fundamental level it will enable the accountant to record day to day transactions in a set of accounting records so any business, however large, can keep track of its financial position.

Life has got much easier for the financial accountants since the advent of computerized accounting systems. These systems will make sure the books balance and will faithfully record whatever you put into them. However this is merely the mechanics—it is the understanding of the principles that is important and the knowledge of how to record what needs to be done to adjust the numbers in the books so that they relate to the financial period under review.

This series of modules will teach you about the range and purpose of financial accounting, will teach you basic double entry bookkeeping, how to make sure that the books balance and how to show the true financial position of the business.

These modules do not go into any detail about complex accounting issues relating to accounting standards, nor do they cover the accounts of complex entities such as groups of companies or partnerships.

Instead they do what it says on the tin—provide a good solid grounding in basic accounting techniques to enable the learner to go from no knowledge at all through to being able to prepare a set of financial statements for a business or organization.

They also include some additional skills training in useful topics such as managing cash in a business, analyzing a set of financial statements to identify problem areas, and how to finance a business. There are questions to enable you to practice your skills and full explanations of all the key issues involved in basic accounting practice.

Once these skills are mastered you will be equipped to tackle some of the more specialized areas of accounting, but the skills you learn here will provide the foundation for the future and will continue to be relevant throughout all your future studies.

Introduction to Management Accounting

Management accounting is one of the key areas of business operations at a practical level. It enables managers to calculate a price for goods and services, it assists in costing processes and production, it is concerned with budgets and forecasting and it enables accountants to see where it all went wrong—or right. It is concerned not simply with counting the past but also with looking ahead and deciding the pathways the business or organization might follow in the future.

It is a tool which provides hard financial information to aid planning and decision making in a business or organization.

As with all skills it is one learned gradually; for example some of the concepts and techniques applied to the measurement of production processes can be complicated and, to some extent, require experience and knowledge but all the complex processes of management accounting are built on a foundation of key principles and skills.

It is these key skills which this course will teach you.

It begins at the beginning with the concepts of cost—something which might be a bit more complicated than you might imagine. How do costs behave? How do they grow and how do we measure them? How do we decide what our breakeven point is, what our profit is or, indeed, how much we should charge for our product or service? Should we accept this contract? Will this venture make us any money? What will our result be next year? What might go wrong and what will the effect be if it does?

All these are questions for the management accountant and all are rooted in the skills and concepts within these ten modules.

This course will teach you the basic concepts of cost accounting. It will enable you to evaluate a capital investment and will introduce you to some wider concepts such as transfer pricing and how to maximize value.

The principles learned on this course will apply throughout any further learning in management accounting. The concepts are universal and are applied every day in businesses all over the world. They are fundamental to business and every manager or entrepreneur should be familiar with these key principles and techniques.

Contributors

John R. Taylor

MSc, FCA

John Taylor has taught accounting and auditing at Leeds Beckett University and before this was a professional auditor for many years. He is the author of various successful auditing, accounting and finance books and currently works as a freelance writer and lecturer in auditing, accounting and management. John Taylor is the lead contributor to this course and his clear and accessible writing style makes this reading a unique and valuable resource.

Liz Crookes

University of Derby

Liz Crookes trained as a Management Accountant qualifying with CIMA and spent several years working in industry before moving into teaching professional courses and finally teaching full-time at the University of Derby. Liz undertook a thorough review of this reading and contributed to the online course materials.

Tony Abdoush

PhD, MSc

Bournemouth University

Tony Abdoush undertook a review of this reading before contributing to the online course materials.

MINDTAP
From Cengage

Fit your coursework into your hectic life.

Make the most of your time by learning your way. Access the resources you need to succeed wherever, whenever.

 Study with interactive tools and resources designed to help you master key concepts and prepare you for class.

 Review your current course grade and compare your progress with your peers.

 Get the free MindTap Mobile App and learn wherever you are.

Break Limitations. Create your own potential, and be unstoppable with MindTap.

MINDTAP. POWERED BY YOU.

cengage.co.uk/education/Mindtap

Introduction to Financial Accounting

PART I

1 Business entities and the need for information

In this module we will consider:

- Types of business entity
- Stakeholders and their interests
- Financial performance and social responsibility
- Agency theory
- Accounting objectives of an organization
- Accounting systems and the organization
- Professional accountancy bodies and the preparation of accounts
- Management accounts and financial accounts
- The Management Information System (MIS)
- Outline of purchases, revenues and payroll systems

Types of business entity

There are many types of business entity ranging from the smallest (a self-employed person) to the largest. In the UK this would be a publicly listed entity known as a public limited company (or 'plc' for short), which is permitted to, but does not have to, have its shares listed on a recognized stock exchange. In other countries there are different forms of company organization, which are too extensive to be listed here.

Stop and think	What are the types of business entity in your country? What laws govern the operations of those entities?

Business entities broadly fall into two types:

1 one that is comprised of people, such as a sole trader business or a partnership
2 one that is a company, which is a legal entity in its own right and is independent of the people who own and run it

Sole traders are small businesses such as tradespeople, plumbers, electricians, small shopkeepers, etc. They work for themselves, keep all their profits and pay tax based on their financial result at the year's end. There are few rules governing sole traders and such businesses are easy to start and stop. In many cases they require little or no investment to set up and are only limited by the amount of effort, skill and time contributed by the individual. Business decisions are made by the individual.

Partnerships are really just a group of sole traders working together in a common business. Partnerships generally are governed by a partnership agreement, which sets out key principles such as:

- how profits are to be shared
- how much capital partners should contribute
- procedures for settling disputes, introducing new partners, etc.

Business decisions can be taken collectively, and partners can bring expertise into the business, thus broadening its scope.

The main problem with these types of business entity is liability for losses. Clearly a sole trader is totally responsible for any losses incurred, as are the partners in a partnership. However in partnership, losses are 'joint and several,' which means that each partner is responsible for the losses of all the other partners; if there are four partners and one can pay and three can't, that one has to shoulder all the losses.

Companies, including limited liability partnerships, are legal entities, which means that they have the capacity to take part in legal actions, to sue and be sued. A company, once set up, goes on until it is liquidated; there are some companies that are several hundred years old. The company is independent of the shareholders who own it and the managers who manage it. Companies are, however, subject to lots of rules and regulations. The owners and directors and their financial statements are a matter of public record.

The main difference between the two types of business organization is limited liability.

LIMITED LIABILITY   Limited liability means that the liability for losses of any owner of a business is limited to their investment in the business. Consequently, if they have invested only £1 in a business their liability for losses is £1 and, in theory, they can simply walk away from any additional losses incurred. However, it is sometimes not quite as simple as that, as we will see later.

Figure 1.1 below summarizes the various types of business entity.

Figure 1.1 Trading organizations

Entity	Key features
Sole trader	Self-employed business owner. No requirement to file accounts so they can be accessed by the public. Accounts needed only for tax purposes.
Partnership	Two or more individuals operating a business jointly. Similar filing and tax rules to sole trader.
Limited liability partnership (LLP)	Similar to a company. It is a partnership which has limited liability. It must file accounts on a public record. Commonly used by large firms of accountants and lawyers.
Limited company (Ltd)	Company in private ownership owned by shareholders and managed by directors. Minimum share capital is £1. Must comply with Companies Legislation. Financial statements must be filed on a public record.
Public limited company (Plc)	Company with shares available to be bought by the public. Often has minimum share capital requirement. Can be listed on a stock exchange. Must comply with Companies Legislation and, if listed, with a stock exchange listing agreement.

Stakeholders and their interests

When people think of accounts they often simply think of the annual financial statements. When asked who uses these accounts, typical replies are:

- the management
- shareholders or owners
- the tax authorities

and there the list often ends.

However there are many more stakeholders than this, and all of them have some use for financial information. So who are the stakeholders in an organization?

A stakeholder can be defined as anyone who has some sort of financial or other interest in the business. Clearly this widens the potential list of information users quite considerably, as Figure 1.2 below shows.

Figure 1.2
Stakeholders in the business

Stop and think   Who are the stakeholders in your or your employer's business? What information do they need:

a. frequently?
b. periodically?

INFORMATION NEEDS OF STAKEHOLDERS

What sort of financial information do these stakeholders need?

Some need detailed day-to-day information, while some need only periodic information. For example, a shareholder in a listed plc might be happy with a set of accounts once a year and a dividend cheque, whereas the management of that plc will want regular management accounting information about the performance of the business on a daily basis.

Many stakeholders require a combination of detailed information and periodic information. For example, employees want their wages and salaries correctly calculated and paid to them on time with a payslip, but they also have an interest in the financial health of their employer, so would be interested in the annual financial accounts.

Requirements can be summarized as in Figure 1.3:

Figure 1.3 Information needs of different stakeholders

Stakeholder	Relevant information
Staff	Wages information, bonus and overtime. Annual accounts.
Owners/shareholders	Information to monitor their investment such as profit statements, annual accounts, etc.
Suppliers	Invoice processing and cheque payments. Information about ability to pay sums owed.
Customers	Sales invoicing, banking of monies and debt collection.
Lenders	Information to enable them to assess the ability of the business to repay and the value of any security for borrowings.
Management	Budgets and management accounting information about how the business is performing.
Government	Taxes, VAT, economic statistics.
Community	Effect on local community, e.g. sponsorship information, employment statistics, etc.

The accounting information system or Management Information System (MIS) must be able to produce all this information.

Note that not all information has to be financial. It could be quantitative information, giving details of units of output, numbers employed, delivery times, etc.

EXAMPLE

You have been approached to become a major supplier to Wibbly Ltd, a large and growing manufacturing company. They have been a customer of yours for some years but have only placed orders from time to time. These orders have been increasing in size recently and they are now proposing that you enter into a monthly supply contract with them.

If you do they promise much larger orders, which would help to grow your business, but they want to extend the credit period from 45 days to 60 days.

REQUIRED

What information would you require before you entered into this sort of commitment?

ANSWER

Your business objective is to grow your own business by increased trade.

Your financial objective is to avoid the risk of a big bad debt if Wibbly cannot pay.

(continued)

You would need reassurance, as a minimum, as to:

- What is the maximum credit exposure you could have with Wibbly?
- What effect might this have on your business if it became a bad debt?
- How strong is Wibbly's cash flow? Does it want to extend the credit period because of cash flow difficulties?
- What is Wibbly's trading situation? Are its markets healthy and is Wibbly's customer base sound?
- What other commitments does Wibbly have on a regular basis; for example, interest on borrowings?
- Was there a previous supplier for these goods? If so who was it and what was their experience of dealing with Wibbly?

You would expect Wibbly to supply most of this information to you so you can make an informed business decision.

Stop and think   Imagine that have been left some money and wish to invest it in a local business. What information would you need to find out about the business before you committed your money?

THE ANNUAL REPORT

Every company is required by law to send accounts to its shareholders.

Module 2 outlines the legal framework which requires this to be done, but the underlying reason is obvious: the shareholders need to have an accounting of what their managers, the directors, have been doing during the year and how successful (or otherwise) they have been.

Companies Legislation and International Accounting Standards (Module 6) set out the format for the Income Statement and the Statement of Financial Position. It does this for two reasons:

- to ensure that all the information shareholders need is included in the accounts
- to ensure that the accounts of different companies are comparable with each other

Company directors are thus not allowed to include, or omit, information from the accounts that might disguise the real financial situation of the business.

Stop and think   If you work for a public company (plc), try and obtain a set of accounts and review how the Income Statement and Statement of Financial Position are set out.

If you don't work for a plc, you can obtain a set of accounts from a library, from the Internet or by contacting a listed public company directly.

What other statements are included in these accounts?

Financial performance and social responsibility

A business does not operate in isolation. The lives of its employees, the businesses of its customers and suppliers and even the community in which it operates are all affected by it to a greater or lesser extent.

When a major employer closes down, the area immediately around it can be severely affected. This has been experienced in many countries, for example, with the loss of traditional manufacturing industries such as mining, steel production and heavy engineering. This decline has had an enormous impact on the economies of the affected areas and the lives of the people who live there.

In the immediate locality increased unemployment means reduced spending, which has a knock-on effect on local shops and leisure facilities. If suppliers to the business don't get paid, their businesses will suffer adverse cash flow effects and they may even be driven out of business in turn. Banks lose money and tighten up lending policies; shareholders who see the value of their investment disappear become reluctant to invest again.

Conversely, when businesses do well, the effect on the wider community is just the opposite. Successful businesses generate new skills and new optimism in their locality, new small businesses spring up, new markets are created and employees and their families have money to spend.

A business thus has a much wider social responsibility than might, at first, be thought, and it is important that the social context in which the business operates is considered to be as important as the market for its goods and services.

Stop and think	What effect did the decision by Nissan to site a manufacturing facility have on the North East region of England? Is there a similar example of either a success or a failure in your area which affected a local community?

Agency theory

Imagine the development of a firm from a small family-owned business to a multinational entity. As the business grows in size, the capacity of one individual or a small group of individuals to manage it declines, and they have to take on help to assist them in both the day-to-day tasks and in devising business strategies for the future.

They need to import skills of accounting, selling, production, they take on more staff, need supervisors, line managers and ultimately have to share power with a board of directors. As the business grows in size and complexity, the role of these managers increases with it to the extent that they are, effectively, running it. When the business raises money by selling shares to outside shareholders, the original owner's interest becomes more and more diluted until the business is owned, effectively, by strangers who see it as an investment not a lifestyle.

Here lies the root of agency theory. The managers or directors are agents for the investors or shareholders, known as principals.

The managers or directors of the business are entrusted with the principals' money, and their role, it is hoped, is:

- to use that investment to create profits that the principals could receive by way of dividend
- to expand that initial capital on behalf of the principals, increasing the value of their investment
- to preserve the assets of the business
- to act always in the best interests of their principals

In return the agents should receive suitable remuneration, concomitant with their status and their level of success in making money for their principals. Thus, everybody should get something out of the arrangement—or so it seems.

In fact, things don't always work out quite as well as might have been anticipated because, as usual, human nature gets in the way.

Agency theory holds that agents do not, necessarily, take decisions in the best interests of their principals. It states that the objectives or goals of principals and agents mostly conflict and, where they do, agents will, naturally, make the choice which benefits themselves the most, choices which may not be the most beneficial decision for the principal. This can be summarized quite simply in Figure 1.4.

Figure 1.4 **Agency theory—differing expectations**

Party	What their expectations are
Principal	• Safe investment
	• Regular dividends
	• Long-term capital growth
	• Maintenance of the value of the business
Agent	• Salary and benefits
	• Maximum bonus
	• Share options
	• Personal success of successful business measured by share price

Agency theory is a relatively simple principle to grasp, but its ramifications are extensive and they have important implications for how organizations conduct themselves and their operational culture.

REAL WORLD
Agency theory—the view from the accountancy profession

The Institute of Chartered Accountants in England & Wales, in November 2006 noted that the 'poor principal' requires high levels of compensation for agents, assuming that no agents can be trusted and that they are likely to attempt to use their principal's assets to make themselves more money.

The ICAEW places importance on independent audits with regard to agents and you can find more out about this here: www.icaew.com/

One of the key differences between principals and agents is the different views of the time horizon each party holds. It is not difficult to envisage that agents incline less towards long-term rewards than do owners. Whilst their rewards might, indeed should, be performance-related, the period over which performance improvement is measured is often relatively short—often only one financial accounting period—so agents can benefit greatly from short-term profitability which may create an illusion of growth rather than real, underlying, organic development.

The extent to which principals don't trust their agents will tend to govern the level of the monitoring mechanisms principals need to create an overview of their agents' activities. This has a direct effect on the establishment of financial systems and reporting mechanisms within the organization.

The relevance of agency theory to financial reporting is that principals need to be sure that such financial information as they do receive in the way of annual financial statements and (for listed companies) quarterly bulletins, is reliable and has not been distorted by the management in an attempt to 'improve' the financial position of the organization, thus increasing their own rewards.

In addition, potential investors need reliable financial information on which to base investment decisions.

Consequently, financial accounting, as opposed to management accounting, is all about producing an historical summary of transactions ordered in such a way that the actions of agents are made accountable to their principals.

Accounting objectives of an organization

There are two key points to remember when considering accounting objectives:

1 Accounting objectives are linked to wider business or organizational objectives.
2 Accounting objectives are linked to stakeholder needs and their objectives.

We have already briefly considered the varying needs of stakeholders and we will look further at the links between business and accounting objectives later. The main accounting objectives of a business are based on the principle of generating information which is:

- accurate
- relevant
- on time
- understandable
- complete
- reliable
- comparable between accounting periods

The system must function efficiently enough to produce the varying kinds and levels of information stakeholders need on a day-to-day basis.

In addition to the production of financial information, the financial or accounting systems must also deal with the day-to-day tasks involved in running the business. For example:

- suppliers need to be paid
- money from customers needs to be collected and banked
- financial records need to be updated daily
- salaries and wages must be calculated and employees paid
- taxes must be calculated and paid to the revenue authorities

In some ways these objectives are the most important ones as, unless the business can meet its day-to-day requirements, its longer term goals will remain unachieved.

Accounting information systems should be designed in such a way as to both record and to produce information that is accurate, timely and relevant and that meets the objectives of both general stakeholders and business management.

Accounting systems and the organization

The accounting system and the information that goes in and flows out of it is the responsibility of the finance function within the organization. This function, however it is described, has the responsibility for producing not only financial information for management but also for dealing with the day-to-day processing of transactions.

This function should be ranked in equal importance to other areas of the business, such as sales or production.

In the context of a typical organizational structure, the finance function sits alongside other operating departments within the organization.

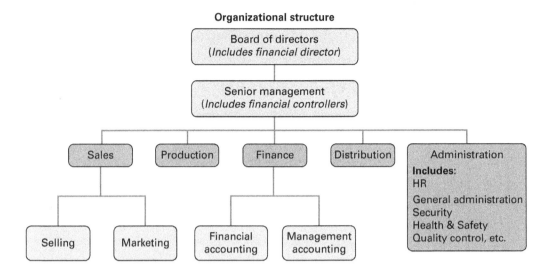

The finance function is usually represented by a financial director who sits on the main board of directors. Below the financial director will be a range of accountants and other staff. The financial director will usually have a professional qualification, as may some of the other accountants in functional areas within the department. A large finance function might look like this:

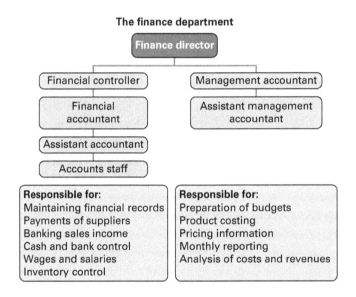

Clearly, the numbers of accountants and accounts staff is very much dependent upon the size of the organization. Very small businesses and charities might have only a part time bookkeeper and a bespoke accounts package running on a single PC, whereas a large manufacturing business might have teams of accountants running separate functions within the department, producing both financial and management information.

Professional accountancy bodies and the preparation of accounts

Most financial directors and senior accountants are members of a professional body.

These are organizations that have the responsibility of overseeing the regulation of the accounting profession and the maintenance of professional standards.

In the UK they are:

- Institute of Chartered Accountants in England and Wales (ICAEW)
- Institute of Chartered Accountants of Scotland (ICAS)
- Institute of Chartered Accountants in Ireland
- Association of Chartered Certified Accountants (ACCA)
- Chartered Institute of Management Accountants (CIMA)
- Chartered Institute of Public Finance and Accountancy (CIPFA)
- Association of Accounting Technicians (AAT)

Some of these bodies, principally ACCA and CIMA, are internationally recognized and there are similar bodies in most other countries.

Members of these organizations work in different sectors and at different levels within the accountancy profession as a whole, but all of them have in common:

- a code of ethics by which members must abide
- a code of professional behaviour to which members must adhere
- a duty of care and confidentiality towards information
- a disciplinary procedure for enforcing standards

Most of these bodies also have a system of continuing professional education (CPE) to ensure technical standards are maintained. This is also known as CPD (Continuous Professional Development).

> **Stop and think**   Look at the finance function within your own organization or place of study.
>
> What is its structure? How does it fit within the overall organizational structure?

Management accounts and financial accounts

At this point it might be useful to draw the distinction between management and financial accounts.

Financial accounts are basically used for reporting. They include the accounts that are sent to shareholders and other stakeholders. They are often produced periodically within an organization but, because they are reporting what has passed, they are of limited value as a management tool.

Management accounts are used by the management as an aid to managing the business. Management accounts include budgets and forecasts, as well as analyses of actual performance against those budgets.

Figure 1.5 summarises the differences.

Figure 1.5 Difference between financial and management accounts

	Financial accounts	Management accounts
Scope	Defined by statute	Decided by management
Format	As set out in Companies Act 2005	In format suitable for management decision-making
Reporting on	Historical data	Future and historical data
Checked by third parties	Yes—audited (subject to size)	No
Used by	Owners and other stakeholders	Management and internal users

The Management Information System (MIS)

The Management Information System (MIS) is designed to produce the financial information the company needs in order to control and manage its financial affairs.

The systems fit together like this:

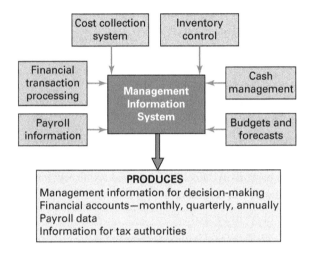

Note at this point that we are referring to a system. This means that information is recorded in a system and the system produces reports and statistics as required. We are not referring to situations where management collects information and produces reports using, say, spreadsheets, which are not part of the system.

WHAT IS THE FUNCTION OF THE MIS?   There are three basic functions:

- Recording—to provide financial data for reporting
- Planning—to provide information to help management plan and make decisions
- Control—to provide information useful to management in the management and control of the organization

Every business has its own information requirements. The more complex the business, the more information will be required; therefore, the MIS tends to be more complex and serve more functions in bigger organizations.

Here are some examples of how the MIS evolves as the business grows and the information requirements of managers grow accordingly.

SMALL BUSINESSES—RECORDING   The primary function of the MIS is one of recording information. In the smallest organizations, this tends to be about as far as the system goes.

Transactions are recorded on a daily basis and summarized periodically into a set of historical accounts. These are used primarily for tax purposes if the business is a sole trader or small partnership.

Primary financial control is based on the bank balance as cash is the key driver of the business.

Data can be prepared and stored on a PC using a bespoke accounts package such as QuickBooks or Sage 1.

MORE COMPLEX BUSINESS—RECORDING AND CONTROL   Once the organization becomes more complex additional information is required to assist in controlling the business.

This might consist of reports about inventory levels, age of debts, cash balances, all still based on historical information. In addition, a basic costing system may be introduced. Reports may be produced weekly or monthly.

They will provide information about outstanding liabilities the business may have, and outstanding debts still to be collected.

Data will require more complex financial processing software and there will begin to be the distinction between financial processing of day-to-day transactions and the recording of management information such as budgets. This is to facilitate the production of management accounts.

EXAMPLE

You are the advisor to the owner and manager of a business that buys chocolates and sweets in bulk and repackages them in small quantities for hotels and conference centres using their 'own name' packaging.

The business employs an accountant and two bookkeepers to maintain the financial records, but you make all the management decisions. Your accountant produces a set of accounts at the end of each month comprising a profit and loss account and a balance sheet showing the result for the month and the cumulative financial position for the year to date.

At the end of each financial year, the accountant produces a set of annual accounts and these are audited.

REQUIRED

The owner/manager has decided that this is not sufficient for her to make management decisions and has asked you to advise at a meeting to be held next week. What points would you make to your client?

ANSWER

You would wish to make the following points as a minimum:

- Financial accounts are of limited use for decision-making, as they only report on what has already happened.
- The business should create a budget and measure itself against that. This can be developed together with overall business objectives.
- The financial accounts don't give any indication on the profitability of individual products. Information about costs and revenues for each product would be useful.
- The budget can be used to control levels of expenditure on overheads, which at the moment are uncontrolled.
- Quantitative information might be useful; for example, showing a reconciliation of the quantities of goods purchased, goods in stock and goods sold.
- Information about cash flows would be useful so a cash budget could be developed. This would enable any surplus cash to be put to use and any borrowings required to be forecast in advance.
- Comparative information would be useful so the business can identify changes from the equivalent month for the previous year.

LARGER BUSINESSES—RECORDING, CONTROL AND PLANNING   The business is in a position to move away from straightforward recording and control information and to introduce planning information into the MIS.

This results in more complex costing analyses, stock control, automatic monitoring against budgets and perhaps daily reporting rather than weekly or monthly reporting.

This requires a full suite of management and financial reporting software and in many cases this will be bespoke to some extent. It may include detailed cost information, such as product costs and pricing, as well as wage analysis and integrated reporting software for financial reporting.

FULLY INTEGRATED SYSTEMS—RECORDING, CONTROL AND PLANNING   The business has integrated all of its systems into an overall management information system.

This incorporates not only the MIS but other systems as well, which are outside the scope of this course.

These might comprise point of sale (POS) recording such as that used by supermarkets, client monitoring for sales and marketing departments, treasury management for investing surplus funds, human resource management, and so on.

The business is highly computer-dependent, with transactions being processed electronically and the use of paper-based procedures kept to a minimum.

Outline of purchases, revenues and payroll systems

Full consideration of each of the key systems for purchasing, recording revenues and processing payroll is outside the scope of this course. However there are two points to note.

All systems have control objectives, i.e. what the system is designed to achieve in terms of the control over transactions.

All systems have within them internal controls to ensure that errors or mistakes are detected as soon as possible and that opportunities for fraud are limited. We will not describe the internal controls in detail, but we will make reference to them. Learners who are interested in learning more about internal controls and systems should look at a manual on auditing.

The reason for including the diagrams of these parts of a financial system is to show how the books of account are integrated and how various systems interact. No system works in isolation. Systems have controls built into them and finance departments spend a good deal of their time monitoring these controls as they process transactions and produce reports.

It would be useful for learners to study these diagrams and familiarize themselves with the outline of these various systems.

Stop and think	Consider one of these systems at your own workplace. Does it work in broadly the same way as the diagram? What internal controls are there? How do they do things differently?
	If you are not in work, can you see any way you might take advantage of these systems? What weaknesses might there be? What would you need to do to circumvent the controls?

PURCHASE SYSTEMS   A purchase system has the following key control objectives (see Figure 1.6):

- To ensure that goods and services are only ordered in the quantity, of the quality, and at the best terms available after appropriate requisition and approval.
- To ensure that goods and services received are inspected and only acceptable items are accepted.
- To ensure that all invoices are checked against authorized orders and receipt of the goods and services in good condition.
- To ensure that all goods and services invoiced are properly recorded in the books.

Figure 1.6 shows the layout of a basic purchases system, most commonly computerized. Internal controls are shown *in italics* on the diagram, but we will not be giving any detailed explanation in the text.

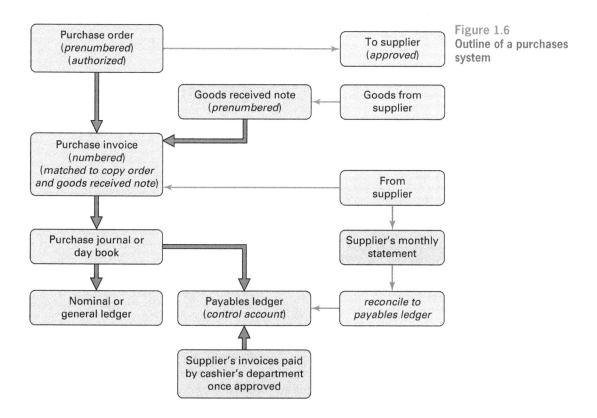

Figure 1.6
Outline of a purchases system

REVENUES   The control objectives of a typical revenues system are:

- to ensure that all customers orders are promptly executed
- to ensure that sales on credit are made only to bona fide good credit risks
- to ensure that all sales on credit are invoiced, that authorized prices are charged and that before issue all invoices are completed and checked as regards price, trade discounts and sales tax
- to ensure that all invoices raised are entered in the books

- to ensure that all customers' claims are fully investigated before credit notes are issued
- to ensure that every effort is made to collect all debts
- to ensure that no unauthorized credits are made to receivables accounts.

Figure 1.7 is the outline of a typical revenues system. Once again, internal controls are indicated in italics.

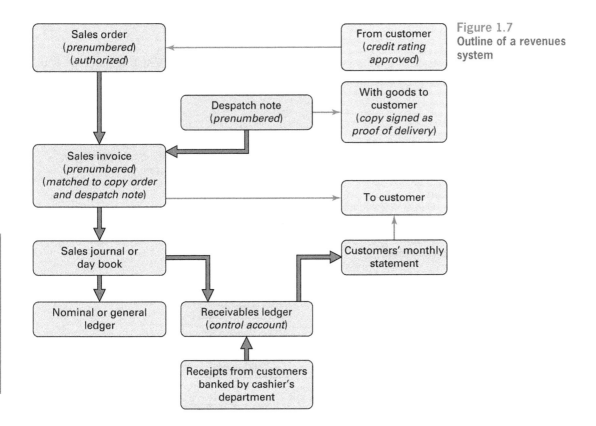

Figure 1.7
Outline of a revenues system

PAYROLL SYSTEM   Payroll—processing the payment of salaries and wages—is for obvious reasons one of the most important systems in an organization. Paying the staff correctly and on time is vital to ensure good relations between the business and its staff. It is also important that any statutory deductions such as tax or social insurance are dealt with correctly according to the law, and any non-statutory deductions such a pension fund payments are made correctly.

Payroll processing must be done in accordance with many rules and procedures, so weaknesses in the system could have serious consequences.

The control objectives of a payroll system are:

- to ensure that wages and salaries are paid only to actual employees at authorized rates of pay
- to ensure that all wages and salaries are computed in accordance with records of work performed, whether in respect of time, output, sales made or other criteria
- to ensure that payrolls are correctly calculated
- to ensure that payments are made only to the correct employees

- to ensure that payroll deductions are correctly accounted for and paid over to the appropriate third parties
- to ensure that all transactions are correctly recorded in the books of account

Figure 1.8 shows the layout of a basic purchases system. Internal controls are shown *in italics* on the diagram but, as before, we will not be giving any detailed explanation in the text.

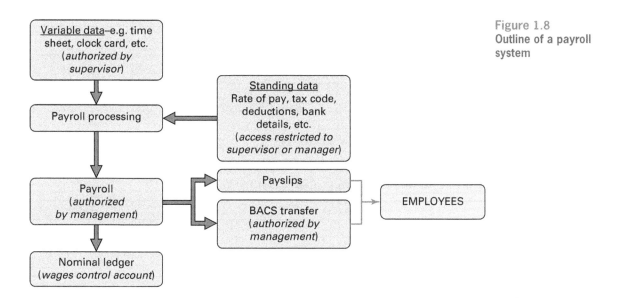

Figure 1.8
Outline of a payroll system

Clearly these are not the only financial systems within an organization, but they will give you an indication of how a finance department operates and the links between different parts of a system and how those systems interact with the outside world. Systems design and control is a massive topic, and interested learners are encouraged to read further.

Stop and think   What effect would it have on a business if the management information system did not grow as fast as the business?

Test yourself

1 Which of the following is not a stakeholder group?

Management	
The local population	
The lender	
Trade receivables	

2 A partnership is two or more people acting together for a common purpose and each partner is responsible for their own share of any liabilities.   **True/False**

3 In a limited company, what is limited?   ✔

The liability of the company for its debts	
The liability of management for debts incurred by the company	
The liability of shareholders for the debts of the company	
The liability of lenders to the company	

4 Directors of a limited company must also be shareholders.   **True/False**

5 The following elements are part of a management information system.   ✔   ✔

	True	False
Payroll		
Customer management		
Costing system		
Inventory recording		

6 The Management Information System produces information for management on costing, budgets and forecasts. Financial accounting forms part of a different system.   **True/False**

7 In most jurisdictions, companies are governed by laws that set out how they should be formed and structured.   **True/False**

8 Which of the following are advantages and which disadvantages of organizational structures?

	Advantage	Disadvantage
Sole traders are free to take advantage of business opportunities, as they are not bound by any legal restrictions		
Companies have limited liability		
Partnerships share risks, but all partners share full risks		

9 Agency theory states that company managers are accountable to shareholders, so should not benefit themselves at the expense of the business.   **True/False**

10 Lenders to a business require information about the business on a regular basis. They are entitled by law to receive copies of all financial statements and management information produced by the company so they can minimize their risk exposure.   **True/False**

In the next module we start to look at the fundamental principles of financial accounting and how these come together to form a set of financial statements.

Test yourself

1 Growbig Plc used to be a medium-sized company trading in agricultural supplies and chemicals such as fertilizers and pesticides. It was owned by a consortium of farmers and growers and on flotation as a public company, they each received shares; these still form the majority of shareholders even though individual shareholdings are relatively small.

On flotation, Growbig also issued shares, which were taken up by institutional investors. There are now four major shareholders who together own about 35 per cent of the company; the remaining shareholders are the original farmers and growers. It used the funds to buy out rival businesses and to expand production of fertilizers and pesticides under its own brand to sell to the general public.

Growbig complies with all the legal disclosure requirements but does not provide shareholders with any other information. Recently there has been adverse publicity with regard to 'dumping' products that are not allowed to be sold in the UK under environmental legislation in various developing countries using a different brand name. There has also been an issue with the lack of health and safety provision in one of their factories overseas that manufactures fertilizer.

Required
- Identify the stakeholders in this company.
- What information would they require:
    - daily?
    - weekly?
    - monthly?
    - annually?

2 You have been asked to advise Mr Siddique, the owner and manager of a family company called Siddique Confections Ltd, which buys chocolates and sweets in bulk and repackages them in small quantities for hotels and conference centres using their 'own name' packaging.

The company's ownership is divided up as follows:

Mr Siddique	45%
Mr Siddique's father	35%
Mr Siddique's mother	10%
Mr Siddique's uncle	10%

Apart from Mr Siddique, none of them take an active part in the business.

The turnover has risen steadily over the years and is now approaching $4 million. The after-tax profit for the last financial year was $800 000. A dividend has been paid out to the shareholders.

The business has simply grown in size, but in essence nothing has changed. Mr Siddique adjusts retail selling prices by the same amount as raw material prices increase, the workforce has expanded as the business has grown and most of the packaging is still done by hand.

The business employs an unqualified accountant and two bookkeepers to maintain the financial records. They use proprietary accounting software to maintain the financial records and to prepare the accounts. The accountant makes any final adjustments manually. The accounts are audited by a local firm and everything has proved satisfactory.

Mr Siddique makes all the management decisions and monitors the progress of his business by monitoring the bank balance.

The accountant produces a set of accounts at the end of each month comprising a profit and loss account and a balance sheet showing the result for the month and the cumulative financial position for the year to date.

At the end of each financial year the accountant produces a set of annual accounts.

Up until now the company has enjoyed good relations with its major customers, but recently two have started to be supplied by a rival company, stating that their prices are cheaper; several others have indicated that they would be looking for price reduction from Mr Siddique in view of what his competitor Choc-O-Munch is offering.

Required

Mr Siddique has indicated that the information he has is insufficient to manage the business properly.

You are asked to advise Mr Siddique as to what kind of information he might need and how it can be provided for him.

2 Reporting the financial position

In this module we will look at:

- The requirement for financial statements

- What is meant by 'financial statements'

- The role of the auditor

- Accounting records—what must be kept

- Accounting data and the hierarchy of information

- Preparing financial information and the fundamental accounting concepts

- The accounting equation

- The distinction between revenue and capital transactions

- What's included in a set of financial statements

The requirement for financial statements

There is a considerable difference, from an accounts preparation point of view, between financial statements prepared for companies, including limited liability partnerships, and those prepared by sole traders, partnerships and other unincorporated bodies such as charities.

For such unincorporated bodies, i.e. those organizations that are not companies, financial statements are prepared at least annually and provided to the owners of the business for information. As, in most cases, the owners and managers of the organizations are often the same people, the need for formal accounting rules is rather unnecessary, so they can be in any format.

Larger partnerships often need more regular information, so might produce monthly or quarterly accounts; for the smallest businesses these are often considered unnecessary, as the owner/managers have a very good idea of their financial position.

As we saw in Module 1, however, every organization has stakeholders, so even the smallest business will have to be accountable to, in particular:

- The tax authorities
- Any lenders to the business
- Any sleeping or non-active partners

For a company or a limited liability partnership, things are very different. The rules for the preparation of financial statements are set out in company legislation and in International Accounting Standards, of which more in Module 6. These rules together set out the form and content of financial accounts.

When approved by the members, i.e. the shareholders, in a general meeting known as the Annual General Meeting, they have to be filed on the public record. Small companies can file a sort of short form financial statement that gives very little away, but the point is that this is a legal requirement and cannot be avoided.

The accounting records must be sufficient to disclose the financial position of the company at any time, with reasonable accuracy.

In practice, with computerized accounting systems, this should not present any difficulty.

It is the responsibility of the directors of the company to ensure that financial statements are prepared, sent to the shareholders annually and filed with the appropriate authorities.

What is meant by 'financial statements'?

Financial statements means:

- the statement of financial position (which used to be known as the balance sheet)
- the income statement (which used to be known as the profit and loss account)
- the statement of cash flows and total recognized gains and losses
- any notes to these statements and notes of the accounting policies adopted

The directors are required specifically to:

- select suitable accounting policies and apply them consistently
- make judgements and estimates that are reasonable and prudent
- state whether applicable accounting standards have been followed (we'll look at these later in this module)
- explain, in the case of larger companies, any departure from accounting standards
- prepare the financial statements on a going concern basis, unless they consider that the business will not be able to continue in the foreseeable future

The role of the auditor

The financial accounts also require to be audited (subject to the size of the business: small companies may not require an audit). This must be carried out by suitably qualified and accredited firms of independent accountants and represent an independent check on the truth and fairness of the financial statements.

The financial statements may:

- contain errors
- not disclose fraud
- be inadvertently misleading
- be deliberately misleading
- fail to disclose relevant information
- fail to conform to regulations

Further, owners of companies must be protected from unscrupulous management who would use the owner's investment for their own benefit and not that of the owner. This is based on agency theory, which we looked at in Module 1.

Potential investors must guard against investing in abuse of limited liability where companies are deliberately set up for speculative or high-risk ventures where the initial investors have very little to lose, and the managers perhaps nothing at all, apart from their employment. If later investors are not aware of company activity, they could be induced to invest in a project that carries a much greater level of risk than the rewards they might achieve would warrant.

The solution to this problem of credibility in reports and accounts lies in appointing independent professionals to investigate the report and report on their findings, because an audit helps to reduce these so-called agency costs, as it protects investors from the actions of predatory managers.

The problems the auditors face are different from those of the directors. Their problems lie outside the area of straightforward bookkeeping and arise when the financial statements incorporate judgements, estimates and opinions.

For example, the accounts might contain an estimate—made by the directors to the best of their ability—of the potential loss on a contract—but is it:

- too much?
- too little?
- or should it not be there at all?

The auditors have to decide what they think, based on the evidence they can gather.

It is straightforward enough for a company to ensure that all the transactions in the books are properly processed, but how do the auditors know that:

- all the transactions that should be included have been included?
- all the transactions that are included are bona fide ones, and not transactions invented by the directors to make the results look good?

They have to check the underlying financial records, together with all the adjustments the directors have made such as provisions and accruals, and form their opinion.

So, because the auditors are expressing an opinion, they use a term of art—'true and fair.' This carries with it implications of honesty, integrity, impartiality and objectivity in the telling of a story, which is what the accounts do, in as understandable a way as possible for the benefit of the people who, after all, own the business or have a significant vested interest in it.

REAL WORLD

The purpose of audit

In one of its **International Standards on Auditing** (ISAs) **ISA 200**: *'Overall objectives of the independent auditor and the conduct of an audit in accordance with international standards on auditing'* the **Financial Reporting Council (FRC)**, which is the body responsible for issuing auditing standards and guidelines in the UK and Ireland, describes how an audit emphasizes the confidence users feel in financial statements.

For more information on ISA 200, you can visit the FRC website here: www.frc.org.uk/, or find out who is responsible for Financial Reporting standards in your country.

Stop and think

Obtain a set of published financial statements either from a company, a library or the internet. Look at the auditors' report.

- How detailed is it?
- What does it contain?
- What does it tell you about the respective roles of auditors and directors?

ACCOUNTING RECORDS—WHAT MUST BE KEPT

A company's accounting records must record all the information the directors need in order to ensure that any financial accounts they prepare for presentation to the shareholders comply with Companies Legislation and accounting standards. For companies it is a legal requirement.

As a minimum, the accounting records for any business other than the smallest should include the books and records summarized in Figure 2.1.

Figure 2.1 Requirement to keep accounting records

Required	Books and records
A record of payments and receipts	Cash book
	Petty cash book
A record of assets and liabilities	Asset register
	Receivables ledger
	Payables ledger
If the company deals in goods	Inventory lists at the period end
	All statements of inventory count from which the inventory listings have been prepared, i.e. the stock count sheets

You do need to be aware of this minimum requirement for maintaining financial records.

This applies to all companies, and it is the responsibility of the company's directors to ensure that proper books and records are kept. The directors must ensure that the accounting records are kept accurately and are up-to-date, so that financial statements can be prepared at any time.

Whilst these legal requirements only apply to companies, it is good practice to ensure that all but the very smallest businesses operate accounting records on similar lines. Nowadays, computerized accounts packages make this a much more feasible proposition for businesses.

Accounting data and the hierarchy of information

In Module 1 we looked at the main functions of a Management Information System ('MIS'). These were:

- recording information
- producing information for planning and control

In this section, we look at what information might be produced for each of those functions. The lists are not comprehensive, but will give an indication of the type of information that the organization might produce for each function. At this stage don't worry too much about the meaning of some of the examples—all will be explained shortly! Figure 2.2 shows the details.

Figure 2.2 **Function of accounting records**

Function	Information examples
Recording	• Cash and bank transactions
	• Recording of invoices for purchases and sales transactions
	• Details of stock (inventory) held for sale or reworking
	• Details of the assets and liabilities of the organization
Planning	• Monthly budgets
	• Pricing and costing information
	• Cash forecasts
Control	• Age of debt analysis
	• Stock movements
	• Goods returned
	• Bank reconciliations
	• Wages analysis

Note that most companies of any size produce detailed financial information regularly as part of their management processes. Management accounts can be in any format, so organizations design a format to suit their purposes. They can be as detailed or as summarized as the people in the organization who use those accounts may need.

HIERARCHY OF INFORMATION   Different users of information need different levels of detail. We will look at this more closely in Part II Introduction to Management Accounting, but for now the broad spectrum of information needs can be summarized as shown below in Figure 2.3.

Figure 2.3 **Hierarchy of information**

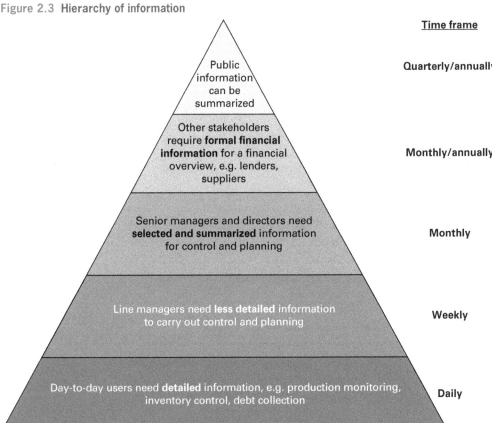

The MIS must be capable of producing the necessary information at all levels and within the time frame required to meet deadlines.

Stop and think

Establish the type and detail of financial information produced by your organization or place of study.

- Where does it go?
- Who gets what?
- What are the time frames for different types of information production?

EXAMPLE

A company delivers training in a variety of business areas nationwide. It has expanded from one office in Rotherham to having twenty branch offices nationwide.

At the moment, each branch office uses a bespoke accounts package to prepare its own accounts monthly. These are sent to head office where the financial director enters them on a spreadsheet and consolidates them together. Accounts are usually available in the third week of the month following the month being reported.

REQUIRED

a) List three reasons why this system needs improvement.

b) Write a list of briefing points for a meeting with the financial director to suggest how the system might be improved.

ANSWER

a) Three points are:

- The accounts for the business are not available until the third week of the month following. This is too late to make quick decisions if management need to look at the performance of the business or a branch office.
- The financial director has to enter the information manually onto a spreadsheet. This can be a cause of errors when transcribing the figures. There would have to be some kind of check to ensure everything was entered correctly.
- Each office is preparing its own financial statements. This means there is no central overview of the performance of each office and no control from head office—they could be concealing a fraud by falsifying figures at the branch office level.

b) Suggested improvements:

- Centralize the financial system so all financial data is processed centrally and taken away from the branch offices. Branch offices can invoice for work performed and send details to head office. They can also notify head office of any unpaid costs at the month end. All other processing to be carried out centrally.
- New software to be written to consolidate all the financial statements of the branch offices automatically so the financial director can dispense with the spreadsheet.

Preparing financial information and fundamental accounting concepts

Financial accounts are always historical. This is known as the historical cost convention. We are reporting what happened in the accounting period just ended. This has implications that arise when a line is drawn through what is, in effect, a continuous flow of transactions, but we will look at this later when we have a greater understanding of the methodology of accounts production.

Financial accounts are prepared in accordance with four fundamental accounting concepts. These are important and must be borne in mind when preparing financial statements at any level.

The fundamental accounting concepts which act as a framework for the production of a set of financial statements are:

- **Accruals**—all financial information relating to the accounting period must be included in the financial statements whether cash has changed hands or not. We will explain this concept in more detail in Module 3.
- **Consistency**—the financial statements will be prepared in the same way every financial period; if they aren't, the reasons why and the effect of any changes must be explained.
- **Prudence**—financial statements will be prepared on a cautious basis; profits and gains will be included only when they are earned. Losses and costs will be recognized when they are likely to happen or have already been incurred. There is a legal duty to pay.
- **Going concern**—the organization for which the accounts are being prepared will continue to be viable for the forseeable future—at least twelve months ahead.

We will come back to these fundamental principles later but for now suffice to say that these four concepts underpin the whole of the methodology of preparing financial statements.

THE ACCOUNTING EQUATION

This is a simple proposition once you understand the concepts that underlie it. The accounting equation is:

$$\text{Assets} = \text{Equity} + \text{Liabilities}$$

The accounts must balance: that is, one side of the equation must equal the other side. Let us deconstruct this a little.

ASSETS   What do we mean by assets? Assets are the things the business uses to do business with, so they include:

- Tangible assets—assets that have a physical existence such as land, buildings, equipment, vehicles, etc.
- Intangible assets—assets that only have a legal existence, such as copyrights, patents, trademarks, etc.
- Current assets—assets where the value changes all the time and that, individually, have a relatively short life, such as:
  - Items of inventory (stock) that are to be bought and sold
  - Receivables—amounts owed by customers for goods and services, which they have bought on credit but which haven't been paid for
  - Bank balances, unless the balance is overdrawn
  - Cash

EQUITY   Equity is basically the owners' collective investment in the business or organization. It includes:

- The amount subscribed to fund the business in the long term
- Any accumulated profits which have not been taken out of the business by the owners

For a company, the amount subscribed to fund the business in the long term is its share capital. This is put into the company by the shareholders, who thus own the business and the funds are expected to stay there.

The shares have a nominal value, say €1 or €10, and this is the amount each shareholder has to pay for each share. So, a company may have a share capital of €10 000 made up of 1000 ordinary shares of €10 each.

Clearly this does not prevent shareholders selling their shares to new shareholders, but this has no effect on the company—one shareholder is simply replaced by another. The fact that shares may change hands for many times their nominal value is irrelevant to the company in terms of its funding—that is simply a transaction between shareholders. In the UK, limited liability partnerships also have a share capital.

Profits are earned each year out of which the shareholders are paid a dividend on their share. This is paid as being so much per share so, for example, a dividend will be paid at the rate of 10 cents per share. The remaining profits after paying the dividend are retained in the company and are described as reserves. We will look at these in more detail in later modules.

For partnerships and sole traders, the capital invested in the business is simply an amount of cash or other assets contributed by the individuals. Here is an example:

EXAMPLE

Flo, Mo, Jo and Wrigglesworth decide to set up a legal firm with themselves as equal partners.
   Each of them should invest £20 000 to start up the business, employ an administrator, buy office equipment and set up a law library.

- Flo and Mo both subscribe £20 000
- Jo subscribes £15 000 plus office equipment valued at £5000
- Wrigglesworth subscribes office space valued at £18 000 plus £2000 in cash

Each of them has subscribed their share of capital but not all in cash; providing all the partners agree on the valuation of the other assets brought into the business all is well.

So the word equity is simply a way of describing the investment the owners have made in the organization.

Remember that the business, even if it is a small corner shop, is separate from the person or individuals who own it. If the proprietor of a business puts some money in to it to start it or help it expand, at some point they want that investment back, so the business owes it to the owners. This is a relatively simple concept in the case of shareholders in a company but it is exactly the same for the partners or owners of a business.

LIABILITIES   What do we mean by liabilities? Some of these are obvious and some need a little explanation. Don't worry too much at this stage—we will develop these further as the course progresses.

Liabilities are what the business owes to third parties, which include the owners of the business be they shareholders, partners or the sole proprietor. Liabilities include:

- Amounts due to suppliers (payables)
- Amounts due to lenders: bank overdrafts, loans, etc.
- Specific amounts of expenditure that have been incurred but have not yet been paid. These are known as accruals and we will look at these in a later module
- Amounts set aside to meet known liabilities, which cannot be precisely quantified. These are known as provisions and we will look at these in a later module.

Assets, equity and liabilities form the accounting equation and are the components of the snapshot of the financial state of the organization at a moment in time called the statement of financial position—of which more later.

The distinction between revenue and capital transactions

Now we have the distinction between assets and liabilities the second difference to understand is between revenue and capital. At this point don't get confused by the use of the word 'revenue' here. Unfortunately accountancy does occasionally attribute different meanings to the same word and this is one of those occasions.

Revenue can be used to mean income or earnings, and we will use it in that context later in the course. In this case we use the word 'revenue' as a form of classification of transactions to distinguish them from another category of transactions, which we call 'capital'.

Sadly, 'capital' is another word with a double meaning because, as we have seen, it can also mean the amount invested in a business by a sole trader or partners. In this case we are using it as a means of classifying transactions that are not revenue.

These transactions have very different characteristics, as Figure 2.4 shows.

Figure 2.4 Characteristics of revenue and capital transactions

	Revenue transactions	Capital transactions
Description	Income and expenditure derived from operating activities in the financial period	Expenditure designed to enhance the infrastructure of the business to improve operating potential
Long-term/short-term?	Short-term—one accounting period	Long-term—over the economic life of the asset
Recurring transactions	Yes	No—one off expenditure
Matching transactions	Yes—income matched with related expenditure	No—capital receipts as a result of asset sales not related to purchases of assets

As we can see, revenue transactions relate entirely to the financial period only, whereas capital expenditure exists for the economic life of the asset so is for the longer term.

Figure 2.5 has some examples of the different types of transactions.

Figure 2.5 Revenue and capital transactions

Revenue transactions (examples)	Capital transactions (examples)
Buying goods and services from suppliers	Investing money in the business or buying shares
Selling goods and services to customers	Buying property or other assets such as equipment or vehicles
Paying for goods and services purchased	Taking out a long-term loan for the business
Receiving money from customers	Selling or scrapping assets no longer needed
Paying salaries and wages	Issuing shares in a company
Repairing or renovating existing property or equipment	
Paying running costs for the business, e.g. heat and light, rent, repairs, etc.	

Stop and think

Which of the following transactions are classed as capital and which are classed as revenue?

- Legal fees to register a trademark
- New roof for the raw materials store
- Expenses claimed by sales staff
- New lathe to replace one that has been scrapped

What's included in a set of financial statements?

How are these recognized in the financial statements? There are two key statements we will look at in this course, which are:

- income statement
- statement of financial position

INCOME STATEMENT   Revenue transactions are recognized in what used to be known as the profit and loss account (P&L) but which is now known as the income statement. This basically looks like this:

	£
The income from sales or commercial activities for the financial period	X
Minus	
The expenditure relating to that income, the costs of goods and services which have been sold in the period	(X)
Minus	
The other costs related to running the business: such things as wages and salaries, rent, light & heat, repairs, etc.	(X)
Leaves	
Profit or loss for the period	X̲

This is broadly, how the income statement looks. We will look again at this in more detail later in the course.

STATEMENT OF FINANCIAL POSITION   Capital transactions are reported in a slightly more complicated way. As we have seen, capital transactions last a lot longer than revenue ones, so they are shown in the financial statements in what used to be known as the balance sheet but is now known as the statement of financial position.

In this statement we include all the assets and liabilities of the business that we looked at earlier in this module.

There are some conventions in the layout of the statement and we will look at these in more detail later; for now we will simply list them. By convention, assets are shown first.

A statement of financial position looks like this.

	£
Tangible assets—Land, buildings, plant, equipment, vehicles, etc.	X
Intangible assets—patents, trademarks, etc.	X
Inventories—stock for resale or reworking	X
Receivables—amounts owed to the organization	X
Bank balances—if in credit	X
Cash held in the business	X
TOTAL ASSETS	X̲
Share capital or owner's capital (if not a company)	X
Accumulated profits or losses from previous accounting periods	X
Profits or losses for the current financial period	X
Long-term loans from lenders	X
Payables—amounts owed by the business to its suppliers of goods and services	X
Specific amounts of expenditure which have been incurred but have not yet been paid (accruals)	X
Amounts set aside to meet known liabilities that cannot be precisely quantified (provisions)	X
Bank overdrafts	X
TOTAL LIABILITIES	X̲

The important point here—and we looked at it at the beginning of this module—is that the sum of all the assets equals the sum of all the liabilities—the statement of financial position balances.

Stop and think

Visit the website of a public company (plc) to find its accounts and review how the income statement and statement of financial position are set out.

What other statements are included in these accounts?

Test yourself

1 Accounting records must be able to disclose the financial position of the company at
   any time.   **True/False**

2 A company's sole accounting records consist of a cash book and bank statements which record
   receipts into the bank account and payments from it. In order to comply with the law, which
   of the following records should it also maintain?   ✔   ✔

Accounting record	Must maintain	Optional
Petty cash book		
Journal		
Receivables ledger		
Purchase day book		

3 The main function of accounting records is the recording of day-to-day transactions.
   This is why financial books and records must be maintained carefully.   **True/False**

4 Line managers generally only need summarized weekly information, whilst assistant
   managers need all the detail daily.   **True/False**

5 Which of the following is not a fundamental accounting concept?   ✔

Fairness	
Consistency	
Going concern	
Historical cost convention	

6 What is the accounting equation? Is it: ✔

Assets + Liabilities = Capital	
Assets = Capital + Liabilities	
Capital = Assets	

7 Which of the following are not current assets?   ✔

Accruals	
Trade marks	
Petty cash	
Inventories	

8 Equity is generally defined as Share Capital + Reserves.   **True/False**

9 The nominal value of a share is the same as its market price   **True/False**

10 Which of these transactions are capital and which are revenue   ✔   ✔

	Capital	Revenue
Selling obsolete inventory for scrap		
Selling an item of plant and equipment		
Issuing shares to existing shareholders		
Taking out a long-term bank loan		

In the next module we look at how we start to construct a set of financial position and introduce the basic principles of double entry—to make the financial statements balance.

Test yourself

1 Calculon plc has the following balances in its books at 31 December 20X7.

CALCULON

	£m
Purchases of goods and materials	1156
Inventories	374
Tangible assets after depreciation	1849
Trade receivables	294
Revenues	2891
Interest paid	92
Trade payables	301
Share capital	125
Accumulated reserves at 1 January 20X7	1534
Administration costs	487
Long-term loan	251
Wages and salaries	936
Accrual for unpaid rent	68
Cash and bank balances	1
Provision for legal costs	22
Bank overdraft	122

Prepare an income account and a statement of financial position at 31 December 20X7 using the layout set out above.

2 Bolington Ltd, a manufacturer of fish processing equipment, has been upgrading their property and equipment to meet new international standards. The work involved:
- repairing and improving some of their existing premises
- demolishing an old factory and building a new building
- installing new equipment in the new factory
- renovating and upgrading existing equipment in the old factory
- renovating their existing office block for administration staff

They incurred costs as follows:

Cost type	£
Building materials	143980
Demolition costs	10150
Delivery of building materials	2754
New plant and equipment	298609
Legal costs—planning and title deeds	12500
Legal costs—resolving dispute with neighbouring business over blocked access	3500
Redecorating costs for the office block	86023
Site preparation costs	24098
Interest incurred on construction loan during the period of construction	88
Renovating and repairing existing equipment	147264

- With the aid of relevant examples, outline your understanding of the difference between capital expenditure and revenue expenditure.
- Calculate the cost of the building to be included in tangible fixed assets of Bolington Ltd.

3 Recording transactions and the trial balance

Introduction to bookkeeping

Accounting records are formed and maintained via the use of double entry bookkeeping. It is hard to historically and geographically place the origins of double entry bookkeeping. Certainly by the 11th and 12th centuries, double-entry systems were being used by merchants in Italy and Germany.

There exists a set of financial account books relating to the affairs of one Amatino Manucci, a Florentine merchant in the 13th century. The books of the Farolfi firm, which employed Manucci for the financial period 1299–1300, show a full double-entry system that would be recognized by accountants today.

The person often cited as the Father of Accounting was a Franciscan friar called Luca Pacioli. He is often erroneously cited as being the person who invented double-entry bookkeeping, but this is untrue. What he did was to describe it in his mathematics textbook *Summa de Arithmetica, Geometria, Proportioni et Proportionalità* published in Venice in 1594—so Pacioli is really the Father of Accounting Textbooks. He published a detailed description of double-entry, thus enabling students to study it.

It is gratifying to know that the antecedents of this course go back over 400 years, at least!

We are looking at a system that has stood the test of time and is used universally to record financial transactions. So how does it work?

REAL WORLD
The view from the investor
'You have to know accounting. It's the language of practical business life. It was a very useful thing to deliver to civilization. I've heard it came to civilization through Venice, which of course was once the great commercial power in the Mediterranean. However, double-entry bookkeeping was a hell of an invention.

'Economists get very uncomfortable when you talk about virtue and vice. It doesn't lend itself to a lot of columns with numbers. But I would argue that there are big virtue effects in economics. I would say that the spreading of double-entry bookkeeping by the Monk, Fra Luce de Pacioli, was a big virtue effect in economics. It made business more controllable, and it made it more honest.'

Source: *Charlie Munger Vice Chairman Berkshire Hathaway*

Principles of double-entry

The principle is quite a simple one. For each accounting transaction there has to be two entries in the books of account: every entry has a counterpart. Using double-entry principles, if a business sells a box of chocolates for €3 cash, it has to account both for the sale of the chocolate for €3 and the €3 in cash it has received. In this way books balance, so the accountants can be assured that the transactions have been included in full.

Books of account are written up using certain conventions. These are universally applicable and date back to the days when double-entry bookkeeping was first used. There is no particular reason why they are written up this way—they just are. You simply have to remember the process: it is just that, a process, similar to wiring an electrical circuit or plumbing in a tap—you just do it this way.

So, for reasons we need not go into, transactions are described as:

- **Debits (Dr)**—which record assets and costs and expenses
- **Credits (Cr)**—which record liabilities and income (sales or revenues)

Dr and Cr are accountants' shorthand for debit and credit.
In the books of account:

- **Debits** are always recorded on the left-hand side of the account
- **Credits** are always recorded on the right-hand side *(Tip: you can remember this because credit has an 'r' in it)*

There is no particular reason for this and no logic; it just is that way. The books of account could be perfectly well written up the other way around and they would still balance, but they would be out of step with the rest of the financial world.

Stop and think

Look at a bank statement. If you have money in the bank this is shown as a credit balance or Cr, on your bank statement—and yet it is an asset, i.e. money in the bank, so surely, shouldn't it be a debit (Dr)? Why isn't it?

We'll give you the answer to that at the end of the module!

Books of account

The books of account of any organization are divided into three sections. Two of these are described as ledgers. A ledger is simply a word for a collection of individual accounts, such as an account for each supplier or customer or accounts for individual types of cost or expense, asset or liability.

Don't worry too much about this at this stage—you'll get used to it as we progress through the module. The three sections are:

- **Cash book**—records the movement of money through the business. **IMPORTANT NOTE**: When accountants refer to 'cash,' they don't just mean coins and notes. Cash is accountant's shorthand for both physical cash (i.e. coins and notes) transactions AND transactions through bank accounts.
- **Nominal ledger**—records assets, income and expenses, so will have accounts headed up things like 'Land and Buildings,' 'Purchases,' 'Repairs,' 'Motor Vehicles,' Revenues, etc.
- The financial statements prepared at the end of the accounting period will, as we will see, be based on the transactions in the nominal ledger.
- **Payables and receivables ledgers**—record details of transactions made on credit with individual suppliers or customers. Old-fashioned textbooks used to call these 'personal accounts' because they related to named individuals or organizations.

The balances on these accounts will appear, in total, on the statement of financial position (Module 2) at the end of the financial period, as they represent either assets (amounts due from customers) or liabilities (amounts due to suppliers).

There are two other ancillary books which we will mention at this stage. These are:

- Day books—simply a listing of transactions for either purchases or sales for each day.
- Journals—used for transfers between accounts.

We will look at the use of day books later in the module. We will meet the journal in Module 4.

Recording simple transactions

We know that each transaction has to have two entries—one debit and one credit—so we can apply this to a simple situation.

Suppose Freda the Florist buys flowers for her shop, paying by bank transfer. She has €2000 in the bank and spends €500. How do we account for this in her books of account?

1 Firstly, the purchase of the flowers is a revenue item (Module 2) and it is a cost to the business, so the first entry is a debit, because it is a cost, in her Purchase of Flowers account. So far so simple.
2 We now have to find a credit. Remember, credits are either income or liabilities. It isn't income, so it must be a liability. If Freda had had an overdraft this would be straightforward enough: her liability to the bank would go up by €500.
3 But she hasn't an overdraft; she has money in the bank. What has happened is that the amount of money in the bank has gone down—part of her bank balance has been converted into flowers. This has made her asset—her bank balance—smaller. Instead of creating a liability, the transaction has made an asset smaller—which, in accounting terms, we can say at this stage is more or less the same thing.

We can illustrate this using what are known in accountancy world as T accounts.

We need, at this stage, two accounts:

- A Purchase of Flowers account
- A cash book to record the transactions that flow in and out of her bank account.

These T accounts record the purchase of the flowers and the outlay of money from her bank.

Purchase of flowers account

	Dr		Cr
Buys flowers	500		

Cash book

	Dr		Cr
Opening bank balance	2000	Purchase of flowers	500

Notice at this point her bank balance has gone down. The bank account shows:

Opening balance (asset)	Debit	2000
Payment for flowers (reducing value of asset)	Credit	(500)
New balance		1500

Now the next step. Suppose Freda goes on to sell those flowers for cash and generates sales of €700.
We need to record the sale, so we need another account—a Sale of Flowers account.
Again, this transaction has two parts:

- Firstly a credit—because it's income—to the Sale of Flowers account
- Secondly the income she has generated from selling the flowers has given her an asset—an increase in her bank balance—so this is a debit

These T accounts show the income from the sale of the flowers and the receipt of money into her bank balance.

Purchase of flowers account

	Dr		Cr
Buys flowers	500		

Cash book

	Dr		Cr
Bank balance	2000	Purchase of flowers	500
Income from sales	700		

Sale of flowers

	Dr		Cr
			700

Notice that the bank balance has gone up again:

Opening balance (asset)	Debit	2000
Payment for flowers (reducing value of asset)	Credit	(500)
Receipts from sale of flowers (increasing value of asset)	Debit	700
New balance		2200

This simple example illustrates the points made above about debits and credits and how we write up the books of account.

Remember:

- **Debits (Dr)**—which record assets and costs and expenses—the opening bank balance and the cost of flowers purchased
- **Credits (Cr)**—which record liabilities and income (sales or revenues)—the income from sales of flowers and, in this case, the reduction in the asset of the bank balance

> **Stop and think**   Think of a transaction you have carried out recently: for example, paying rent, buying petrol or food. How would you record such a transaction if you kept books of account like Freda?

This is as simple as double-entry bookkeeping gets, and if everything in the business world was bought and sold for cash, all we'd need would be a cash book and some simple ledger accounts. However, life is rarely so obliging, so we have to be able to record transactions on credit where no cash changes hands at the time of the transaction, but does so at a later time.

Don't be confused by the use of the word 'credit' here. This is yet another occasion where accountants use the same word in two different ways. This use of the word credit relates to the granting of time to pay—'buy now pay later', i.e. the ordinary everyday meaning of the word. It does not relate to the credit side of a set of accounting records.

Entering details of a transaction in the accounting records is known as posting. Entering the details of an invoice or a bank transaction into the accounting records is known as posting it.

Accounting for purchase transactions on credit

Moving away from simple cash–based transactions, we need to insert a step into the recording of transactions. This step is to account for the fact that invoices will not be paid straight away, so we have to keep a record of what is due to the business by customers and what the business owes suppliers of goods and services.

To do this we need to introduce one of the ancillary books we mentioned earlier—the day books. There are two of these:

- Purchase day book
- Sales day book

They are simply a list of each day's transactions with some analysis of what the transaction is for. Computerized systems may not have a separate book but the software will record the details for entry into the ledger. In any event, summaries of these will feed into the financial statements. The information to be recorded in a day book is shown in the table at Figure 3.1.

Figure 3.1 **Day book contents**

Information included in day book listing	Comment
Date of transaction	The day book is started afresh every day so transactions can be identified and traced by date, as well as by name of relevant customer or supplier
Name of customer or supplier	Obviously
Their account code	It's easier if all accounts in a ledger are given a number or an alphanumeric identity so that a computerized system can process the details. So the purchase or payables ledger might have accounts identified as Smith's Building Supplies Code number S101, Smith's Joinery Supplies might be S105 and Smith's Taxis S110, for example
Amount for goods or services	This is the amount either as a total or, if the invoice is for several different categories of goods or services, there might be a separate entry for each item coming to the total of the invoice pre-sales tax
Sales tax	If appropriate—not all businesses might pay sales tax, but those that do have to record it separately
Nominal or general ledger code	This completes the double-entry and records what the transaction is for, i.e. in a purchase day book it would analyze what the invoice was for, e.g. materials, repairs, light and heat, rent, etc. In a sales day book it would record the product sold or what the income source was

So how do we record transactions on credit?

To do this, in addition to the day books, we have to introduce the ledgers that we mentioned earlier. Remember, a ledger is simply a collection of individual accounts, so in posting credit transactions involving purchasing we need to introduce:

- **Nominal ledger**—records assets, income and expenses, so will have accounts headed up things like 'Land and Buildings,' 'Purchases,' 'Repairs,' 'Motor Vehicles,' Sales, etc.
- **Payables ledger**—records details of transactions made on credit with individual suppliers

Let us look at an example:

MacRusty Ltd is an engineering company making water tanks and piping. It has the following transactions in a week:

MACRUSTY
Purchase day book
List of transactions—w/c 15 October 20X8

Date	Name	Payables ledger account code	Steel	Bolts	Welding rods	Paint	Wood	Engineering sundries	Subtotal	Sales tax	Total
15-Oct	Massive Metals	M094	2500	150					2650	530	3180
15-Oct	Woodly	W010					640		640	128	768
16-Oct	Engineering Stuff	E004						2120	2120	424	2544
16-Oct	Massive Metals	M094	3700						3700	740	4440
17-Oct	Greys Paints	G076				735			735	147	882
18-Oct	Strictly Steel	S062	5023						5023	1005	6028
19-Oct	Welders Supplies	W002			376				376	75	451
	TOTAL		11223	150	376	735	640	2120	15244	3049	18293
	Nominal code		*S11*	*B04*	*W01*	*P06*	*W02*	*S03*		*V01*	

Before we move on let's just look at a few features of this extract from the accounting records:

- Each supplier has a code—so Massive Metals is M094, Woodly is W010, etc. This relates to their individual accounts in the payables ledger.
- There is a column for each category of expense.
- We've included sales tax in these examples because, for all but the smallest businesses, it is a fact of life. Sales tax is shown separately; what we want to show in the financial statements is the amount net of tax. This is because the sales tax is owed to the government so it is not a cost to the company. Instead it is a liability they have to pay based on the difference between what the business charges to customers and what they are charged by suppliers.
- At the foot of each column once they have been totalled up at the end of the week is a nominal ledger code. This shows where the expense cost is to go to in the accounting records, so Steel is S11, Bolts B04, etc.

Now what we have here is, in fact, the double-entry for these invoices. We have a code for the supplier's account in the payables ledger and a code for the account in the nominal ledger. But which is the debit and which is the credit?

Remember the rule:

- Debits are assets and expenses
- Credits are liabilities and income

so here we have:

Debit expense − Nominal ledger − steel, bolts, welding rods, etc.
Credit liabilities − Payables ledger − amounts due to the individual suppliers

Let's look just at the first transaction on the list: the invoice from Woodly for £640 plus £128 sales tax, a total of £768. This is the double-entry, using the principles set out above. By convention debits are shown first—looks neater!

Remember the nominal ledger records the details of what was bought and the payables ledger who it was bought from.

So the transactions to record that invoice are:

Debit—nominal ledger—wood	640
Debit—nominal ledger—sales tax	128
Credit—payables ledger—Woodly	768

So the nominal ledger records the expense of wood and the liability of sales tax, and the payables ledger records the full amount due to Woodly. As the payables ledger records the transactions with the supplier, it shows the whole of the invoice, including the tax, that has to be paid.

The use of the day book is the intermediate step that makes it possible to enter credit-based transactions into the accounting records in groups of invoices. Of course, it is also possible to just enter one invoice without using a day book and the double-entry is the same.

Debit expense
Credit liabilities

If we write up the books properly for these transactions they look like this:

PAYABLES LEDGER

Massive Metals M094

Dr			Cr
	15-Oct	Invoice	3 180
	16-Oct	Invoice	4 440

Woodly W010

Dr			Cr
	15-Oct	Invoice	768

Engineering Stuff E004

Dr			Cr
	16-Oct	Invoice	2 544

Greys Paints G076

Dr			Cr
	17-Oct	Invoice	882

Strictly Steel S062

Dr			Cr
	18-Oct	Invoice	6 028

Welders Supplies W002

Dr			Cr
	19-Oct	Invoice	451

NOMINAL OR GENERAL LEDGER

Steel S11

		Dr	Cr
43027	PDB	11 223	

Bolts B04

		Dr	Cr
43027	PDB	150	

Welding Rods W01

		Dr	Cr
43027	PDB	376	

Paint P06

		Dr	Cr
43027	PDB	735	

Wood W02

		Dr	Cr
43027	PDB	640	

Engineering Sundries S03

		Dr	Cr
43027	PDB	2 120	

Sales Tax V01

		Dr	Cr
43027	PDB	3 049	

What we have here is a record of expense incurred in the nominal ledger and a record of amounts due to suppliers in the payables ledger.

The next step is to pay the suppliers. At an appropriate point in the financial period, the bills have to be paid. The finance team will decide which suppliers will be paid and which may be held over to the next period or payment run.

Looking at MacRusty the finance team decide to pay their key suppliers:

- Massive Metals—first invoice only
- Strictly Steel
- Welders Supplies

The rest can wait.

Let us assume that MacRusty has 12 450 local currency in the bank.

Where payment is concerned there are only two parties involved:

- The paying company—in this case, MacRusty
- The organization or person being paid—in this case Massive Metals, Strictly Steel and Welders Supplies

Consequently with payments there is no need to involve the nominal ledger as this is just there to record the expense. Instead we record details of the payment in the cash book and the supplier's account in the payables ledger. Remember 'cash' is accountant's shorthand for all transactions involving physical cash as well as payments through the bank by cheque or bank transfer.

So they decide to pay the key suppliers listed above.

The transaction double entry for making the payment is this.

Debit − Account in the Payables ledger
Credit − Cash book

The logic for this is quite straightforward. Making the payment reduces liabilities. As a liability is always shown as a credit balance, the account has to be debited to reduce the credit amount.

Similarly with the cash book; if the organization has money in the bank, this will be shown as a debit because it is an asset. Making the payment reduces the asset, so it must be shown as a credit. If the organization does not have money in the bank and is therefore overdrawn, this will be shown as a credit balance on the account and making payments will only increase the overdraft, so the credit amount will get bigger.

They make the payments and the double-entry looks like this:

PAYABLES LEDGER

Massive Metals M094

		Dr			Cr	
30-Oct	Paid	3 180	15-Oct	Invoice	3 180
			16-Oct	Invoice	4 440

Strictly Steel S062

		Dr			Cr	
30-Oct	Paid	6 028	18-Oct	Invoice	6 028

Welders Supplies

		Dr			Cr	
30-Oct	Paid	451	19-Oct	Invoice	451

CASH BOOK

Cash book

	Dr			Cr	
01-Oct Balance at bank	12 450	30-Oct Massive Metals	3 180
		Strictly Steel	6 028
		Welders Supplies	451

Here we can see that the amounts due to the suppliers have been paid and the amount shown as an asset in the cash book has been reduced.

Assets (i.e. the bank balance) and liabilities (i.e. the amounts due to suppliers) have been reduced by the same amount, so the accounts are still in balance.

PURCHASE RETURNS AND REFUNDS   It may be that goods delivered are faulty, incorrectly invoiced or not what was ordered and they are sent back to the supplier as not required. It may be that services provided are not of the right standard or incomplete and the customer demands a refund.

It would not be good practice to simply throw the supplier's invoice away because it was not going to be paid. For one thing the supplier will probably have posted their invoice into their receivables ledger, so the supplier's receivables ledger and the customer's payables ledger would not agree.

Consequently, the procedure is to post the supplier's invoice in the usual way and request a credit note from the supplier to cancel the invoice.

Credit notes can be entered into the purchase day book as a negative invoice, but many systems have a separate day book called the purchase returns day book (PRDB), which acts in the same way as a purchase day book.

Once the supplier's credit note is received, it is posted into the payables ledger, but the opposite way to the invoice.

EXAMPLE

Topsy Ltd has received three invoices for goods from their supplier, Franklin plc:

Invoice number 967	€2653.98
Invoice number 978	€1794.74
Invoice number 982	€3659.48

On inspection, the goods ordered and invoiced with invoice number 978 proved to be faulty, so Topsy returned them to Franklin and requested a credit note. This arrived as:

Credit Note Number 74   €1794.74

How should these be posted in the books of Topsy?

The payables ledger account for Franklin in the payables ledger will look like this when everything is posted:

PAYABLES LEDGER

Franklin plc

Credit Note 74	1794.74	Invoice number 967	2653.98
		Invoice number 978	1794.74
		Invoice number 982	3659.48

The purchases account in the nominal ledger will look like this:

NOMINAL LEDGER

Purchases

Invoice number 967	2653.98	Credit Note 74	1794.74
Invoice number 978	1794.74		
Invoice number 982	3659.48		

As can be seen, the credit note cancels the appropriate invoice, so the correct amount is paid to Franklin when due.

Stop and think

If possible, review the processes in your organization for faulty goods or services. How are they identified in the first place? What documentation is there? How are any returns accounted for?

If not possible, review an occasion when you had cause to return an item or complain about a service to obtain a refund. How was it handled by the supplier? What documentation did they ask for? Was it successful?

DISCOUNTS

Suppliers often offer a discount for early payment. If the customer takes advantage of the discount, this will present a small accounting problem, because on the payment of an invoice the amount paid will be less than the amount of the invoice. If an invoice has been received from a supplier for €100 with 5 per cent discount for payment within 10 days (known as a 5/10 discount) the customer will only pay the supplier €95. How to account for the remaining €5?

In double-entry bookkeeping, all things are possible and the solution is quite straightforward. We create an account in the nominal ledger called discount received and debit the supplier's account in the payables ledger with the discount.

Here's an example. Topsy and Franklin again!

Topsy Ltd has received three invoices for goods from their supplier Franklin plc.

Invoice number 967	€2653.98
Invoice number 978	€1794.74
Invoice number 982	€3659.48

Franklin has offered Topsy a 5 per cent discount for early payment. Topsy decides to pay invoice number 967 early and claims a discount of €132.70.

The payables ledger account for Franklin in the payables ledger will look like this when everything is posted (including the credit note posted earlier!):

PAYABLES LEDGER

Franklin plc

Credit note 74	1794.74	Invoice number 967	2653.98
Payment invoice 967	2521.28	Invoice number 978	1794.74
Discount received	132.70	Invoice number 982	3659.48

The accounts in the nominal ledger will look like this:

NOMINAL LEDGER

Purchases

Invoice number 967	2653.98	Credit note 74	1794.74
Invoice number 978	1794.74		
Invoice number 982	3659.48		

Discount received

| | | Franklin Ltd | 132.70 |

Discounts received are usually shown separately in the income account, as they represent financial savings rather than a reduction in the price of items purchased. This keeps the cost of goods sold (cost of sales) as a full value, and shows the benefit to the business of early payment to suppliers.

Accounting for sales transactions on credit

Now MacRusty, to survive as a business, must sell something and earn some money, and this must be accounted for. The principles of recording sales on credit and income from customers are exactly the same as for recording purchases on credit and payments to suppliers, except that the double-entry is the other way around.

In this case invoices to customers are shown as debits. Why? Because they create an asset, i.e. an amount due from the customer to the business. When the customer pays, the amount due from them goes down and the cash in the bank goes up.

We use a sales day book to list invoices in exactly the same way as we used a purchase day book. Let us look at some transactions involving sales by MacRusty.

Sales day book
List of transactions—w/c 15 October 201X

Date	Name	Sales ledger account code	Large tanks	Mini tanks	Wide-bore pipe	Bespoke pipe	Subtotal	VAT	Total
15-Oct	Dooboy Drainage Solutions	D167	596				596	119	715
15-Oct	Pipemasters	P027			2789		2789	558	3347
16-Oct	Birt Plumbing	B016				394	394	79	473
17-Oct	Nakimoto	N002		2900			2900	580	3480
18-Oct	Pipemasters	P027				698	698	140	838
19-Oct	Winterhalter	W012	1950				1950	390	2340
								0	0
TOTAL			**2546**	**2900**	**2789**	**1092**	**9327**	**1865**	**11192**
	Nominal code		*SO1*	*SO2*	*SO3*	*SO4*		*VO1*	

We now need to post these into the receivables ledger and the nominal ledger. Remember the double-entry shown above; for the first transaction, sales of large tanks to Dooboy Drainage Solutions the double-entry is:

> Debit — Receivables ledger — Dooboy Drainage Solutions — £715
> Credit — Nominal ledger — Sales of tanks   — £596
> Credit — Nominal ledger — VAT   — £119

Posting up all the transactions for that week, the receivables and nominal ledgers look like this:

RECEIVABLES LEDGER
Dooboy Drainage Solutions D167

		Dr	Cr
15-Oct	Invoice	715	

Pipemasters P027

		Dr	Cr
15-Oct	Invoice	3347	
18-Oct	Invoice	838	

Birt Plumbing B016

		Dr	Cr
16-Oct	Invoice	473	

NOMINAL OR GENERAL LEDGER
Sales—Large Tanks SO1

Dr	Cr	
	19-Oct Sales day book	2546

Sales Mini Tanks SO2

Dr	Cr	
	19-Oct Sales day book	2900

Sales Wide Bore Pipe SO3

Dr	Cr	
	19-Oct Sales day book	2789

Nakimoto N002		
	Dr	Cr
17-Oct Invoice	3480	

Sales Bespoke Pipe S04		
Dr		Cr
	19-Oct Sales day book	1092

Winterhalter W012		
	Dr	Cr
19-Oct Invoice	2340	

Sales Tax		
Dr		Cr
19-Oct Purchase Day book	3049	19-Oct Sales day book 1865

Notice that the sales tax account in the nominal ledger is the same one we used in the earlier example for purchases; there will ideally only be one account, so the details for the tax return can be extracted when the time comes.

Now the customers are going to pay, so we have to account for sales receipts. Again, the parties to the transaction are:

1 The customers, Dooboy Drainage Solutions
2 The business, MacRusty

The double-entry is confined to the receivables ledger and the cash book.

Three customers decide to pay MacRusty for the goods they have bought:

- Nakimoto
- Winterhalter
- Pipemasters (one invoice)

So the double-entry looks like this:

RECEIVABLES LEDGER

Dooboy Drainage Solutions D167		
	Dr	Cr
15-Oct Invoice	715	

Pipemasters P027			
	Dr		Cr
15-Oct Invoice	3347	30-Oct Cash book	3347
18-Oct Invoice	838		

Birt Plumbing B016		
	Dr	Cr
16-Oct Invoice	473	

Nakimoto N002			
	Dr		Cr
17-Oct Invoice	3480	30-Oct Cash book	3480

Winterhalter W012			
	Dr		Cr
19-Oct Invoice	2340	30-Oct Cash book	2340

CASH BOOK

Cash book					
		Dr			Cr
1-Oct	Balance at bank	12450	30-Oct	Massive Metals	3180
30-Oct	Winterhalter	2340		Strictly Steel	6028
30-Oct	Dooboy	3347		Welders Supplies	451
30-Oct	Nakimoto	3480			

There is only one cash book, so we use the same one as we used for the purchases example above.

By posting these entries the asset of receivables—amounts due from customers—has transmogrified into the asset cash, so the bank balance has gone up as the receivables go down. The overall asset position has remained the same.

GOODS RETURNED AND REFUNDS   It may be that a customer returns goods delivered because they are damaged, incorrectly invoiced, not what was ordered or for another acceptable reason, or a customer demands a refund for services which are incomplete or inadequate.

It is not good practice to not invoice the customer or to simply cancel the invoice through the books; the correct practice, as we saw with payables, is to issue a sales credit note.

Using the example we looked at in the section on payables above, we can look at the same transactions but this time from the point of view of the selling company Franklin.

EXAMPLE

Franklin Ltd has sent three invoices for goods to their customer Topsy Ltd plc.

Invoice number 967	€2653.98
Invoice number 978	€1794.74
Invoice number 982	€3659.48

On inspection, the goods ordered and invoiced with invoice number 978 proved to be faulty so Topsy returned them to Franklin and requested a credit note. This was sent:

Credit note number 74	€1794.74

How should these be posted in the books of Franklin?

The Receivables ledger account for Topsy in the Payables ledger will look like this when everything is posted:

RECEIVABLES LEDGER

Topsy Ltd			
Invoice number 967	2653.98	Credit Note 74	1794.74
Invoice number 978	1794.74		
Invoice number 982	3659.48		

The sales account in the nominal ledger will look like this:

NOMINAL LEDGER

Sales			
Credit Note 74	1794.74	Invoice number 967	2653.98
		Invoice number 978	1794.74
		Invoice number 982	3659.48

As can be seen, the credit note cancels the appropriate invoice so the correct amount is received from Topsy when due.

Also, the books of both Topsy and Franklin have both recorded the same transactions, consequently when the time comes to pay, both companies have a clear idea of what is being paid for and can agree outstanding balances.

DISCOUNTS

Companies frequently offer discounts for early payment and these have to be accounted for. They do this to avoid the finance cost of carrying receivables, as they have worked out it is cheaper to give up 5 per cent of their sales price as a discount than have to fund the whole amount for, say, 45 days through bank borrowing. This is a calculation which has to be looked at carefully as, obviously, giving a discount represents a cost to the selling company.

In the earlier part of the module we saw the transactions between Topsy Ltd and Franklin plc in the books of Topsy.

Now let us look at those same transactions in the books of Franklin plc. In this case the discount is allowed to Topsy by Franklin, so is called discount allowed.

Here are the transactions with Topsy (including the credit note). Topsy pays invoice 967 and claims a 5 per cent discount of €132.70.

RECEIVABLES LEDGER

Topsy Ltd

Invoice number 967	2653.98	Credit Note 74	1794.74
Invoice number 978	1794.74	Payment invoice 967	2521.28
Invoice number 982	3659.48	Discount allowed	132.70

The Sales account in the nominal ledger will look like this:

NOMINAL LEDGER

Sales

Credit Note 74	1794.74	Invoice number 967	2653.98
		Invoice number 978	1794.74
		Invoice number 982	3659.48

Discount allowed

Topsy Ltd	132.70	

As you can see, the discount is posted as a debit because it is a cost to Franklin plc. This cost is shown as a separate line in the income account, so that:

- sales are shown at their full value
- the cost of discounts can be monitored and considered by management

Again, the books of both Topsy and Franklin are in accordance.

Balancing the account

A core skill for accountants is to be able to balance an individual account or the cash book. This has to be tackled in simple steps, but once mastered is quite straightforward. We do this at the end of each financial period for which we wish to prepare financial statements, e.g. monthly accounts. The cash book might be balanced more frequently, e.g. daily or weekly, so the business can work out how much cash it has. Computerized systems will show the balance on an individual account, but the accountant needs to know how to do it.

Let us use the cash book from MacRusty as an example.

Here is where we left it, with sales and purchase details and an opening balance from the previous period.

BALANCING THE CASH BOOK

ALL ENTRIES POSTED

Cash book

		Dr			Cr
1-Oct	Balance at bank	12450	30-Oct	Massive Metals	3180
30-Oct	Winterhalter	2340		Strictly Steel	6028
30-Oct	Dooboy	3347		Welders Supplies	451
30-Oct	Nakimoto	3480			

Step 1—we add up both the debit and credit sides to see which has the highest total. Obviously with few entries this is quite easy, but it is not necessarily so obvious if there are a considerable number.

In this case the debit side has the highest total.

STEP 1

ADD EACH SIDE

Cash book

		Dr			Cr
1-Oct	Balance at bank	12450	30-Oct	Massive Metals	3180
30-Oct	Winterhalter	2340		Strictly Steel	6028
30-Oct	Dooboy	3347		Welders Supplies	451
30-Oct	Nakimoto	3480			9659
		21617			

Step 2—We subtract one total from the other and that is the balance on the account. The balance is the number that makes the totals on each side equal.

This is described as the 'balance carried down' or 'balance c/d' for short.

STEP 2

PUT IN THE AMOUNT TO MAKE BOTH SIDES EQUAL

THIS IS THE BALANCE TO BE CARRIED DOWN (c/d)

TO THE NEXT ACCOUNTING PERIOD

Cash book

		Dr			Cr
1-Oct	Balance at bank	12450	30-Oct	Massive Metals	3180
30-Oct	Winterhalter	2340		Strictly Steel	6028
30-Oct	Dooboy	3347		Welders Supplies	451
30-Oct	Nakimoto	3480			9659
				Balance c/d	11958
		21617			21617

Step 3—We carry the balance down to the opposite side of the account as the opening balance for the next financial period.

STEP 3
THIS IS THE ACCOUNT BALANCED WITH A
DEBIT BALANCE TO START THE NEW
PERIOD

		Cash book				
		Dr				*Cr*
1-Oct	Balance at bank	12450	30-Oct	Massive Metals		3180
30-Oct	Winterhalter	2340		Strictly Steel		6028
30-Oct	Dooboy	3347		Welders Supplies		451
30-Oct	Nakimoto	3480				9659
				Balance c/d		11958
		21617				21617
1-Nov	Balance b/d	11058				

If you follow the logic of what we have done in Steps 1–3 it becomes fairly obvious. The debit side had the biggest total at the end of the previous financial period, and all we have done is reinstate it as a net figure (debits minus credits) at the start of the next period.

The balance on the cash book at the end of the financial period is thus a debit of £11958. The total has dropped slightly from the beginning of the earlier period due to having paid more to suppliers than we have received in from customers.

We will come back to this but at this stage we can point out that, apart from the bank balance, we have other assets and liabilities in the receivables and payables ledgers:

Assets—Balance on receivables ledger accounts.

	£
Dooboy	715
Pipemasters	838
Birt Plumbing	473
	2026

Liabilities—Balances on payables ledger accounts

	£
Massive Metals	4440
Woodley	768
Engineering Stuff	2544
Greys Paints	882
	8634

We will look at these types of balances again when we come to consider the statement of financial position in which they will appear.

Stop and think

Computerized accounting systems, even those specifically designed for small businesses, will do all this automatically. All you have to do is data entry. Do you think you need to understand the processes, or doesn't it matter anymore because the computer does the work? If the latter, how would you know if anything had been entered incorrectly? How would you know how to correct it?

Creating the trial balance

The first step in creating a set of financial statements is to balance the books, and to do this we extract what is known as a trial balance. In reality, modern computer systems will automatically balance the books as they do not permit one-sided entries into the system, but nevertheless it is important that any student of accounting understands the principles underlying the trial balance, what it is used for and how it contributes to production of a set of financial statements.

And remember, just because the books balance doesn't mean they're right—it just means that all the transactions are in there somewhere!

The trial balance or TB for short, is simply a list of the balances on all the accounts in the books and the cash book. To illustrate how we do this let us look at a more comprehensive example and work through it.

EXAMPLE—BOTTLES LTD

STEP 1

Bottles Ltd has raised £10000 by issuing shares for cash. From this, Bottles Ltd has purchased equipment for £6000 and inventory (stock) for £2000.

Share capital account		
	Issue of shares	10000

Cash book			
Share issue	10000	Purchase of equipment	6000
		Purchase of inventory for sale	2000

Fixed asset—Equipment	
Equipment purchased	6000

Inventory	
Inventory purchased	2000

The money raised is invested by the shareholders and is owed back to them. It is therefore a liability and is shown on the credit side of an account called share capital in the nominal ledger.

The debit is a receipt into the cash book, creating the opening bank balance—an asset—and therefore a debit balance.

Bottles Ltd has bought equipment for £6000 and inventory for £2000. These are assets and are thus shown as debits in their respective accounts. The credit in the cash book represents a reduction in the bank balance of Bottles Ltd.

Note that all these transactions are recorded in the nominal ledger of Bottles Ltd. At this point Bottles has had no dealings with suppliers or customers and none of the transactions has involved credit.

Note also that, in this example, we are using a summary account in the nominal ledger for all payables and receivables. This is purely to save space and to simplify the example.

STEP 2

Bottles Ltd sells half the stock for £4000 cash and buys another £5000 worth on credit. It pays wages to staff of £1000.

Sales account

		Cash sales	4000

Cost of sales

Cost of inventory	1000		

Inventory

Inventory purchased	2000	Cost of sales	1000
Inventory purchased	5000		

Cash book

Share issue	10000	Purchase of equipment	6000
Cash sales	4000	Purchase of inventory for sale	2000
		Pay wages	1000

Payables

		Purchase of inventory	5000

Wages

Wages paid	1000		

Sales

		Cash sales	4000

Looking at the transactions in detail:

- Bottles Ltd sells half the inventory for £4000 cash. This is the first trading transaction. The sales represent income and this is a credit into the sales account.
- The sale is for cash and increases the bank balance.
- Half of the value of the inventory is transferred from the stock account to an account called Cost of sales. This is because it is no longer inventory, but is the cost to the business of what has been sold.
- Bottles Ltd buys £5000 worth of stock on credit. This represents both a liability which Bottles Ltd has incurred and an asset which Bottles Ltd has acquired. The liability is thus recorded as a credit in the payables account and the asset as a debit in the inventory account. Note that no money has changed hands, so the bank balance is not affected.
- Bottles Ltd pays wages of £1000. This is a straightforward expense payment, so the transaction is a debit in the wages account and a credit in the cash book to reflect the reduction in the bank balance.

(continued)

STEP 3

Bottles Ltd makes sales of £3000 on credit. The cost of sales is £1500.

Sales account

		Cash sales	4000
		Credit sales	3000

Receivables account

Sales on credit	3000		

Inventory

Inventory purchased	2000	Cost of sales	1000
Inventory purchased	5000	Cost of sales	1500

Cost of sales

Cost of inventory	1000		
Cost of Inventory	1500		

No money has changed hands, so the cash book is not affected. Instead Bottles Ltd has created income which is recorded as a credit in the sales account. Bottles Ltd has also created an asset, which is a debt due to Bottles Ltd to be collected at a future date. This is a debit in the receivables account.

STEP 4

So we now have all the transactions recorded and just to simplify the situation here are all the accounts fully written up with the transactions we have just included.

Share capital account

		Issue of shares	10000

Cash book

Share issue	10000	Purchase of equipment	6000
Cash sales	4000	Purchase of inventory for sale	2000
		Pay wages	1000

Fixed asset—Equipment

Equipment purchased	6000		

Inventory

Inventory purchased	2000	Cost of sales	1000
Inventory purchased	5000	Cost of sales	1500

Payables account

		Purchase of inventory	5000

Receivables account

Sales on credit	3000		

Sales account

		Cash sales	4000
		Credit sales	3000

Cost of sales

Cost of inventory	1000		
Cost of Inventory	1500		

Wages

Wages paid	1000		

All the transactions have now been recorded in the cash book and nominal ledger. In order to complete the trial balance, we have to balance all the accounts individually.

STEP 5

The first step is to balance all the accounts that contain more than one transaction. This is done as shown.

Share capital account

		Issue of shares	10000

Cash book

Share issue	10000	Purchase of equipment	6000
Cash sales	4000	Purchase of inventory for sale	2000
		Pay wages	1000
		Balance c/d	5000
	14000		14000
Balance b/d	5000		

Fixed asset—Equipment

Equipment purchased	6000		

Inventory

Inventory purchased	2000	Cost of sales	1000
Inventory purchased	5000	Cost of sales	1500
		Balance c/d	4500
	7000		7000
Balance b/d	4500		

Payables account

		Purchase of inventory	5000

(continued)

Receivables account

Sales on credit	3000		

Sales account

		Cash sales	4000
Balance c/d	7000	Credit sales	3000
	7000	Balance b/d	7000

Cost of sales

Cost of inventory	1000		
Cost of Inventory	1500	Balance c/d	2500
	2500		2500
Balance b/d	2500		

Wages

Wages paid	1000		

Once we have done this for all accounts, we can make a list of them. This is the trial balance and it looks like this:

Bottles Ltd
Trial balance

	Dr	Cr
Share capital		10000
Cash book	5000	
Fixed assets—Equipment	6000	
Inventory	4500	
Sales		7000
Cost of sales	2500	
Wages	1000	
Receivables	3000	
Payables		5000
	22000	22000

Note that both sides have the same total. In this way we can be certain the books balance.

Note that does not mean that the trial balance is correct: items could be included in the wrong account for example and, providing they have been posted correctly, the books will still balance.

Consequently, the trial balance has to be reviewed before we go on to prepare the financial statements.

Answer to stop and think

As we promised we'd do, here is the answer to why, on your bank statement, the money you have in the bank is always shown as a credit (Cr) when money in the bank is an asset. Yes, it is an asset, but it's your asset, not the bank's. It's your money and the bank owes it to you, so for the bank it is a liability, hence a Cr. If, conversely, you are overdrawn, you owe the bank money, so that is an asset to the bank; it is a Dr as far as the bank is concerned.

Test yourself

1 Toby runs a shop selling model railways. He has an overdraft at the bank of £1000. He buys some model trains for £300 and sells them for £700. He then buys track for £200, model figures for £150 and model railway carriages for £600 all in cash. He sells a train and carriages for £400 and some track for £100. He then opens an account with a model train supplier from which he acquires some more track for £200 and a model controller for £250 on credit. The supplier offers him a 2% discount for prompt payment which Toby claims. What is Toby's cash balance once these transactions are completed?

2 Basket Ltd has a customer called Wilter. At the beginning of Period 4, Wilter owed Basket R4500. In Period 4 Basket sent Wilter invoices for goods sold amounting to R8000. At the end of Period 4, Wilter owed basket R5150. How much has Wilter paid Basket in Period 4?

3 Which of the following statements is correct?
   a) A trial balance shows the financial position of the business
   b) A trial balance is a list of balances in the books
   c) A trial balance shows all the entries in the books
   d) A trial balance is a special account in the nominal ledger

4 Which of the following transactions is correctly recorded?

Transaction	Debit account	Credit account
a) A customer, Bilton & Co, pays $6000 for the previous month's invoices	Bilton in the receivables ledger	Cash book
b) Bought equipment for £12000 cash	Tangible assets equipment	Cash book
c) Received invoices from supplier Doris plc of €9750 for goods supplied on credit	Materials purchased (inventory) in nominal ledger	Doris plc account in payables ledger
d) Sold goods on credit to Moggeridge Ltd	Sales account	Moggeridge Ltd in receivables ledger

   Answer
   i. a), b), c)
   ii. b), c)
   iii. b), c), d)
   iv. a), b), d)

5 The receivables ledger account for Maximum Concrete, a supplier to Megabuild plc, shows the following transactions in May 201X. They sent invoices as follows:

1 May—	€20347
3 May—	€19730
9 May—	€24930
17 May—	€6200
25 May—	€17211

   Megabuild disputed the invoice of 9 May, and Maximum Concrete sent them a credit note for €4318. On 10 May Megabuild paid them €40077 and on 30 May another €20612.
   What is the balance on Megabuild's account with Maximum Concrete?

6 Which of the following transactions is correctly recorded?

Transaction	Debit account	Credit account
a) Introduced capital into the bank	Cash book	Capital introduced
b) Sold an item of plant on credit	Equipment sales	Payables ledger
c) Returned some goods to supplier Milton & Co	Milton & Co in payables ledger	Purchases returns in nominal ledger
d) Make loan repayments by direct debit	Long-term loan in nominal ledger	Cash book

Answer
  i. a), c), d)
  ii. a), b), d)
  iii. b), c), d)
  iv. a), b), c)

7 Jimmy Ltd has extracted the following from its accounting records:
Capital £144 000 Tangible assets £239 000, Intangible assets £45 000, Receivables total £126 000, Payables total £198 000, Bank overdraft £38 000, Short term loan £87 000, Inventories £57 000. You have been asked to produce a Trial Balance for Jimmy Ltd.

8 True or false:
Debits record assets and income?   **True/False**

9 The cost of sales account in the books of Twinkle Ltd shows the following transactions in Period 9:
Brought forward from Period 8 €287 600, Inventory sold at cost Period 9 €47 398, Returned to supplier as faulty €1863, Miscellaneous cash purchases €13 756. What is the balance on Twinkle's cost of sales account at the end of Period 9?
a) €350 617
b) €334 998
c) €346 891
d) €319 359

10 Milo has an account with a supplier called Plastic Pipes. At the beginning of Period 4, the balance on the account with Plastic Pipes in Milo's books was $18 456. Milo paid half of that balance off in Period 4 and returned goods to Plastic Pipes amounting to $839. At the end of Period 4, the balance on the account with Plastic Pipes in Milo's books was $23 060. How much had Milo bought and been invoiced for in Period 4?
a) $15 510
b) $14 671
c) $23 899
d) $5463

In the next module we will move on from the trial balance to creating a set of financial statements for an enterprise, and we will see how the trial balance is adjusted to take account of the actual financial position at the period end, rather than simply what has gone through the books. We will look at expanding on what we have learned in Module 2 and making accounting adjustments to recognize items that are not included in the financial records but which should be.

Test yourself

1 Bert Wibble runs a small joinery business with his son called Wibblewood Ltd. They carry out general joinery work and also fit kitchens for major national kitchen supply company called Megakitchen. They are contractors for that company and are paid when the work is complete.
    They have trade accounts with various suppliers for wood and other materials necessary for their work. They run two vans for work.

Generally, they are paid directly by customers for domestic joinery work, sometimes in cash and sometimes by cheque. Customers can also pay via electronic banking by bankers' direct credit.

During May 20X8 they had the following transactions:

Date	Detail	Amount (£)
1 May	Invoiced Megakitchen two installations	4540
2 May	Purchased wood from Woodyco on credit	356
3 May	Petrol for van—paid cash	50
4 May	Received electronic transfer from customer Jones for supply and fit new door	267
6 May	Paid cash from customer Pike for installing bookshelves	125
8 May	Purchased wood and brackets from Woodyco on credit	248
10 May	Received from Megakitchen	2517
13 May	Petrol for van—paid cash	67
15 May	Purchased new drills and equipment from Toolshop	85
17 May	Received electronic transfer from customer Wilson for supply and fit new window	1890
18 May	Paid Woodyco with 5% discount	1273
20 May	Invoiced Megakitchen two installations	4270
23 May	New tyre for van—paid cash	140
25 May	Sent Megakitchen credit note for incorrect invoice—Invoice £4540 should be £4450	90
30 May	Paid Toolshop	167
31 May	Paid cash to labourer for disposal of waste	200

At the beginning of the month Megakitchen owed them £2517 for installations, and they owed Woodyco £1340 and Toolshop £167.

Prepare the T accounts to record the transactions and balance each account.

2 Bodyclock Ltd sells fitness equipment, provides personal training and runs a small gym to train triathlon and marathon runners. Members of the gym pay monthly subscriptions by direct debit. Bodyclock purchases food and training supplements from a supplier called Fittit plc.

Bodyclock employs trainers to run courses on a contract basis and pays them monthly for courses run in the previous month. Bodyclock rents the building in which it operates for £750 per month.

At 31 July 20X8 a trial balance of Bodyclock was extracted as follows:

Bodyclock Ltd—Trial balance at 31 July 20X8 (€)

Gym equipment	22560	
Amount owed to Fittit		2362
Rent outstanding		750
Balance at bank	1890	
Share capital		5000
Accumulated profits		15438
Amount owed to contract trainers		1250
Amount due from members—subscriptions not paid	350	
	24800	**24800**

In August 20X8 Bodyclock had the following transactions:

Date	Detail	Amount (€)
1 August	Paid rent	750
3 August	Subscriptions received	125
5 August	Purchased supplies from Fittit plc on credit	189
9 August	Income from classes etc in cash from previous week	1789
10 August	Paid trainers	1250
10 August	Subscriptions received	225
15 August	Income from classes in cash	2162
16 August	Paid Fittit	1287
17 August	Purchased supplies from Fittit on credit	456
18 August	Purchased supplies from Bodywarm Ltd on credit	375
22 August	Income from classes in cash	956
26 August	Received short term loan from bank	5200
27 August	Purchased new training equipment	5000
28 August	Invoices from trainers	1200
29 August	Income from classes in cash	835
30 August	Paid loan interest	100
31 August	Paid Fittit	237

Using the information above:
- prepare the T accounts for Bodyclock
- balance off all accounts
- prepare the trial balance

4 Control accounts and adjustments

In this module we will consider:

- Control accounts
- Wages control account
- Adjusting the trial balance
- Depreciation of assets
- Provision for doubtful debts

It is important that any adjustments to the accounting records are carried out fairly and with a view to presenting as accurate a picture as possible of the financial position of the business for the financial period.

Clearly in many cases there is a matter of judgement. Decisions have to be made, as we will see, about the size of a possible provision for unknown costs, or the impairment to the value of an asset, but by and large these decisions have to be made based on the best information available and without any intention to distort the financial statements. However, from time to time things may go astray.

REAL LIFE
Tesco

After a warning from a whistleblower regarding the mis-booking of payments from suppliers and business costs, British supermarket Tesco was in crisis mode in September 2014. These changes had artificially inflated its profits by £250 million in the first half of the year, and the CEO was forced to bring in forensic accountants and lawyers to examine its books.

Specifically, payments from suppliers for in-store promotions and bonuses were accelerated when Tesco hit sales targets. Figures were also blurred over out of date food and stock theft.

(continued)

This type of thing isn't necessarily unusual in the industry. In an article on this matter, Graham Wearden described how, "It is common practice in the industry to agree a cost price with a supplier at the start of the year but to receive a discount at a later date based on hitting sales targets. Deciding when to book these payments is 'art rather than science,' according to one industry insider, but the margin for error would never be expected to be of the magnitude reported by Tesco.

"'Lots of different businesses flex when they choose to put certain cheques in the bank to hit quarterly targets,' said Kantar Retail analyst Bryan Roberts of the supplier payments. 'This is mobile money not related to the timing of sales. But it's robbing Peter to pay Paul because if you bring it forward you would have to compensate in the following period.'"

Of course, the company itself wasn't the only business that raised eyebrows in this matter. Pricewaterhousecoopers, the famous auditing firm, had analysed and signed off the accounts on Tesco's annual reports.

Overall, these practices wiped £2 billion of the value of Tesco almost instantly and saw the matter reported to the Financial Conduct Authority.

Source: *Tesco loses £2bn in value as investigation of profit overstatement begins. Graham Wearden 20/09/2014 Guardian online*

Stop and think

There have been many frauds and distortions over the years involving manipulation of financial accounts, many of which have been extensively documented. The classic fraud is that of Enron in the USA, but you can identify many others. For example, there has been Parmalat in Italy, Satyam in India, Toshiba and Olympus in Japan. Identify such a fraud and consider how it was carried out. What do you think was in the minds of the people who carried it out? What motivated them to do so? Do you think they anticipated getting caught and the consequences that might follow?

Control accounts

In Module 3 we looked at the payables and receivables ledgers and how invoices both for purchases and sales are written into the ledgers, thus recording the financial position of the organization with its suppliers and customers.

In a large organization, the number of accounts in a payables or receivables ledger may run into many thousands; indeed in very large businesses such as banks, credit card companies, internet suppliers, and water and power companies, the number of customer accounts runs into millions.

Clearly it is not possible to include every account in a trial balance when the financial statements for a particular period are being prepared. What is needed is a summary of all of the individual accounts in each of the payables or receivables ledgers. This summary is called a control account.

Control accounts are held in the nominal ledger. The reason for this is that when a trial balance is prepared from the nominal ledger, the balances on the payables and receivables ledger are automatically included in the trial balance.

Let us consider a purchase day book. We have seen one before for MacRusty in Module 3.

Here is the example:

MACRUSTY
Purchase day book
List of transactions—w/c 15 October 20X8

Date	Name	Payables ledger account code	Steel	Bolts	Welding rods	Paint	Wood	Engi- neering sundries	Subtotal	VAT	Total
15-Oct	Massive Metals	M094	2500	150					2650	530	3180
15-Oct	Woodly	W010					640		640	128	768
16-Oct	Engineering Stuff	E004						2120	2120	424	2544
16-Oct	Massive Metals	M094	3700						3700	740	4440
17-Oct	Greys Paints	G076				735			735	147	882
18-Oct	Strictly Steel	S062	5023						5023	1005	6028
19-Oct	Welders Supplies	W002			376				376	75	451
									0	0	0
	TOTAL		**11223**	**150**	**376**	**735**	**640**	**2120**	**15244**	**3049**	**18293**
	Nominal code		**S11**	**B04**	**W01**	**P06**	**W02**	**S03**		**V01**	

We can see from the list of transactions that invoices to the value of €18293 have been posted into the credit of MacRusty's payables ledger.

Because the payables ledger control account is a summary of the payables ledger, the total of €18293 is posted into the credit of the payables ledger control account in the nominal ledger.

This can cause confusion in the mind of learners, because obviously the individual invoices making up that €18293 have also been posted into the credit of the individual supplier's accounts in the payables ledger. So instead of double-entry have we got triple-entry?

The answer, obviously, is no. The control accounts are, effectively, a memorandum or ancillary account, which is just used for accounts preparation to avoid the tedium of having to list thousands of individual accounts.

Payables control account

Total of payments made to suppliers from the cash book	Total of Invoices posted from purchase day book in the period
Total of credit notes received from suppliers from purchase day book	
Total of discounts received	

Similarly the receivables control account will include this in any given financial period

Receivables control account

Total of invoices posted from sales day book in the period	Total of amounts received from customers from cash book
	Total of credit notes given to customers from sales day book
	Total of discounts allowed

The key point is that the balance on the control account must always equal the total of all the balances on the individual payables or receivables accounts.

If it does not, then either something has been posted to the control account that is not in the ledger, or something is in the ledger but not in the control account. This can happen with manually written books of account, but is virtually impossible with computerized accounting systems where invoices, payments, discounts and credit note postings are automatically written into the control account when being entered in the appropriate ledger.

Let us look at an example.

EXAMPLE

West Ltd has the following entries in its account books for June 20X8:

		$
Purchase day book	Invoices posted to payables ledger	215 893
Purchase returns day book	Credit notes posted to payables ledger	3 298
Cash book	Payments to suppliers	189 375
Discounts received	Discounts due to prompt payment	1 769

The total of payables ledger balances at the beginning of June 20X8 was $187 394.
The payables control account in the nominal ledger of West Ltd therefore looks like this:

		Balance brought down	187 394
Credit notes from PRDB	3 298	Invoices from PDB	215 893
Payments to suppliers	189 375		
Discounts received	1 769		
Balance carried down	208 845		
	403 287		403 287
		Balance b/d	208 845

In essence, the payables ledger control and the receivables ledger control accounts are written up in exactly the same way as an account for an individual supplier or customer would be, except using totals instead of individual invoices or payments.

Stop and think	As we include the control accounts in the nominal ledger, can we extract a trial balance without including the balances in the payables and receivables ledger? Using the same principles could we establish a cash book control account in the nominal ledger? If we did all this, could we not extract all the balances from the nominal ledger at the end of a financial period and the two sides would automatically balance?

Wages control account

Wages and salaries can be problematic when an employer deducts tax and social security or national insurance payments at source. In some cases, other items are also deducted from the payment of wages and salaries before the employee receives the net payment. These can include such deductions as:

- pension fund payments
- court orders to pay alimony or child support

- trade union subscriptions
- employee share ownership schemes

All of these, of course, are deducted with the consent of the employee.

The employee receives a net payment, so what the employee gets looks like this:

			£
Gross pay—month 3			2250
Deduct	Taxation	243	
	National insurance	135	
	Pension fund	90	
	Trade union sub	5	473
Net pay			1777

In addition, the employer will make additional national insurance and pension fund contributions, so these have to be accounted for.

With a considerable number of employees, it is necessary to summarize the payments using a wages control account. The reasons for this are:

- taxation and national insurance have to be paid over to the tax authorities
- pension fund deductions to the pension fund
- trade union subscriptions to the trade union
- net pay to all the employees

The totals have to be calculated and checked to the payroll each week or month depending on the frequency of payment. In larger organizations, a payroll department will deal with the individual amounts payable to employees and a computerized payroll system will produce the payroll and calculate the relevant totals for entry in the books of account.

The wages control account is designed to ensure that the payments made to the employees and the relevant bodies for deductions equals the total gross pay plus the employers contributions.

EXAMPLE

Hubert Ltd has the following payroll entries for Month 4:

	£
Gross wages	50 750
Income tax	8 000
Employee national insurance	2 000
Employer national insurance	2 030
Employee pension contributions	800
Employer pension contributions	800
Trade union fees	600

Using a systematic approach, you can break these figures down into who gets paid what.

(continued)

1 The employees will receive net wages of £39 350
   This amount is calculated by subtracting any employee deductions from the gross wage.
   Gross Wages − Income Tax − Employee National Insurance − Employee Pension − Trade Union Fees
   £50 750 − £8000 − £2000 − £800 − £600 = £39 350
2 The tax authorities will receive £1030
   This amount is calculated by adding up any of the figures which will need to be paid to them.
   Income Tax + Employee National Insurance + Employer National Insurance
   £8000 + £2000 + £2030
3 Pension providers will receive £1600
   This amount is simply calculated by adding the two pension figures together.
4 Trade union will receive £600

The double-entry is as follows:
The income account will ultimately need to record the total amount of wages and other costs paid by the business. We thus have a wages expense which is the total gross pay. in this case £50 750 plus the employer's contributions to national insurance and pension. The total wage expense is:

$$50 750 + 2030 + 800 = 53 580$$

This needs to go to the debit of the wages cost account, or it could be split to go to the debit of a national insurance employer's contribution account and a employer's pension fund contribution account if the business wanted to keep control of these costs separately.

In the interest of brevity, we will lump them all in one account.

As this is an expense, it is a debit.

The credit goes into the wages control account, thus:

Wages cost—expense account

Gross pay and employer's contributions Month 4	53 580		

Wages control account

		Month 4 Gross pay	53 580

The next step is to pay the wages. Payment is net pay, so this is £39 350. The debit for this is to wages control and the credit is, of course, the cash book recording the payment:

Wages control account

Net pay	39 350	Month 4 Gross pay	53 580

Cash book

		Net pay Month 4	39 350

The next step is to deal with the amounts due to the tax authorities and the pension fund.

These will be paid later than the net pay, so we cannot enter them in the cash book; instead we open an account in the payables ledger for the tax authorities and the pension fund and enter a credit in those accounts. The debit again goes to wages control.

We have calculated above that the amount due to the tax authority is £12030, the pension fund is due £1600 and the trade union £600

Wages control account

Net pay	39 350	Month 4 Gross pay	53 580
Taxation	12 030		
Pension	1 600		
Trade union	600		

Tax authority

		Deductions Month 4	12 030

Pension fund

		Deductions Month 4	1 600

Trade union

		Deductions Month 4	600

If everything has been posted correctly, the wages control account will balance.

Wages control account

Net pay	39 350	Month 4 Gross pay	53 580
Taxation	12 030		
Pension	1 600		
Trade union	600		
	53 580		53 580

When the time comes to pay the tax authorities, the pension fund and the trade union these can be dealt with in the normal way by:

Dr	Tax authority	12 030		
	Pension fund	1 600		
	Trade union	600		
			Cr Cash book	14 230

This can look quite complicated at first, but a moment's thought will show that what we are doing is simply creating a credit in an account—the wages control account—which is to balance the debits of the total wages costs for a period, and then using that account to set up a debit for the payment and the liabilities for deductions. It is quite an elegant solution to what can be a complex set of entries where payrolls are rather large and there are dozens of different types of deduction. It is a way of keeping track of everything.

If the account does not balance, something has gone wrong and will have to be investigated.

Stop and think

Look at a payslip you have had or see if you can find an example of one online. How many entries are there on it? Can you identify what they are and how they would all be posted into the wages and salaries system?

Adjusting the trial balance

When preparing financial statements, the trial balance is just the starting point, though an important one. Once the trial balance, or TB for short, is prepared we know that the books balance. As we saw in Module 3, in reality, with computer-based systems, it is virtually impossible for the books not to balance, as the systems will not permit the posting of only one side of the double-entry.

Once we have the trial balance, we can go on to prepare the final accounts. To do this, however, we have to make some adjustments to the figures in the trial balance before we have the final picture.

It is a fundamental accounting principle that accounts are prepared on an accruals basis (Module 1). This means that we have to adjust the records of what has been processed through the books of account for what is not included, to ensure that the accounts for the financial period properly reflect the actual result for the period, not simply what has been put through the books. As such, further double entries in the ledger will be required.

These consist of adjustments for:

- items that are not included
- items that relate to a different accounting period
- the writing down of asset values—depreciation and amortization
- the disposal of assets
- valuation of inventory

We will deal with each of these in turn.

ACCRUALS

The accounts an organization prepares cover a fixed amount of time. They may be annual accounts covering a year, or monthly management accounts. Because of this, we need to record in those accounts all expenses and income that relate to the accounting period, but only to that accounting period.

Accruals are costs which have been incurred but not yet invoiced, or income which is earned but hasn't yet been received. The word 'incurred' is another accountancy jargon word. What it means is that the expense is committed: the organization is legally bound to pay it even if an invoice or other demand for payment has not been received.

ASSETS AND LIABILITIES   For example, the business takes a delivery of raw materials to be processed. The business has accepted the materials and may have even started to use them, so has to pay for them and is simply waiting for the invoice to arrive. The cost of those materials has to be included in the financial statements, so the accountants anticipate the invoice and make an accrual in the raw materials purchased account in the nominal ledger.

Note an important point here: the materials are on the premises, so we have to include them in inventory. If we include them as an asset in our accounts, we must also include the liability to the supplier so that we do not distort the financial statements. If the invoice hasn't been received we must accrue it in our accounts.

The organization must establish in their accounting systems procedures for identifying goods or services delivered but not invoiced, so that period end accruals can be identified. In Module 1 we looked at the outline of a basic purchasing system and the internal controls within it. Part of that control mechanism is a process of capturing accruals and, in particular, purchase accruals.

Several frauds have taken place whereby purchase accruals have been deliberately left to fall into the following financial period whilst inventories have been included in the current period. This actually distorts two financial periods: the current one, which has more assets than liabilities and the following one, which has more liabilities than assets. This means costs are understated in the current period creating overstated profits. If managers' pay is linked to profit, managers may benefit financially by manipulating the figures. The problem for managers carrying out this manipulation of results is that, having distorted the results for Year 1 by pushing costs into Year 2, they then have to distort Year 2 by even more to take account of the costs from Year 1. This goes on and on until it becomes ludicrous and the fraud is exposed.

THE NEED FOR ACCRUALS   If a cost has been incurred that relates to the financial period but the invoice for it has not been received or processed, we must make an accrual. For example, a business must pay its electricity bill. If the electricity is billed quarterly in arrears and the quarter end doesn't coincide with the financial year end, there will have to be an accrual for the period which falls within the financial year.

We can illustrate this with a timeline. Suppose we are preparing financial statements for twelve months and the final quarter's electricity bill is not received until after the year's end, too late to be posted into the books. The timeline illustrates the point.

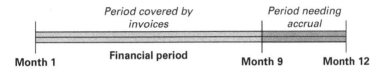

Here, we have paid for nine months of electricity, having been billed quarterly in arrears. We have yet to be invoiced for the last quarter. If our annual bill was £12 000 then we could estimate the amount to be accrued as one quarter of the annual bill, namely £3000. By doing so we reflect the full year's cost of electricity despite having only paid three quarters' worth at the end of our financial year. The theory being that if the business hypothetically closed down right at the period end that amount would still have to be paid by the business.

Once the invoice arrives, it will be matched against the accrual so the expense is not recorded twice. We will see how this is done shortly.

Income might be earned but not yet received. For example, interest on an investment might be *receivable* (another technical word meaning capable of being received or due) but it has not been paid over.

EXAMPLE

North Ltd's financial period end is 31 March. It has to pay insurance on all its properties, plant and vehicles. The insurance charge is €24 000 per year. The insurance company invoices twice a year. The financial period is the year to 31 December. The insurance company has not sent its invoice for the second half of the year.
How should North account for the missing invoice?

ANSWER

An accrual must be made for €12 000.
The entries in North's insurance account in the nominal ledger will look like this:

Nominal Ledger

1 The accrual for the invoice for the second half year is entered in the accounts

Insurance	
01-Jan-17 Insurance to 31 July 2017	12 000
Accrual—Insurance to 31 Dec 2017	12 000

(continued)

2　The cost of insurance is now correct at €24000, which will be charged to the income account, BUT there is a problem. The accrual has only one entry, and we know there must be two—so how do we deal with this?

Insurance

01-Jan-17 Insurance to 31 July 2017	12000	Charge to income statement	24000
Accrual—Insurance to 31 Dec 2017	12000		
	24000		24000

3　The accrual is carried down to the opposite side of the account. As a credit balance it will appear as a payable in the statement of assets and liabilities

Insurance

01-Jan-17 Insurance to 31 July 2017	12000	Charge to Income Statement	24000
Accrual—Insurance to 31 Dec 2017	12000		
	24000		24000
		Accrual b/d Insurance to 31 Dec	12000

4　When the invoice finally appears it will be processed like this.
The accrual is cancelled out in the nominal ledger by the actual invoice.
This makes sure that the full insurance cost ends up in the correct financial period.

Insurance

01-Jan-17 Insurance to 31 July 2017	12000	Charge to income statement	24000
Accrual—Insurance to 31 Dec 2017	12000		
	24000		24000
01-Jan-17 Insurance to 31 Dec 2017	12000	Accrual b/d Insurance to 31 Dec	12000

PAYABLES LEDGER

Slow Insurance Company

	01-Jan-18 Insurance to 31 Dec 2017	12000

Exactly the same process can be used to accrue income earned but not received.

Let us assume that an organization has made a loan of €200000 on 1 June, on which it receives interest at 6% per annum payable quarterly in arrears in February, May, August and November. Interest of €12000 is therefore due for this financial period.

The accounting period is the year to 31 March and the latest instalment of interest was paid in February. One month's interest is due for the period from the end of February to the end of March. The accrual is €1000 (one quarter's interest [€3000] divided by 3). The accounting entries for the interest accrual will look like this:

Nominal Ledger

1　The accrual for the interest due for the last month of the financial year is entered in the accounts

Interest

	Interest paid to end February	9000
	One month to 31 March	1000

2 The cost of insurance is now correct at €24 000, which will be charged to the income account, BUT there is a problem. The accrual has only one entry, and we know there must be two—so how do we deal with this?

Interest

Income to income statement	10 000	Interest paid to end February	9 000
		Accrual One month to 31 March	1 000
	10 000		10 000

3 The accrual is carried down to the opposite side of the account. As a debit balance it will appear as a receivable in the statement of assets and liabilities

Interest

Income to income statement	10 000	Interest paid to end February	9 000
		Accrual c/d One month to 31 March	1 000
	10 000		10 000
Accrual b/d One month to 31 March	1 000		

4 When the interest is paid it will be processed like this.
The accrual is cancelled out in the nominal ledger by the receipt. It is effectively split, with €1000 being included in the previous financial period, leaving a net €2000 for the current period.

Interest

Income to Income Statement	10 000	Interest paid to end February	9 000
		Accrual c/d One month to 31 March	1 000
	10 000		10 000
01-Apr Interest to 31 March 2017	1 000	31-May Interest on loan	3 000

CASH BOOK

31-May Interest on loan to XX Ltd	3 000	

Again the aim is to make sure that the accounting period includes all the expense and income that relate to it and that, at the end of it, the statement of financial position includes all the amounts the organization owns and owes and all that is due to it.

Stop and think

Can you make inquiries in your organization or place of study as to how they capture accruals, i.e. how do they know what to accrue?

Otherwise, what sort of system do you think should be established to make sure that all outstanding accruals have been identified and quantified?

PREPAYMENTS

Prepayments are, effectively, accruals in reverse. These arise when a payment is made in advance, i.e. it is effectively an overpayment made in the current year.

This is an adjustment that is made for costs which have been paid in advance. The easiest way to illustrate this is by example. Suppose the organization rents its business premises. Its financial period end is 31 March and the rent is due on 1 January. The organization pays six months' rent on 1 January. At 31 March, three months of the rent relates to the financial period just ended and three months relates to the next financial period—so that three months is prepaid.

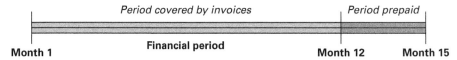

As we have already seen it is a fundamental accounting principle that a set of financial statements for any given period contain only the transactions for that period. Expenditure that relates to a future period therefore has to be carried forward into that period.

This is done by including the excess payment as a receivable, i.e. a sum due back to the business, the theory being that if the business hypothetically closed down right at the period end that amount would have to be refunded to the business.

EXAMPLE

A gain we find North Ltd, which started in business on 1 March and rents a factory from the local council at a rent of £12 000 per year.

This time rent is paid in advance and North has so far paid 15 months' rent.

North's year end is 28 February.

REQUIRED

How should North account for the rent overpaid?

ANSWER

North will have paid £15 000 in rent.

As the total rent for the year is £12 000, North will have to create a prepayment for £3000.

The entries in North's rent payable account will look like this:

Nominal Ledger

1 The rent has been paid for 15 months

Rent			
Rental payment	15 000		

2 North's rent for the financial year is only £12 000, so £3000 has been paid in advance at the financial period end. This is a prepayment

Rent			
Rental payment	15 000	Prepaid rent	3 000

3 The correct rent can be charged to the income account, and the £3000 prepayment carried down into the next period as a receivable.
The logic is that if the business closed at the end of the financial period, the £3000 would be refundable.

Rent

Rental payment	15000	Prepaid rent c/d	3000
		Income account	12000
	15000		15000
Prepaid rent b/d	3000		

As you can see once again, there are two entries for the prepayment. The amount of the prepayment is credited to the nominal ledger rent account in order to reduce the debit entry for the expense.

As we need two entries, the prepayment has to be carried down (c/d) to the next accounting period, and it will be included in the statement of financial position as a receivable.

VALUATION OF INVENTORY   In compliance with IAS 2, inventories are valued at the lower of cost and net realizable value: in other words the lower of what the items cost to buy or what they could be sold for on the open market.

If inventories are damaged or obsolete, they must be written down to resale or scrap value, or if they are worth nothing then they must be written off altogether.

Here is an example: This is an extract from an inventory count and valuation exercise:

Product	Quantity/Units	Cost per unit £	Selling price/unit £	Selling costs £
A	915	2.10	4.75	0.35
B	3110	0.90	0.85	
C	5100	1.45	1.50	0.15

Note that:

- Product A is valued at £2.10 per unit—its original cost
- Product B is valued at £0.85 per unit as the selling price is lower than the cost price
- Product C is trickier as the selling price is higher than the cost price but there are selling costs, so it will be valued at £1.50 − £0.15 = £1.35 per unit

PROVISIONS

In some cases, there are situations when costs have been incurred but it is not possible to quantify them with any reasonable degree of certainty. In these cases, the accountants make an estimate based on what information they have available and a 'best guess' based on experience.

For example, suppose the business is involved in a court case where they are being sued by an irate customer for damages caused by supplying faulty goods. It is possible that any legal fees involved can be estimated with reasonable certainty (the lawyers will supply that information) so an accrual can be made for legal fees but the amount of damages a judge might award were they to lose the case is less certain. An estimate, a provision, for damages is made and included in the financial statements.

Once the real figure is known, it can be offset against the provision so the damages are not included in the financial statements twice. We will look at how this is done later.

Provisions are an estimate of costs that might be incurred but that cannot be accurately quantified. It is an estimate, based on what information is available, of a liability which the business may have to meet in the future.

Examples of provisions are:

- an estimate of future bad debts
- estimated losses on contracts in progress
- estimated damages from a court case

The accounting entries for provisions are exactly the same as those for an accrual, so there is no need to repeat the example. They are treated as payables in the statement of financial position and charged to the income account as an expense.

Depreciation of assets

Nearly all businesses have some form of asset with which they carry on their business. These may be:

- tangible assets such as property, equipment, vehicles, computers, etc.
- intangible assets such as copyrights, trademarks, patents. etc.
- goodwill on the acquisition of a business (we will look at this separately)

There are two considerations we must take into account when looking at this question of depreciation.

First is the fact that all assets lose value over time. Even property (that is buildings, not land) loses value over time. It may be that some property built by the Romans, the ancient Egyptians or the Normans in the 10th century are still with us, but the real facts are that modern buildings are not built to last any more than a vehicle or item of equipment is. All tangible assets, except land, have a shelf life and this varies according to the type of asset. Land is the exception—it has no shelf life and is not subject to depreciation.

Consequently, what has to be determined is the economic life of the asset—that is its productive useful life as an asset to be used in the business. This is different from its physical life—a piece of equipment may well go on working long after its first owner has parted with it. It is the period of time that the assets has value to the organization. Land is considered to have an infinite economic life—presumably on the basis that no more of it is being made, so it will always have a use.

Some assets—motor vehicles, computers, software—may have a relatively short economic life of say three to four years; however other assets like equipment, machinery, furniture and fittings, etc., may be thought of as having a much longer economic life—say 10–15 years.

Secondly, assets may become impaired—that is:

- no longer of use, or as much use, to the business as they were when first acquired
- where the market value of the asset has declined significantly so that, were it to be sold, the amount received would be significantly less than the value at which it is being carried in the books

Accordingly, all assets (except freehold land) have to be depreciated in the financial statements to some degree. We will look at the question of impairment in more detail a little later.

Another factor to take into account when looking at depreciating assets is the residual value. At the end of its useful life an asset may have some resale or scrap value. For example, an item of equipment may be no longer of use in a factory because it is too old or to slow for the current level of production—however it may be of use in a smaller business, so it could be sold on at a secondhand value. This resale or trade in value, or its scrap value, is known in accounting as the residual value, i.e. the value that is left once the item has been fully depreciated.

CALCULATING DEPRECIATION   There are many ways to calculate depreciation, but in practical terms the two basic methods that are the most commonly used are:

- straight line
- diminishing balance

Under the straight line method, the value of the asset is written off down to its residual value, if there is one, over its estimated useful life by equal amounts each year.

Under the diminishing balance method, the net value of the asset after deducting both the accumulated depreciation of previous years plus the residual value is depreciated each year.

EXAMPLE

North has fixed assets amounting to £200 000. North decides that a depreciation rate of 20% per annum is appropriate. There is no residual value.

It can't decide whether to write off on a straight line or on a diminishing balance basis, so asks for a comparison of calculations.

REQUIRED

Calculate the depreciation on both bases.

ANSWER

Depreciation—straight line or reducing balance?

	Straight line	Net book value of asset	Diminishing balance	Net book value of asset
Asset value	200 000		200 000	
Depreciation				
Year 1	40 000	160 000	40 000	160 000 Both methods produce the same result in the first year
Year 2	40 000	120 000	32 000	128 000 Reducing balance method is based on (200 000 − 40 000) × 20%
Year 3	40 000	80 000	25 600	102 400 Reducing balance method is based on (200 000 − 40 000 − 32 000) × 20%
Year 4	40 000	40 000	20 480	81 920 Reducing balance method is based on (200 000 − 40 000 − 32 000 − 25 600) × 20%
Year 5	40 000	0	16 384	65 536 ...and so on
Year 6			13 107	52 429
Year 7			10 486	41 943
Year 8			8 389	33 554
Year 9			6 711	26 844
Year 10			5 369	21 475
			and so on....	

(continued)

As you can see, the straight line method is a simple write-off of the same amount each year. The net book value (its original cost minus the total depreciation to date) declines in equal annual amounts. This method might be suitable for assets with a relatively short useful economic life, such as computers or motor vehicles.

In contrast, the diminishing balance method gives a proportionally higher write-off during the earlier years and writes the asset off over a longer period. This is more likely to reflect the reality of the life of assets such as plant and machinery or commercial vehicles, which tend to have a much longer life. As the asset ages, the amount of depreciation written off each year reduces. In our example, after ten years the asset still has a net book value of £21 475.

The choice of which method to use and the estimates of economic life are up to the organization, and most will use a combination of both to write down their tangible asset values each year. The overriding consideration is that whichever method is chosen it must be:

- fair and reasonable in the context of the particular type of asset
- must be applied consistently year after year—once started the same basis must be continued unless there is an overriding reason for changing

IMPAIRMENT   Essentially, the value of an asset to the business is considered to be impaired if the asset is no longer useful because it is obsolete or damaged in some way, or is no longer fit for purpose in the market in which it is required to function.

For example, if the market for widgets measures them according to a statutory standard specification, all the machinery-making widgets will be designed to produce them according to that measurement. If the standard statutory specification changes and the machinery cannot be adapted, it suddenly becomes obsolete and its value plummets, perhaps to a scrap value. Accordingly, the value of the machine must be written down in the books to that scrap value. The value is impaired.

So whilst previously the machine might have been depreciated according to a fixed formula, i.e. on a straight line or diminishing balance basis, there must now be an extra amount written off the value of the machine in the books of account, which is known as an impairment loss.

Stop and think

Look at the price of a new car, then consider the value after 6 months. How different are the two values? Why is a nearly new car worth so much less than a new car after so little time?

Is the rate of depreciation on a new car unrealistic? In accounting we often depreciate cars on a straight line basis—is this the best way?

DOUBLE-ENTRY   How do we actually enter the depreciation and any impairment loss through the books of account? We need to think about two things.

In the books of account, the assets are shown as debits and they appear in the statement of financial position at the financial period end. The amount of depreciation written off those assets must therefore be a credit, and will also appear in the statement of financial position so that the:

Value of the asset (i.e. cost or revalued amount) − Accumulated depreciation = Net book value

At the same time, depreciation and any impairment loss is also a cost to the business. This is to reflect the loss in value of assets due to the passage of time or other considerations, such as obsolescence or other factors giving rise to impairment.

Because depreciation is a cost, it will be shown as a debit in the income account. So we have double-entry, which is:

Debit: Depreciation − Income account

Credit − Accumulated depreciation − Statement of financial position

EXAMPLE

In 20X6, a new company Winkle Ltd acquired tangible fixed assets amounting to a cost of R350 000. This is divided into:

- Equipment   R245 000
- Computers   R50 000
- Motor vehicles   R55 000

The rates of depreciation being used are:

- Equipment—15 per cent pa on a diminishing balance basis
- Computers—straight line over four years
- Motor vehicles—straight line over three years

One year's depreciation was charged last year.
None of the assets have a residual value.
During the current financial period 20X7, Winkle purchased a new machine for R60 000. A full year's depreciation is charged in the year of purchase. We need to calculate the depreciation due for 20X7 and show the accounting entries.

ANSWER

The fixed assets schedule will look like this:

Winkle Ltd
Tangible assets

	Cost of assets at 20X6	Purchase of assets	Cost of assets at 20X7	Depreciation 20X6	Depreciation 20X7	Total depreciation at 20X7	Net book value at 20X7
Equipment	245 000	60 000	305 000	36 750	40 237	76 987	228 013
Computers	50 000		50 000	12 500	12 500	25 000	25 000
Motor vehicles	55 000		55 000	18 333	18 333	36 666	18 334
	350 000	**60 000**	**410 000**	**67 583**	**71 070**	**138 653**	**271 347**

The calculations include the following:

- In real life, assets will be depreciated individually and organizations will keep records of the cost and depreciation of each individual asset.
- Clearly, an asset cannot be depreciated more than its original cost.
- Where there has been an addition and the whole of the assets are to be depreciated for a full year, the calculation is reasonably straightforward. The calculation for the equipment depreciation is:

$$\text{Cost} - \text{R245 000} + \text{addition R60 000} - \text{Accumulated depreciation R36 750} = \underline{\underline{\text{R268 250}}}$$

$$\text{R268 250} \times 15\% = \underline{\underline{\text{R40 237}}}$$

(continued)

- If the new addition is to be depreciated for a part year, the depreciation on it would be calculated separately, but as stated above, in real life each individual asset would be depreciated separately in any case.
- Computers and motor vehicles are depreciated on a straight line basis, so the depreciation is the same each year until they are fully written off.
- The total depreciation debit will be written off in the year to the income account (we will look at this further in Module 5).
- The depreciation credit in the accumulated depreciation accounts is carried forward year after year and will appear in the statement of financial position at the end of the financial period.

Depreciation calculations and the double-entry are reasonably straightforward once the underlying logic is understood.

Winkle Ltd
Tangible assets
Double-entry
Depreciation—Income Account

Depreciation charge for 20X7	71 071		

Depreciation—Equipment

		Brought forward from 20X6	36 750
		Added for 20X7	40 237
			76 987

Depreciation—Computers

		Brought forward from 20X6	12 500
		Added for 20X7	12 500
			25 000

Depreciation—Motor vehicles

		Brought forward from 20X6	18 333
		Added for 20X7	18 333
			36 666

This will become more apparent in Module 5 when we construct a set of financial statements.

AMORTIZATION   Amortization is another accountants' word and simply means depreciation of an intangible asset. An intangible asset is something that has value but no physical presence. Examples are such things as patents and trademarks. If there is a cost associated with creating the intangible asset, the cost has to be written off over a period of years—generally its estimated economic life. That write-off is called amortization and it is dealt with in exactly the same way as depreciation.

DISPOSAL OF A TANGIBLE FIXED ASSET   When a tangible fixed asset is sold, three things need to happen:

- The cost has to be written out of the tangible assets cost account.
- The accumulated depreciation relating to that asset has to be written out of the accumulated depreciation account.
- The proceeds of sale have to be accounted for.

To do this, we use a fixed assets disposals account. Here is an example.

EXAMPLE

Boggly Plc has sold its whanging machine to a smaller company, Hooper Ltd, for parts. The whanging machine originally cost £250000, but Boggly have had it a long time and it has been depreciated, so now has a net book value of £22000. Hooper has agreed to pay Boggly £25000 for the machine.

The entries in the disposal of fixed assets account are:

Disposal of fixed assets

Cost of whanging machine	250000	Accumulated depreciation	
		Whanging machine	228000
		Proceeds of sale	25000
		Loss on sale	3000
	250000		250000

- The debit for the loss on sale is the income account.
- The debit for the sale proceeds is either the cash book, if it has been received, or a receivables account in the name of Hooper Ltd.
- The cost of tangible assets is credited with the cost of the whanging machine
- Accumulated depreciation is debited with the depreciation on it.

In short, all the entries relating to the machine are collected in one account and the resultant loss or profit on sale transferred to the income account when the financial statements are prepared.

Provisions for doubtful debts

The provision for doubtful debts is made using the same principles and the double-entry is the same as for an ordinary provision but the method of calculation or estimation is rather different.

Any organization that is owed money for goods or services supplied is never totally sure it will be paid in full until the money is in the bank. There may be every reasonable expectation that the outstanding amount, the receivable, will be paid in full but it is never absolutely sure.

This can be because:

1 There is a dispute about the amount charged as not having been previously agreed, e.g. the invoice quotes a price greater than that shown on a price list
2 An agreed discount has not been given
3 The invoice is incorrectly calculated
4 The services or goods supplied have been rejected or refused in whole or in part
5 The customer is short of funds and cannot pay in accordance with agreed credit terms
6 The customer has become insolvent and cannot pay at all or can only pay a small proportion of the outstanding amount

In the case of the first four items on the list the usual way of dealing with the issue, once it has been resolved with the customer, is by means of a credit note. We looked at this in Module 3.

That situation is all very well; where there has been a mistake on an invoice or a dispute about what was provided and the issue can be resolved with a credit note. But what about the last two situations on the above list, where the customer has a reduced ability to pay?

This is where the prudent accountant will look to make a provision for doubtful debts in the financial statements. This is not suggesting that the debt will never be paid but rather allowing an estimation of the cost of the debt if it goes bad. Actual bad debt is covered below. Firstly, however, the prudent accountant will prepare what is known as an aged debt analysis from the receivables ledger. In reality, most accounting software packages will prepare such an analysis as a report, so it's not particularly difficult.

It works like this.

Here is the receivables ledger account for Megablast plc in the books of Mightybig plc:

Receivables ledger
Megablast plc-MO12

Balance brought forward from August		12850			
(includes €3250 from June in dispute)					
2-Sep	Invoice	2500	12-Sep	Received	7000
7-Sep	Invoice	12600	19-Sep	Received	5100
9-Sep	Invoice	9900	30-Sep	Received	44600
12-Sep	Invoice	22100			
16-Sep	Invoice	18750	Balance c/d		67700
23-Sep	Invoice	19250			
30-Sep	Invoice	26450			
		124400			124400
1-Oct	Balance b/d	67700	3-Oct	Received	45700
4-Oct	Invoice	9250	16-Oct	Received	21050
7-Oct	Invoice	11800	30-Oct	Received	42400
12-Oct	Invoice	3950			
19-Oct	Invoice	16250			
22-Oct	Invoice	22200	Balance c/d		40630
31-Oct	Invoice	18630			
		149780			149780
	Balance b/d	40630			
8-Nov	Invoice	12970	4-Nov	Received	18630
12-Nov	Invoice	18250	23-Nov	Received	40860
15-Nov	Invoice	9640			
22-Nov	Invoice	13780	Balance c/d		51750
30-Nov	Invoice	15970			
		111240			111240
1-Dec	Balance b/d	51750			

The balance on the account at the end of November is €51750. However, what we need to discover is how one arrives at that figure. We do this by matching the receipts from Megablast to the invoices Mightybig has sent them. There are several key points to note here:

1 The receipt of €7000 on 12 Sept and the receipt of €5100 on 19 Sept pay off the opening balance of €12850 except the €3250 in dispute + the first invoice in September of €2500.
2 The other receipts in September can be matched against invoices so that the balance at the end of September of €67700 is made up of €3250 not paid as part of the opening balance + three invoices (€18750 + €19250 + €26450).

3 In October the first receipt of €45 700 pays of the two invoices in September for €19 250 + €26 450. The earlier invoice for €18 750 has not been paid as part of that payment.

4 For the remainder of October and November, receipts from Megablast can be matched against invoices quite easily.

5 At the end of November there is a balance of €51 750 on the account of Megablast. This consists of:

Invoice not paid from pre September	3 250
Invoice not paid from September	18 750
November invoice	13 780
November invoice	15 970
	€51 750

In this situation it may be recognized that the two earlier invoices may not be paid. It may be that Mightybig will end up sending credit notes to cancel the invoices in dispute, but whilst the dispute continues the amount owed by Megabuild is uncertain—Mightybig might persuade them to pay part of the invoices.

The point here is that Mightybig cannot uphold an asset in its financial statements, i.e. the amount due from Megablast, at a value that is not recoverable. It is possible that Megablast does not owe €51 750 but some smaller number, so to carry a value of €51 750 in the statement of financial position would be to overstate the assets of the business. Prudence dictates that the disputed invoices should be provided for at this stage.

This exercise is carried out for all accounts in the receivables ledger.

At the end of the whole analysis of the receivables ledger, the accountant will have produced a schedule which looks like this:

Mightybig

Aged debt analysis (extract)

Account number	Account name	Total	Current	Over 30 days	Over 60 days	Over 90 days	120 days +
A345	Alphastone	3 400	3 400				
A358	Arrow	10 745	9 400	1 345			
B257	Binkle	20 690	2 390	9 600	8 700		
B980	BBB Const	13 158	4 598			8 560	
C100	Crinkle	3 114	497	92	450	1 100	975
D095	Doggle	19 574	19 574				
M012	Megablast	51 750	29 750			18 750	3 250
N033	Nutter	52 389	52 389				
R897	Russell	35 147	1 256	33 891			
Z083	Zeta	21 965	21 965				
		231 932	145 219	44 928	9 150	28 410	4 225

Assuming the terms of trade are that invoices should be paid within 30 days, as can be seen from the schedule, there are several accounts which are over the 30-day limit. Accounts for:

- Binkle—€8700
- BBB—€8560
- Crinkle—€3114—because it has continually defaulted on payments
- Megablast—€22 000

These are causes for concern.

Now there might be good and sufficient reasons why these amounts have not been paid on time and, if there are, the accountants might decide that no provision is necessary as the amounts will be paid in full eventually.

If not, a provision is required. In this case the accountant decides to provide for all the debts shown above, a total of €42 374.

In an ongoing business, there will probably already be a provision in the nominal ledger so it is necessary to update it for the new one.

The double-entry for the provision for doubtful debts is this.

Provision for doubtful debts

NOMINAL LEDGER
PROVISION FOR DOUBTFUL DEBTS

		Provision for doubtful debts b/d from previous period	31 458
Provision for doubtful debts current period c/d	42 374	Charge to income account	10 916
	42 374		42 374
		Provision for doubtful debts b/d	42 374

The way to complete the double-entry is to include the provision as a debit on the account in the current period, so it is carried down as a credit to offset against the receivables asset.

Note that any increase (or decrease) in the provision is charged to the income account so that the account balances.

In the statement of financial position, the receivables are shown as a net figure, e.g.

Receivables	2 567 897
Provision for doubtful debts	(124 743)
	2 443 154

so that the receivables are shown at their recoverable amount.

BAD DEBTS   If a debt is beyond recovery—say the customer goes into liquidation with no assets and no hope of recovery—there is no point in making a provision for a doubtful debt. The debt is more than doubtful—it has gone for good.

Consequently, the only thing to do is to write it off to the income account. The double-entry is:

Dr Income account − Bad debts written off
Cr Customer account in the receivables ledger.

The main thing to remember is also to make an entry in the receivables ledger control account to ensure it will still agree to the list of balances.

Test yourself

1 Noggle Ltd has the following balances in its accounting records:

Opening balance on purchase ledger control	126 471
Payments to suppliers per cash book	99 360
Discounts received	349
Closing balance on purchase ledger control	158 240

How much was posted from the purchase day book for invoices in the period?

2 Jakeways Ltd has the following entries from its Month 2 payroll:

Gross pay	346 789
Income tax	42 814
Social insurance	51 287
Pension fund	22 742
Employer social insurance contributions	82 765
Employer pension fund contributions	64 981

Using a T account, create the wages control account.

3 Jiminy plc rents three factories in different parts of the country. Jiminy's period end is 30 June. It has paid rent as follows:
  ● North—paid rent of £15 000 for three months in advance on 2 May
  ● West—monthly rental is £2000 but nothing paid since January due to dispute with landlord
  ● South—Quarterly rent paid in arrears on 31 August of £9000

What accounting adjustments does Jiminy need to include in its Rent Account?

4 Boggis Trucks Ltd has a fleet of vehicles comprising large and small vans for deliveries nationwide. At 31 March 20X7, the value of the fleet at cost was R3 279 000 with accumulated depreciation of R1 945 725. During 20X8, Boggis purchased new vans at a cost of R485 000 and sold several that originally cost R385 000 and had been depreciated down to R98 000. The sale proceeds were R153 000. Depreciation is straight line 25 per cent on cost and new vehicles are depreciated in full in the year of acquisition but not in the year of sale.

Using T accounts, calculate the profit or loss on sale of vehicles and write up the cost and accumulated depreciation accounts.

5 The purpose of a provision is to ensure that costs and revenues are included in the correct accounting period.   **True/False**

6 Massive Ltd wants to make a bad debt provision for the current year of $236 400, based on a review of its receivables at the end of the financial year. It already has a provision brought forward from last year of $181 500, but part of that has now had to be cancelled because the money from the customer unexpectedly came in. That amounted to $21 750. If Massive makes those entries to its provision for doubtful debts account, what will be the charge to the income account for the financial year?

7 Whipple Ltd has extracted the following information for the year ended 31 March 20X7:

Business rates—owing from previous year	£1 200
Paid in 20X7	£5 600
Prepaid in 20X7	£900
Insurance—Prepaid from last year	£250
Paid in year	£1 500
Prepaid in 20X7	£300
Materials purchased	
Opening accrual	£7 051
Invoiced in 20X7	£165 376
Closing accrual	£9 239

Prepare the T accounts for rates, insurance and materials purchased.

8 Winterbottom Ltd has made a one-year loan to a sister company, Flatbottom Ltd, of £150 000, on which it is to receive interest at 10 per cent per annum. Flatbottom has so far paid five instalments of £13 750, but should have paid seven up to the end of Winterbottom's financial year in September 20X8. Enquiries indicate that Flatbottom is in financial difficulties and is undergoing a cash crisis, which the directors have described as 'temporary'.
   i. What action should Winterbottom take in respect of this situation?
   ii. What entries should it put through its books?

9 Megablast plc has bought an item of equipment for $1 250 000.

   It estimates that the equipment has a useful life of 10 years and a residual value of $100 000.

   It wants to know the effect on its annual financial statements of depreciating the asset on a straight line or reducing balance basis.
   i. Calculate the depreciation over ten years
   ii. Explain the difference between the two approaches

10 Which of these statements are true or false?

	True	False
A sales day book is part of the double-entry system.		
'Posting' entries into the accounting records is a shorthand way of saying entering transactions in the books of account.		
If wages control account has been completed correctly, both sides should balance.		
Purchase credit notes are credited to the supplier's account in the payables ledger.		

In the next module we will bring all this together to create an income statement and a statement of financial position from the trial balance. If you are unsure of how these adjustments work or how a trial balance is prepared now is the time to review Modules 3 and 4 before we move on!

Test yourself

1 Monty Ltd carried out the following transactions:

Feb 1	Sold goods on credit to Jason	R6789
Feb 2	Sold goods for cash to Olsen	R2756
	Sold goods on credit to Mason	R1793
Feb 3	Sold goods on credit to Jason	R2987
Feb 4	Returned goods from Olsen	R734
Feb 8	Sold goods on credit to Williams	R3897
Feb 9	Sold goods on credit to Mason	R5128
Feb 10	Cash sales	R1287
	Goods returned from Mason	R934

The opening balances on the receivables account included Mason R1200, Jason R657 and Williams R1245.

All three paid off their opening balances in this period of February.

At the end of February, Monty Ltd learned that Williams had gone into liquidation and it was doubtful if the debt would be paid.

A dispute has arisen between Monty Ltd and Jason over the invoice on Feb 3. Jason states that the prices were inflated and was only going to pay R2650. Monty claims that they had informed Jason of the price increase but decides to make a provision for a doubtful debt anyway.

a. Write up the entries in Monty's books including a sales day book and the ledger accounts and bring down the balances.

b. If Jason subsequently agrees to pay the full amount what entries will be needed to revise the situation in Monty's books?

2 Potterton Ltd extracted information from its financial records at 30 September 20X8 as follows:

a. Payroll details Week 31:

Gross pay	42789
Income tax	3146
Social insurance	4124
Pension fund	5962
Employer social insurance contributions	7725
Employer pension fund contributions	8320

b. The rent account hadn't been completed correctly. Rent of £24 500 had been paid in the financial period, but the amount brought forward from the previous year of a prepayment of £2100 had not been included on the account. Potterton account staff calculated that the rent paid of £24 500 included £2000 for October 20X8.

c. Motor insurance for the company vehicles had been paid amounting to £8350, but £1500 was in respect of an adjustment for the previous year, which had been included in the account. This left £2100 owing at 30 September 20X8.

d. The purchase ledger control account did not agree to the list of balances. Investigations revealed the following:
- The list of balances totalled £28 691
- The payables control account was £35 483
- Discounts allowed of £1790 had been omitted from the control account
- A credit note for £765 had been entered twice into the supplier's account in the ledger but only once in the control account
- Payments to a supplier of £3678 due to M. Hurst had been posted to Hurst Motors instead in the payables ledger
- A balance of £4237 for Xylonix Ltd had been missed off the list of payables balances.

As a member of the finance team at Potterton, you have been tasked with:
a. Preparing the wages control account for Week 31 and posting the entries into the books of account (use T accounts).
b. With use of a T account showing how the rent account and the motor insurance account should be written up.
c. Reconciling the list of balances from the payables ledger to the payables control account.

5 Creating a set of financial statements

In this module we will show how a set of financial statements is prepared from a trial balance and how the adjustments detailed in this module and in Module 4 are used in preparing the final accounts.

In particular we will look at:

- Reconciling the bank and the cash book
- The journal
- Accounting for intangible assets
- Accounting for goodwill
- Preparation of the income statement
- Preparation of the statement of financial position
- Appropriations of profit
- Adjusting the trial balance
- Using an extended trial balance in Excel
- Financial reporting—GAAP and International Financial Reporting Standards

We are now moving to a point when we can bring all that we have learned from previous modules together to create a set of financial statements.

This is the end point of recording information in the financial records, making adjustments for accruals, prepayments and provisions, depreciating assets and generally amending the financial records to tell the story of how the organization has performed financially in the accounting period.

At this stage we are looking only to create a simple set of financial statements. There is a good deal of complexity that is outside the scope of these modules and so we will not be considering the finer points of International Financial Reporting Standards, accounting for groups of companies or partnerships.

Instead we will stick to the basics and if these are fully understood, more complex issues dealt with later in another course will be more easy to grasp.

Before we start to prepare our set of financial statements we must undertake some more tasks and become familiar with another book of account, the journal.

Reconciling the bank and the cash book

Almost everybody has a bank account, and the bank will prepare a statement showing the transactions that have gone through the bank account and the current balance either in hand or overdrawn.

However the statements can only show transactions that have actually been processed by the bank: it obviously knows nothing of unbanked income or payments that might have been issued but which have not yet passed through the account.

Accordingly, the bank statement may be out of step with the cash book, which records transactions right up to the period end, some of which the bank knows nothing about.

Consider a situation where payments and receipts are made by cheque or where sales income is received in cash or by cheque. It might be that:

● cheque payments to suppliers have been issued and entered into the cash book but the cheques have not yet been presented by the supplier as they are in transit
● takings have been counted and entered into the cash book as receipts but have not yet been taken to the bank

Modern electronic banking systems have made this situation much easier as transactions are pretty much instantaneous, so they will go through the bank account more or less at the same time the payments are entered into the company's books of account. Almost invariably, though, there is a time delay between some payments and receipts entered in the cash book which have not yet been included on the bank statement.

Accordingly, before the financial accounts can be prepared it is necessary to reconcile the balance shown by the cash book to that shown on the bank statement at the end of the accounting period attributable to timing differences.

This is done by checking the transactions for, say, the last couple of weeks of the accounting period between the cash book and the bank statements. This will show items which are in the cash book and not on the bank statements and vice versa. It might be that standing orders and direct debits have not been included in the cash book, so these can be written in to the cash book and won't form part of the reconciliation.

Once these have been included, any differences will be due to timing.

In the reconciliation the bank balance can be adjusted for:

● Cheques that have been issued are included in the cash book, but that have not been presented to the bank (known as unpresented cheques)
● Receipts or lodgements that are included in the cash book but that have not been banked (known as uncredited lodgements)

Here is an example of how it might work.

EXAMPLE

At 30 June 20X8, the bank statement of Bolington Ltd showed a balance of €84 258. The balance shown by Bolington's cash book was a debit balance of €81 747.

Checking the transactions between the cash book and the bank statement for the two weeks prior to the period end revealed the following:

● A standing order for property rental of €3000 paid on 28 June 20X8 had not been included in the cash book
● Takings amounting to €7234 from trading on 29 and 30 June were not banked until 1 July
● Cheque payments amounting to €12 745 had been made but the cheques had not been presented at the bank

The reconciliation between the balance in the cash book and the bank balance is carried out like this.

First of all, we have to make sure the cash book is properly written up and complete so we have to write in the standing order. This will reduce the debit balance as it is a payment entered in the cash book as a credit.

	€
Balance per cash book	81 747 Dr
Deduct: Standing order not entered	(3 000)
Revised balance	€78 747 Dr

We now have the cash book balance we are reconciling to and we can complete the bank reconciliation.

	€
Balance per bank statement	84 258 Cr
Deduct: Unpresented cheques (reduces bank balance)	(12 745)
	71 513
Add: Uncredited lodgements (increases bank balance)	7 234
	€78 747 Cr

Clearly, if the bank balance had been overdrawn the unpresented cheques would be added to increase the overdraft and the uncredited lodgements deducted in order to facilitate the reconciliation.

Using exactly the same information as the previous example, except that the cash book balance is now a credit balance of €86 769 and instead of the bank balance being in credit it is overdrawn, the revised reconciliation looks like this:

Balance per cash book	(86 769) Cr
Add: Standing order not entered	(3 000)
Revised balance	(89 769) Cr

We now have the cash book balance we are reconciling to and we can complete the bank reconciliation.

Balance per bank statement	(84 258) o/d
Add: Unpresented cheques	(12 745)
	(97 003)
Deduct: Uncredited lodgements	7 234
	(89 769) o/d

The journal

The journal is simply a way of recording transfers between accounts. Before computerization it was generally a book—hence the name—but in computerized systems of course it is simply a list of transactions within the computer that must be evidenced separately.

However, it is clear that use of the journal could be of benefit to anyone wanting to manipulate the financial statements or to hide suspicious transactions. Consequently, in most organizations, any journal entry has to be controlled, for example:

- evidenced by some form of voucher or document giving reasons for the transaction
- authorized by a third party who can confirm the entry is a valid one
- numbered so the transaction can be traced

Journals are also used to post adjustments to the financial statements at the period end, such as:

- Depreciation
- Inventory totals
- Provisions and prepayments
- Write-offs and other reductions in asset values

Note any adjustments at the period end will complete the accounts and add the double entry required after adjustments to the trial balance. Again an explanation should be recorded and the journals authorized, even if they are routine transactions.

Here is an example of a journal voucher for a journal entry writing off a bad debt from the receivables ledger account RL 4567 to the Bad Debts account in the nominal ledger account NL 0345.

Jnl number	Account	Account name	Amount Dr	Amount Cr
1234	NL 0345	Bad Debts	2467.86	
1234	RL 4567	Dotty Plumbers		2467.86
Comment				
Balance written off—Dotty Plumbers in liquidation—no prospect of recovery				
Prepared by........		**Authorized by........**		

Accounting for intangible assets

We have so far dealt with assets which are tangible; that is, you can see and touch them.

Examples of such assets are:

- property
- machinery
- fixtures and fittings
- motor vehicles

We have seen how these appear on the statement of financial position and are depreciated annually using an appropriate method.

There are, however, assets that cannot be touched and seen but nevertheless belong to the company and using which the company can earn income and will require adjustments just as tangible assets.

Examples of this kind of asset are:

- patents
- trademarks
- brands
- computer software

Accounting for intangible assets is a major topic in itself and the accounting is outside the scope of this book. However, we will look at the principles of accounting for goodwill and for other intangible assets.

Most intangible assets are bought or created. For example:

- A company will invest in research in order to create a product which it then patents
- Companies employ programmers to create new software, e.g. for gaming or business applications
- Companies engage in marketing campaigns to create a brand

In these cases the value of the assets is related to its ability to earn future revenues. A patent can be licensed to manufacturers and royalty income received, computer software and brands represent saleable products.

The accounting treatment is to write off the value of such assets over what is considered to be their useful life. This is known as amortization and is the same as depreciation calculated on a straight line basis.

However if the value of the assets suffers a permanent reduction in value for some reason, its value will have to be written down to its estimated value, even if this means a greater charge to the income statement than the annual amortization charge.

Accounting for goodwill

Goodwill arises when one business buys another for more than the value of its assets.

If one company wishes to buy the whole of another business, it would expect to buy the assets at a valuation and probably take over some liabilities. That places a value on the net assets.

However, the value of a business is more than the sum of the value of its assets. A successful business has a reputation, it has a list of customers and it has a track record of successful trading.

The owners of such a business would want to reflect the value of what, broadly, might be called the business's reputation reflected in the selling price, and it is this that forms the basis of the valuation of goodwill.

EXAMPLE

A company buys a business for €1 million. The fair value of its premises is €550000, its plant etc is €150000, and it has receivables and inventories of €30000 and payables of €40000.
Calculate the value of goodwill.

ANSWER

The calculation is as follows:

Purchase price		1 000 000
Fixed assets		
Property	550 000	
Plant	150 000	
Inventory and receivables	30 000	
	730 000	
Payables	(40 000)	
		690 000
Goodwill		310 000

The rules for financial reporting require the value of goodwill to be reviewed annually and if it has declined the loss must be written off in the income statement.

The income statement and statement of financial position

At this point we have looked at all the adjustments we can make to a trial balance in order to create the income statement and statement of financial position.

Remember these are:

- accruals
- provisions
- prepayments
- depreciation
- provisions for doubtful debts
- journal adjustments

Once we have all these, we are ready to start.

We need to look at what these two statements show and what their purpose is. Remember the distinction between capital and revenue transactions? The income account deals in revenue transactions for the financial period and the statement of financial position summarizes the capital position of the organization.

REAL LIFE
The importance of communicating financial information

General purpose financial reports represent economic phenomena in words and numbers. To be useful, financial information must not only be relevant, it must also represent faithfully the phenomena it purports to represent. This fundamental characteristic seeks to maximize the underlying characteristics of completeness, neutrality and freedom from error. Information must be both relevant and faithfully represented if it is to be useful.

Classifying, characterizing and presenting information clearly and concisely makes it understandable. While some phenomena are inherently complex and cannot be made easy to understand, to exclude such information would make financial reports incomplete and potentially misleading. Financial reports are prepared for users who have a reasonable knowledge of business and economic activities and who review and analyze the information with diligence.

Source: 'Conceptual Framework for Financial Reporting 2010'
Approved by the International Accounting Standards Board—September 2010

In summary:

- The income statement shows the results of the organization's financial activities for the financial period. It shows the income earned and all the costs relevant to that income.
- The statement of financial position is a snapshot in time. It shows the financial position of the business at a particular time. It shows the assets and liabilities of the business at the period end.

INCOME STATEMENT

The income statement shows the results of the organization's activities for the period.

The key components of an income statement are:

Income statement	Includes
Income	Sales/turnover/revenue Rental income Interest received
Cost of sales	Opening and closing inventory Purchases Cost of production
Overheads/costs	Wages Administration expenses Premises costs Marketing and advertising costs
Finance costs	Interest on loans and overdrafts Hire purchase interest Leasing payments
Depreciation	Depreciation

There are accounting conventions as to how the income statement and statement of financial position are presented.

The income statement is, broadly, always presented in the following format:

Revenues		XX
Cost of sales—see below		(XX)
Gross profit		XX
Overheads	XX	
Finance costs	XX	
Depreciation	XX	
		(XX)
Net profit (or [loss]) for the period		XX

COST OF SALES The cost of sales is what it says it is: it represents the cost of items sold in the accounting period. Accordingly, it includes:

- The opening inventory, i.e. what was available to be sold or made into saleable items at the end of the last accounting period
- The purchases for the year, i.e. what has been bought in order to provide products for sale
- The closing inventory. This is deducted from the total of the opening inventory and the purchases, as it represents items purchased but not sold in the accounting period, i.e. that are still in the warehouse or on the shelf in the shop.

So cost of sales is calculated like this:

Opening inventory	XX
Add: purchases	XX
	XX
Less: closing inventory	(XX)
= Cost of sales	XX

THE STATEMENT OF FINANCIAL POSITION

The statement of financial position is a statement of the assets and liabilities of the business at a particular time. It includes the following:

Statement of financial position	Includes
Tangible fixed assets	Written-down values (i.e. after charging depreciation) of Property Plant and equipment Vehicles etc.
Intangible assets	Patents, trademarks, goodwill, etc.
Current assets	Inventory and work in progress Trade receivables Prepayments Bank balances Cash in hand
Current liabilities	Trade payables Accruals and provisions Short-term loans less than one year Amount of long-terms loans repayable within next twelve months Bank overdrafts
Long-term loans	Commercial mortgages and longer-term borrowings
Owners investment	Share capital Capital accounts of partners or sole traders
Reserves	Accumulated profits from the current and previous years

The statement of financial position is also conventionally presented in a certain way.

Tangible assets		XX
Intangible assets		XX
Total		XX
Current assets		
Inventories	XX	
Receivables and prepayments	XX	
Bank balances	XX	
Cash in hand	XX	
	A	XX

Current liabilities

Payables and accruals			XX
Bank overdraft			XX
		B	XX

Net current assets (A-B)	XX
Total assets	XX

Financed by:

Share capital or capital account	XX
Reserves	XX
Shareholders' funds	XX
Long-term loans	XX
	XX

The totals of both parts of the statement of financial position must be the same.

As you can see the statement of financial position shows the assets and liabilities with which the organization carries on its activities as one total, and then shows how those assets and liabilities have been funded as the other.

APPROPRIATIONS OF PROFIT

Once a profit has been identified, the company will have to make a provision for corporation tax payable on those profits. This is calculated in accordance with the tax rules and the provision is included in the income statement and in the statement of financial position as an accrual.

The company then has to decide whether or not to pay a dividend to its shareholders.

This is at the discretion of the directors and they will take two factors into account:

- the need to retain profits in the business to strengthen the statement of financial position
- the cash requirement needed to pay the dividend

If they decide to pay a dividend to the shareholders, they will declare an amount per share and include this in the income statement as an appropriation of profit.

The income statement will look like this:

Net profit	XX
Provision for corporation tax	(XX)
Profit after tax	XX
Proposed dividend	(XX)
Profit retained transferred to reserves	XX

The dividend is described as 'proposed,' because the shareholders will approve its payment at the Annual General Meeting and the dividend will be paid after that. This is, of course, some months after the end of the financial period.

So how do we go about creating a set of financial statements? This requires us to extract a trial balance and then adjust it for all the transactions not in the books or ones that are in the books but which relate to other accounting periods.

Adjusting the trial balance

The best way to do this is to work though examples, and then try it for yourself.

EXAMPLE

This is the summarized trial balance of North Ltd at 31 March 20X7, which is the financial year end.

Trial balance of North Ltd at 31 March 20X7

	Dr	Cr
Share capital		100 000
Office costs	20 000	
Distribution costs	30 000	
Balance at bank	40 000	
Tangible assets—equipment	220 000	
Tangible asset—vehicles	66 000	
Depreciation—equipment		100 000
Depreciation vehicles		50 000
Inventory	44 500	
Sales		924 000
Property costs	35 000	
Rental costs	70 000	
Purchases	580 000	
Wages paid	115 000	
Reserves		48 500
Receivables ledger control account	71 000	
Payables ledger control account		69 000
	1 291 500	1 291 500

There are some adjustments that are required as follows:

- Two months' rent is due at £1000 per month.
- Purchase invoices for materials amounting to £12 000 have not been processed.
- Depreciation on fixed assets is 10% straight line on equipment and 25% reducing balance on vehicles. Vehicles are depreciated from the month of purchase.
- Property costs amounting to £1500 have been paid in advance.

- A new vehicle was purchased on 30 March for £12000, but the invoice has not been processed.
- Closing inventory is £46 700

REQUIRED

Prepare the income statement and statement of financial position at 31 March 20X7.

ANSWER

The first thing that has to be done before we can start to create the financial statements is to account for all the adjustments. We will look at this on an account by account basis. If you are not sure about the double-entry for this, please revise the section in Module 4.

These are the adjustments for all the accruals and prepayments:

The first account to amend is rental costs for the accrual of rents due

Rental costs

Balance per trial balance	70000	Income statement	72000
Accrual c/d—2 months rent	2000		
	72000		72000
		Accrual b/d	2000

The balance on the rental costs account, after adjusting for the accrual, is transferred to the income statement

Purchases

Balance per trial balance	580000	Income statement	592000
Accrual c/d—Invoices not processed	12000		
	592000		592000
		Accrual b/d	12000

Again the balance on the rental costs account, after adjusting for the accrual, is transferred to the income statement

Property costs

Balance per trial balance	35000	Prepayment c/d	1500
		Income statement	33500
	35000		35000
Prepayment b/d	1500		

(continued)

We need to account for the new vehicle

Tangible assets—vehicles

Balance per trial balance	66 000	Balance c/d	78 000
Accrual c/d—new vehicle	12 000		
	78 000		78 000
Balance b/d	78 000		

In this case the balance on the account is not transferred to the income statement as vehicles are assets and thus appear on the statement of financial position.

After dealing with these, the next step is to calculate the depreciation on the tangible assets and calculate the charge for the year.

If you are not sure about the double-entry for this, please revise the section in Module 4.

We need to deal with the new asset and calculate the depreciation for the year.

Cost

	At 1 April 20X6	Added	Disposals	At 31 March 20X7	
Equipment	220 000			220 000	
Vehicles	66 000	12 000		78 000	
	286 000	12 000		298 000	

Depreciation

	At 1 April 20X6	Added	Disposals	At 31 March 20X7	
Equipment	100 000	22 000		122 000	10% straight line
Vehicles	50 000	4 250		54 250	25% reducing balance
					(see calculation below)
	150 000	26 250		176 250	
Net book value	136 000			121 750	

Calculation of vehicle depreciation

Existing vehicles

Cost	66 000		
Depreciation	(50 000)		
	16 000	× 25%	4 000
New vehicle cost	12 000	× 25%	250
			4 250

Once we have made all the adjustments to the trial balance, we can start to assemble the income statement and statement of financial position.

The income statement will look like this. Note that it is described as the income statement for the year ended 31 March 20X7, as it covers the full year.

Notice also that we include the closing inventory for the first time as it forms part of the cost of what has been sold in the year.

North Ltd
Income statement for the year ended 31 March 20X7

	£	£
Sales		924000
Cost of sales		
Opening inventory	44500	
Purchases	592000	
	636500	
Less: Closing inventory	(46700)	(589800)
Gross profit		334200
Overheads		
Wages paid	115000	
Office costs	20000	
Distribution costs	30000	
Property costs	33500	
Rental costs	72000	
Depreciation	26250	296750
		37450

The statement of financial position summarizes, at a moment in time, the financial circumstances of the business. Accordingly, it incorporates all those balances of assets and liabilities outstanding at the end of the financial period.

Thus, it includes:

- the closing inventory
- the net book values (cost minus depreciation) of all the assets, tangible and intangible
- accruals and prepayments adjusting the trial balance
- receivables and payables ledger balances
- cash book balance

North Ltd
Statement of financial position at 31 March 20X7

		£	£
Tangible assets—net book value			121750
Current assets			
	Inventory	46700	
	Receivables	71000	
	Prepayments	1500	
	Balance at bank	40000	
		159200	
Current liabilities			
	Payables	69000	
	Accruals*	26000	
		95000	
Net current assets			64200
			185950
Share capital			100000
Reserves			48500
Profit for the year			37450
			185950

*Note: Includes the accruals for purchases and rental costs plus the £12000 for the new vehicle

Because this is the culmination of the work we have done so far, we will look at another example. What we have considered so far has mainly related to the financial statements of companies, so let us look at another example—this time a partnership. The reason for this is that a partnership is simply two or more sole traders operating together, so if we look at partnerships we also include sole traders.

PARTNERSHIP ACCOUNTS   Partnership accounts can become complex when we have to prepare accounts involving changes in partnerships or adjustments to profit shares, but these are outside the scope of this course. Instead let us look at a simple partnership where the partners share profits 50/50 but have, perhaps, contributed different amounts to set up the business.

Here is a trial balance and some information about a partnership involving two individuals, Ben and Sue; the business name is Florizel Garden Centre. Ben and Sue share profits and losses equally and make up financial statements to 31 October each year.

At 31 October 20X8, part of their trial balance included these balances.

	Dr	Cr
	$	$
Capital account—Ben	4 000	
Capital account—Sue	1 000	
Accumulated profit share—Ben		16 423
Accumulated profit share—Sue		16 423
Drawings—Ben	12 865	
Drawings—Sue	14 937	

Notice that this is a partnership between Ben and Sue so there are some significant differences between these financial statements and those of a company.

- Both partners subscribed some initial capital to get the business off the ground—in this case Ben $4000 and Sue $1000.
- Both share profits equally, so their share of profits earned so far is credited to their capital accounts.
- When partners or sole traders take money or goods from their business; this is known as drawings. Their capital accounts are debited with the amount they have withdrawn and, if the drawings are in cash the cash book is credited; if it is goods they have taken for their own use this is credited to purchases account, usually with a journal entry so:

> Dr Drawings
> Cr Purchases goods for own use at cost

Why purchases at cost and not revenues at full price? Because the owners cannot make a profit out of themselves; what they have taken from their business is the cost of something the business has bought.

So here is the full trial balance for Ben and Sue's business, Florizel Garden Centre.

FLORIZEL GARDEN CENTRE
TRIAL BALANCE AT 31 OCTOBER 20X8

	Dr $	Cr $
Revenues		227669
Office costs	12648	
Purchase of plants, soils and fertilizers	109721	
Marketing and advertising	2680	
Balance at bank	2376	
Tangible assets—equipment	28000	
Tangible asset—vehicles	45000	
Depreciation—equipment		7200
Depreciation vehicles		19000
Inventory—plants, fertilizers and soil for resale	21350	
Repairs to property and equipment	6237	
Light, heat and power	8914	
Insurance	5900	
Rental costs	14000	
Wages expense	33729	
Legal fees	525	
Leasing payments	3750	
Short-term loan		8000
Payables ledger control account		22917
Capital account—Ben		4000
Capital account—Sue		1000
Accumulated profit share—Ben		16423
Accumulated profit share—Sue		16423
Drawings—Ben	12865	
Drawings—Sue	14937	
	322632	322632

At 31 October, the following adjustments were required

1) Wages costs totalling £1178 for week ended 31 October 20X8 were not recorded in the cash book until 1 November
2) Invoices for light, heat and power were paid to 31 December 20X8. The prepayment is $740
3) Rental costs of $1200 were unpaid at 31 October 20X8
4) A leasing payment was made on 1 November relating to the previous month of $341
5) Short-term loan interest had not been included in the cash book amounting to $400
6) Closing inventory was $23980
7) Depreciation of vehicles is 25% straight line and on other assets is 10% reducing balance
8) They have been informed that they have to pay a fine for polluting an underground stream but they do not know precisely how much it will be. Their lawyers estimate it will probably be about $750.

We can now amend the individual accounts for the adjustments.

First we must update all the accounts for accruals, prepayments, etc.

Wages expense

Per TB	33 729	Income account	34 907
Accrual c/d	1 178		
	34 907		34 907
		Accrual b/d	1 178

Light, heat and power

Per TB	8 914	Prepaid	740
		Income account	8 174
	8 914		8 914
Prepayment	740		

Rental costs

Per TB	14 000	Income account	15 200
Accrual	1 200		
	15 200		15 200
		Accrual b/d	1 200

Leasing payments

Per TB	3 750	Income account	4 091
Accrual	341		
	4 091		4 091
		Accrual c/d	341

Fines and penalties

Provision	750	Income account	750

Once these are done, we can move on to fixed assets and journal adjustments.

Then we must calculate the depreciation

Tangible assets		
Equipment cost	28 000	
Accumulated depreciation	(7 200)	
	20 800	
Depreciation at 10%	(2 080)	(2 080)
Net book value	18 720	
Motor vehicles cost	45 000	
Accumulated depreciation	(19 000)	
	26 000	
Depreciation 25% straight line	(11 250)	(11 250)
	14 750	
Depreciation for the year		(13 330)

And we need a journal entry to deal with the short-term loan interest

Dr Loan interest	400	
Cr Cash book		400

Bringing it all together, we can create the income account and the statement of financial position.

Now we can prepare the income account and statement of financial position

FLORIZEL GARDEN CENTRE—INCOME ACCOUNT FOR THE YEAR ENDED 31 OCTOBER 20X8

		$	$
Revenues			227 669
Opening inventory		21 350	
Purchases		109 721	
		131 071	
Closing inventory		(23 980)	107 091
Gross profit			120 578
Wages		34 907	
Light, heat and power		8 174	
Rental costs		15 200	
Office costs		12 648	
Repairs		6 237	
Insurance		5 900	
Legal fees		525	
Marketing and advertising		2 680	
Provision for fine		750	
Leasing payments		4 091	
Loan interest		400	
Depreciation		13 330	104 842
Net profit for the year			15 736
Split	Ben		7 868
	Sue		7 868
			15 736

FLORIZEL GARDEN CENTRE—STATEMENT OF FINANCIAL POSITION AT 31 OCTOBER 20X8

Tangible assets

	Cost	Depreciation	Net book value	
Equipment	28 000	(9 280)	18 720	
Vehicles	45 000	(30 250)	14 750	33 470
	73 000	(39 530)		

Current assets

Inventories			23 980	
Prepayments			740	
Cash at bank	(2 376 − 400)		1 976	
			26 696	

Current liabilities

Trade payables			22 917	
Accruals and provisions (1 178 +1 200+341 +750)			3 469	
Short-term loan			8 000	
			34 386	
Net current liabilities				(7 690)
				25 780

Partners capital accounts

	Ben	Sue	
Initial capital	4 000	1 000	
Accumulated profits	16 423	16 423	
Share of profit for the year	7 868	7 868	
	28 291	25 291	
Drawings	(12 865)	(14 937)	
	15 426	10 354	25 780

Note the partner's capital accounts where, in a set of company accounts, share capital and reserves normally fund the assets.

Using an extended trial balance in Excel

Clearly the methodology used above is fine for illustrating how to adjust a trial balance in order to prepare a set of financial statements, but in the real world accountants need a quicker and more foolproof way of doing it, a way that can also be computerized.

This is the extended trial balance or ETB.

This is a spreadsheet that has a trial balance at one end and a set of financial statements at the other, and in between are all the adjustments needed to turn one into the other.

Many accounting packages will produce a set of financial statements as part of their reporting structure, so as these become more sophisticated for even the smallest business, accountants are probably using ETBs less and less. However, it is a skill and one that should be understood as it requires a sound grasp of double-entry bookkeeping to set the ETB up in the first place.

The ETB can take some time to set up but the advantage of it is that once all the formulae are in it can be used over and over again; a management accountant preparing monthly accounts can use the previous month's ETB and simply insert the current numbers into the spreadsheet.

If a new account is needed a line can be inserted and the formulae copied over.

The advantage of an ETB is that it should always balance if it has been properly prepared, i.e. if the formulae are correct. It is possible to check the adjustments made to each nominal ledger account and track through any changes.

The best way to illustrate this is by way of example, so let us rework the above example of North Ltd, this time using an ETB.

There are some key points to follow:

- The layout is flexible but the broad approach should be followed.
- The formulae used in the columns for the income statement and the statement of financial position should follow the rules of double-entry, so an expense line could have

Balance per TB + Accrual − Prepayments + Journal Dr − Journal Cr

for example.

- Care has to be taken setting up the formulae and this can be the trickiest part of the ETB. If it's complicated, use a T account to get the double-entry clear then rework it into a formula.
- Closing inventory appears twice—once in the income statement as a credit and once in the statement of financial position as a debit. How this is done in the ETB is flexible and this is just one layout.
- The totals of some of the columns are added separately to make the statement of financial position balance.

The great advantage of an ETB is that it brings all the adjustments together in one place and they can be tracked through the ETB. Journal columns will balance so there is no possibility of a one-sided adjustment and accrual and prepayment columns can be supported by working schedules.

This is what it will look like:

	Trial balance					Journal entries				Income account		Statement of financial position	
	Dr	Cr	Provisions	Prepayments	Inventories	Dr	Cr	Payables	Receivables	Dr	Cr	Dr	Cr
Share capital		100000											100000
Office costs	20000									20000			
Distribution costs	30000									30000			
Balance at bank	40000											40000	
Tangible assets—equipment	220000											220000	
Tangible asset—vehicles	66000							12000				78000	
Depreciation—equipment		100000					22000						122000
Depreciation vehicles		50000					4250						54250
Inventory	44500				46700					44500	46700	46700	
Sales		924000									924000		
Property costs	35000			1500						33500			
Rental costs	70000		2000							72000			
Purchases	580000		12000							592000			
Wages paid	115000									115000			
Depreciation						26250				26250			
Reserves		48500											48500
Receivables ledger control account	71000											71000	
Payables ledger control account		69000											69000
	1291500	1291500	14000	1500	46700	26250	26250	12000	0	933250	970700	455700	393750
Profit										37450			37450
										970700	970700		
Provisions													14000
Payables													12000
Prepayments												1500	
												457200	457200

This is obviously quite a simple example, but it provides a basic illustration of how an ETB works.

Stop and think   Try and rework Ben and Sue's partnership accounts using an ETB. The principles are the same as for North.

Financial reporting—GAAP and International Financial Reporting Standards

When financial statements are being prepared for issue to shareholders they have to comply with two sets of rules, these being:

- any Companies Act legislation detailing the form and content of company accounts
- various financial reporting standards (FRSs) of differing applicability

There are differing sets of rules, which lead to different disclosures and this can make matters quite complicated. Fundamentally, it depends on:

- whether or not the company for which financial statements are being prepared is listed on a recognized stock exchange
- How big an unlisted company is—some very large well-known organizations are still private companies, for example the world's largest private company is Cargill, which deals primarily in US agriculture and which has revenues in excess of $135bn; well-known names like Dell, Bosch and Mars are also privately-owned companies.
- Which country has jurisdiction in terms of accounting rules

Listed companies and larger unlisted companies tend to have to comply with International Financial Reporting Standards (IFRS Standards) issued by the International Accounting Standards Board (IASB), which have now been adopted by over 100 jurisdictions worldwide. In each jurisdiction where the standard has been adopted, IFRS Standards tend to be mandatory for listed companies and some larger unlisted companies, permissible for all unlisted companies and increasingly permissible for smaller and medium-sized enterprises (SMEs).

Smaller, unlisted entities may have a choice of reporting standard. For example, in the UK and Ireland IFRS Standards are mandatory for listed companies and what are known as Generally Accepted Accounting Principles (GAAP), issued by the Financial Reporting Council, apply to all other businesses. In the UK and Ireland, the standards that make up GAAP are known as Financial Reporting Standards (FRSs) and there is a variant for smaller companies called the Financial Reporting Standard for Smaller Entities (FRSSE).

South Africa uses variants on the IFRS Standards, and the United States requires domestic public companies to use US GAAP.

Clearly this whole issue is far from straightforward and anyone preparing financial statements for anything other than a small family company will need to be clear on precisely which rules are to be applied.

The reason why this is important is that these rules set out how the income statement and the statement of financial position are to be set out and how particular aspects of disclosure are to be calculated. For example, complexities arise in areas such as leases, intangible assets, long-term contract work in progress and issues involving valuation of tangible assets.

Clearly, the rules for a company listed on a recognized stock exchange are more onerous than those for a family company issuing its annual accounts to its family shareholders, but good practice dictates that the same rules should be followed throughout.

It is beyond the scope of this course to detail the various rules relating to the presentation of financial statements. Interested learners should obtain a set of public company accounts and look at them for themselves. This will give a good indication of the complexity of modern financial disclosure—some say to the point of incomprehensibility for the untrained reader!

Test yourself

1 At the end of Month 4 of the financial year, Harris Ltd, a small business, is reconciling the balance shown in the cash book with the bank statements. Harris establishes that unpresented cheque payments amounting to £3768 have not gone through the bank before the period end, and a banking of cash of £5250 has also not been credited by the period end. However, Harris also discovers that a direct debit of £2750 has not been included in the cash book and that a payment of £540 had been entered as £450 in error. The balance shown by the cash book before any adjustments was a debit balance of £22 160 and the balance shown by the bank statements a credit balance of £17 838.

   Prepare the bank reconciliation at the end of Month 4.

2 Which of these statements are true or false?

	True	False
The journal is used as a way of posting entries into the financial records. It can be used by fraudsters to manipulate financial records if not properly controlled.		
Amortization is a way of capitalizing intangible assets.		
The statement of financial position records the value of the business in terms of its assets and liabilities at a particular point in time.		

3 Burbler plc has just bought the business of Winterbottom Ltd. At the date of the acquisition, Winterbottom's statement of financial position was:

	€
Tangible assets—net book value	729 000
Inventories	92 000
Receivables	187 830
Payables	112 650
Cash and deposits	7 250

However, Burbler successfully argued that:

- The value of tangible assets was under depreciated by €150 000
- Part of the inventory amounting to €25 000 was obsolete and should be scrapped
- A bad debt provision of €13 000 was needed against the receivables
- A provision was required against a possible legal action of £32 000

Burbler paid €800 000 for Winterbottom.

What is the value of goodwill Burbler will hold in its statement of financial position?

4 Parris has the following extracts from its accounting records. Purchases £198 356, credit notes from suppliers, £2536, opening inventory £11 275, closing inventory £9081.

What is Parris's cost of sales?

5 Buster owns a secondhand bulldozer that he doesn't really need, which originally cost him R98 000. It has been depreciated over four years on a straight line basis at 10 per cent per year. He has had an offer of R45 000 to buy the bulldozer. Should he accept it?

6 Wilma runs a pet grooming business and makes up accounts to 31 March each year. Her electricity bills for the current financial 20X8 year are:

Date received	Date paid	Period covered	Amount £
2 June 20X7	4 July 20X7	1 March to 31 May 20X7	981
4 September 20X7	9 October 20X7	I June to 31 August 20X7	863
8 December 20X7	5 January 20X8	I September to 30 November 20X7	811
6 March 20X8	2 April 20X8	1 December to 28 February 20X8	928

Wilma estimates that her electricity for March to be about £360.

What figure should be included in Wilma's light, heat and power cost for the year to 31 March 20X8 (to nearest £)?

7 Red Snapper Ltd sells fish and seafood to shops and restaurants. At 30 June 20X8, it extracted the following balances from its accounting records:

Discounts allowed to customers	341
Revenues	189 349
Purchases of fish and seafood	44 560
Telephone and postage	2 854
Light & heat	8 287
Delivery costs	4 598
Purchase returns	2 750
Discounts received from suppliers	967
Interest received	76
Rent	10 450
Administration costs	12 980
Inventory at 1 July 20X7	3 821

Red Snapper had not been invoiced for insurance due to an oversight. The cost was £856. In addition, the rent paid is only for eleven months so one more month is due. Closing inventory amounted to £3081.

Prepare Red Snapper's income account for the year ended 30 June 20X8.

8 Bloater Ltd sells timber, and at 31 March 20X8 had the following information extracted from the financial records.

	€
Revenues	144 822
Purchases	106 010
Sales credit notes issued	722
Purchase credit notes received	3 720

Inventory at 1 April 20X7 was €8364 and at 31 March 20X8 was €10 198.

What is Bloater Ltd's gross profit?

a) 43 644

b) 36 204

c) 37 648

d) 45 088

9 Hudebrass Ltd, a manufacturer of metal fittings has an overdrawn balance at the bank of $287 691 at the end of Period 4. Its overdraft limit is $300 000, but Hudebrass is confident it will not go over the limit and thus be charged additional interest and an unarranged overdraft fee of $1000. The finance department are recording a credit balance in their cash book of $308 511 and have reported this to the chief accountant, who tells them they're wrong and they'd better sort out the difference as soon as possible.

   Examination of the records reveals that bank direct payments of $21 820 had not been included in the cash book, but a payment of $42 640 recorded in the cash book in Period 4 had not been received by the bank until Period 5.

   Prepare the bank reconciliation at the end of Period 4 to inform the chief accountant of the position.

10 Which of these statements are true or false?

	True	False
Reducing balance depreciation weights the charge towards the early years of owning an asset when the depreciation is the greatest.		
It is always a good idea to make a general provision for doubtful debts of, say, 5 per cent of the receivables balances to cover any doubtful ones we don't know about.		
IFRS Standards are issued by the IAASB.		
An ETB is a method of preparing a set of accounts by simply entering all the figures on a spreadsheet and adding them across into the appropriate column.		

In the next module we will move away from accounts preparation and consider the characteristics of various types of business organization, the principles of corporate governance including the duties of directors, the different methods of financing a business and the role played by the auditors.

Test yourself

1 The following trial balance was extracted from the books of Snagglepuss Ltd on 30 September 20X8:

SNAGGLEPUSS TRIAL BALANCE AT 30 SEPTEMBER 20X8

	Dr	Cr
	£	£
Land	198 540	
Property	256 000	
Depreciation of property		25 600
Plant equipment and vehicles	78 530	
Depreciation—Plant equipment and vehicles		39 265
Inventory as at 1/10/20X7	26 180	
Receivables control account	61 670	
Payables control account		57 160
Bank and cash	11 985	
Payroll deductions liability		4 740
Sales tax liability		7 130
Revenues		557 820
Purchases	317 450	
Sales returns	22 980	
Purchase returns		17 965
Rental costs on office space and equipment	41 840	
5% long-term bank loan		151 000
Interest charged by supplier on overdue balances	1 780	
Provision for doubtful debts at 1/1/20X7	4 050	
Discounts allowed	2 540	
Discount received		1 850
Advertising and media costs	3 150	
Light and heat	6 520	
Telephone and internet	2 220	
Insurance	17 850	
Rates, water charges and refuse collection	7 950	
Wages and salaries	103 740	
Employers pension contributions	12 150	
Long-term loan interest	3 050	
Bad debts written off	4 110	
Share capital		50 000
Reserves		271 755
	1 184 285	**1 184 285**

The following information, which has not been accounted for above, is also available:

1 The inventory count as at 30 September 20X8 showed closing inventory valued at £21 540.

2 Included in the insurance costs above is £14 400, which relates to the year ended 31 December 2013.

3 Telephone and internet charges are consistent at £222 per month. The figure included in the trial balance above does not include telephone and internet charges for August and September 20X8.

4 Snagglepuss reviewed the receivables balances as at 30 September 20X8, and decided the following:
  • An additional £2150 of receivables balances should be written off as irrecoverable
  • An additional provision for doubtful debts needs to be made of £3650 in addition to what has already been provided.

5 Property is depreciated at 2 per cent straight line. All plant, equipment and vehicles are depreciated at 10 per cent reducing balance.

6 During the year a second had item of plant was sold for £2000. Its original cost was £8000 and the accumulated depreciation was £7400.

Prepare:
a) The statement of profit and loss for the year ended 30 September 20X8.
b) The statement of financial position as at that date.

2 Harry Harrison is a sole trader who has been in business for some years as a wholesaler of toys and games. His trial balance at 31 March 20X8 is as follows:

HARRY HARRISON
TRIAL BALANCE AT 31 MARCH 20X8

	Dr	Cr
Capital account		25 000
Drawings	9 100	
Accumulated profits		25 635
Bad debts written off	1 250	
Repairs	1 520	
Land and buildings	200 750	
Depreciation—buildings		78 210
Plant and equipment	154 410	
Depreciation plant and equipment		12 150
Vehicles	74 100	
Depreciation—vehicles		34 250
Trade receivables	74 320	
Trade payables		41 970
Inventory at 1 April 20X7	13 120	
Bank balance		7 130
Employer's deductions liability		3 150
Accruals		780

(continued)

HARRY HARRISON
TRIAL BALANCE AT 31 MARCH 20X8

	Dr	Cr
Revenues		613410
Purchases	312400	
Sales returns	1780	
Purchase returns		2950
Van running costs	3250	
Light heat and power	6410	
Telephone and internet	7520	
Insurances	14420	
Property costs	5250	
Wages costs	96295	
5% bank loan		135000
Loan interest	3740	
	979635	**979635**

The following additional information, which has not been accounted for is available:

1 Closing inventory has been calculated at £11450

2 Included in insurance is £2220 for Harry Harrison's personal household insurance

3 Property costs are £350 per month. On 28 March, Harry Harrison paid an invoice for April—June 20X8 of £1050

4 On 31 January 20X8 Harry sold a delivery van for £11000. It had originally cost £31000 and had been depreciated by £24455. None of these entries were in Harry's books.

5 Depreciation is as follows:
   Property—2 per cent straight line
   Equipment—5 per cent reducing balance
   Vehicles—15 per cent straight line

   Prepare an income account and statement of financial position for Harry Harrison at 31 March 20X8.

6 The accounts of limited companies

In this module we will consider:

- Business entities
- Not-for-profit organizations and charities
- Principles of corporate governance
- The duties of directors
- Financing a business
- Gearing/leverage
- The role of the auditors

Business entities

Internationally there are many and various forms of business entities, and it would be impossible to list them all. To simplify matters, we'll consider that organizations fall into some basic categories:

- Unincorporated entities—sole traders, partnerships, charities (unincorporated associations that are usually non-profit-making)
- Incorporated entities—companies
- Other—government or official bodies related to government-type entities

Within these three categories lie a multitude of different forms, but it is only necessary to understand those that relate to the local business environment. However, there are commonalities. For instance, sole traders, partnerships and unincorporated associations (that is, groups of people who come together for a common purpose) have limited legal status and, in many jurisdictions, it is the proprietors, partners or representatives who have to bring any legal actions in their own name.

They are fully liable for all the debts of the entity. Partners have what is known as joint and several liability, which means that if one partner is unable to pay, all the other partners are liable for their share of any debts in addition to their own.

Contrast an incorporated body, which is recognized as a legal person; this means it can act at law in its own name. Mr Bodger the Builder, sole trader, has to go to court as an individual to sue customers for money owed. Bodger the Builder Limited can sue customers in the name of Bodger the Builder Limited—it is a legal person.

Whilst sole traders and partnerships tend to be more or less the same the world over, there are a tremendous variety of corporate forms. They can have different types of board structure, different forms of capital requirement, different internal rules, etc. Space does not permit detailed expositions of worldwide corporate structures!

In most countries where businesses operate, they tend to fall into these broad categories as illustrated in Figure 6.1.

Figure 6.1 **Types of business entity**

Type of business	Funded by	Notes
Sole trader	• Own funds • Investment from friends and family • Bank loans and overdrafts	• Personal assets are at risk if business fails
Partnership	• Capital invested by partners • Bank loans and overdrafts	• Partners jointly and severally liable for debts • Personal assets at risk if business fails
Limited liability partnership (LLP)	• Capital invested by partners • Bank loans and overdrafts	• Partners' liability limited by agreement • LLP regulated by partnership agreement • In some jurisdictions financial statements are available to public
Limited company—private	• Issue of shares • Bank loans and overdrafts	• Number of shareholders can be as low as one • Liability of the members (shareholders) is limited to their investment in the business • Restrictions on rights to transfer shares
Limited company—public	• Has the right to issue shares to public • Bank loans and overdrafts	• Minimum share capital • No restriction on rights to transfer shares

As stated above, there are a myriad of company forms worldwide, some of which have very open structures where there is a great deal of investor information available; some, on the other hand, are completely private where even finding out who owns the company may be extremely difficult.

We will look in more detail at financing later.

Not-for-profit organizations and charities

Not-for-profit organizations are distinguished from profit-focused entities through three main characteristics:

- Their objectives are usually based around a social, cultural, religious, philanthropic, welfare or environmental reason
- Most not-for-profit organizations do not have external shareholders providing risk capital for the business. They do not distribute dividends or profits, so any profit (or surplus) that is generated is retained by the business as a further source of capital.
- Many are bodies which are owned by their members, such as cooperatives

Many such organizations do make a profit every year but describe their profit as a 'surplus' rather than a profit; either way it is still an excess of income over expenditure.

Most, but not all, public sector organizations do not have profit as their primary objective and exist to provide public benefit. These include such bodies as healthcare providers, police authorities, social services, etc. These are funded through forms of taxation and are governed by government or quasi-government bodies and elected officials.

Private sector examples include most forms of charity, religious and self-help organizations, such as housing associations that provide housing for low income and minority groups, scientific research foundations and environmental groups. These groups can vary in size from very small charitable bodies to international organizations such as Médecins Sans Frontières, Oxfam or Greenpeace.

CORPORATE FORM   Not-for-profit organizations can be established as incorporated or unincorporated bodies. The common business forms include:

- in the public sector, they may be departments or agents of government
- some public sector bodies are established as private companies limited by guarantee. This is a corporate form whereby there are no shareholders, merely guarantors who undertake to pay a certain amount of money in the event of the company going into liquidation.
- in the private sector they may be established as cooperatives, industrial or provident societies (a specific type of organization owned by its members), by trust, as limited companies or simply as clubs or associations

A cooperative is a body owned by its members, and usually governed on the basis of 'one member, one vote.' A trust is an entity specifically constituted to achieve certain objectives. The trustees are appointed by the founders to manage the funds and ensure compliance with the objectives of the trust.

OBJECTIVES AND PERFORMANCE   As with any type of organization, the objectives of not-for-profit organizations are laid down by the founders and their successors in management. Unlike profit based entities, however, the broad strategic objectives of not-for-profit organizations will tend not to change over time: they were created for a specific purpose and that is what they will continue to do unless and until that purpose becomes obsolete or redundant.

For example, a charity formed for the relief of pit ponies ceased to have any purpose once pit ponies stopped being used in mines. The charity either has to be wound up, or new charitable objectives established, which can be far from straightforward as they are generally bound by their founding constitution.

It is important to recognize that, although not-for-profit organizations do not maximize profit as a primary objective, many are expected to be self-financing and, therefore, generate profit in order to survive and grow. Even if their activities rely to some extent on external grants, the providers of this finance invariably expect the organization to be as financially self-reliant as possible.

As the performance of not-for-profit organizations cannot easily be assessed by conventional accounting, as they do not behave in the same way as a commercial operation, it often has to be assessed with reference to other measures. Most not-for-profit organizations rely on measures that estimate the performance of the organization in relation to:

- economy—the ability of the organization to optimize the use of its productive resources
- efficiency—how well the organization uses its resources to achieve its outputs. For example, most charitable bodies have a very low level of administration cost—the bulk of any funds collected being used for charitable purposes.
- effectiveness—the extent to which the organization achieves its objectives

Where the organization has public accountability, performance measures can also be published to demonstrate that funds have been used in the most cost-effective manner.

Stop and think	Consider a charity that you have personal experience of. What are its objectives, how is it funded? Obtain a set of financial statements and compare them with a profit-based organization—notice the differences in approach, descriptions and presentation.

MANAGEMENT   The management structure of not-for-profit organizations resembles that of profit-based entities, though the terms used to describe certain bodies and officers may differ somewhat.

While limited companies have a board of directors comprising executive and non-executive directors, many not-for-profit organizations are often managed by a council or board of management whose role is to ensure adherence to the founding objectives. In recent times there has been some convergence between how companies and not-for-profit organizations are managed, including increasing reliance on non-executive officers (notably in respect of the scrutiny or oversight role) and the employment of career executives to run the organization on a daily basis.

Next, we will look at the management of larger organizations, which have greater impact on the economic environment. This is the regulation of the management of companies—a process known as corporate governance.

Principles of corporate governance

The key principles of what is today known as corporate governance were established by Sir Peter Cadbury. After some major corporate scandals in the UK in the 1980s, he was commissioned to come up with some good practice proposals which would:

- reinforce the responsibilities of executive directors
- separate the role of chairman and chief executive
- strengthen the role of the non-executive director
- make the case for audit committees of the board
- restate the principal responsibilities of auditors
- reinforce the links between shareholders, boards and auditors

This Cadbury duly did, and his report issued in 1992 (imaginatively entitled The Cadbury Report) formed the foundation of what was to become a part of the UK Stock Exchange Listing Agreement, which all companies wishing to have their shares listed on the London Stock Exchange must comply with. The principles set out by Cadbury have been gradually adopted internationally, and form the core of corporate governance practice and legislation in many countries of the world.

The definition of corporate governance most often quoted is the one contained in the Cadbury Report:

'...the system by which companies are directed and controlled'

This definition was all very well for the time, but as the various reports post-Cadbury have refined and enhanced his initial concepts, so the definition of what corporate governance actually is has also been refined. In research carried out among UK institutional investors: the definition which found the most favour was:

'the process of supervision and control intended to ensure that the company's management acts in accordance with the interests of shareholders' (Parkinson, 1994)

The modern multinational company has considerable power and influence, which it can bring to bear on the everyday lives of ordinary people.

REAL LIFE
Corporate power
In 1932 Adolf Berle and Gardiner Means published *The Modern Corporation and Private Property*. In it they said:

> 'The property owner who invests in a modern corporation so far surrenders his wealth to those in control of the corporation that he has exchanged the position of independent owner for one in which he may become merely recipient of the wages of capital... [Such owners] have surrendered the right that the corporation should be operated in their sole interest...'

> 'The economic power in the hands of the few persons who control a giant corporation is a tremendous force which can harm or benefit a multitude of individuals, affect whole districts, shift the currents of trade, bring ruin to one community and prosperity to another. The organizations which they control have passed far beyond the realm of private enterprise—they have become more nearly social institutions.'

> 'Have we any justification for the assumption that those in control of a modern corporation will also choose to operate it in the interests of the owners? The answer to this question will depend on the degree to which the self-interest of those in control may run parallel to the interests of ownership and, insofar as they differ, on the checks on the use of power which may be established by political, economic, or social conditions... If we are to assume that the desire for personal profit is the prime force motivating control, we must conclude that the interests of control are different from and often radically opposed to those of ownership; that the owners most emphatically will not be served by a profit-seeking controlling group.'

Those who doubt this should consider:

- The effect on the high street of a new out-of-town hypermarket
- The influence of Starbucks on coffee consumption
- The influence of McDonalds and Burger King on the nation's eating habits and the behaviour of its children
- The economic power of oil companies

Consequently, we can understand the need for trust and what happens when trust is violated and:

- owners and others are misled or lied to
- secrets are concealed not for honourable commercial motives but out of shame or for the personal protection of guilty individuals, and
- companies engage in behaviour which ethical individuals would consider to be unethical or immoral

Consequently, there is a need for us to trust the individuals who wield real commercial power and to trust what they tell us. As we saw in Module 1, the management of companies has become separated from their ownership and the implications are that managers can pursue their own agenda, sometimes at the expense of longer-term considerations.

The power wielded by executives of large multinational corporations is considerable and whilst, in theory, they remain accountable to shareholders, the reality is that most of those shareholders are large institutional investors—insurance companies, pension funds, etc.—who are primarily interested in maximizing returns of income in the form of dividends and in capital growth in the form of an increased share price.

Executives who fail to produce a strong dividend performance and an increasing share price are vulnerable.

REAL LIFE

The alternative view—Milton Friedman

This was written in the 1960s:

> 'Few trends would so thoroughly undermine the very foundations of our free society as the acceptance by corporate officials of a social responsibility other than to make as much money for their shareholders as they possibly can.'

We doubt any manager of a large business would publicly at least, espouse these views. Times have changed.

Source: Milton Friedman, (1962) *Capitalism and Freedom*, University of Chicago Press, Chicago, Ill

There are three key issues around modern corporate responsibility we need to bear in mind:

1 The influence of corporate culture, set by senior management, on the behaviour of individuals and how dysfunctional organizations can, in striving to meet corporate goals, compel individuals to engage in behaviour which outside work they would find reprehensible and unacceptable. This includes behaviour such as bullying, lying, theft, corruption, sabotage, evasion of responsibilities and fraud. There also needs to be consideration of how individuals who may wish to avoid this kind of behaviour or who wish to act ethically may be forced out of the organization or ostracized within it.

2 The conflict between the perceived duty of a director to maximize value for the shareholder, however 'value' is defined, and actions that may be ethical but which could be costly and reduce shareholder value. An example of this may be, for example, the directors involving the company in schemes to reduce tax payments through the use of tax havens that are perfectly legal and preserve profits in the company but that deprive the home nation of much-needed tax revenues, which could be used to fund social welfare programmes.

3 How modern companies are coming under pressure to take on some of the responsibilities of ownership and to act like corporate citizens with a moral code. The attitudes espoused by Milton Friedman, above, are, at least publicly, frowned upon by most corporate managers nowadays and most would acknowledge that they owe something to the wider community and have some level of social responsibility that is greater than the compulsion of regulation. Cynics may point out that demonstrated social efforts make good PR and that's why companies do it, but that's not the point—the point is that it **is** good PR because contemporary western society has expectations of companies and are pleased to see them met, even if the company uses the occasion to boast.

Stop and think

Do you agree with Milton Friedman that the primary objective of a company is to make money?

At what point should a responsibility to society outweigh the objective of making money? How far should businesses sacrifice money making opportunities in order to benefit society?

KEY PRINCIPLES OF CORPORATE GOVERNANCE   Accordingly, corporate governance codes tend to stress key principles as shown in Figure 6.2.

Figure 6.2 **Principles of corporate governance**

Principle	What it means
Discipline	Corporate discipline is a commitment by a company's senior management to adhere to behaviour that is universally recognized and accepted to be ethical and fair. This includes a company's commitment to the underlying principles of good corporate governance, particularly at senior management level.
Transparency	Transparency is considered to be a key aspect of good corporate governance. It is the ease with which an independent outsider is able to analyze a company's actions, understand its economic fundamentals and the non-financial aspects relevant to the business. It reflects whether or not investors and other stakeholders can obtain a true picture of what is happening inside the company.
Independence	Independence is the extent to which mechanisms have been put in place to minimize or avoid potential conflicts of interest that may exist, such as dominance by a strong chief executive or large shareowner. These mechanisms range from the composition of the board, to appointments to committees of the board and external parties such as the auditors. The decisions made, and internal processes established, should be objective and not allow for undue influences.
Accountability	Individuals or groups in a company, who make decisions and take actions on specific issues, need to be accountable for their decisions and actions. Mechanisms must exist and be effective to allow for accountability. These provide investors with the means to query and assess the actions of the board and its committees.
Responsibility	Responsibility is linked to accountability and relates to behaviour that allows for corrective action and for penalizing mismanagement. While the board is accountable to the company, it must act responsively to and with responsibility towards all stakeholders of the company.
Fairness	The systems that exist within the company must be balanced in taking into account all those that have an interest in the company and its future. The rights of various groups have to be acknowledged and respected. For example, minority shareowner interests must receive equal consideration to those of the dominant shareowners. Equally the company must act fairly with regard to all its employees and key stakeholders (Module 1), including suppliers and customers.
Social responsibility	A well-managed company will be aware of, and respond to, social issues, placing a high priority on ethical standards. A good corporate citizen is increasingly seen as one that is non-discriminatory, non-exploitative, and responsible with regard to environmental and human rights issues. Research shows that a company is likely to experience indirect economic benefits such as improved productivity and corporate reputation by taking those factors into consideration.

Good corporate governance should not be a show of respectability and responsibility towards shareholders where company management make empty statements about being good corporate citizens whilst polluting the environment and denying employee rights.

As we have seen, very large organizations wield huge influence over the lives of millions of people and irresponsible behaviour by senior management can have very damaging effects on the environment and on the lives of ordinary people. Figure 6.3 illustrates just three examples, but there are others ranging from exploding Samsung Galaxy Note 7 phones to financial scandals involving executives at BT in Italy. The numbers involved are huge and the effects range from widespread (Volkswagen/Concordia) to more localized, involving employees, suppliers and disappointed customers.

Figure 6.3 Corporate scandals

Volkswagen

In September 2015, the US Environmental Protection Agency (EPA) found that many VW cars being sold in America had a 'defeat device'—or software—in diesel engines that could detect when they were being tested, changing the performance accordingly to improve results. The German car giant has since admitted cheating emissions tests in the US.

Concordia

The UK Competition and Markets Authority (CMA) said it had provisionally found that Concordia had 'abused its dominant position to overcharge the NHS' by hiking the price of liothyronine, used to treat patients with an underactive thyroid, by nearly 6000 per cent between 2007 and 2017.

The regulator said the NHS had spent more than £34 million on the drug last year, up from about £600 000 in 2006. The amount it paid per pack rose from £4.46 in 2007 to £258.19 by July 2017. The price of a single pill went up from 16p to £9.22, even though production costs remained broadly stable during that period.

Bell Pottinger (BPP Communications Ltd)

During 2016 and 2017, a sustained 'dirty campaign' by the firm came to light, in which BPP played on racial animosity in South Africa, including the creation of fake news, in order to benefit its client Oakbay Investments, which is controlled by the controversial and influential Gupta family in South Africa and had strong ties to President Zuma's government. In 2017, the resulting scandal saw the firm disgraced and expelled from its professional body. It collapsed in late 2017 and was placed into administration. Most of its staff in offices around the world lost their jobs.

Duties of directors

The duties of directors can be summarized as being to act in the best interests of the company and its shareholders. Best practice corporate governance suggests that executive directors' (those that manage the business on a daily basis) performance is reviewed annually by non-executive directors, who can bring an independent view to the performance evaluation and the CEO and chair of the board should also have a formal review.

They should have been appointed directors on merit and be rewarded accordingly, based on the performance of the company.

This latter point has been the cause of some controversy, as it has led some commentators to observe that this encourages greed and is an incentive for directors to act in their own short-term interests to boost performance by sharp business practice and hide losses.

Others feel that only by incentivizing individuals will they perform at their best.

Suffice to say all directors have duties that they should observe and, in most countries, these are enshrined in law or in mandatory codes of practice. These are:

1 Act within powers

Directors must act in accordance with the company's constitution, and only exercise their powers for the purposes for which they were given.

2 Promote the success of the company

They must act in the way they consider, in good faith, would be most likely to promote the success of the company for the benefit of its members as a whole. 'Success' will generally mean a long-term increase in value, but fundamentally it is up to each director to decide, in good faith, whether it is appropriate for the company to take a particular course of action.

When considering what is most likely to promote the success of the company, the legislation states that a director must have regard to:
- the likely consequences of any decision in the long term
- the interests of the company's employees
- the need to foster the company's business relationships with suppliers, customers and others
- the impact of the company's operations on the community and the environment
- the desirability of the company maintaining a reputation for high standards of business conduct
- the need to act fairly as between members of the company

This list is not exhaustive, but is designed to highlight areas of particular importance to responsible business behaviour.

3 Exercise independent judgement
Directors must exercise independent judgement and make their own decisions. This does not prevent them from acting in accordance with the company's constitution or an agreement into which the company has entered.

4 Exercise reasonable care, skill and diligence
They must exercise the same care, skill and diligence that would be exercised by a reasonably diligent person with:
- the general knowledge, skill and experience that may reasonably be expected of a person carrying out the same functions in relation to the company
- the general knowledge, skill and experience that they actually possess

The expected standard is measured against both objective and subjective yardsticks. A director's actual understanding and abilities may not be enough if more could reasonably be expected of someone in his or her position.

5 Avoid conflicts of interest (a 'conflict situation')
Directors must avoid a situation in which they have, or could have, an interest that conflicts, or may conflict, with the interests of the company. This applies in particular to the exploitation of any property, information or opportunity, regardless of whether the company could take advantage of it.

There are other specific duties imposed on directors including:
- those relating to the preparation, content, circulation and filing of the company's annual reports and accounts
- restrictions and conditions placed on transactions between a director and the company and loans made by the company to a director
- a duty of confidentiality to the company and must use or disclose the company's confidential information only for the benefit of the company
- responsibility for ensuring that the company complies with its obligations relating to the health, safety and welfare at work of its workers, under health and safety legislation. Similarly, obligations arise under environmental legislation, money laundering and anti-corruption legislation.

Financing a business

Financing any business is critical. To get started a business, however small, will need some initial capital to get it off the ground. Indeed this is true of any venture, be it a sole trader starting up a business as a window cleaner (need to finance a squeegee and a ladder), someone setting up a charity for the relief of distressed armadillos (fees to register it, legal costs, letterhead etc) or an entrepreneur setting up a new airline.

It is all a matter of degree or scale.

There are basically four ways to finance any business where cash is required:

- using your own money
- persuading others to invest in your venture
- borrowing the money from a lender
- obtaining grants from specific bodies in special situations

Most people, when setting up a small business, use a combination of these. For example, they may introduce their savings, go into partnership with a like-minded person who shares their ambition and borrow some money from a bank. In certain situations, grants may be available for start-up ventures in rural areas, technical product development, restoration services for old buildings, etc., but these tend to be rather specialized and often come with conditions and restrictions.

A sole trader investing their own money in the business creates capital and this will be reflected on the statement of financial position. What profit they make is added to their capital as it represents a growing investment in the business. What individuals take out of the business is known as drawings.

It is important to understand that for unincorporated organizations, owners or partners do not receive a salary or any form of emolument. What they take out of the business is, in effect, a reduction of their capital investment in it.

This structure is also true of partnerships where a separate capital account will be maintained for each partner.

Larger businesses need larger investment, and this is where the company comes in, for one simple reason: limited liability.

Setting up in business as a sole trader or partnership carries with it a risk. That risk is that should the business fail the owners are responsible for the debts of the business, including repayment of any loans or overdrafts. This can mean that personal assets are at risk: the family home, the family car, the computer, television and furniture all could be sold in bankruptcy proceedings to repay debts.

However, setting yourself up as a limited liability company immediately provides the protection of limited liability. All that the individual shareholder is liable for is any amount unpaid on their shares, which could be a minimal amount.

Gearing/leverage

Most businesses of any size are funded by a combination of money which is 'free' (partners' capital, shares) and money which carries an interest charge (bank loans and overdrafts). When we use the expression 'free' in this context it does not, of course, mean that there is never a return for investors—far from it. Investors in a business will want some form of dividend return, although research indicates that most investors in stocks and shares prefer to see the value of their investment grow rather than as an it being an investment to generate an income.

The point about 'free' investment is that the income return on the investment, in the form of a dividend, is at the discretion of the management of the business. In hard times they may choose to pay a very low dividend, or indeed, not pay one at all.

In contrast, a loan or an overdraft has an interest cost, which has to be met, come what may. So even in hard times when money is tight, the interest burden on the loan or overdraft still has to be met, as do agreed repayments of a loan or reduction in an overdraft.

In addition to this, the financial disclosures of financing costs and dividends are different. Financing costs—bank interest and costs—are shown as a deduction from profits, so are included in the calculation of the profit or loss before tax of the business—known in accounting jargon as above the line. Interest payments are tax deductible, whereas dividends are not.

In contrast, dividends are classed as an appropriation of profit that is after the pre-tax profit—so are shown below the line.

Remember the layout of a simple income statement:

		R,000s	
Revenues		1000	
Cost of sales	(400)		
Other costs and expenses	(200)	(600)	
Operating profit		400	
Finance costs		(150)	
Profit before taxation		250	'the line'
Taxation		(50)	
Profit after taxation		200	
Dividend		(50)	
Retained profit		150	

As can be seen, finance costs form part of operating profit, whilst dividends do not. Why is this relevant?

Well, as we will see later in Module 8, profit before taxation forms part of several key accounting ratios used by financial analysts to determine the financial health of a company. Generally the greater the profit before tax, the better the ratios look. If you are a director being rewarded on performance, having net profit as high as possible is a good thing.

The role of the auditors

As we have seen, shareholders own the business and managers (or directors) manage the business. Consequently, shareholders use an independent expert to give an opinion on whether the accounts of their company, which the managers prepare, show a true and fair view of the financial position of the company and that the financial statements are properly presented and comply with company law and relevant accounting standards. These experts are the auditors.

There are several issues underlying this, not just the need for owners of the business to receive reliable information:

- Agency theory tells us that directors are motivated to show good results on the basis that it will benefit them directly in the short term.
- Shareholders need realism and information about the business they own, and that information has to be validated by an independent expert.
- It is totally impractical for shareholders to check accounts in detail.
- The auditors will also report on whether proper books and records have been kept and on any weaknesses in the accounting systems.

However, there is an underlying dilemma for the shareholders in that the auditors are paid by the company, which is controlled on a day-to-day basis by the directors—who agree the audit fee. Consequently, auditors may well be tempted to look favourably on the actions of the directors so as to retain their valuable client.

The integrity and independence of the audit firm is paramount, and there is a whole system of controls and rules binding audit firms to act in an independent and ethical manner.

The auditors' job is to gather evidence to prove that:

- profits and losses are properly stated
- assets and liabilities belong to the company and are shown at their correct values
- accounting entries are properly recorded in the correct accounting period

To do this they:

- review the accounting records and controls
- ask for explanations from directors, managers and staff of the company
- obtain details from third parties such as banks and legal representatives

During the course of their work, auditors may be involved in:

- discovering weaknesses in the financial systems
- checking compliance with laws and accounting standards
- discovering frauds or errors

WHAT DOES 'TRUE AND FAIR' MEAN?   The report of the auditors will always use words such as 'true and fair' or 'presents fairly' to describe the financial statements. An auditor's report contains an opinion paragraph, which in the UK will read something like:

'In our opinion the financial statements give a true and fair view of the state of the company's affairs as at 31 March 20X8 and of its profit for the year then ended.'

There are variations on this form of wording internationally but suffice to say at some point the auditors have to nail their colours to the mast and make a decision as to the validity of the financial statements they have just audited. So, what does 'true and fair' mean?

It is perhaps easier to state what it does not mean. It does not mean that the financial statements are:

- correct
- totally accurate
- free of errors

It means that the accounts are a reasonably fair representation of the company's performance and of its assets and liabilities at the balance sheet date. It accepts that there may be some errors, mistakes or inconsistencies in the financial statements but that none of these are significant enough, either singly or collectively, to cast doubt on the validity of the financial statements as a whole. Auditors have a jargon word for this: any error or mistake considered significant enough to affect the economic decisions of a reader of the financial statements is classed as material.

RIGHTS OF AUDITORS   In order to carry out their role auditors have certain rights, without which a proper financial audit would be impossible. Key rights are:

- right to all necessary information and explanations they consider necessary
- full access to company records
- entitlement to receive notice of meetings, attend and speak.

Remember that the auditors are acting for the shareholders and report to them. They are not a management resource, nor are they a rubber stamp for the actions of the directors. They are, in many ways, an executive arm of good corporate governance and their role is critical in informing and reporting on the financial health of the company.

That role becomes increasingly more significant where standards of corporate morality are, or are seen to be, declining. Corporate scandals in the UK, US, Europe, India and Japan involving misrepresentation, corruption and theft on a huge scale have increased the demand from both investors and regulators for auditors to be more efficient and more demanding of their clients in terms of their visible adherence to ethical principles and practical internal control systems.

Throughout history there have always been thieves and deceivers. There have always been those who seek to profit at the expense of others. At one level then, auditors and managers are on the same side as they seek to protect the organization's assets or to catch the offender and, hopefully, see them punished. Where auditors and managers part company is where it is the manager who seeks to enrich themselves at the organization's expense in a way that the auditor would expose as illegal or immoral because, in that case, it is depriving the owners of the business of what is rightfully theirs.

When managers distort the financial statements so that their share options sell out at a good price, where they create fictitious assets to hide their own depredations, where they stick their noses so far into the trough that their feet leave the ground is where the external auditor is there to step in and expose this bad behaviour, this immorality, this betrayal of trust.

It has to be said that, in the case of most corporate scandals the auditors have played an insignificant role and they have often been duped by unscrupulous managers but the point is that without an audit function, however ineffective it is at uncovering fraud or misrepresentation, things could be a great deal worse for shareholders.

Test yourself

1 Charities are usually unincorporated associations limited by guarantee.   **True/False**

2 What is the main objective of a social enterprise?
   a) Running a business to create social benefits
   b) Providing a public service
   c) Maximizing profits
   d) Generating cash to donate to charities

3 One advantage of a sole trader business is:
   a) The owners have limited liability
   b) It is easy to raise capital
   c) The owner is independent
   d) Decisions and responsibilities can be shared

4 Transparency is a key aspect of good corporate governance.   **True/False**

5 Which of the following is NOT a feature of a private limited company?
   a) Shares can be sold to raise capital
   b) The business continues after the death of the shareholders
   c) Shares are listed on a stock exchange so can be easily bought and sold
   d) The owners of the business have limited liability

6 Directors have a fiduciary responsibility to safeguard the assets of the business.   **True/False**

7 Once a private limited company reaches a certain size, it might wish to change its status to a public limited company and offer its shares to the public. One of the drawbacks of doing this is:
   a) Reduced efficiency as more staff and managers have to be employed
   b) Loss of control by the original owners
   c) Employees have a greater say in how the business is run
   d) The government takes a greater interest in the activities of the company

8 Joint and several liability means that each partner is responsible for all the debts of a business.   **True/False**

9 There are three measures commonly used to assess the performance of not-for-profit organizations: economy, efficiency and effectiveness. Which definition fits each of these descriptions?

Definition	Defines
'More bang for your buck.'	
'Make the best use of what you've got.'	
'Hit the target every time.'	

10 Auditors use the words 'true and fair' to mean accurate and free from material errors.   **True/False**

In the next module we will look at the importance of cash flows within an organization and how a business can maximize its cash flow to reduce dependence on borrowed funds.

Test yourself

1 Extract from the financial statements of Megablast Ltd regarding corporate governance:
   'Mr Tidyman is the Chief Executive Officer and board chairman of Megablast. He appoints and maintains a board of six executive and two non-executive directors, one of which is his father, the former Chairman of Megablast, Sir Roger Tidyman.

   The board sets performance targets for the senior managers in the company, but there are no formal targets for directors and the company does not have a remuneration committee. Mr Tidyman carries out a review of board policies annually in conjunction with the non-executive directors. Salaries for executive directors are set and paid by Mr Tidyman based on his assessment of all the board members, including himself. There is no formal measure of actual performance of individual directors.

Internal controls in the company are monitored by the senior accountant, although detailed review is assumed to be carried out by the external auditors; Megablast does not have an internal audit department. Annual financial statements are produced, providing detailed information on past performance.'

Required

Write a report for Mr Tidyman to:

(a) Explain why Megablast does not meet international codes of corporate governance.

(b) Explain why not meeting the international codes may cause a problem for Megablast.

(c) Recommend any changes necessary to implement those codes in the company.

2 Sally Svenson, a qualified accountant, is the finance manager of a small family company called Wintergreen Ltd, a company that sells aircraft components to aircraft repairers and airlines. The company is a family-owned business and there are five shareholders, three of whom are active in the business. Dave, Ethel and Joe are the directors; there are no outside directors and Sally is the most senior manager.

The company has revenues of some $6.2 million and the latest financial statements showed a profit after tax of $1.2 million.

The company is owned as to:

Dave Wintergreen—founder and CEO	25%
Ethel Wintergreen—his wife and a director	25%
Joe Wintergreen—their son and a director	20%
Misha Begum—family friend	15%
Madge Mulligan—family friend	15%

Madge Mulligan helped with initial finance but does not take any active part in the business, apart from attending the annual general meeting. She has indicated that she wants to sell her shares to the other shareholders. Misha is happy to be a passive shareholder.

The company is close to sealing a deal with a large airline for a supply of parts. If successful, it would mean a significant boost to profits and cash flow as the business expands. The annual general meeting is coming up and Sally has the audited accounts. She has also prepared some cash flow forecasts and projections for the next financial year.

Dave and Joe Wintergreen have come to see her to ask her not to include anything in the projections relating to the new contract.

Sally is of the opinion that this is so they can buy Madge's shares off her cheaply before the business expands and profits increase. She is unhappy about doing this.

Required

Write a report covering the following issues:

i. Sally obviously has an ethical concern, but is it valid in view of the fact the contract has not been signed yet?

ii. The CEO, Dave Wintergreen, has said that they don't need to bother with corporate governance nonsense as it is a small private company owned by the family, so they can do what they like. Is this true and, if true, is it advisable?

iii. How is the governance of a company structured like this affected by the fact that it has a predominance of family shareholders and family management?

7 Cash flows

In this module we will consider:

- The importance of cash flow
- Cash and cash equivalents
- Cash flow reporting in financial accounts
- Preparing the cash flow statement

The importance of cash flow

It is often said that 'cash is king,' because without cash even the largest business will fail. The reason is simple: only cash will pay the bills. If a business cannot generate sufficient cash to pay its way, it cannot go on.

The budding business entrepreneur would do well to understand that there is a big difference between cash and profit.

Here is a simple example to illustrate the point.

EXAMPLE

Hugo has £50. He uses £20 to buy some coloured pens, of which he sold half for £35.
In cash terms, however, Hugo has:

Day 1	£
Initial cash	50
Purchase of pens	(20)
Sale of pens	35
Closing cash balance	65

So Hugo's asset value has gone up from £50 to £65 because of the profit he made on his sale of the pens, all of which he realized in cash. In fact, as we will see, Hugo did better than it might at first appear because he still has half his stock of pens left to sell.

In accounting terms, Hugo's income statement will look like this:

	£
Sales	35
Cost of sales ($\frac{1}{2} \times £20$)	(10)
Profit	25

Note that the cost of sales relates to the amount of pens sold, i.e. half of what Hugo bought, so only half of the cost is included in the income statement. The remaining cost of the pens Hugo bought is inventory for sale the next time.

So Hugo's little statement of financial position will look like this:

	£
Assets	
Inventory	10
Cash	65
Assets	75
Capital	
Hugo's initial capital	50
Profit	25
	75

So Hugo's capital has increased by £25 because of the profit he has made, and this is reflected in the cash he has and the stock of pens he still has to sell.

Flushed with success Hugo spends £40 buying more pens but the next day's trading is poor, and he only sells half of his total inventory for £35.

His cash position now looks like this:

Day 2	£
Opening cash balance	65
Purchase of pens	(40)
Sales	35
Closing cash balance	60

His income statement for the next period of trading looks like this:

	£
Sales	35
Cost of sales $(10 + 40) \times \frac{1}{2} =$	(25)
Profit	10

His statement of financial position reveals something interesting:

	£
Assets	
Cash	60
Inventory	25
	85
Capital	
Opening balance	75
Profit for the period	10
	85

Hugo's business is growing on paper, but his cash balance has declined from £65 to £60. The cash he had was used to buy additional inventory but sales were not up to expectations so he was left with an increased inventory (up from £10 to £25) and a lower cash balance.

If Hugo continues to spend and sales do not generate sufficient cash to cover the outlay, he may well end up with a lot of pens but no cash! Hugo still has a viable business and his wealth has increased by £35 because of the two profits he has made in the first and second trading periods, i.e. £25 + £10. Consequently he is now worth £85 from his initial £50 starting point.

This simple example shows that, whilst the income statement and the statement of financial position measure flows of wealth, the cash flow statement measures the movement of cash over time and is of critical importance in managing the business.

Even the largest companies can run into difficulties when the cash runs dry. Figure 7.1 has some examples.

Figure 7.1 Cash flow problems affect even the largest companies

Monarch airlines

Monarch was the largest airline ever to have ceased trading in the UK. The causal factors of Monarch's demise were a combination of factors such as strong competition on routes to southern Europe from other low-cost rivals, excess capacity on many routes forcing down prices and affecting profit margins, terrorism in Libya and uncertainty in Egypt causing a massive downturn in tourism to those countries, and Brexit causing the depreciation of the UK pound, which increased operating costs (i.e. fuel costs, aircraft leasing costs, airport landing fees).

Toys'R'Us

Toys'R'Us has filed for bankruptcy protection in the US and Canada after running up $5 billion (£3.7 billion) of debts and struggling to compete in the age of internet shopping.

The world's largest toy store chain said it had filed for bankruptcy protection in the US in order to restructure its debts and plan for long-term growth.

Carillon

Carillion, a major construction group, issued its third profit warning in five months in November and said it was heading towards a breach of debt covenants and would need fresh capital.

The firm went into liquidation, citing costly contract delays and a downturn in new business at the company, which handles major infrastructure projects for the British and other governments.

Cash and cash equivalents

What do we mean by cash? Obviously notes and coins are cash and bank balances that are accessible on demand are also cash, but businesses often hold other forms of investment, which can be classified as a cash equivalent. Why is this?

Cash equivalents are short term investments that are highly **liquid**—that is, easily and quickly convertible into cash. They have to be:

- short-term
- readily convertible into cash
- very low risk of a change in value, i.e. a stable investment that isn't affected by a volatile market or by being converted into cash.

So cash and cash equivalents can include:

- a bank current account
- a bank deposit account
- an overdraft—negative cash—which is available for funding the business
- treasury bills
- short-term government bonds
- money market funds

Cash does not include:

- a high interest bank deposit account where the funds are 'locked in' for six months or longer
- equity investments listed on a stock exchange, because there is volatility in the share price so the amount receivable on sale cannot be established precisely

So fundamentally cash is a highly liquid asset which can be made available for trading purposes.

REAL LIFE
Trouble at HTC in 2013

Taiwanese smartphone maker HTC halted at least one of its four main manufacturing lines, accounting for at least a fifth of total capacity, and outsourced production as a sales slump put pressure on its cash flow, according to sources with direct knowledge of the situation.

The company, whose woes have been exacerbated by supply chain constraints and internal turmoil, reported its first-ever quarterly loss in October 2013 and its cash flow from operations dropped to a negative US$707.27 million as of the end of June 2013.

HTC initially denied it was shutting down any production, in Taiwan or elsewhere, and declined to comment on whether it was in discussions to outsource production.

'HTC is not shutting down nor has plans to sell any of its factory assets,' the company said in an emailed response to queries. 'HTC has a very strong balance sheet and will provide the latest financials in our upcoming earnings call to investors and the broader community.'

Manufacturing has been halted since at least August 2013 on the line, housed in a facility called Building H, while production continued at a nearby plant known as TY5.

Most of the assembly lines in HTC's Shanghai factory, which can produce two million phones a month, were also out of production, one of the sources said, with only a small number of phones being produced for sale inside China.

'HTC's cash flow is not doing well. It has to do something soon to generate cash,' said one of the sources with direct knowledge of the manufacturing sale plan.

At the end of June 2013 HTC's cash position decreased to T$48.1 billion from T$55.5 billion a year earlier as cash flow turned negative. Its balance sheet also shows that bill payments increased while less money came in from customers. Receivables increased by T$7.9 billion, but accounts payable dropped T$7.8 billion.

HTC's return on assets (ROA)—an indicator of how effectively a company uses its assets to generate earnings—is expected to turn negative this year at –0.69 per cent, the first time since 1999. ROA last year was 8.1 per cent.

Source: *South China Morning Post.* 'HTC scales back production amid cash flow problems'—23 October 2013

Cash flow reporting in financial accounts

The various statements recording cash flows are keenly studied by analysts for the reasons outlined above: they will be looking to see how much cash the organization is generating from its activities.

The income statement and statement of financial position are the first port of call for anyone examining a set of statutory financial statements, and they will give the analysts detailed information about the profitability of the entity and its asset value. However, as we have seen, financial statements are prepared on an accruals basis and include estimates and judgements made by management as to, for example:

- the inclusion or otherwise or certain costs or revenues, e.g. provisions and accruals
- the inclusion or otherwise of profits or losses in connection with contract work in progress
- the valuation of assets

There have been many and various instances where financial statements have been manipulated by unscrupulous management in order to present a favourable picture to shareholders and often, incidentally, to trigger bonus payments for themselves.

It is not to say that close examination of the cash flow statements will suddenly reveal that the management have been cooking the books—far from it, as these statements are, after all, derived from the same source as the rest of the accounts—but it does present the numbers in a different way, which can shed light on what has actually happened from a cash perspective.

The reason for this is that the statements start and end with cash balances—cash and cash equivalents—and show how they have changed from the beginning to the end of the financial period. Cash doesn't lie. What the cash flow statement actually does is reconcile:

The balance of cash and cash equivalents at the beginning of the financial period = X

minus

The balance of cash and cash equivalents at the end of the financial period = Y

The statement seeks to explain **X—Y**. In other words, to answer the question: *'What has happened to the money?'*

In many ways, the cash flow statement is the most important part of the financial statements as a whole because it shows the movement in the financial position of the business in quite stark detail by showing where the money went. As we've said before, businesses do not go under purely through making accounting losses; they go under because they cannot pay their debts.

Let us look at how a cash flow statement for financial accounts is constructed.

By convention, cash flows are either inflows (receipts), which are represented as a positive number, or outflows (costs, expenses and purchases, etc.), which are represented as a negative number shown in brackets.

In most cases it is easy to establish the cash flow as either a positive or negative number.

There are other key aspects of cash flow forecasts that have to be understood in order to balance the cash flow statement.

SOME NUMBERS HAVE TO BE CALCULATED   One of the key aspects of preparing a cash flow statement for financial accounts is that some of the numbers have to be calculated. The reason is that what we need to establish is the amount of actual cash paid out, not the movement in a provision. As we saw in Module 3 a provision is an accounting construct: based on real information it's true, but it does not represent a movement of cash. The best way to illustrate this is with an example.

One of the most common calculations of this type which has to be performed is the calculation of tax paid.

EXAMPLE

At the beginning of the accounting period the financial accounts of a company showed a tax liability in payables of €102000. At the end of the financial period, the accounts showed a liability of €95000. The statement of income showed a charge of €100000. How much tax was actually paid?

Well, obviously one way would be to simply look at the tax account in the nominal ledger and work from there, but there is a technique that is widely used in other situations, which can be adopted if that isn't possible.

To answer this the easiest way is to reconstitute the tax account in the nominal ledger and we can use the T account method to make this easy.

So we have a situation that looks like this:

TAX ACCOUNT

		Opening provision b/d	102000
		Charge to income account	100000
Closing provision c/d	95000		

At this stage it is obvious that the two sides don't balance out—they are not equal. In the absence of any other adjustments the difference between the two sides must be the tax paid. Remember the double-entry:

Dr Tax paid

Cr Cash book

so completing the double entry the T account would look like this:

TAX ACCOUNT

		Opening provision b/d	102000
		Charge to income account	100000
Tax paid	107000		
Closing provision c/d	95000		
	€202000		€202000
		Closing provision b/d	95000

The actual amount of tax paid was €107000. The charge to the income account of €100000 is, in fact, made up of two parts. Firstly, the tax liability for the previous year was underprovided by €5000 (provision of €102000—actual tax paid of €107000) plus the €95000 provision for the current tax year.

This doesn't affect the cash flow but might affect how the financial statements are presented.

For our purposes the number to be included in the cash flow statement is the actual tax paid of €107000.

SOME COSTS AREN'T CASH AND SOME ADJUSTMENTS AREN'T EITHER Depreciation and amortization, as we saw in Module 4, is a way of writing down the carrying or written down value of tangible and intangible assets in the statement of financial position. It is a calculation carried out by the accountants and is largely there to write down asset values to reflect the passage of time.

It is not cash and has no part in a cash flow statement, so will need to be added back to the profit or deducted from the loss for the period when we come to do the calculation. More about this later.

Similarly, asset values can be amended by revaluations. Again, a revaluation isn't cash, so this is something else, which has to be adjusted for in the calculation.

Let us look again at the technique we used above, but in this case we'll look at tangible assets and in particular plant and equipment.

Again, we can use T account to make this easy. One point to be made here is that, if this was being done in real life there would be separate accounts for depreciation and revaluation surpluses, etc., but we've combined them together here in the interests of clarity and simplicity.

Here's an example:

EXAMPLE

A t the beginning of the accounting period a company had plant and equipment with a carrying or written-down value of £500000. There was a depreciation charge for the year of £65000. Assets with a carrying value of £76000 were sold during the year and finally some of the equipment was revalued recording a surplus of £25000.

At the end of the financial year the carrying value of plant and equipment was £660000.

How much cash was spent on plant and equipment in the financial period?

To answer we must create, in this case, a composite T account.

PLANT AND EQUIPMENT

Opening balance b/d	500000	Depreciation charged	65000
Revaluation surplus	25000	Disposal of assets	76000
		Closing balance c/d	660000

Remember these are assets so the opening balance is a debit. Depreciation and the sale of assets reduces that value, so they are credits. We looked at these in Module 4.

The revaluation surplus increases the value, so this too is a debit. The double-entry for this is:

Dr Tangible assets
Cr Revaluation reserve

Both these appear in the statement of financial position.

Clearly this account doesn't balance and, in the absence of any other adjustments, the missing number must be the assets purchased.

PLANT AND EQUIPMENT

Opening balance b/d	500000	Depreciation charged	65000
Revaluation surplus	25000	Disposal of assets	76000
Assets purchased	275000	Closing balance c/d	660000
	800000		800000
Closing balance c/d	660000		

The key entry for the cash flow is the assets purchased of £275000.

Preparing the cash flow statement

The reporting standard here is International Accounting Standard 7, '*Statement of Cash Flows*,' which details how the statement of cash flows should be presented.

It classifies cash flows into three headings:

i. Operating activities
ii. Investing activities
iii. Financing activities

Just to make it confusing, operating activities can be presented in two different ways—both of which obviously produce the same result, but which report different information. The approaches are:

Direct method	Shows the actual cash flows from operating activities, e.g. receipts from customers, payments to suppliers and staff, payment of expenses, etc.
Indirect method	Starts with the profit or loss for the accounting period and adjusts it for non-cash items such as depreciation, etc. It also adjusts for changes in the values of current assets and liabilities to reflect the movement of cash through the business.

The indirect method is the one most usually adopted, but it can be difficult to understand some of the concepts involved in its preparation. The direct method involves only cash—cash paid in and cash paid out. The indirect method calculates cash movements by inference. This is the tricky part of the calculation.

For example, suppose the value of trade receivables at the beginning and end of the financial period has gone up from R200 to R300. Because these are receivables, the business hasn't got the cash. It's increased its assets but not by cash so this, effectively, represents an outflow of cash as the balance of receivables has to be funded by the business until the cash comes in. Similarly, if the balances have gone the other way, so the value of receivables has declined in the period by R100; this is an inflow of cash as the customers have paid up and don't owe so much.

The best way to illustrate this is with a worked example.

Here is an extract from a set of financial statements:

Income statement

	Year 2
Revenues	500
Cost of sales (materials)	(240)
Staff costs	(100)
Depreciation	(40)
	120

Statement of financial position

		Year 2		Year 1
Non-current assets				
Tangible assets		470		500
Current assets				
Inventory	60		40	
Receivables	65		75	
Cash and bank balances	175	300	50	165
Total assets		770		665
Current liabilities				
Trade payables		55		70
Non-current liabilities				
Long-term loan		500		500
Total liabilities		555		570
Net assets		215		95

DIRECT METHOD

It has to be said that this is not a common way of presenting cash flow statements, but it does have value and can be used for smaller, less complex organizations.

Under the direct method, cash flows arising from transactions are calculated and included in the forecast. The flows are calculated broadly in accordance with the income statement, and the cash flow statement thus records the gross flows of cash through the business.

The cash flows have to be calculated. Remember that financial statements are prepared on an accruals basis and transactions are carried out on credit. Accordingly, for example, the amount shown as revenues in the income statement is not the cash received from customers, it is what has been invoiced to customers—and some of those invoices haven't been paid.

So, we have to work out the cash movements as follows:

CASH RECEIVED FROM CUSTOMERS   This can be established by adjusting for opening and closing receivables. We assume that some of the cash received is last year's invoices (trade receivables) being paid plus what we sold in the year minus this year's trade receivables—which haven't been paid yet.

So the calculation is:

Opening receivables—Year 1	75
Sold in year—Revenues	500
Closing receivables—Year 2	(65)
Cash received from customers	510

CASH PAID TO SUPPLIERS   This is a slightly more complicated calculation, as it also has to take into account the movement in inventory values between the two years. This is because we assume that the opening inventory was used first so there was no need to buy more but at the end of the period the business had bought materials, which it was storing for use or sale in the next period. So we have a two-part calculation, firstly to establish the cost of purchases and secondly to work out how much actual cash changed hands.

Thus:

Cost of inventory sold in the period	240
Minus—opening inventory	(40)
Plus—closing inventory	60
Purchases of materials	260

Having worked out the value of materials purchased, we can calculate the cash movement.

Purchases in period	260
Add: Opening payables	70
Less: Closing payables	(55)
Cash paid to suppliers	275

STAFF COSTS   Staff are paid for the period they work and, for this purpose, we can assume that the amount shown in the income account is what was actually paid.

TANGIBLE FIXED ASSETS   The value of tangible fixed assets has changed in the year and only part of that can be accounted for by depreciation. The difference must be accounted for by the purchase and sale of fixed assets, so we can reconcile the movement thus:

Opening tangible assets	500
Depreciation	(40)
Purchase of assets	10
Closing tangible assets	470

The purchase of new assets is also a cash movement, so we have to include this in the cash flow; depreciation is not so we exclude that. Depreciation is an accounting construct and just a paper adjustment to asset values shown in the statement of financial position.

So the direct method cash flow statement looks like this:

Cash received from customers	510
Cash paid to suppliers	(275)
Staff costs	(100)
Purchase of assets	(10)
Cash flow	125

Which we can agree to the movement in the bank balance:

Opening balance	50
Closing balance	175
Net inflow of cash	125

INDIRECT METHOD

The indirect method is the one more frequently used. It differs from the direct method insofar as it does not show the gross cash movement of revenues and costs, but starts with operating profit and makes adjustments to that for:

- increases or decreases in the values of current assets and liabilities
- non-cash items such as depreciation, losses on disposals of assets etc.
- other one-off costs such as tax payments, interest payments and purchases and sales of assets

Using the same information as the example above, we can prepare a cash flow statement, using the indirect method thus:

Operating profit	120
Add: Non-cash items	
Depreciation	40
	160
Increase in inventory	(20)
Decrease in receivables	10
Decrease in trade payables	(15)
Cash flow from operations	135
Cash flow from investing activities	
Purchase of tangible assets	(10)
Increase/decrease in cash	125

The key to understanding when to add and when to subtract from operating profit is to determine the effect on the cash flow.

Consider an increase in inventories. An increase in inventories means that the business has spent more cash on inventories that have not yet turned into receivables and thus not yet turned into cash. This results in a cash outflow and outflows are deducted from operating profit. Conversely, if there was a decrease in inventories, then this would represent an inflow of cash, because the business had spent less on inventories than in the previous year.

Increases in trade receivables demonstrate that less cash has been received from trade receivables than the previous year, which represents an outflow and thus a deduction from operating profit in the statement.

Conversely, an increase in payables means that we have paid less to trade payables than in the previous year, resulting in more cash being kept in the bank meaning an inflow, so an addition to operating profit in the cash flow statement.

The example shown above deals only with operating activities but a more comprehensive cash flow statement for a larger operation would, as outlined above under the provisions of International Accounting Standard 7 'Statement of Cash Flows,' classify cash flows into three headings:

i. Operating activities
ii. Investing activities
iii. Financing activities

What we need to look at now is a much more comprehensive example illustrating all three types of activity. We will use the example Tattibogle set out below and work through each stage using the indirect method to illustrate the process.

Firstly, we need to consider the income account for the current period and the statement of financial position for the current and previous financial periods.

Here are the income account and statement of financial position for Tattibogle plc, which we will use to prepare a cash flow statement:

Tattibogle plc
Income statement for the year

	£m
Revenue	1892
Cost of sales	(841)
Gross profit	1051
Operating costs	(442)
Administration costs	(293)
Marketing, distribution and sales costs	(87)
Loss on disposal of equipment	(29)
Depreciation and amortization	(19)
Operating profit before tax	181
Interest receivable	35
Finance costs—interest payable	(20)
Profit before tax	196
Taxation	(51)
Profit after tax retained	145

Tattibogle plc
Statement of financial position

	Year 2		Year 1	
	£m	£m	£m	£m
Property plant and equipment—cost	279		256	
Accumulated depreciation	(44)	235	(51)	205
Intangible assets	185		185	
Amortization	(34)	151	(27)	158
Total non-current assets		386		363
Current assets				
Inventories	171		63	
Trade receivables	247		263	
Cash and bank balances	230		183	
	648		509	
Current liabilities				
Trade payables	201		182	
Interest payable	22		18	
Taxation payable	58		49	
	281		249	
Net current assets		367		260
Non-current liabilities				
Long-term loan		(138)		(153)
Net assets		615		470
Share capital		75		75
Retained earnings		540		395
		615		470

Notes

1 During the year the company purchased additional plant and equipment costing £93m.
2 The company sold a redundant property for £22m. The original cost was £70m and the accumulated depreciation was £19m.

What we are looking to do is to establish the changes in the financial position of the business between the two financial accounting periods. The changes are caused by the operating and other activities during the year (Year 2) so we can look at what has changed, how it has changed and account for the differences in our cash flow statement.

The first thing to do therefore is identify the differences between the statement of financial position for Year 2 and that for Year 1. This will identify many of the amounts required for the cash flow statement—but not all! For example, it gives us:

- The change in all of the current assets and liabilities, including the change in bank and cash balances, which is the figure we are reconciling to.
- It gives us the changes in tangible and intangible assets, which have to be accounted for—we will look at this in more detail later.
- There are items such as interest and dividends where the actual cash movement has to be calculated.

Tattibogle plc
Statement of financial position

	Year 2		Year 1		Difference increase or	
	£m	£m	£m	£m	(decrease) in asset value	Note
Property plant and equipment—cost	279		256			
Accumulated depreciation	(44)	235	(51)	205	30	1
Intangible assets	185		185			
Amortization	(34)	151	(27)	158	(7)	2
Total non-current assets		386		363		
Current assets						
Inventories	171		63		108	3
Trade receivables	247		263		(16)	3
Cash and bank balances	230		183		47	4
	648		509			
Current liabilities						
Trade payables	201		182		(19)	3
Interest payable	22		18		(4)	5
Taxation payable	58		49		(9)	6
	281		249			
Net current assets		367		260		
Non-current liabilities						
Long-term loan		(138)		(153)	15	7
Net assets		615		470	145	
Share capital		75		75		
Retained earnings		540		395		
		615		470		

Let us look at the movements in more detail. The note numbers refer to the points below.

NOTE 1—TANGIBLE ASSETS   The movement in tangible assets of a net amount of £30 million is made up of several items. Obviously, depreciation is one but the business also sold some assets at a loss during the financial year, so this also has to be accounted for. This can get quite complicated so it is necessary to follow the logic here.

Let us take tangible assets as a whole and look at the transactions in a comprehensive T account:

Tangible assets

Cost brought forward	256	Accumulated depreciation	51

We now have to dispose of the assets sold. The entries will be debited/credited to a disposal of assets account elsewhere in the nominal ledger to complete the double-entry, but we are only concerned with the total of tangible assets.

Tangible assets

Cost brought forward	256	Accumulated depreciation	51
Depreciation on assets sold	19	Cost of assets sold written off	70

We can now add the assets purchased and the depreciation for the year.

Tangible assets

Cost brought forward	256	Accumulated depreciation	51
Depreciation on assets sold	19	Cost of assets sold written off	70
Cost of assets purchased	93	Depreciation for the year	12
		Balance c/d	235
	368		368
Balance b/d	235		

In the cash flow statement, the individual movements have to be accounted for to enable a full explanation to be given to the reader as to what has happened in the year.

The disposal of fixed assets is accounted for in the cash flow statement by showing the sale proceeds of £22 million and the loss on sale £29 million separately. This gives an overall £51 million, which is equivalent to the original cost of £70 million minus the accumulated depreciation of £19 million. This accounts for those aspects of the adjustments on disposal shown above. We show the purchase of new assets and the depreciation separately.

NOTE 2—INTANGIBLE ASSETS   The only movement here is amortization. There has been no change to the cost of these assets.

NOTE 3—CURRENT ASSETS AND LIABILITIES   These are shown separately in the cash flow statement.

NOTE 4—CASH AND BANK BALANCES   This is the movement in liquid funds to which we are reconciling.

NOTE 5—INTEREST PAID   We looked at this in the first part of this module. What we must establish is how much cash was involved. We have the opening position, the charge to the income statement and the amount owing at the end of the year—so how much did we actually spend on interest in the year?

We could use a T account as we did earlier or we can simply work the number out arithmetically.

	£m
Balance of interest owed brought forward from Year 1	18
Charge to income account—current year	20
	38
Amount outstanding at the end of Year 2	(22)
Amount of interest paid	16

NOTE 6—TAXATION PAYABLE   Exactly the same process is applied to the tax liability—how much was actually paid out. The calculations are:

	£m
Balance of tax owing from Year 1 brought forward	49
Charge to income account—current year	51
	100
Balance outstanding at the end of Year 2	(58)
Amount of tax paid	42

NOTE 7—LONG-TERM LOAN   There has been movement here and, in the absence of other information we have to assume it is because part of the loan has been repaid. This is clearly a cash movement so we must account for it in the statement.

If we put all this together we can produce the statement of cash flow thus:

Tattibogle Plc

Cash flow statement

Operating profit before tax		181
Add: Non-cash items		
Depreciation and amortization		19
Loss on sale of equipment		29
		229
Increase in inventories		(108)
Decrease in trade receivables		16
Increase in trade payables		19
		156
Interest receivable		35
Interest paid		(16)
Taxation paid		(42)
Cash generated from operations		133
Investing activities		
Proceeds of sale of assets	22	
Purchase of tangible assets	(93)	
Repayment of long term loan	(15)	
Cash flow from investing activities		(86)
Increase in cash and bank balances		47
Opening balance		183
Closing balance		230
		47

As can be seen, the layout records cash flows from operating and investing activities. There were no changes to the capital structure—other than loan repayments in the ordinary course of business—so there were no financing activities this time. Had there been a share issue or another loan, this would be included separately.

What does this statement tell us? The key number which leaps out is the increase in inventories. This is tying up a lot of cash, so should be investigated. Otherwise the movements are not majorly significant and are all helping the cash position.

The loss on disposal of assets was, presumably, expected by management and did not constitute a major cash drain. The company was able to purchase some new assets and make its loan repayments and still generate cash from its activities.

It seems all is well with the company at the moment—but management has to constantly review the situation if cash generation suddenly starts to become cash outflow.

FREE CASH FLOW

Free cash flow is defined as:

Operating cash flow−gross capital investment

It measures the ability of the business to fund expansion or the addition of new assets through cash generation from operations.

If that number is negative and the business still wishes to expand, the most obvious route is to borrow money, and this can have significant effects on the ability of the business to service its debt and also to generate a sufficiently good return to ordinary shareholders.

Consider this: A business that has inventory of £150 000 is funding that amount for the length of time it takes the inventory to be turned into cash. If the inventory is held for 30 days before being sold and the customer takes 45 days to pay, the company is funding 75 days of holding that potential cash in another form. Clearly some of that funding is by taking credit from suppliers—but the rest has to be found from borrowings or capital.

Shortening the period of stockholding and collecting debts more quickly can speed up the amount of free cash available to the business and cut the requirement for borrowing significantly.

We look at this again in the next module when we look at ratio analysis.

Test yourself

1 Boggis Ltd has tangible assets at the beginning of the year with a net asset value of $1.456 million. During the year assets with a net asset value of $287 000 were sold for $350 000. At the end of the financial year the net asset value of the tangible assets was $1.550 million. What is the value of assets purchased in the year?

2 Wilbur prepares accounts to 31 December each year. At 31 December 20X8 his statement of financial position recorded the following current assets and liabilities.:

	20X8	20X7
	€	€
Inventories	52 846	49 372
Trade receivables	98 462	101 638
Trade payables	78 286	62 357

His operating profit for the year was €243 865 after deducting depreciation of €52 850 and adding a profit on sale of tangible assets of €7750. What is Wilbur's cash flow from operations for the year ended 31 December 20X8?

3 Trevor's tax account at 31 March 20X8 showed a brought forward provision of $88 000. The tax charge for the current period is estimated to be $97 500. The charge to the income account is $95 500. How much tax did Trevor pay in cash in 20X8?

4 Which of these statements are true or false?   ✔   ✔

	True	False
If the value of trade receivables goes down from one year to the next, this represents a cash inflow.		
The direct method of cash flow accounting starts with net profit.		
There is a paradox that a business can appear to grow whilst at the same time running out of cash.		
An increase in inventories increases asset values and therefore cash.		

5 Purchases on credit during the year 20X8 were £14 million. Trade payables at the start of the year were £3.5 million and at the end of the year were £4.1 million. How much cash was paid to suppliers in the year?

6 Splodge Ltd has an operating profit of R6 million which includes a depreciation charge of R0.5 million. During the year, inventories increased by R1.2 million, trade payables declined by R0.75 million and trade receivables by R0.9 million.

What was the cash flow from operations of Splodge during the year?

7 Which of these statements is true or false?

	True	False
If opening receivables are £3 million, closing receivables are £2.5 million and we invoiced £8 million in the year, the cash from customers must be £6.5 million.		
If the provision for the dividend for 20X7 was $500 000, the provision for the dividend for 20X8 was $650 000 and the charge to the income statement for dividends was $675 000, the amount paid to the shareholders in cash was $525 000.		
Cash equivalents includes term deposit accounts.		

8 Pilot plc made a provision for a dividend on its ordinary shares at the end of 20X7 of €4 250 000. It actually paid out €4 680 000 as the provision had been incorrectly calculated. The provision for 20X8 is €4 190 000. How much is the charge to the income account for 20X8?
   a) 4 620 000
   b) 4 740 000
   c) 3 760 000
   d) 4 260 000

9 Bugle Ltd has tangible fixed assets at the beginning of 20X8 of $987 000 at cost. Assets with an original cost of $78 000 were sold during the year and at the end of 20X8 the balance on the cost of tangible fixed assets account was $1 022 000. How much was spent on acquiring new assets during the year?
   a) $43 000
   b) $113 000
   c) $35 000
   d) $121 000

10 Hubert Ltd has an operating profit of R9 million which includes a depreciation charge of R1.2 million. During the year Inventories decreased by R1.3 million, trade payables increased by R1.1 million and trade receivables increased by R0.5 million.

What is the cash flow from operations of Hubert in 20X8?

In the next module we will look at how to analyze a set of financial statements and how to spot warning signs. We will look at horizontal and vertical analysis and ratio analysis to reveal the financial story told by the accounts.

Test yourself

1 The accountant at Geronimo Ltd has prepared an income statement and statement of financial position at 31 March 20X8.

He has told you that he doesn't really know how to do cash flow statements but needs one for inclusion in the information to go to the board of directors. He has asked you to prepare one.

The information he has provided is as follows:

Geronimo Ltd

Income account for the year ended 31 March 20X8

	$m
Revenues	640
Cost of sales	(286)
Gross profit	354
Interest received	10
Loss on disposal of equipment	(16)
Depreciation	(78)
Administration costs	(14)
Selling and distribution costs	(12)
Operating profit	244
Interest cost	(12)
Profit after interest	232
Taxation	(78)
Profit after interest and taxation	154

Statement of financial position at 31 March 20X8

	20X8	20X8	20X7	20X7
	$m		$m	
Tangible assets—cost		450		300
Tangible assets—depreciation		(180)		(120)
		270		180
Intangible asset		140		200
		410		380
Current assets				
Inventory	60		44	
Trade receivables	54		48	
Cash and bank	96		16	
	210		108	
Trade payables	42		40	
Interest payable	18		22	
Taxation payable	24		18	
	84		80	
Net current assets		126		28
Total assets		536		408
Share capital		288		280
Retained earnings		208		98
		496		378
Long-term loan		40		30
		536		408

Notes:

1. A dividend of $44m was paid during the year. The retained earnings increased as to:

Retained earnings at 31 March 20X7	98
Profit for 20X8	154
	252
Dividend paid	(44)
	208

2. During 20X8 the company purchased tangible assets amounting to $188m
3. During 20X8 the company sold tangible foxed assets for $4m. Their original cost was $38m and the accumulated depreciation was $18m
4. The company sold the rights to an intangible asset for $60m. There were no additions in the year

Required

i. Prepare a statement of cash flows using the indirect method
ii. Write a short commentary summarizing the key points

2 Ricardo's Restaurants Ltd need to provide some information for the bank. They have produced an income account and a statement of financial position and have attempted a cash flow forecast.

The information they have prepared is as follows:

Ricardo's Restaurants Ltd

Income account for the year ended 30 June 20X8

	£000's
Revenues	250
Cost of sales	(87)
Gross profit	163
Depreciation	(10)
Administration costs	(45)
Advertising and promotion	(26)
Operating profit	82
Interest cost	(6)
Profit after interest	76
Taxation	(21)
Profit after interest and taxation	55

Ricardo's Restaurants Ltd

Statement of financial position at 31 March 20X8

	20X8	20X7
	£000's	£000's
Tangible assets—cost	203	149
Tangible assets—depreciation	(40)	(30)
	163	119

Current assets				
Inventory	22		19	
Trade receivables	27		24	
Cash and bank	6		8	
	55		51	
Trade payables	14		12	
Interest payable	9		11	
Taxation payable	12		9	
	35		32	
Net current assets		20		19
Total assets		183		138
Share capital		10		10
Retained earnings		153		98
		163		108
Long-term loan		20		30
		183		138

Ricardo's Restaurants Ltd

Cash flow statement for the year ended 30 June 20X8

Profit for the year			55
Add depreciation			10
			65
Increase in inventory		(3)	
Increase in receivables		(3)	
Increase in payables		2	
Interest paid		(6)	
Taxation paid		(21)	(31)
			34
Purchase of fixed assets			(54)
			(20)
Movement in cash balances	At 20X7		8
	At 20X8		6
			2

There were no other adjustments in the year.

Ricardo can't balance his cash flow statement and has asked you to check it and correct it so it balances.

8 Analyzing and interpreting financial statements

In this module we will consider:

- Horizontal and vertical analysis of financial reports

- Ratio analysis

- Profitability ratios

- Efficiency ratios

- Financing ratios

- Investor ratios

- Limitations of ratio analysis

In this module we are moving away from creating financial statements to examining and analyzing what has been prepared. Financial statements are there to tell a story. They are an historical reporting of the financial health or otherwise of the organization and, as such, need to tell a consistent and understandable tale.

On the dark side, there have been many instances of management manipulation of financial statements, so it is also useful to have a toolkit which might flag anomalous or odd results, which could give cause for concern or raise what fraud investigators call a 'red flag.'

The form of analysis of financial statements takes two forms:

- Horizontal and vertical analysis
- Ratio analysis

If used carefully, these will give an understanding of what has happened in the financial period and help to tell the story of the financial dealings of the organization in some detail.

However, a note of caution. Any analysis of an organization's financial statements is only as good as those financial statements. If they are prepared carefully using a recognized financial reporting framework (International Accounting Standards, International Financial Reporting Standards, etc.), and audited by suitably qualified auditors in accordance with International Standards on Auditing, then it is fairly certain that the numbers are reliable, and consequently that any analysis of ratios will provide a convincing and reliable story of what happened in the financial period.

Horizontal and vertical analysis of financial reports

Arranging the financial statements for a series of accounting periods, be they annual financial statements or monthly management accounts is a way of identifying trends.

There are two types of analysis to be performed: horizontal and vertical. Note that these are not mutually exclusive; the object is to perform both types of analysis as they reveal different facets of the accounts.

HORIZONTAL ANALYSIS   In horizontal analysis, as shown in Figure 8.1, the financial statements for several accounting periods are set out in horizontal format, and the movement period on period is identified.

What we are looking for are unusual or anomalous movements that might indicate a problem area. Clearly the effects of economic factors such as inflation or interest rates, which might affect the organization over time, will have to be factored into these calculations, as will changes in business practice or structural changes in the organization.

For example, we might be looking for increases between periods in one set of numbers that are not matched by concomitant increases in related numbers, e.g. income has increased by 20 per cent, but allied costs such as cost of sales or selling costs have only increased by less than 10 per cent. This would call for an investigation of both these sets of numbers as increases in income would be expected to drive increases in costs.

Figure 8.1 Horizontal analysis

	20X5	20X6	20X7	20X8	% Change 20X5–20X6	% Change 20X6–20X7	% Change 20X7–20X8
Income statement							
Revenues	248000	257000	286000	294000	3.6	11.3	2.8
Cost of sales	219000	224000	255000	258000	2.3	13.8	1.2
Gross profit	**29000**	**33000**	**31000**	**36000**	13.8	(6.1)	16.1
Administration costs	9500	9000	8000	10000	(5.3)	(11.1)	25.0
Selling and marketing costs	12000	11000	12000	15000	(8.3)	9.1	25.0
Interest	4000	3000	2000	1500	(25.0)	(33.3)	(25.0)
Taxation	1000	2000	3000	2800	100.0	50.0	(6.7)
Net profit	**2500**	**8000**	**6000**	**6700**	220.0	(25.0)	11.7
Statement of financial position							
Cash and bank	3000	7000	4000	1500	133.3	(42.9)	(62.5)
Inventories	9000	12000	14000	18000	33.3	16.7	28.6
Receiveables	20000	17000	19000	23300	(15.0)	11.8	22.6
Total current assets	32000	36000	37000	42800			
Non-current assets	169000	167000	172000	173000	(1.2)	3.0	0.6
Total assets	**201000**	**203000**	**209000**	**215800**			
Payables	25000	22000	24000	29000	(12.0)	9.1	20.8
Other current liabilities	1800	2000	2000	1100	11.1	0.0	(45.0)
Loans	19000	15000	13000	9000	(21.1)	(13.3)	(30.8)
Share capital and reserves	156000	164000	170000	176700	5.1	3.7	3.9
Total liabilities and share capital	**201800**	**203000**	**209000**	**215800**			

In Figure 8.1, we can see that revenues have continued to rise year on year for the four years under review, but gross profit has fluctuated year on year. For example, between 20X6 and 20X7 there was negative growth, so we could look at the gross margin for those years to see if that sheds any light on the reasons why. For the four years under review the gross margin, calculated by the formula (of which more later):

$$\text{Gross profit} \div \text{Revenues} \times 100$$

was:

20X5	11.7%
20X6	12.8%
20X7	10.9%
20X8	12.2%

Here is part of the answer: the gross margin in 20X7 dipped well below previous levels. The next step is to find out why, and why the business was able to more than recover its margin in 20X8. Was it seeing off a competitor in a price war or was there a more prosaic explanation?

The statement of financial position reveals another interesting story.

- Cash and bank balances have declined in successive years.
- Inventories have increased year on year. Is the business carrying too high a level of inventory?
- Receivables have increased dramatically between 20X7 and 20X8, whereas revenues have remained broadly constant. Is there a problem collecting money from customers?
- The rate of increase in payables is outstripping the increases in cost of sales year on year. Is this a deliberate policy to take extra credit or is a shortage of cash preventing them from paying suppliers?

All these factors should be investigated.

VERTICAL ANALYSIS   Vertical analysis of results is based on the proportion that selected costs are of a base figure, usually revenues in the case of the income statement or total assets in the case of the statement of financial position. These can be compared year on year to indicate any illogical or unusual changes which are not explained by known trading patterns.

Figure 8.2 shows the format of vertical analysis:

Figure 8.2 **Vertical analysis**

	20X5	20X6	20X7	20X8	Costs as % of revenues			
					20X5	20X6	20X7	20X8
Income statement								
Revenues	248000	257000	286000	294000				
Cost of sales	219000	224000	255000	258000	88.3	87.2	89.2	87.8
Gross profit	29000	33000	31000	36000				
Administration costs	9500	9000	8000	10000	3.8	3.5	2.8	3.4
Selling and marketing costs	12000	11000	12000	15000	4.8	4.3	4.2	5.1
Interest	4000	3000	2000	1500	1.6	1.2	0.7	0.5
Taxation	1000	2000	3000	2800	0.4	0.8	1.0	1.0
Net profit	2500	8000	6000	6700				

					% of Total assets			
					20X5	20X6	20X7	20X8
Statement of financial position								
Cash and bank	3000	7000	4000	1500	1.5	3.4	1.9	0.7
Inventories	9000	12000	14000	18000	4.5	5.9	6.7	8.3
Receivables	20000	17000	19000	23300	10.0	8.4	9.1	10.8
Total current assets	32000	36000	37000	42800				
Non-current assets	169000	167000	172000	173000	84.1	82.3	82.3	80.2
Total assets	**201000**	**203000**	**209000**	**215800**				
Payables	25000	22000	24000	29000	12.4	10.8	11.5	13.4
Other current liabilities	1800	2000	2000	1100	0.9	1.0	1.0	0.5
Loans	19000	15000	13000	9000	9.5	7.4	6.2	4.2
Share capital and reserves	156000	164000	170000	176700	77.6	80.8	81.3	81.9
Total liabilities and share capital	**201800**	**203000**	**209000**	**215800**				

In this case, the costs show a broad level of consistency as far as the income statement is concerned, with an increase in selling and marketing costs being noticeable in 20X8. This may have an influence on revenues or profitability. As far as the statement of financial position is concerned, as we saw with the horizontal analysis, cash and bank balances are declining rapidly as a proportion of total assets with receivables, inventory and payables assuming an increasingly large proportion. Inventories have risen considerably over the four years being reviewed with both receivables and payables going back to 20X5 levels. The level of payables is increasing, which might reflect the increase in inventories.

Ratio analysis

The use of analytical review, or ratio analysis as it is sometimes known, is a powerful tool in the accountant's toolbox. Auditors have known for some time about the effectiveness of analytical review as part of the audit process—indeed ISA 520 *Analytical Procedures* requires auditors to use analytical techniques as part of the audit planning process, as a method of testing and as part of the overall review process at the end of the audit.

The purpose of analytical procedures is to help in telling the story of the financial statements, prepared by the directors, to gather evidence to show that the relationships between the numbers in the accounts are reasonable and logical and bear out what is known from other sources about the events of the accounting period.

They can be analyzed into groups. Different groups of ratios can be used for different forms of analysis. These groups are:

- profitability ratios
- efficiency ratios
- financing ratios
- investor ratios

The ratios listed here are the basic ratios needed to analyze a set of financial statements and to tell the story of the financial period.

REAL LIFE
The analysis of Global Crossing—manipulation of financial accounts fraud

Professor Massod D Beneish of Indiana State University in the USA investigated the extension of the use of analytical review in detecting fraud by considering the effect that manipulation of revenues or understatement of costs had on the appropriate asset accounts.

His theory, outlined in a paper in 1999, was based on the analysis of 74 companies. These were known manipulators identified through Securities & Exchange Commission (SEC) enforcement actions or news media reports. He refined the number of firms to include only those which had restated earnings at the request of auditors or as a result of an investigation. This is to eliminate firms who corrected errors made in quarterly filings or which traded in areas where comparison with a source of non-manipulated data could not be made.

The source of non-manipulated data was 1708 firms in Standard & Poor's COMPUSTAT database sorted by industry and year to match the accounts of known manipulators.

The results of this are shown below together with comparative results for super manipulator Global Crossing Ltd.

Global Crossing was a telecoms company which filed for bankruptcy in January 2002. Data relating to the accounts for 1998 and 1999, which were prior to Global Crossing's collapse in 2002, have been included for comparison.

The key ratios developed by Beneish (which we won't detail) are:

1 DSRI—Days' sales in receivable index
2 GMI—Gross margin index
3 AQI—Asset quality index
4 SGI—Sales growth index
5 TATA—Total accruals to total assets

Index type	Non-manipulators	Manipulators	Global Crossing
Days sales in receivables index	1.031	1.465	3.436
Gross margin index	1.014	1.193	1.177
Asset quality index	1.039	1.254	1.170
Sales growth index	1.134	1.607	3.964
Total accruals to total assets	0.018	0.031	−0.069

Source: Beneish, 1999, and Golden Skalak & Clayton, 2006

Interestingly, given the comparisons above, the alleged crime of Global Crossing was artificial inflation of revenues. The ratios for sales can be seen to be well out of line with those of non-manipulators.

This demonstrates that judicious use of accounting ratios—which need not be the specialized ones devised by Beneish—can provide an indication of problems which need to be investigated.

Profitability ratios

These ratios are designed to highlight management performance measured in terms of the profitability of the enterprise in relation to the level of assets employed in it and the efficiency with which management have used the assets of the organization.

We look at two of these ratios below—namely:

- Gross margin (gross profit percentage)
- Net margin percentage, which is the profit before interest and tax (known as **PBIT** or operating profit)

These give a good indication of the overall profitability of the operational side of the business. These ratios can be applied to individual products or activities, analyzed over geographical sales area or in any other way the management information system can provide data. This, of course, is not available to the general public or the potential investor so they have to be satisfied with the summary information in the published financial statements.

GROSS PROFIT PERCENTAGE OR GROSS MARGIN (GP%)

$$\frac{\text{Gross profit} \times 100}{\text{Trade revenues}}$$

This is one of the most useful ratios as it represents the profit made by the organization from selling its goods and services excluding indirect costs. If the organization's pricing structure and type of customer base remain consistent, this margin should remain reasonably constant whatever the level of activity, i.e. if sales double the cost of sales should also rise proportionally so the margin will remain the same despite the increase in activity. It includes the levels of turnover and inventory. Significant fluctuations in this ratio may indicate areas where additional investigation could be required.

NET MARGIN OR OPERATING PROFIT MARGIN PER CENT

$$\frac{\text{Profit before interest and tax (PBIT)} \times 100}{\text{Revenues}}$$

This represents the operating profit on business activities after taking account of expenses relating directly to business operations. The points made above concerning the gross profit margin apply equally to this ratio.

Two other ratios which can be used to provide more information on management performance are:

- Return on capital employed (ROCE)
- Return on shareholders' funds (ROSF)

These give an indication of the return generated from the assets used in the business. Consider this—if a potential investor has €10 000 to invest they want three things:

- security of investment
- a return on their money
- capital growth

An organization should want the same thing: they wish to keep the entity viable, generate the best return possible and make the entity bigger, if possible, by re-investing and growing the business. These ratios measure how successful management have been in achieving at least one of those objectives: the generation of a return on investment.

RETURN ON CAPITAL EMPLOYED (ROCE)   This is one of the major operating ratios and is seen as a measure of management efficiency. It can be calculated in two ways, both of which should generate the same answer.

One way to do it is:

$$\frac{\text{Profit before interest and tax (PBIT)} \times 100}{\text{Ordinary share capital} + \text{Reserves} + \text{Non-current liabilities}}$$

or it could be:

$$\frac{\text{Profit before interest and tax (PBIT)} \times 100}{\text{Total assets} - \text{current liabilities}}$$

The first basis of calculation is probably the best. This ratio provides a calculation of the return, i.e. the PBIT that management are generating on the capital in the business provided by the ordinary shareholders, other suppliers of long-term finance and generated by the business itself. Obviously the higher this is the better. It gives a broad indication of how well the finance in the business is being used to generate profit.

RETURN ON SHAREHOLDERS' FUNDS (ROSF)   Also known as return on equity, a variation of ROCF is the return on that part of the financing of the business provided by ordinary shareholders. It is broadly the same basis as ROCE, but uses profit for the year (i.e. after interest and tax, as this is what is attributable to ordinary shareholders). Anything relating to shareholders other than ordinary shareholders has to be eliminated. So, for example, if there are preference shareholders the dividend due to them has to be excluded, as, of course, does their shareholding.

The calculation is:

$$\frac{\text{Profit for the year} \times 100}{\text{Ordinary share capital} + \text{Reserves}}$$

Efficiency ratios

These show aspects of the statement of financial position assets and liabilities. They are a measure of how efficiently management is controlling its current assets and liabilities in terms of its liquidity (i.e. its ability to generate cash) and working capital. They can highlight changes in operational practice, such as worsening credit control, as well as providing indicators or audit areas warranting investigation.

Key ratios are:

CURRENT RATIO

$$\frac{\text{Current assets}}{\text{Current liabilities}}$$

The current ratio measures the ability of the organization to meet its immediate liabilities. It is a ratio of liquidity and a ratio greater than 1 indicates that liabilities can be covered through realization of current assets. This ratio must be reviewed in relation to those ratios related to other elements of current assets and liabilities.

QUICK RATIO OR ACID TEST

$$\frac{\text{Current assets} - \text{Inventories}}{\text{Current liabilities}}$$

This ratio is another liquidity ratio, but excludes inventories. The logic behind this is that, in a crisis, receivables and cash are more liquid than inventories which have to be sold and the cash collected before liabilities can be met. It measures the ability of the organization to meet its current liabilities out of liquid resources.

INVENTORY TURNOVER

$$\frac{\text{Cost of goods sold}}{\text{Average inventory}}$$

This represents the number of times the inventory is turned over in the period. This is important as money tied up in inventory is not able to be used for anything else so, broadly, the more frequently it is turned over (into receivables and cash) the better.

INVENTORY DAYS

$$\frac{\text{Closing inventory} \times 365}{\text{Cost of sales}}$$

This represents the inventory turnover ratio expressed as days. The formula can also be written as:

$$\frac{365}{\text{Inventory turnover}}$$

In commercial terms this ratio is relevant because days in inventory represent money tied up but also increase the risks of obsolescence, damage and storage costs.

RECEIVABLES DAYS

$$\frac{\text{Trade receivables} \times 365}{\text{Credit sales}}$$

This ratio records the number of days it takes the organization, on average, to collect its trade debts from customers.

PAYABLES DAYS

$$\frac{\text{Trade payables} \times 365}{\text{Cost of sales}}$$

This represents the number of days the organization takes to pay its trade payables.

Financing ratios

These relate to the financing of the business. Key ratios are:

DEBT/EQUITY (LEVERAGE OR GEARING)

$$\frac{\text{Long-term liabilities} + \text{Preference share capital}}{\text{Ordinary share capital} + \text{Reserves}}$$

This ratio represents the proportion of the business funded by debt, i.e. long-term loans and preference shares compared with shareholders equity. There are many variations on this ratio which tend to centre around the definition of debt so one basis should be adopted and used consistently. One version includes all liabilities including trade payables and overdrafts, which can be considered to be short-term financing but the most accepted formula confines itself to structural funding such as long-term loans and forms of share capital.

These loans are classed as structural funding because as they are paid off they are replaced by new loans—in other words the organization chooses to use loan financing to fund its operations rather than raising share capital.

Preference share capital is included because it has the characteristics of loan finance: it carries a fixed dividend which it has a right to ahead of any dividend payable to the holders of ordinary shares, hence the name preference shares.

One note of caution here.: The accounting standards require a short-term loan or that part of a long-term loan due for repayment within one year to be classified as a current liability so it is necessary to include that amount in long-term liabilities for this purpose.

NET DEBT   There is another variation on the gearing ratio, which is called net debt. The logic for this is that organizations have liabilities such as bank overdrafts or other financing obligations such as forms of asset financing as well as cash and cash equivalents, which earn them interest.

So instead of just including long-term debt and preference share capital, the net debt calculation includes all interest bearing liabilities minus cash and cash equivalents.

So the formula here is:

$$\frac{\text{Net debt (i.e including loans and overdrafts)}}{\text{Ordinary share capital} + \text{Reserves}}$$

INTEREST COVER   If an enterprise is heavily funded by loans and overdrafts instead of ordinary share capital the question of being able to meet interest obligations arises.

This ratio indicates by how much the interest payable is covered by the operating profit. The formula is:

$$\frac{\text{Operating profit (before interest and tax)}}{\text{Interest payable}}$$

Usually there is very little problem where the organization is making good profits but, as we saw in Module 6, where an entity is heavily funded by loans and debt, the interest charge can become a major problem if insufficient profits are made to cover the liability.

Investor ratios

At this point we move away from management ratios and look at two ratios that are used by investors to judge a company's performance.

These are earnings per share (EPS) and the price/earnings (P/E) ratio.

EARNINGS PER SHARE   This relates to the amount of a company's earnings available to ordinary shareholders. So the measure is of the profit after taxation, minus any preference dividend, divided by the number of ordinary shares.

$$\frac{\text{Profit after taxation, interest and preference dividend}}{\text{Number of ordinary shares in issue}}$$

Here is an example of the calculation.

EXAMPLE

Biggasplash has the following share structure:

Ordinary shares	1 000 000 ordinary shares of £1 each	1 000 000
8% preference shares of £1 each		500 000
		£1 500 000

Biggasplash has made a profit for the year of £900 000 on which tax is payable of £160 000. The earnings per share calculation is thus:

Profit for the year	900 000
Less: Tax payable	(160 000)
Preference dividend	(40 000)
Profit available to ordinary shareholders	£700 000
Number of ordinary shares	1 000 000
Earnings per share	0.70 pence

This measure is often seen as a fundamental measure of the performance of an ordinary share in the company. Note that this is not what a shareholder might receive—that would be a dividend on the ordinary shares—but it is a measure of the value of an ordinary share. Again, the trend is significant: an investor would be hoping to see this increasing year on year, and this would be a guide to potential investors of the investment value of ordinary shares in the business.

There is an analogy between EPS and ROCE (see earlier), which is a similar measure. Company managers can focus on increasing EPS without giving significant consideration to the needs of the company as a whole. Increasing the ordinary share capital with a new issue might be good for the business if it replaces interest-bearing debt with equity funding, but it would dilute the EPS (more shares in issue) so managers might be reluctant to do this if it was likely to deter potential investors by affecting the share price.

If the business is expanding and the free cash (Module 7) does not cover the increase in assets, the answer is likely to be borrowing more money. EPS might continue to increase but the ROCE may start to fall as this ratio includes all forms of capital including borrowings—and this is a warning sign for the business.

PRICE/EARNINGS RATIO   This is applicable only to companies listed on a recognized stock exchange where a share price for ordinary shares is readily available.

The ratio is:

$$\frac{\text{Market price per ordinary share}}{\text{Earnings per share}}$$

What it indicates is a measure of confidence the market has in the business. For instance, if the P/E ratio is high, investors are more likely to invest because there is an indication of confidence in the future earning power of the business. This can, of course, be misplaced, but generally it is a good indicator that investors will be prepared to pay more for a share in the business.

EXAMPLE

Suppose the market price of the shares of Biggasplash from the example above is £2.10, the EPS is 0.70 and the P/E is 3. What investors will want to see is:

- How does that compare with similar companies?
- What is the trend—upwards or downwards?

Once you have familiarized yourself with the basic formulae, we can look at a worked example.

EXAMPLE

Figure 8.3 is a set of accounts for Binkle plc, a manufacturer of flat-packed furniture. We have an income statement and a statement of financial position for the current financial period under review and for the previous period to act as a comparison.

Figure 8.3 Binkle plc accounts

BINKLE PLC
Income statement for the year ended 31 March

	2X18	2X17
	£m	£m
Revenues	2649	2582
Cost of sales	(1086)	(1162)
Gross profit	1563	1420
Administration costs	(834)	(729)
Selling and marketing costs	(211)	(148)
Operating profit	518	543
Interest payable	(23)	(19)
Profit before taxation	495	524
Taxation	(110)	(121)
Profit after taxation	385	403

(continued)

BINKLE PLC
Statement of financial position at 31 March

Assets	£m	£m	£m	£m
Non-current assets				
Land and buildings		1309		997
Plant and equipment		898		742
		2207		1739
Current assets				
Inventories	277		258	
Receivables	261		298	
Cash and bank balances	64		78	
	602		634	
Current liabilities				
Trade payables	249		193	
Taxation	158		113	
Loan repayable within 1 year	48		47	
	455		353	
Net current assets		147		281
Total assets		2354		2020
Share capital				
Ordinary shares of £1		500		500
Reserves		1617		1232
		2117		1732
Long-term loan		237		288
Total equity and liabilities		2354		2020

NOTES

1 All sales and purchases are made on credit
2 At the period end, the market price of the shares was £2.76 (2X17 £3.02)
3 At the period end, trade receivables were £258 m (2X17 £294 m)
4 At the period end, trade payables were £241 m (2X17 £189 m)

Using these figures we can calculate the ratios.

Ratio calculations

	2X18		2X17	
Gross profit percentage				
$\dfrac{\text{Gross profit} \times 100}{\text{Trade revenues}}$	$\dfrac{1563 \times 100}{2649}$	59%	$\dfrac{1420 \times 100}{2582}$	55%
Net margin percentage				
$\dfrac{\text{Profit before interest and tax (PBIT)} \times 100}{\text{Revenues}}$	$\dfrac{518 \times 100}{2649}$	20%	$\dfrac{543 \times 100}{2582}$	21%
ROCE				
$\dfrac{\text{Profit before interest and tax} \times 100}{\text{Ordinary share capital} + \text{Reserves} + \text{Non-current liabilities}}$	$\dfrac{518 \times 100}{500 + 1617 + 237 + 48}$	22%	$\dfrac{543 \times 100}{500 + 1232 + 288 + 47}$	26%

ROSF

$\dfrac{\text{Profit for the year} \times 100}{\text{Ordinary share capital} + \text{Reserves}}$	$\dfrac{385 \times 100}{500 + 1617}$	18%	$\dfrac{403 \times 100}{500 + 1232}$	23%

Current ratio

$\dfrac{\text{Current assets}}{\text{Current liabilities}}$	$\dfrac{602}{455}$	1.3	$\dfrac{634}{353}$	1.8

Quick ratio

$\dfrac{\text{Current assets} - \text{Inventories}}{\text{Current liabilities}}$	$\dfrac{602 - 277}{455}$	0.7	$\dfrac{634 - 258}{353}$	1.1

Inventory turnover

$\dfrac{\text{Cost of goods sold}}{\text{Average inventory}}$	$\dfrac{1086}{(277 + 258) \div 2}$	4.1 Times		

Inventory days

$\dfrac{\text{Closing inventory} \times 365}{\text{Cost of sales}}$	$\dfrac{277 \times 365}{1086}$	93 Days	$\dfrac{258 \times 365}{1162}$	81 Days

Receivables days

$\dfrac{\text{Trade receivables} \times 365}{\text{Credit sales}}$	$\dfrac{258 \times 365}{2649}$	36 Days	$\dfrac{294 \times 365}{2582}$	42 Days

Payables days

$\dfrac{\text{Trade payables} \times 365}{\text{Cost of sales}}$	$\dfrac{241 \times 365}{1086}$	81 Days	$\dfrac{189 \times 365}{1162}$	59 Days

Gearing

$\dfrac{\text{Long-term liabilities} + \text{Preference share capital}}{\text{Ordinary share capital} + \text{Reserves}}$	$\dfrac{237 + 48}{2117}$	0.13	$\dfrac{288 + 78}{1732}$	0.19

Earnings per share

$\dfrac{\text{Profit after taxation, interest and preference dividend}}{\text{Number of Ordinary shares in issue}}$	$\dfrac{385}{500}$	0.77 Pence	$\dfrac{403}{500}$	0.81 Pence

Price earnings ratio

$\dfrac{\text{Market price per ordinary share}}{\text{Earnings per share}}$	$\dfrac{2.76}{0.77}$	3.58	$\dfrac{3.02}{0.81}$	3.73

What does this tell us about the results for this company?
There are some clear points of interest:

- Gross profit percentage has gone up by 4 per cent. This is good, but is a significant increase, so it could be that the closing inventory is quite high. This could be an error in valuation or miscounting so should be investigated, particularly in view of the inventory days ratio, which has gone up from 81 days to 93 days—a big increase.
- Net margin percentage has stayed broadly the same. If the gross margin is correct this means that indirect costs such as administration, selling and marketing and general overheads have increased, thus negating the increase in gross margin.
- Return on capital employed (ROCE) and return on shareholders' funds (ROSF) have both declined, which indicates that assets are being used less efficiently by management.

(continued)

- Both the current and the quick ratios have declined. Although the current ratio is still reasonably healthy at 1.3 against 1.8 last year, it indicates that overall liquidity is declining. The quick ratio at 0.7 (20X7 1.1) demonstrates this quite starkly as it means that, if it had to, the business could not meet all its current liabilities out of liquid assets such as cash and receivables. This would be a worrying trend for management, particularly coupled with the decline in ROCE. However, it should be noted that the gearing ratio has improved as long-term debt has been repaid, so it is likely that the business has been using cash to repay debt.
- Receivables days have shortened from 42 to 36, and payables days have increased from 59 days to 81 days. This supports a decline in liquidity, as the business is clearly trying to collect amounts due from customers more quickly whilst holding back payments to suppliers.
- As we have already mentioned, inventory days have increased from 81 to 93 days, which needs investigating. Inventory turnover is 4.1 times per year; unfortunately we don't have the figure for last year but what it shows is that, on average, it is taking three months to sell the inventory they are holding which is quite a long time. If the inventory figure is correct, this has contributed to the decline in liquidity as more money than previously is being tied up in inventory rather than circulating to fund the business.
- Gearing has improved as the business is generating good profits and it has obviously been able to repay loans. This has affected liquidity in the short term but could lead to longer-term benefits.
- The investor ratios are not of direct concern to operational management, although many boards of directors do worry inordinately about the share price and the return to investors. They have declined slightly in the current year but not significantly so would not immediately be raising warning flags—unless there was further deterioration in the current period to 20X9.

Overall the ratios have told a story about the financial results and flagged up a possible area, inventory valuation, for management to investigate. This highlights the importance of ratio analysis in the review of financial accounts and is both a guide to management of possible areas of concern and a stimulus for future action.

Limitations of ratio analysis

There are important caveats when using analytical procedures:

- All the information used must be reliable. Analytical procedures are the analysis of relationships and are commonly used to indicate trends over time. Comparison numbers have to be as reliable as the ones being reviewed, so that the story they tell is based on fact, not subjective opinion or inadequate or incomplete data.
- The source of the figures must be homogenous. For example, if the business has grown by acquisition over a period of years, the business in year seven may be radically different from the business in year one. In this case the numbers must be disaggregated in order to provide a valid comparison.
- Analytical procedures raise questions, but they rarely provide answers. Indicators thrown up using these techniques must be followed through and investigated in detail and, where possible, explanations received for the apparent anomalies.
- A ratio is of very limited value in isolation. Simply saying, for example, that a business's gross profit per cent (or gross margin as it is sometimes called) is 51.2 per cent means little. Is that good? How do we know? What was last year's gross profit per cent? What is the gross profit per cent of a comparable business? Consequently, there has to be a context for the number produced and it has to be placed in conjunction with other ratios to tell the whole story.
- The ratios calculated will vary from industry to industry and organization to organization, so it is the trend analysis that is important, not the size of the number calculated.

- Many of the ratios will not be affected by activity levels, so the fact that the enterprise has grown in size would not, necessarily, affect some of the ratios. Changes year on year in others could be partially explained by business activities, e.g. a change in the sales mix of products. Unexplained movements should be investigated further.
- There may be sound business reasons for variances and differences from one period to another. For example, gross profit percentages may have changed as a result of market conditions rather than because of errors in inventory figures, but the changes would indicate an area for further investigation.
- More analysis is not necessarily better analysis. A simple set of ratios well chosen will tell the story.

Clearly it helps to have a good working knowledge of the operational circumstances of the organization and the likely effect on the accounts of its activities. This enables the identification of the trading or operational factors that are likely to have an effect on figures in the accounts. Knowledge of the circumstances of the business can be the context within which fluctuations in numbers and ratios can be explained.

For example, a sudden reduction in gross profit percentage might be as a result of a known price war, resulting in a forced reduction in selling prices. The drop may then not appear to be anomalous. However, an unexpected change in a GP percentage without a commercial or other reason may be an indicator that, for example, the closing inventory is under- or over-stated. In any case it should be investigated.

Some aspects of accounting may be complex and difficult to be absolutely confident about, for example, the valuation of long-term work in progress in construction companies. Whilst there are accounting rules regarding the taking of profits and the recognition of losses, there remains a degree of subjective opinion in the process of valuation, in particular the percentage completion of contracts.

Where the organization is engaged in complex or specialized activities, it is even more important that the accountant becomes as familiar as possible with the organization's activities and discovers as much as is feasible about the underlying principles on which the accounts are based. Disaggregating the numbers will be more successful than looking at the entity as a whole. Figures can be compared, for example:

- by business unit
- by activity
- over time
- by region

This enables the investigator to identify trends and fluctuations. Of course these may be a natural part of the trading pattern, for example seasonal fluctuations, on the other hand sudden movements prior to the end of a reporting period may be grounds for suspicion, particularly as the scale of movements may not be consistent, i.e. the corrupt management may need to make big adjustments one quarter to meet a profit target, but a smaller one in the next quarter, so the adjustments are not as large.

Test yourself

1 Wonderboy Ltd has the following working capital amounts in its statement of financial position:

	€
Inventory	19 340
Trade Receivables	23 580
Trade Payables	17 431
Cash in hand	1 245
Bank Overdraft	12 897

The quick ratio (to two decimal places) is:

a) 2.46

b) 1.35

c) 1.45

d) 0.82

2 Robin's inventory at 31 March 20X7 was $405 000. By the end of the following financial year, 20X8, it had gone up 10 per cent. The cost of sales for that year was $1 506 700. What is the inventory turnover in days?

3 Tootles Ltd has the flowing working capital items in its statement of financial position.

Inventory	217 540
Trade receivables	188 600
Cash and bank balances	3 200
Trade payables	221 300

The company has recently received some information from its bank that benchmarked industry average ratios for similar businesses to Tootles Ltd.

Those benchmarks were:

Current ratio	1.62:1
Quick ratio	0.93:1

Which of the following statements is true?

a) Tootles' ratios are both higher than the industry average

b) Tootles' current ratio is higher than the industry average, but its quick ratio is lower

c) Tootles' ratios are both lower than the industry average

d) Tootles' current ratio is lower than the industry average, but its quick ratio is higher

4 XYZ Ltd. supplies you the following information regarding the year ending 31 December 20X8.

Credit sales	R200 000
Sales returns	R10 000
Opening inventory	R25 000
Closing inventory	R30 000

The gross profit ratio is 25 per cent.

What is the cost of sales?

5 Flighty Ltd has receivables in its statement of financial position of $437 206. Its revenues for the year ended 31 March 20X8 were $3 407 396. Seventy per cent of the revenues were credit sales.

Receivables turnover in days is:

a) 46.8 days

b) 32.7 days

c) 66.9 days

d) 18.3 days

6 Hollogica Ltd has the following information extracted from its financial statements by an investment analyst:

Net profit after interest and tax

Number of ordinary shares issued

Market price per share £4.20

Calculate the price/earnings ratio and the earnings per share.

7 If trade payables in a set of accounts are £55 000, opening inventory is £90 000, purchases of materials are £236 000 and closing inventory is £94 000; how many days, on average, does the business take to pay its suppliers?

8 Zebedee Ltd has capital employed as follows:

	$
Ordinary share capital	3 000 000
Reserves	13 850 000
Long-term loan	4 750 000

For the year ended 31 March 20X8 the profit before interest and tax was $1 250 000. What is the return on capital employed?

9 Wubbles plc has the following capital structure:

Ordinary share capital	1 000 000 shares of £1 each
Reserves	2 739 400
Long-term loan	2 000 000

What is the gearing of this business?

10 Which of these statements are True or False?   ✔   ✔

	True	False
When trading hits a recession, low-geared businesses have an advantage because they do not have to meet a high level of interest payments.		
The liquidity ratios measure long-term solvency of an organization.		
Gross profit margin is gross profit × 100 ÷ revenues.		
Vertical analysis is based on the change in the financial statements from year to year.		

In the next module we will look at business financing in more detail and consider the effect of borrowing on liquidity. We will also look at some more specialized sources of finance and capital structures and consider how Islamic finance, with its prohibition of charging interest, works.

Test yourself

1 There are two businesses, Yoshi Ltd and Pogo Ltd, both very similar retailing enterprises, which are looking for some management and possibly financial support. You have been brought in to consider the business case for both businesses and report.

The information you have consists of a table of ratios—shown below:

Ratio	Yoshi Ltd	Pogo Ltd
Current ratio	1.8:1	1.3:1
Quick ratio	1.6:1	0.8:1
ROCE	21%	18%
ROSF	32%	21%
Inventory turnover	5 times	18 times
Receivable days	58 days	22 days
Payable days	49 days	44 days
Gross profit percentage	40%	18%
Net profit percentage	10%	10%

Required

i. Explain briefly how each ratio is calculated
ii. Write a short report on what these ratios tell you about the way each business is run. One business prides itself on personal service and one on competitive pricing for example. Which do you think is which, and why?

(ACCA)

2 Here is financial information in respect of two businesses:

Statement of financial position at 30 June 20X8

	Business A		Business B	
	£'000s	£'000s	£'000s	£'000s
Land		80		260
Buildings	120		200	
Less: Depreciation	(40)	80	–	200
Plant and equipment	90		150	
Less: Depreciation	(70)	20	(40)	110
Current assets				
Inventories	80		100	
Trade receivables	100		90	
Bank and cash balances	–		10	
	180		200	
Current liabilities				
Trade payables	110		120	
Bank overdraft	50		–	
Loan at 10% p.a	100		130	
	260		250	
Net current assets/(liabilities)		(80)		(50)
		100		520
Capital at 1 July 20X7		100		300
Profit for the year		30		100
		130		400
Less: Drawings		(30)		(40)
		100		360
Land revaluation		–		160
		100		520
Income account (extract)				
Revenues		1000		3000
Cost of sales		400		2000

Required

i) Produce a table of eight ratios calculated for both businesses.
ii) Write a report briefly outlining the strengths and weaknesses of both businesses. Include a comment on any major area where simple use of figures could be misleading.

(ACCA)

9 External business finance

Businesses are financed in a remarkable number of ways. There are forms of capital and loans with varying terms, there are arrangements that involve deferred purchase of assets and self-financing by the business itself, which we will look at in Module 10.

Clearly detailing the complexities and details of arcane forms of share capital is both tedious and unnecessary, but it is necessary to understand the principles behind various forms of financing and the advantages and disadvantages of each one.

In this module we will look at the varying types of external finance available to a business and examine the advantages and disadvantages of each one.

But first—businesses have changed because of the rise of the internet and forms of social media. To take one example, it is now possible for a vlogger to make money through YouTube. The initial investment is either very small or nonexistent; all they need is a video camera and an idea. Money is made either by becoming a YouTube partner, thus allowing them to insert advertisements either side of your video, or by persuading retailers to advertise with you. Some individuals have made a considerable amount of money through vlogging with virtually no monetary input.

Stop and think   Could you start a YouTube channel? What would you need? How hard would it be to build a following?

However, there are thousands of videos uploaded every day, consumers of videos are becoming more sophisticated and demanding and, unless you can come up with a unique concept, it's probably already been done.

What we are looking at in this module is the more traditional business form, but the use of the internet and social media should not be forgotten. The internet has already created a huge online market and, consequently, suppliers to that market spring up creating new business opportunities. However, the internet is simply a form of delivery of the product: the basic rules of business apply just as much to Amazon as to any other business which requires more than a video camera and a hot idea.

REAL LIFE
Amazon

Amazon is an internet-based operation that did not exist 25 years ago. Founded in 1994 as an online only book store, it has expanded into many markets including publishing, IT (e.g. Kindle, Echo), film and TV. In 2015 it was rated the fourth most valuable company in the world.

Amazon's only multibillion-dollar acquisition was the $13.7 billion purchase of Whole Foods Market, which was sealed in 2017. Amazon.com announced in June it planned to issue debt to finance its proposed $13.7 billion deal to buy Whole Foods Market. Amazon confirmed that the debt offering would be private. The debt is set to be broken into seven parts, ranging from 3-year notes to 40-year notes, analysts said.

Amazon had previously issued bonds in 2012 and 2014, and is reported to have $8.75 billion in debt. It has now made an offer to acquire Ring for approximately $1.2–$1.8 billion.

Source: *CNBC Feb 2018*

Sources of finance

The key to successful business finance is to utilize the right finance at the right time and not to be trapped into a situation where the costs of finance outweigh the benefits.

In the beginning when a new business is starting up it is most likely that the initial capital will come from personal funds of the owner(s), possibly supported also by a bank loan. The bank loan will probably require a personal guarantee from someone that, in the event of the business failing, they would pay up the balance of the loan and the bank would get its money back.

The initial subscription of funds could be in the form of a direct amount of cash or assets put into the business to start it off or a subscription for shares in a new company. Either way the structure is uncomplicated and easy to manage.

As the organization gets bigger and more complicated, the requirements for financing it will change. Generally, finance comes from two sources:

- Internal finance—reinvestment of cash generated from operations
- External finance—bankers and investors

Consider the broad stages of development of a successful business shown in Figure 9.1:

Figure 9.1 **Business stages of development**

STAGE	DEVELOPMENT	FINANCED BY
1	**Business start-up**	• Savings of proprietors
		• Investment by friends/family
		• Small bank loan
2	**Initial growth**	• Reinvested cash from trading
		• Increased bank borrowing
		• Lease/hire of assets
		• Invoice discounting/debt factoring
3	**Expansion—takeover of another business(s)**	• Reinvested cash from trading
	Increased number of outlets	• Increased share capital
		• Increased bank borrowing
4	**Business becomes public**	• Offer of shares to public—listing on stock exchange
		• Replace bank borrowings with investment from shareholders
5	**Continued expansion**	• Reinvested cash from trading
		• Bank borrowing for specific projects and working capital
		• Further issues of shares to fund expansion

Clearly there are three themes here:

• Internal finance
• Share capital
• External finance in the form of bank borrowing

We will look at internal finance in Module 10. For now we will concentrate on external funding from banks and other investors.

External sources of finance

There are more of these than might initially be thought. There are of course the main ones—investors and bankers—but there are also others, principally:

• Leasing companies
• Hire purchase finance
• Debt factors
• Grants

The expanding business has several sources of finance in addition to any it may generate internally.

Some of these, principally bank overdrafts, debt factoring and invoice discounting are, essentially, short-term finance, which we will look at in Module 10.

We can summarize overall long-term external finance in Figure 9.2:

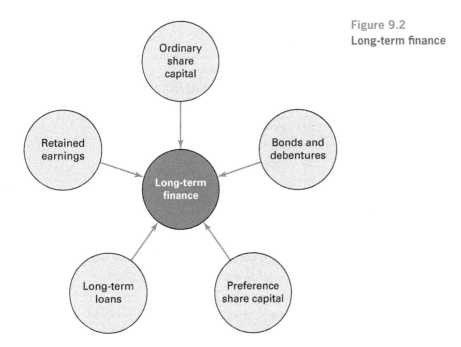

Figure 9.2
Long-term finance

Once the initial start-up phase is past, and the business requires some serious finance for expansion, it will need more than the combined savings of friends and family and a start-up loan from the bank.

Stop and think	Have you bought an asset on deferred terms—for example, a house or a vehicle? How was the deal structured? What were the considerations about affordability, the length of term, etc. that went through your mind before you signed?

It will need some structural funding which will only come from a longer-term loan arrangement and, hopefully, some investment from outside investors.

To obtain this the business will have to demonstrate that it has:

- A profitable trading history evidenced by audited financial statements
- Strong internal checks and controls on its management information systems
- Accurate and timely management information
- Experienced and knowledgeable management
- Good corporate governance

However good the product or service on offer, no investor is going to risk their money in a business with weak management, poor accounting controls and limited external scrutiny and advice.

Investing is always a risky business—there is no guarantee of success, so investors will always seek to minimize their risk exposure whenever possible and will always favour well-managed businesses over poorly-managed ones, even if the products for the poorly-managed business are superior—the logic being that a badly-managed business will, sooner or later, run aground.

These principles apply to both the investor in shares and a lender—at the end of the day it's all about risk.

Share capital

There are two main forms of share capital:

- ordinary shares
- preference shares

Ordinary shares are the most common form of shareholder investment. They are issued with a nominal or 'face' value which could be £1 or €1. In some jurisdictions, shares can be issued with no nominal value. When shares are issued it is usually at or above the nominal value.

The market value of ordinary shares bears no relation to the face value.

The key factors favouring ordinary shares are:

- There is no fixed rate of dividend—any dividend paid is decided by the directors and approved or otherwise by the shareholders themselves. Any dividend is paid out of profits available for distribution, i.e. after other investors such as banks and preference shareholders have been paid.
- The liability of an investor is limited to the amount they pay or subscribe for their shares. Consequently, an investor can quantify their level of risk exposure.
- If the company is listed on a stock exchange there is a ready market for the shares and investors can take profits or limit losses as long as there are buyers or sellers of the shares.
- The potential gain on their investment is not limited at all. If the shares do well, investors can make a considerable amount of money from their investment. Should an investor have been shrewd enough to buy shares in Apple or Google at a very early stage, for example, they would have seen an immense rise in the value of their shareholding.
- Ordinary shares carry rights. Shareholders can attend an annual general meeting and question the board of directors. They are entitled to vote on various matters affecting the company, principally the election or re-election of directors and auditors, and are entitled to receive financial information about the company in the form of audited annual financial statements and shareholder bulletins.
- Additional shareholders' rights include the opportunity to participate in new issues of shares. In a liquidation they could receive a share of any assets realized by the liquidators if there is anything left after all other liabilities have been paid.

Ordinary shares can be listed on a recognized stock market. There are advantages and disadvantages to this. Figure 9.3 highlights the advantages:

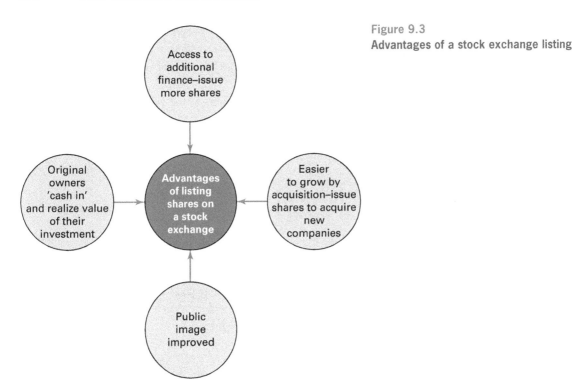

Figure 9.3
Advantages of a stock exchange listing

However there are also some serious disadvantages which should be considered before contemplating a listing. Figure 9.4 shows the disadvantages:

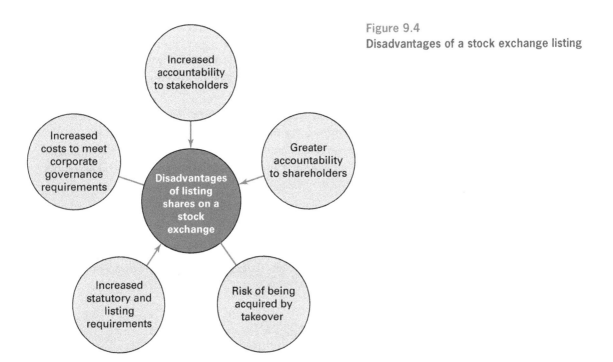

Figure 9.4
Disadvantages of a stock exchange listing

Whilst a stock exchange listing gives the company access to a much wider pool of investors and makes it much easier to raise additional capital, there are some wider considerations to bear in mind.

There will be a much greater focus on good corporate governance in listed companies. For example, this could mean that:

- The company has to recruit several non-executive directors.
- It has to create various committees to be open and transparent about such matters as directors' remuneration and the composition of the board.
- It has to publish a great deal of additional information to shareholders, who may well try to hold the company/board accountable should results not meet expectations.
- There are increased statutory and non-statutory requirements to be met—for example in most jurisdictions the stock exchange has its own set of rules a company must comply with in addition to any statutory requirements.
- Ultimately if the company does well it may become a takeover target and be acquired by another company or a rival. If the shares are publicly listed there is nothing to prevent an acquiring company buying them and ultimately taking over the whole enterprise. This might be contrary to the wishes of the original owners and founder but there is little they can do.

Stop and think	Look at a specialized financial newspaper or magazine or read the business pages of a good quality daily newspaper or online website. What type of information about the value of shares in a company is being considered? What information are companies expected to give to financial journalists? Do they get more information than shareholders?

Bonus and rights issues

There is often confusion between a bonus issue and a rights issue of shares. The distinction is actually quite straightforward.

A bonus issue, also known as a scrip issue or a capitalization issue, is an offer of free additional shares to existing shareholders. A company may decide to distribute further shares as an alternative to increasing the dividend payout. Bonus shares are issued according to each shareholder's stake in the company. For example, a three-for-two bonus issue entitles each shareholder three shares for every two they hold before the issue. A shareholder with 1000 shares receives 1500 bonus shares ($1000 \times 3/2 = 1500$).

Bonus issues are given to shareholders when companies are short of cash and shareholders expect a regular income. Shareholders may sell the bonus shares if they wish to raise funds. Bonus shares may also be issued to restructure company reserves. The double-entry is:

Dr Retained reserves

Cr Share capital

so the company is using its own reserves to finance the share issue. Clearly the overall total of share capital and reserves remains the same, so issuing bonus shares does not involve cash flow. It increases the company's share capital but not its net assets.

Because there are more shares in circulation the market price may drop. In addition, the level of dividend per share may also drop in future years, which may also discourage investors.

A rights issue does involve cash as it is an issue of rights to a company's existing shareholders that entitles them to buy additional shares directly from the company in proportion to their existing holdings, within a fixed time period. In a rights issue, the price at which each share may be purchased is generally at a discount to the current market price. Rights are often transferable, allowing the holder to sell them on the open market.

In a rights issue, a company offers to sell shares to existing shareholders. Each shareholder receives one right for each share it owns. This is a right, and not an obligation, and a shareholder can choose to:

- exercise the right by purchasing shares by the date listed on the offer letter
- do nothing and ignore the opportunity
- sell their rights to another person

Companies generally offer rights when they need to raise money, for example to pay off debt, purchase equipment or acquire another company. A company can use a rights issue to raise money if there are no other viable financing alternatives. This is common during economic slowdowns when banks become reluctant to lend to companies.

A rights issue will reduce gearing if the money is used to replace borrowings, which could be beneficial in times of economic slowdown where heavy dependence on bank finance can hit profits and cash flows.

The benefit of a rights issue to shareholders is that shares are generally offered at a discount. Sometimes this discount can be quite considerable; it all depends on how much a company feels it needs to encourage its shareholders to participate in the rights offering.

A shareholder who does not take up the rights issue will find their shareholding, and consequently their voting rights diluted proportionally; conversely a shareholder who takes the rights up is investing more in the company, which generally means they are happy with the future prospect for the business.

The share price may drop as more shares are on the market.

How does it work?

EXAMPLE

Josephine owns 1000 shares in Maxiblast plc, each of which is worth £5.50 on the stock exchange. The company is in a bit of financial trouble and needs to raise cash to cover its debt obligations. Maxiblast therefore announces a rights issue, in which it plans to raise £30 million by issuing 10 million shares to existing investors at a price of £3 each. This issue is a two-for-five rights issue, in other words, for every five shares you hold, Maxiblast is offering another two at a deeply discounted price of £3. This price is 45 per cent less than the £5.50 price at which Maxiblast stock trades.

Josephine has three options when considering what to do in response to the rights issue. She can:

1 Take up the rights issue in full
2 Ignore it
3 Sell the rights to someone else

OPTION 1—TAKE UP THE RIGHTS ISSUE IN FULL

To take advantage of the rights issue in full, Josephine would need to spend £3 for every Maxiblast share that she was entitled to purchase under the issue. As Josephine holds 1000 shares, she can buy up to 400 new shares (two shares for every five already owned) at the discounted price of £3, giving a total price of £1200.

Although Josephine is buying at a discount, the new issue of shares will dilute her holding and the value will drop accordingly. Whilst it isn't possible to predict the new market price, a rough calculation would be:

1000 existing shares at market value £5.50	5500
400 new shares at £3	1200
Value of 1400 shares	6700
Value per share	6700 ÷ 1400 = £4.79

This is known as the ex-rights price.

Josephine has acquired a larger holding at a discounted price and, should Maxiblast do well the share price may well return to its pre-rights value of £5.50 in time.

OPTION 2—IGNORE THE RIGHTS ISSUE

Josephine may not have the £1200 to purchase the additional 400 shares at £3 each, so she can always let the rights expire. However, if she adopts this course of action her shareholding will be diluted by the extra shares issued and the value is bound to drop as a result of the issue.

OPTION 3—SELL THE RIGHTS TO OTHER INVESTORS

In some cases, rights are not transferable; these are known as 'non-renounceable rights.' But in most cases, the rights allow a shareholder to decide whether to take up the option to buy the shares or sell the rights to other investors or to the underwriter, i.e. the bank or finance house that is underwriting the issue; they will take up the value of any shares left unsold. The value will be relatively low.

The key, from the investors' point of view, is to understand the purpose of the additional funding before accepting or rejecting a rights issue. There should be an explanation of why the rights issue and share dilution are needed.

It can be a quick fix for a weak statement of financial position, but investors will need to be sure that any underlying weaknesses in the company's performance are being addressed by management.

Preference shares

Preference shares represent a lower risk profile to the investor but, in return, generate a fixed return that may be lower than the dividend paid to ordinary shareholders. They are called preference shares because their dividend comes first before any ordinary dividend is paid, so if there is only enough after-tax profit to pay a preference share dividend, the ordinary shareholders will get nothing. They generally carry no voting rights and, in many respects, are akin to loans. They may have a fixed repayment term or, alternatively, a company may choose to repay them.

Should the company go into liquidation, preference shareholders can receive a share of any residual funds ahead of ordinary shareholders. This is a rather dubious benefit because, in most cases, when a company goes into liquidation, there is very little left after the banks have taken their share and the other creditors have claimed any residue.

Preference shares have become of limited value to companies as a source of finance for three reasons:

- Bank borrowing rates are at relatively low levels, so borrowings tend to be preferred. Preference shares and bank loans tend to be very similar from a corporate perspective.
- Preference share dividends are not tax-deductible but interest payments are, so this represents a considerable benefit.

- Holders of preference shares would look to a return better than that offered to savers by financial institutions so preference share dividends have to be higher than rates available to bank savers, which still makes them probably lower than borrowing rates but, as they are not tax deductible, more expensive overall.

Consequently, preference share issues have been considered to be an expensive option for companies.

Borrowings

Borrowing from a bank is a primary source of finance. Essentially this falls into two types: long- and short-term. Long-term loans are structural; they are there for the purchase of major assets such as property and land, major items of fixed plant and equipment, etc. Short-term borrowings consist of bank loans and overdrafts and are a source of finance for, broadly, day-to-day operations.

LOANS AND OVERDRAFTS   Borrowing from a financial institution such as a bank is a very common way of financing a business. Finance can take the form of a mixture of loans—both long- and short-term and an overdraft facility.

An overdraft is a flexible form of borrowing that fluctuates daily. The advantage for the business is that it only pays interest when the overdraft is used. The downside for the business is that:

- an overdraft arrangement can be varied by the bank without notice
- an overdraft is normally repayable on demand

Generally the overdraft facility—the amount that is available to the customer—is reviewed annually and the bank will maintain the arrangement; however if the customer persistently exceeds the limit, the lender may take the view that their finance is at risk, withdraw the facility and demand repayment.

Loans can be taken out for specific purposes, such as the construction of a factory, in which case the loan will match an asset, or simply as general financing for the whole enterprise.

When considering lending a bank will look at the business and carry out a review. This will include:

- An assessment of the quality of the management—are they experienced, what is their track record like, what qualifications do they have?
- An assessment of the products and services of the business and the market in which it operates
- An overview of the competition the business faces in the market and the barriers to entry
- A review of the financial statements and cash flows of the business
- A review of budgets and cash forecasts paying particular attention to the assumptions on which they are based

Consequently, businesses tend to maintain a working relationship with lenders, keeping them informed of business developments so that remedial action can be taken before matters hit a crisis point. In major cases, a lender might insist on having a representative attend board meetings as a non-executive director in order to keep abreast of what the business is doing.

Fixed and floating charges

Lenders will also look to get some form of security for their borrowing, which will take the form of a charge or mortgage. These take two forms:

- fixed charges
- floating charges

A fixed charge is secured on specific assets of the business and this is most usually land and buildings, but can also include larger items of fixed plant and equipment.

A floating charge is not fixed to any particular asset but is a charge over all the assets of the business including current assets such as inventory, receivables and cash. It crystallizes—or becomes fixed—when the business defaults on the loan and the lender is looking to recover its money by repossessing assets and selling them off.

COVENANTS   The lender will also set out the terms of any loan finance and these are what is known as loan or banking covenants. Typically, they can include:

- the rights of lenders to receiver regular information such as monthly management accounts
- the requirement that all assets be insured
- a requirement to achieve certain profit levels or levels of income based on budgets and forecasts
- minimum liquidity or gearing levels
- a restriction on further borrowing
- restricting the right to sell assets subject to the fixed charge without the consent of the lender
- restrictions on dividend payments and director's bonuses

Significant breaches of these covenants can, as the ultimate sanction, require the immediate repayment of all outstanding loans, which could force the business into liquidation and a sale of assets at a discount. In practice this is relatively rare as a lender would rather have a live client than a dead one—so there would be the possibility of trading out of difficulties or selling the business as a going concern with repayment of the loans as a condition of sale.

PERSONAL GUARANTEES   Lenders are only too aware of the major advantage of a limited company being that the risk to the owners—the shareholders—is limited to their investment in shares. In the case of a small business where the investment in shares can be as little as £1, for example, the lender is assuming a greater level of risk than the owner of the business.

Consequently, in the case of small businesses, lenders will often require a personal guarantee from either the shareholders/proprietors or some third party that, in the event of the business defaulting, they will repay any outstanding borrowings.

This can mean that personal assets such as homes, vehicles or other assets of value will be at risk if the business fails. It overcomes the problem, from a lender's perspective, of limited liability and acts as their security for any borrowings.

CONVERTIBLE LOAN NOTES   These are loan notes issued that give the holder the right to convert them to ordinary shares at a guaranteed value and time. Once the notes are converted the shares can be sold at a higher price than was paid on conversion. The advantage for the investor is that initially they have a loan on which interest is paid and, if the business is successful, the investor can convert into ordinary shares.

If the business is successful and the conversion is made, the business does not have to outlay any cash to redeem the notes as they then become shares. The only downside is that issuing further shares dilutes original holdings and possibly a lower dividend per share as there are more ordinary shares in issue.

ADDITIONAL TYPES OF FINANCE   There are many and various forms of finance available to businesses, which we will not detail here. For information these are:

- Debentures—these are financial instruments issued by a company, which carry a fixed rate of interest and are redeemable at a specific date. They are, essentially, loans. In the UK these are secured against assets of the business, but in other jurisdictions, such as the USA, they are unsecured. Debentures may be convertible to ordinary shares at a set rate or not convertible, in which case they are repaid by the company.

- Deep discount bonds—loan notes issued for a fixed term at a substantial discount to their nominal value, which will be redeemed at their nominal value when they mature. These generally carry a low rate of interest.
- Zero coupon bonds—these are similar to deep discount bonds, except no interest (known in jargon terms as the coupon) is paid on them.
- Mortgages—this is a loan secured on a fixed tangible asset invariably land and/or buildings.

Interest payments

There is a complicated formula used for working out loan repayments, which, for the sake of completeness only, is:

$$P = \frac{r(PV)}{1 - (1 + r)^{-n}}$$

Where:

P = Payment

PV = Present value—the original amount of the loan

R = Interest rate per period

N = Number of periods

Learners should not try to remember this, as there is an easier way, which involves the use of annuity tables. Someone has gone to the trouble of working out the calculations for a range of interest rates and periods, and these are available in the form of annuity tables.

Here is an example:

Suppose a business takes out a loan of €500 000 at 5 per cent for 12 years.

The annuity factor for 12 per cent over 5 years is 3.605.

The annual payment each year is therefore:

$$\frac{500\,000}{3.605} = €138\,696$$

The borrower will repay €693 480 (i.e. €138 696 × 5) over five years in equal instalments.

You do not have to worry at this stage about these calculations—this is for information only!

Borrowing and the effects of gearing

The ratio of borrowed money to equity finance is known as gearing, or alternatively leverage, which is a US term coming into more common use.

When times are hard, borrowed money can work against the organization simply because it has to pay interest on the money. Businesses do not fail because they make accounting losses; they fail because they run out of money and cannot pay their bills. If loan repayments cannot be met and the bank calls in the loan, the company will fail unless it is able to refinance in some way.

Let us consider the capital structure of two companies of the same size:

Suppose two companies have the following capital structure:

	Co A	Co B
Capital structure		
Share capital	1000	2000
Loans	1000	____
	2000	2000

Loan carries interest at 5 per cent p.a.

Dividends paid at 3 per cent.

In a normal trading year their results look like this:

	Co A	Co B
Revenues	150	150
Cost of sales and expenses	(55)	(55)
Operating profit	95	95
Finance costs	(50)	—
Operating profit	45	95
Dividend	(30)	(60)
	15	35

When things go wrong in times of depression results drop.

Co A income and COS (cost of sales) drop by 10 per cent.

	Co A	Co B
Revenues	135	135
Cost of sales and expenses	(50)	(50)
Operating profit	85	85
Finance costs	(50)	____
Operating profit	35	85
Dividend	(30)	(60)
	5	25

Clearly Company B has a much more flexible capital structure. Not only are its financing costs lower, which protects its profits, when business turns down in a depression it does not have to pay a dividend at all, or at most a very small one, so its financing costs are much reduced.

Having said that, not paying a dividend will affect the share price as nervous investors may take it as a sign the company is in trouble so, in most cases, companies often will pay a dividend even when they are in trouble financially.

The problem is that loan finance is considerably easier to obtain than raising capital from investors. Banks will lend in a considerably more generous way than investors, who require lots of information and may need to be cajoled into parting with yet more money. From an investors' point of view, the level of gearing is an indicator of the level of risk. A high level of gearing means that interest payments must be met before a dividend is paid so, in difficult times, there may not be sufficient profit available for a dividend.

REAL LIFE

UK water companies need to adjust gearing ratios

Highly leveraged water companies could be forced to seek additional equity to replace borrowings because of increased regulatory pressure, including possible licence changes, according to Moody's Investors Service (Moody's).

The credit rating agency has published a water sector comment. This follows a speech from the chairman of the water industry regulator who challenged companies to improve their financial resilience and adjust dividend policies. He focused on aggressive financial structures and questioned the financial resilience of highly leveraged companies with gearing in excess of 70 per cent.

Moody's listed companies with highly leveraged financing structures including Anglian Water, Southern Water, Thames Water, Yorkshire Water, Affinity Water and South East Water.

But Moody's warned shareholders may be 'reluctant' to inject additional cash considering estimated lower returns from 2020 onwards.

Source: *Utility Week 7.3.18* 'Highly leveraged water firms could seek fresh equity'

Islamic finance

Islamic finance refers to the means by which enterprises in the Muslim world, including banks and other lending institutions, raise capital in accordance with Sharia, or Islamic law. It also refers to the types of investments that are permissible under this form of law. Islamic banking is growing rapidly worldwide, and is something anyone working in finance should be aware of.

Central to Islamic banking and finance is an understanding of the importance of risk sharing as part of raising capital and the avoidance of *riba* (usury) and *gharar* (risk or uncertainty).

Islamic law does not view money as an asset, but instead as a tool for measuring value. It follows therefore that it is not permitted to make money out of money, for example, by charging interest on a loan. This is considered to be usury and is not permitted *(haram)*.

Accordingly, Sharia-compliant *(halal)* finance consists of a form of banking in which the financial institution shares in the profit and loss of the enterprise that it underwrites. Of equal importance is the concept of *gharar*, which is defined as risk or uncertainty. In a financial context it refers to the sale of items whose existence is not certain, so examples of *gharar* would be forms of insurance, such as the purchase of premiums to insure against something that may or may not occur or derivatives used to hedge against possible outcomes.

Although they cannot charge interest, the banks can profit from helping customers to purchase a property using an *ijara* or *murabaha* scheme. With an *ijara* scheme, the bank makes money by charging the customer rent; with a *murabaha* scheme, a price is agreed at the outset that is more than the market value. This profit is deemed to be a reward for the risk that is assumed by the bank.

The main categories within Islamic finance are:

- *Ijara* is a leasing agreement whereby the bank buys an item for a customer and then leases it back over a specific period.
- *Ijara-wa-iqtina* is a similar arrangement, except that the customer is able to buy the item at the end of the contract.
- *Mudaraba* offers specialist investment by a financial expert in which the bank and the customer share any profits. Customers risk losing their money if the investment is unsuccessful, although the bank will not charge a handling fee unless it turns a profit.
- *Murabaha* is a form of credit that enables customers to make a purchase without having to take out an interest-bearing loan. The bank buys an item and then sells it on to the customer on a deferred basis. In many cases, a value will be agreed between the bank and the buyer that is in excess of the market price. The buyer pays the higher price, often on deferred terms, and the difference represents a surplus that substitutes for interest payments.

- *Musharaka* is an investment partnership in which profit-sharing terms are agreed in advance, and losses are pegged to the amount invested.

Sharia law allows investment in company shares as long as those companies do not engage in lending, gambling or the production of alcohol, tobacco, weaponry or pornography. Investment in companies may be in shares or by direct investment (private equity).

Traditional insurance is not permitted as a means of risk management in Islamic law. This is because it constitutes the purchase of something with an uncertain outcome (a form of *ghirar*), and because insurers use fixed income—a form of *riba*—as part of their portfolio management process to satisfy liabilities.

A possible Sharia-compliant alternative is cooperative (mutual) insurance. Subscribers contribute to a pool of funds, which are invested in a Sharia-compliant manner. Funds are withdrawn from the pool to satisfy claims, and unclaimed profits are distributed among policy holders. Such a structure exists infrequently, so Muslims may avail themselves of existing insurance vehicles if needed or required.

Clearly when considering finance, an organization has many options and the advantages and disadvantages of each must be carefully evaluated and considered. There is a danger in relying too much on borrowings rather than equity but, on the other hand, borrowings are more flexible and can be tailored to the organization's requirements.

In every case, however, the liabilities have to be met, whether these be dividend payments to ordinary shareholders, interest and capital repayments to banks or redemption payments to bond holders, so organizations must ensure that funds are available to meet these liabilities.

Test yourself

1 Which of the following is true or false?

	True	False
A stock exchange listing will improve the owner's control over the business.		
Listing shares on a stock exchange improves a company's image.		
A stock exchange listing gives access to a wider pool of finance.		
A stock exchange listing requires stakeholders to be given more information than if the company were not listed.		

2 Snagglepus plc, a listed company, needs to raise finance and has declared that it will make a rights issue. It has an issued share capital of £1 million and the ordinary £1 shares are currently trading at £5.50 each. Snagglepus proposes a 1:4 issue at £4.40 per share.

Percy owns 170 000 shares. If he decides to take up the rights issue how much will he have to pay for his shares?

3 Owl Ltd has the following capital structure:

	€000s
Share capital—ordinary shares of €1 each	1500
5% preference shares of €1 each	500
Accumulated profits	2800
Long-term loan at 6%	750
Short-term loan at 6.8%	125

What is Owl's gearing or leverage ratio?

4 Which of the following is true or false?

	True	False
Preference shares carry voting rights so can influence dividend policy.		
Lenders will want to see a profitable trading history before lending to a business.		
One of the disadvantages of a stock exchange listing is the risk of becoming a takeover target.		
A debenture is a type of ordinary share but redeemable at a fixed date.		

5 Bigbusta plc has a share capital of R1 500 000 in ordinary shares of R0.50 each. At the close of business on 31 March, the price stood at R3.46. It has announced a rights issue of 1:5 at a price of R2.80.
To take up the rights a holder of 50 000 shares will have to pay:
   a) R56 000
   b) R140 000
   c) R28 000
   d) R14 000

6 Which of the following is true or false?

	True	False
Under Islamic finance, loans do not carry interest so they are much cheaper than loans from non-Islamic banks.		
Listing the company on a stock exchange can result in the founders of the business being able to realize their investment.		
Preference shares are a preferred form of raising capital as they are under the control of the company.		
Islamic finance differs from Western finance models because there is a prohibition on charging interest on loans.		

The following information relates to Questions 6 and 7
Wimpole Ltd and Harcourt Ltd have the following capital structures:

	Wimpole $	Harcourt $
Share capital	20 000	2 000
Accumulated profits	50 000	50 000
Long-term loans	5 000	23 000
Total	75 000	75 000

The long term-loans carry interest at 6 per cent.
Both companies make a profit before interest and tax of $15 000. Tax is payable at 30 per cent on profits.

7 Calculate the after-tax profit of both companies and the return on equity shareholders funds (ROSF).
   (You may need to look at Module 8 to remind yourself of the formula.)

8 Both companies suffer a major downturn in profits. All other information remains the same, but pre-tax profits drop to $8000.
   i. Recalculate the effect on the ROSF for both companies.
   ii. What is the major cause of the difference between the performance of the two companies?

9 Which of the following is true or false?   ✔   ✔

	True	False
Convertible loan notes can be converted to ordinary shares at an advantageous value.		
A bonus issue and a rights issue are the same thing except a bonus issue involves more shares.		
Stakeholders can influence company policy by voting at an AGM.		
A zero coupon bond does not carry interest.		

The following information relates to Questions 10 and 11

Boris Ltd and Doris Ltd are two companies with the following capital structures:

	Boris $	Doris $
Share capital	200 000	30 000
Accumulated profits	150 000	150 000
Long-term loans at 10 per cent	25 000	150 000
5 per cent preference shares	75 000	120 000
Total	450 000	450 000

The trading profit for the current year is $40 000.

10 Calculate the gearing for both companies

11 Ignoring taxation, calculate the return on capital employed (ROCE).

In the next module we will examine how organizations fund their activities from their internal resources. We will look at working capital management and see how companies can generate funds by simply managing their net current assets and liabilities.

Test yourself

1 Hamish Ltd has applied for a bank loan of £250 000 at 7 per cent to purchase a new Glimping machine. Hamish's statement of financial position for the current year looks like this:

	£
Tangible assets—net book value	250 000
Net current assets	30 000
	280 000
Share capital	50 000
Accumulated profits	80 000
Long-term secured loan at 6 per cent	150 000
	280 000

Hamish Ltd has a good relationship with the bank. It has a small overdraft facility of £10 000, which it has used only occasionally. It is well managed and the profit for the current year was £20 000 after tax and loan interest. It is a family company and all the shareholders are active in the business. All the profits are ploughed back into the business.

To support the loan application, the company has sent to the bank a copy of its last audited financial statements and a brochure about the Glimping machine.

However, the bank has not automatically approved the loan as the company had hoped it would.

Required

i. What would be the effect on the company's resources if the loan was granted?

ii. What additional information might the bank require to assist it with the loan decision?

2 Megablast plc is looking to raise finance for a major expansion of its operations. This will involve acquiring the business of a rival company—Miniblast plc—building a new factory and expanding its old one with new robotic equipment. Overall it is looking to raise some $300 million.

The latest statement of financial position can be summarized as:

	$m
Tangible assets—net book value	280
Net current assets	170
	450
Share capital—ordinary $1 shares	100
Accumulated profits	100
Long-term secured loan at 7 per cent	250
	450

The income account showed after-tax profit of $65 million, out of which the company paid a dividend to ordinary shareholders of $3 million. The current market price of the shares is $2.50.

The board are considering two financing options:

1) An issue of 300 000 $1 preference shares at 6 per cent fixed for ten years
2) An additional bank loan at 7 per cent

Required

i. What would be the effect on the financial position of Megablast of these two options?

ii. Is there a third course of action which the board could consider? If so, what is it and how would it work?

10 Working capital management

In this module we will consider:

- What is working capital?
- Managing inventories
- Managing receivables
- Cash management
- Managing payables
- Leasing and hire purchase

In this module we will look at the way a business finances itself from its own resources. Ideally an enterprise will have two forms of capital:

- Long-term structural funds
- Short-term operational funds

These serve two different purposes. As we saw in Module 9, long-term funding is used to finance the purchase of assets and for the initial capital requirements of the business. It is structural finance insofar as it forms the core long-term financing of the business.

Short-term funding is there to finance the day-to-day operational cycle of cash flows.

Figure 10.1 gives examples of the two different types of funding:

Figure 10.1 Funding types

Funding	Examples
Long-term structural funding	• Equity share capital
	• Long-term loans
	• Preference shares
	• Debentures and loan notes
	• Retained earnings

(continued)

Funding	Examples
Short-term funding	• Short-term loans
	• Overdrafts
	• Leasing and hire purchase
	• Debt factoring
	• Invoice discounting
	• Cash flows from operations

We looked at long-term structural funding in Module 9 so here we are considering short-term funding derived from the management of working capital. So what do we mean by working capital?

REAL LIFE
Deloitte—strategies for improving your cash management

Big Four accounting firm Deloitte has published a series of guides to improving working capital management—in one, they say:

'As with any cultural shift, embedding a cash management culture within your organization requires management buy-in. Companies that succeed at this effort typically define their objectives up front, assign responsibility to people across the organization and then track progress using monthly cash flow metrics.

'To encourage adoption, it's imperative to establish, communicate and implement standard policies across the organization. Cash management policies should focus on budgeting, forecasting and financing and indicate how to handle day-to-day activities such as collections, procurement/ordering and payment. Keep in mind, too, that cash flow management is not just a finance issue; it's an operational issue. All departments—from sales and marketing, procurement and production to finance and treasury—must coordinate for optimal results. To drive this point, many leading companies actually link staff compensation to achieving specific cash flow targets.'

Source: Deloitte—'Strategies for improving your working capital management'

What is working capital?

Working capital is basically net current assets which involve the movement of cash; in other words:

- Inventories
- Trade receivables
- Cash and bank balances
- Bank overdrafts
- Short-term loan finance
- Trade payables

For this purpose therefore it does not include non-cash items such as:

- Provisions
- Accruals
- Prepayments

How then do we use these as a form of funding to finance day-to-day operations?

Figure 10.2 illustrates the working capital cycle whereby funds from customers are used to pay suppliers to provide more materials to create product to sell to customers, and so on.

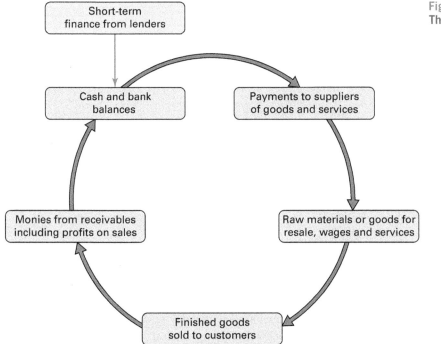

Figure 10.2
The working capital cycle

Stop and think   In your organization or an organization that you know, does the working capital cycle work this way if the organization is not a manufacturing business? What if it was an advertising agency or a firm of accountants? Would the same considerations apply?

Notice that cash is generated from the process of buying and selling or the provision of services. Clearly there are costs other than the purchase of raw materials and services such as:

- Wages
- Administration costs
- Services such as light, heat, water and power
- Sales and distribution costs
- Repairs and ancillary maintenance costs, etc.

All of these have to be met and paid for. That is why working capital management requires additional funding in the form of overdrafts and loans to meet shortfalls in cash generation from operations.

We will look at this in detail later in the module, but for now we can summarize the approach to working capital management as one of control. Control over inventory levels, ensuring customers pay on time, taking the maximum credit from suppliers and ensuring that overdrafts and short-term loan finance is used carefully to avoid excessive interest charges.

Figure 10.3 summarizes the approach:

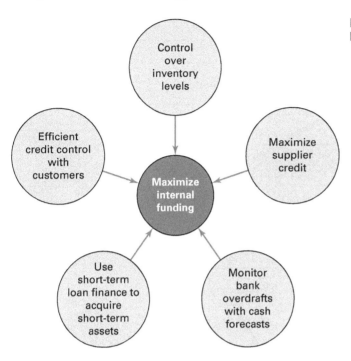

Figure 10.3
Maximizing internal funding

The object is to ensure that internal cash flows are maximized so that day-to-day operations can progress with a minimum funding requirement. Borrowing money involves paying interest. Whilst interest rates are low this may not be a particularly onerous cost, but if rates start to rise the cost of borrowing may assume greater significance. Organizations that do not have the right levels of control over their operations will suffer excess finance costs and, more importantly, may have to increase borrowings to finance their working capital.

There is an upper limit, set by the lender, of how much can be borrowed and the objective is not to reach it so avoiding putting the business under financial pressure.

OPERATING CASH CYCLE (OCC)   The operating cash cycle, or OCC, is broadly the length of time required to fund working capital from the purchase of goods for inventory to the receipt of funds from the customer from the sale of those goods.

Clearly the length of time varies with the type of business. A supermarket, for example, mainly deals in cash or instant card payments so it has a very short OCC. Service-based businesses such as lawyers do have an OCC because the individual lawyers have to be paid their salaries and this may happen before the client is billed and pays the bill. However, it is more true of manufacturers and wholesalers who order goods from suppliers on credit terms, store them and then sell them on credit to customers. Let us look at an example.

EXAMPLE

Vrooom plc imports motor vehicle parts. The business is funded through a combination of bank loans and overdrafts. Vrooom's sales revenue is £29 million per year on credit. Purchases of parts are £15 million per year, also on credit.

Working capital according to the latest statement of financial position is:

	£m
Inventories	3.0
Trade receivables	5.2
Trade payables	1.4

The OCC for Vrooom is:

Inventories days	£3.0 m ÷ £15 m × 365 =	73 days
Receivables days	£5.2 m ÷ £29 m × 365 =	65 days
Payables days	£1.4 m ÷ £15 m =	(34) days
		104 days

Vrooom has to finance its working capital for 104 days; this is, basically, the cost of inventories and outstanding receivables for over three months that requires them to find short-term finance such as an overdraft. This costs money, which reduces their net profit. In addition, Vrooom is paying its suppliers in advance of receiving money from customers: a negative cash flow.

Looking at Vrooom's performance, some simple cash management would improve its financial situation considerably.

EXAMPLE

C ontinuing on the case of Vrooom from the Example above, it has recently been the case that, unsurprisingly, Vrooom has been at its overdraft limit and has occasionally exceeded it, thus incurring excess interest charges and penalties from the bank. The bank has refused to increase the overdraft limit and has advised Vrooom to reduce its spending and restrict its operations so the overdraft will come down.

Vrooom has asked its auditors to advise on how this can be done.

The auditors examined the financial statements of similar companies to Vrooom and has identified some working capital ratios as follows:

Inventory turnover period	31 days
Trade receivables days	51 days
Trade payables days	48 days

On this basis the auditors have shown the directors that the overdraft can be reduced considerably through better working capital management as follows:

	Current level	Target level	Saving
Inventory days	**£3.0 m**	31/365 × £15 m = **£1.27 m**	£1.73 m
Receivables days	**£5.2 m**	51/365 × £29 m = **£4.05 m**	£1.15 m
Payables days	**£1.4 m**	48/365 × £15 m = **£1.97 m**	£0.57 m
TOTAL INCREASED FUNDING			**£3.45 m**

Thus, by taking steps to reduce the levels of inventory carried, collect receipts from customers more quickly and take a little more credit from suppliers, the business is able to generate almost £3.5 million of additional funding to reduce the overdraft. All these actions are within management control so should be able to be carried out quite quickly providing the right information is available.

In order to be able to exercise that control, the business requires to have a good management information system (MIS) able to provide the right financial information as required. It needs to have, as a minimum:

- An inventory system recording inventory levels for each item carried. This must be verified regularly with actual inventory counts to ensure that it does not drift away from what is actually there in stock
- A receivables ledger with the ability to produce an aged debtors report at any time
- A payables ledger with the ability to produce an aged creditors report at any time
- A revenues system that can analyze sales by item to record sales levels as part of inventory control
- A cash book recording transactions in a format suitable for inclusion in a cash forecast

Let us look at these in more detail.

Managing inventories

Most businesses inventories, except purely service-based ones such as lawyers, accountants, cleaners, medical professionals, etc., will form a significant part of their statement of financial position.

In Module 8 we looked at a couple of ratios which give managers an indication of stockholding levels. These were:

INVENTORY TURNOVER

$$\frac{\text{Cost of goods sold}}{\text{Average inventory}}$$

This represents the number of times the inventory is turned over in the period. This is important, as money tied up in inventory is not able to be used for anything else so, broadly, the more frequently it is turned over (into receivables and cash) the better.

INVENTORY DAYS

$$\frac{\text{Closing inventory} \times 365}{\text{Cost of sales}}$$

This represents the inventory turnover ratio expressed as days.

In commercial terms this ratio is relevant because days in inventory represents money tied up but also increases the risks of obsolescence, damage and storage costs.

The key to managing inventory is to:

a) hold as little as possible in stock compatible with efficient operation of the business
b) turn the inventory over as many times as possible in the financial period; in other words not have it sitting on the shelves for too long

Manufacturing businesses and retailers all carry significant levels of inventory in one form or another. The problem with inventory is that it is, in effect, dead money—if it has been paid for.

EXAMPLE

A retail food business buys 1000 tins of beans on 30 days credit from a bean supplier. If they sell the beans within 30 days, they can happily pay the supplier as the tins of beans have been turned into cash. However, if it does not sell those beans within 30 days the supplier still wants paying. Suppose it has only sold 10 tins.

The money from the sale of 10 tins will go towards paying the supplier but the supplier needs to be paid for 1000 tins so, unless the 10 tins have been sold at a huge profit, there will be a shortfall in funds which has to be financed.

Thus the business had to use, perhaps, a bank overdraft to pay the supplier and this will only be cleared when the remaining 990 tins are sold. The longer this takes, the more interest the business pays and the lower its overall profit on the transaction.

Using the above example, if the business knew or could forecast that it would only sell 10 tins it could only order 10 tins from the supplier and not have 990 tins sitting on its shelves that it has had to pay for and are costing money to finance.

Efficient inventory management can be seen operating in many locations. For example, supermarket chains barcode all their stock lines. Why? Well, let us go back to the retailer with 1000 tins of beans in the example above.

This is how the system works in outline for retailers:

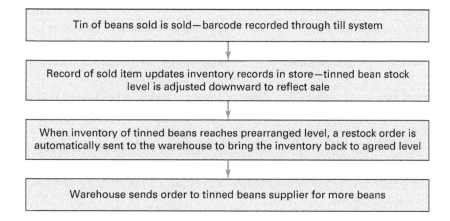

The use of the barcode-based stock recording system means:

- The business knows how many tins of beans it has on its shelves at any one time
- If order and reorder levels are set the system will automatically trigger an order for more tins of beans when the level drops dangerously low
- If the item is perishable or has a limited shelf life, the system will be able to flag up stocks of goods which may become unsaleable and will have to be written off, which is a net loss to the business.

Control over inventory levels is the fundamental basis of inventory management. Retailers can use barcode systems; for manufacturers this is why inventory control systems such as just in time (JIT) were invented.

JUST IN TIME   JIT is a work flow approach used by a lot of manufacturing companies and retailers.

The idea is that the manufacturer or retailer maintains very low inventory levels and the components needed for production or items for resale are delivered to the business just in time to be used or sold. Clearly this requires a very close cooperation with suppliers and a confidence in them that they will be able to deliver what is needed at the right time and to the right place.

Any delay in delivery can mean a halt to production or no goods for sale, with a consequent cost to the business.

Large and sophisticated manufacturers maintain production scheduling software to plan production and pass that information to suppliers through electronic data interchange (EDI) so the suppliers know what is needed and when. Suppliers often share the site with the manufacturer and maintain their own warehousing on site, so they are able to deliver quickly. Supplies are delivered directly to the production line so, for example, a manufacturer of train carriages might have the seats for a carriage delivered to the correct manufacturing area within a very narrow time slot so the workers on the line can install the seats without any delay or stopping the production line.

The supplier thus carries all the stockholding cost but in return will have a guarantee to supply and will be paid promptly.

There are advantages and disadvantages to JIT-type systems as shown in Figure 10.4.

Figure 10.4 Advantages and disadvantages of JIT stock system

Advantages	Disadvantages
Limits levels of inventory to be carried so reducing storage costs	Requires a sophisticated production scheduling system to schedule production in a way that is achievable by the workforce
Requires close working relationship with suppliers and exchanges of information. This enables a team-focused approach in order to achieve agreed targets	Failure of suppliers to deliver can mean delays to production or no sales with consequent cost implications
Costs of holding inventory are with the supplier not with the customer	All output is based on orders so there is no capacity for meeting unexpected orders
Inventory does not become obsolete or out-of-date	Requires a very careful choice of suppliers as they are critical to the customer's operations.
Levels of inventory match demand so excess inventory levels caused by a downturn in demand are avoided	It can be difficult to change suppliers because of the close working relationship required as it will take a new supplier some time to install and adapt its systems to actively operate the customers' JIT requirements efficiently

So, whilst JIT is a very flexible and efficient system it requires a lot of planning and cooperation to work successfully and is not without risk.

Overall inventory management, if successfully carried out, can free up a good deal of cash for the business. It does however require constant monitoring based on good data from the MIS in order to avoid running out of key inventory items at a critical time.

Managing receivables

Receivables are amounts due from customers and, as part of the contract with those customers, the terms of trade should be clearly expressed. These set out the number of days credit from the date of invoice will be allowed before the invoice becomes due for payment.

A ratio that we saw in Module 8 shows the number of days it takes the organization, on average, to collect its trade debts from customers:

$$\frac{\text{Trade receivables} \times 365}{\text{Credit sales}}$$

Ideally the number of days taken to collect the debts should be less than the number of days credit taken from suppliers (see below). This will generate a positive cash flow.

Commonly the level of credit offered is between 30 and 60 days, but terms of trade vary, so it is a matter of either agreement with a customer or common business practice.

The key to managing receivables is called credit control. This involves identifying customers who have not paid within the agreed timescale and sending them reminders to pay.

There is usually a multi-stage system involved in credit control as follows:

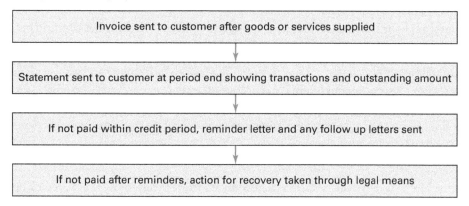

Any reminder letters and follow-up letters can become increasingly strident starting with a gentle reminder that payment may have been overlooked to threats of legal action if the amount due is not paid within a specified period. This is something the business has to decide. Clearly, taking legal action against a customer is a last resort but if the customer will not pay and there is no justifiable reason why not they are not a customer the business wants.

CASH DISCOUNTS   Debt collection can be improved by offering customers a cash discount for prompt payment. However, this represents a cost to the business as it is forgoing part of its profit on the transaction as it will receive less from the customer than the original value of the goods sold. Cash discounts to improve cash flow can represent an expensive form of finance. There are alternatives to cash discounts which we will look at later, principally involving the use of finance companies to take over the receivables position.

AGED RECEIVABLES ANALYSIS   This is quite simply an analysis of the amounts due from customers over time. Here is an example:

AGED DEBT ANALYSIS—EXAMPLE

Customer	Customer ref	Total due	30 days	30–60 days	60–90 days	90 days +
Alphonse	A0012	3 153.26	1 237.47	1 848.45	67.34	
Bertrand	B897	6 868.99		5 983.01	498.00	387.98
Claudine	C003	8 754.00	8 754.00			
Dupont	D932	15 778.00	8 396.00	7 382.00		
Ermintrude	E902	439.00				439.00
Francois	F189	10 251.19	7 629.89	2 387.00	234.30	
Gregory	G176	17 266.00	9 649.00	7 493.00	124.00	
Henri	H005	2 084.00	1 245.00	839.00		
Ivan	I765	17 620.00	9 738.00	7 361.00	521.00	
		82 214.44	**46 649.36**	**33 293.46**	**1 444.64**	**826.98**
Debt %			56.74%	40.50%	1.76%	1.01%

Looking at this analysis, we can see that Bertrand and Ermintrude owe amounts for over 90 days. These could be disputed amounts; if so, the dispute should be settled by either them paying a reduced amount or the debt being cancelled with a credit note. The amounts are minimal in the context of the overall sum of receivables.

However, just over 40 per cent of the amounts due are over 30 days. This could be that the average time being taken is, say 40 days, but it may be that the average time taken is 60 days. Either way this is quite a high percentage of debts due in excess of the terms of trade so represents an opportunity to exercise some credit control and get the money in more quickly.

Clearly Bertrand is a worry as they have no current debt and all the amounts due are over the credit period, so this debt needs immediate attention.

Credit control has to be handled carefully, as it is a matter of being diplomatic but also firm because you are funding their liability until it is paid.

DEBT FACTORING AND INVOICE DISCOUNTING   Debt factoring and invoice discounting are two ways to improve cash flow from receivables, insofar as both promise to release cash early from receivables so businesses do not have to wait out the credit period until they are paid.

Debt factoring involves a finance company 'buying' the invoicing from the business at a discount. The factoring company then collects the sums due in full.

Key features are:

- The factoring company 'buys' the invoices at a discount and pays the business, thus speeding up cash flow.
- The factoring company then chases the customer for payment and collects the debt in full.
- Factoring companies will be selective when reviewing a receivables ledger and will only buy invoices in respect of customers with strong credit ratings, i.e. those unlikely to default.
- The discount can vary from 1 per cent to as much as 10 per cent dependent on the work involved for the factor and the quality of the customers. Consequently, it can be an expensive form of finance.
- If a customer defaults, this is normally handled by the factoring company, but this has to be agreed in advance. Mistakes in invoicing may result in clawback of funds advanced.
- Customers are aware that debts are being handled by a factoring company.

With invoice discounting the position is rather different. With discounting the business is able to borrow money from a financial provider based on the invoices issued. Companies will offer advances of up to 80 or 90 per cent of the invoiced value almost straight away after the invoice is issued. When it is paid the company reimburses the financial provider.

The financial providers often charge a fee for this service in addition to interest on the money advanced by the discounter.

In the case of discounting customers are not aware of the funding arrangement.

There are some advantages and disadvantages of these funding approaches summarized in Figure 10.5.

Figure 10.5   Debt factoring and invoice discounting advantages and disadvantages

Advantages	Disadvantages
Provides cash early and obviates need to fund the receivables credit period	Can be costly forms of finance
Early receipt of cash can be used to fund project or pay suppliers promptly taking advantages of discounts	Customers may see the use of debt factors as indicative of poor cash flow and possible financial trouble
Does not require ownership of assets to act as security for borrowings	Can be difficult to end the arrangements because the business comes to rely on early cash flow
Cash available is linked to levels of invoicing so funding is related directly to activity levels—no danger of taking out funding that outstrips the ability to pay	Discounting requires the business to have a strong credit control function to ensure debts collected promptly
Factors will research new customers and advise on credit rating	Factors will only deal with customers with proven credit history. Poor quality customers or new customers without a proven track record may not be included in factoring arrangements. Bad debt risk can remain with business.

Cash management

As mentioned in earlier modules, using the term 'cash' is accountants' shorthand for both cash and bank transactions. Clearly if a business deals in cash it has a positive cash flow so is in a good position to fund its working capital assuming it takes credit from suppliers. Supermarkets and other retailers are generally cash businesses.

Other types of business will generally not be cash positive but will require some form of short term funding—generally involving an overdraft. The purpose of the overdraft is to bridge the gap between cash receipts and cash payments.

Overdrafts have some key features as shown in Figure 10.6.

Figure 10.6 Overdrafts—key features

Amount	As agreed with lender up to fixed limit
Repayment	Fluctuates with movements in bank account. May not be needed at certain times. Repayable in full on demand from the lender
Interest	Fluctuates according to level of overdraft used. Based on bank base rate plus a percentage.
Purpose	Short-term borrowing to finance working capital and cover shortfalls in cash generation
Secured	Depends but usually included as part of a lenders floating charge (see Module 9)

Many businesses are quite content to run a permanent overdraft as they take the view that the return they generate from operations funded by the overdraft outweighs the interest they pay on it.

With an overdraft, however, there are costs to be considered. The main ones are:

- arrangement fees
- maintenance fees/charges
- interest
- unauthorized borrowing fees
- covenant compliance costs
- professional advice

An arrangement fee is a one-off administration charge payable to the lender to arrange the overdraft facility.

There are also maintenance fees or charges made by the lender to cover the maintenance of the facility; this is usually a monthly cost.

Interest will vary depending on risk of default. Due to the flexible nature of overdrafts the most common type of interest rate charged will be variable (e.g. a margin over bank base rate or London Interbank Offered Rate [LIBOR]).

A higher rate will be charged if the business goes over its overdraft limit so that the overdraft becomes unauthorized. Businesses exceeding their authorized facility may be charged unauthorized borrowing charges such as unpaid fees and a utilization fee. These are often capped by banks to reduce a business's exposure but can still add up to a significant amount.

In some instances, and more often for larger facilities, the cost of borrowing can be reduced if the overdraft is secured, as the risk to the lender will generally be lower. The security provided by the borrower will often be by way of a floating charge over business assets.

This also applies when covenants or other information are required by the lender as a condition of providing the overdraft facility and of its continued availability. Information such as current management accounts and/or cash flow projections can be requested on a regular basis, which will be agreed prior to sanctioning.

Legal fees will vary depending on if other services are provided, the complexity of the business, its size and risk to the lender. Fees are likely to apply when a personal asset, such as a jointly owned property, is provided as security.

OVERDRAFT OR LOAN?   Overdrafts are a good source of short-term finance as they are flexible and fluctuations in the level of overdraft tends to tie the cost of an overdraft to the levels of trading activity. When the business generates cash, the overdraft levels are minimized;- when it needs funds the overdraft goes up.

However for more stable funding—often for the medium and longer term—a loan is usually the preferred option.

A loan has several advantages over an overdraft, the primary one being that it is fixed and the repayment schedule is known.

The problem with an overdraft is that it is repayable on demand so the organization can never be entirely confident that its funding is secure in the longer term. A loan is made by agreement with the lender so providing the terms of the loan are adhered to the funding is secure for the period of the loan. Figure 10.7 shows the differences between overdrafts and loans.

Figure 10.7 **Overdrafts and loans compared**

Overdraft	Loan
Terms agreed with lender and set out in letter or finance agreement	Terms agreed with lender and set out in letter or finance agreement
Repayable on demand	Fixed term providing terms complied with
Level varies with cash flow of borrower	Fixed amount repayable in instalments
Interest rate can fluctuate and interest cost depends on the level of utilization of the facility	Interest rate fixed by loan terms
Generally secured as part of floating charge	Loans can be secured by fixed charge on specific assets
Generally not included as part of gearing ratio	Will be included as part of gearing ratio

Generally, businesses use a combination of overdrafts and loans to finance their operations. The exact proportion of each type of finance depends on the business's operational needs.

Managing payables

Trade credit is one of the main sources of short-term finance for businesses of any size from small to large. Inventories can be purchased on credit terms that represent, at least in most countries, an interest-free loan from the supplier.

The ratio that we saw in Module 8 shows the average time the organization takes to pay its trade payables thus:

$$\frac{\text{Trade payables} \times 365}{\text{Cost of sales}}$$

Managing trade payables involves negotiating with suppliers for:

- Period of trade credit before payment of invoices is due
- Credit limit—how much can be outstanding at any one time
- Discount arrangements

- Arrangements for delivery
- Arrangement for return of damaged or unsatisfactory items
- Possible extended credit terms for specific periods, e.g. where a business is seasonal it may be a supplier has to offer extended credit for a period

In some jurisdictions suppliers may charge interest on overdue amounts but this is not necessarily conducive to harmonious relations between supplier and customer. On the other hand, it is not good practice for customers to constantly pay later than the agreed credit terms.

However, many suppliers will offer a discount for early or prompt payment. The loss of the discount by not paying either early or on time may be a lost opportunity to reduce purchasing costs and increasing margin, so this requires careful management. It may be that cash flow considerations make early payment unprofitable, but it should always be considered.

Whether or not to take advantage of supplier discounts depends on several factors such as:

- Will the payment to the supplier increase an overdraft? If so, how much extra interest would be payable?
- If the payment to the supplier is reduced by the discount what use can be made of the funds? What rate of return would the business get on it?

For example, a business might be offered a discount expressed as 2/10 net 45. This means that a 2 per cent discount will be offered if payment is made within 10 days, otherwise the whole amount is due within 45 days. So if the supplier sends an invoice for R1000, the choice is to pay R980 in ten days or R1000 in 45 days. If the business has to borrow the R980 as part of an overdraft arrangement, there will be an interest cost for that amount for the 35 days before the whole amount would have come due anyway.

If interest rates are low this may not be an issue; borrowing R980 at, say, 6 per cent for 35 days is only about R6 but there are other considerations such as could that R980 be put to better use for 35 days than being paid to a customer to save R20?

This is a cash flow decision, which has to be made where substantial discounts are on offer.

Leasing and hire purchase

There is one other form of finance that can be mentioned which is not strictly working capital but is related to the acquisition of assets and that is the option of leasing or hire purchase.

Leasing is a form of rental of assets whereby a business pays a monthly fixed amount for the provision of an asset. This is commonly used for motor vehicles. At the end of a set time period the asset may be exchanged for a new one and a new leasing contract arranged, or the lessee has an option to buy the asset at an agreed amount. These types of arrangement are classed as finance leases.

Hire purchase (HP) is a form of deferred payment, whereby a borrower acquires an asset on deferred terms, paying by instalments over a fixed period until a final payment secures ownership of the asset.

The two types of finance are very similar in essence, the main difference being that with a leasing contract the lessor has possession of the asset but never owns it, whereas under an HP contract the hirer owns the asset once the last payment is made.

In accounting terms assets purchased under HP agreements can be capitalized and depreciated. The interest charged is a revenue expense as it is a finance cost. The outstanding amount of capital under an HP contract is included in current liabilities (if the amount is payable in less than one year) and is gradually written off as payments are made.

The double-entry can be a little complicated so here is an example:

EXAMPLE

A business buys an asset for $10000 on a hire purchase arrangement.
The period of the contract is 4 years and the interest rate is 4 per cent pa. The total sum borrowed is thus $10000 + $1600 interest = $11600

Over 4 years the monthly repayment is $241.66 of which the interest component is:

$$\frac{1600}{11600} \times 241.66 = \$33.33$$

Making the monthly capital repayment $208.33.
So the initial double entry looks like this:

Fixed asset account

Asset purchased with HP	10000		

HP liability account

		Amount due to HP company	11600

HP deferred interest account

Interest due to HP company	1600		

When an instalment is paid there needs to be two transactions:

1 A payment of capital + interest to the HP company
2 A transfer of the interest component from the HP deferred interest account to HP interest expense in the income statement.

The entries look like this:

HP liability account

Instalment paid	241.66	Amount due to HP company	11600

HP deferred interest account

Interest due to HP company	1600	Transfer of interest	33.33

HP interest expense

HP interest expense transferred	33.33		

Cash book

		Instalment paid	241.66

The HP interest expense is written off to the income account at the end of each financial period.

Accounting for leases can be more complex and the full accounting requirement is outside the scope of this module.

The first thing to establish is whether or not the lease is a finance lease or an operating lease.

The difference is that a finance lease transfers all the risks and rewards of ownership to the lessee—in other words, it is as if they own the asset in question. So they have the right to use it for the whole of its effective economic life but they have to insure it, repair it and use it as if it belonged to them. Other indicators that a lease is a finance lease include:

- At the inception of the lease the present value of the minimum lease payments amounts to substantially all of the fair value of the asset
- The lease agreement transfers ownership of the asset to the lessee by the end of the lease
- The leased asset is of a specialized nature
- The lessee has the option to purchase the asset at a price expected to be substantially lower than the fair value at the date the option becomes exercizable

An operating lease is any lease that is not a finance lease. Quite often operating leases are really rental agreements where the lessor still has a responsibility for maintaining the asset. Operating lease costs are expensed to the income statement as they are incurred.

Accounting for finance lease is a little bit more complicated than accounting for HP transactions. In accounting terms, the double-entry initially is:

Dr Non-current assets
Cr Lease liability

The amount to be capitalized is the fair value of the asset (i.e. its cost on the open market) or the present value of the accumulated lease payments. The present value is the value of a future expense or income expressed in terms of today. For example, £100 in two years' time is worth less than £100 today because of the time value of money. Accordingly, a discount rate is applied to discount £100 in two years to today's value—known as the present value. Accordingly, all the future lease payments can be discounted back to a value in today's terms and this is the amount to be capitalized if the fair value of the asset is not known.

When payments are made against the liability, there is a finance cost involved that has to be expensed and this is where the complexity is involved. There are various ways of calculating interest expense. In the example below, we use a simple method but the accounting standard FRS 102 recognizes various actuarial methods, which are outside the scope of this module.

Here is an example of a leasing transaction:

EXAMPLE

On 1 April 20X7, Snodgrass Ltd entered into an agreement to lease a machine that had an estimated life of four years. The lease period is also four years, at which point the asset will be returned to the leasing company. Annual rentals of $5000 are payable in arrears from 31 March 20X8. The machine is expected to have a nil residual value at the end of its life. The machine had a fair value of $14 275 at the inception of the lease. The lessor includes a finance cost of 15 per cent per annum when calculating annual rentals.

How should the lease be accounted for in the financial statements of Snodgrass for the year end 31 March 20X8?

ANSWER

The lease should be classified as a finance lease as the estimated life of the asset is four years and Snodgrass retains the right to use this asset for four years in accordance with the lease agreement therefore enjoying the rewards of the asset.

(continued)

The first thing to do is to capitalize the asset and the associated lease liability. We use the fair value of the asset. Note the lease liability is not the sum of lease payments or a present value—it is simply the credit to make the books balance!

Dr Property, plant and equipment	14275
Cr Finance lease obligations	14275

The asset can be depreciated as if it was owned by Snodgrass—here we use straight line for simplicity.

Dr Depreciation expense ($14275/4 years)	3568
Cr Accumulated depreciation	3568

The finance element of the lease, the interest, is calculated separately. In the first year it is $14\,275 \times 15\% = \$2141$. In Year 2 it is $\$11\,416 \times 15\%$.

Year	Capital	Interest	Payment	Balance
20X8	14275	2141	(5000)	11416
20X9 (b/fwd)	11416	1712	(5000)	8128

Income statement (extract) – 20X8	
Depreciation	3568
Finance costs	2141

Statement of financial position (extract) – 20X8	
Non-current assets	
Property, plant and equipment—net book value **(14275 – 3568)**	10707
Non-current liabilities	
Lease obligation *(amount payable after Year 2, i.e. more than one year)*	8128
Current liabilities	
Lease obligation *(amount payable in Year 2, i.e. within one year)*	
Capital	
(11416 – 8128)	3288

Thus, accounting for finance lease is more complex than accounting for HP transactions because of the need to identify the finance element in the lease.

Both hire purchase and leasing are used extensively to finance asset purchases and are forms of short-term finance that are tailored specifically to the asset being purchased.

Test yourself

1 Which of the following statements are True or False?   ✔   ✔

	True	False
Retained earnings are a form of short-term funding as they arise from year to year.		
Debt factoring requires a well-managed receivables ledger with customers having good credit histories.		
An important part of credit control is an aged creditors report.		
Working capital is simply current assets and current liabilities.		

2 Smoothly Duzzit Ltd has the following operating ratios:

Receivables days	63
Payables days	41
Inventory days	38

What is the operating cash cycle for Smoothly Duzzit?
a) 142 days
b) 60 days
c) 66 days
d) 72 days

3 The following information is available for Winterease Ltd:

Revenues	£96 m
Cost of sales	£53 m

   Extract from the statement of financial position shows the current level of receivables to be £18 million. A benchmark figure from a rival company shows that the average receivables days was 50. How much could Winterease save if its receivables days reached the benchmark figure (to nearest whole £ million)?

4 Which of the following statements are True or False?

	True	False
Just-in-time systems are dependent on suppliers performing to contract.		
Automatic re-order levels are a good way of maintaining optimum inventory.		
Credit control is based on an aged receivables analysis.		
One of the problems with invoice discounting schemes is ending the arrangement.		

5 Hoopla Ltd has bought an asset on an HP arrangement. The period of the contract is 5 years and the interest is 6 per cent p.a. The asset cost R365 000. The monthly interest payment (to nearest whole R) is R1825.   **True/False**

6 Hubert plc has the following entries in its financial statements:

Revenues	€290 000
Cost of sales	€174 000
Inventories	€51 000
Receivables	€51 000
Payables	€49 000

   Calculate the efficiency ratios for Hubert plc and the OCC.

7 The following information is available for PottyCo Ltd:

Revenues	£12 m
Cost of sales	£5 m

Extract from the statement of financial position shows the current level of inventory to be £1.4 million. A benchmark figure from a rival company shows that the average inventory days were 60. How much could PottyCo save if its inventory days reached the benchmark figure (to nearest whole £)?

8 Which of the following statements are True or False?

	True	False
An operating lease and a finance lease are much the same.		
Present value is the value of a series of future monthly payments expressed at today's value.		
It is always best to take supplier's discounts.		
One of the problems with an overdraft is that it is repayable on demand.		

9 Wibble plc has the following entries in its financial statements:

Revenues	$63 m
Cost of sales	$28 m
Receivables	$7 m
Inventories	$4 m
Payables	$3 m

Calculate the OCC for Wibble. Is it:
a) 131.7 days
b) 50.7 days
c) 92.1 days
d) 53.5 days

10 Which of the following statements are True or False?

	True	False
Debentures and loan notes are structural funds but the interest cost is a revenue expense.		
JIT arrangements are able to meet both regular and unexpected demands for product.		
The working capital cycle and the operating cash cycle are more or less the same thing.		
Invoice discounting provides early availability of cash from customers.		

This is the end of the course. We hope that it has been enjoyable and instructive and that the content has provided a good grounding into the fundamentals of financial accounting.

Clearly there is a lot more to learn in more advanced courses, as accounting is a wide and varied subject. However, if the basics are learned thoroughly more advanced topics should hold no terrors for the student as much can be worked out from first principles.

We trust that you have enjoyed working through these modules.

Our companion course is Introduction to Management Accounting.

Test yourself

1 The financial statements of Willebrod Ltd are shown below.

Willebrod Ltd

Income account for the year ended 31 December 20X8

	$000	$000
Revenues		1640
Cost of sales		
Opening inventory	284	
Purchases	1136	
	1420	
Closing inventory	(332)	1088
Gross profit		552
Administration expenses	240	
Selling and distribution costs	190	430
Operating profit		122
Interest paid		(64)
Profit before taxation		58
Taxation		(14)
Profit for the year		44

Statement of financial position at 31 December 20X8

Non-current assets		
Property, plant and equipment		728
Non-current assets		
Inventories	332	
Receivables	528	
Bank and cash	48	
	908	
Non-current liabilities		
Payables	318	
Taxation payable	14	
	332	
Net current assets		576
		1304
Ordinary share capital		600
Reserves		704
		1304

Purchases and sales are all made on credit terms—there are no cash sales.

Required

a) Calculate the operating cash cycle (OCC) for Willebrod.

b) Management consider that the OCC is far too long as forecasts indicate more challenging trading conditions to come. Consultants suggest the following might be appropriate targets:

i.   Inventory days   85

ii. Receivables days   45

iii. Payables days   60

Assuming Willebrod can hit these targets how much additional internal funding will it be able to generate?

c) Suggest three actions Willebrod management can take to implement the change to the shorter OCC.

2 Maxipod plc has terms of trade requiring its customers to pay invoices in full by the end of the month following delivery. Thus, if goods are delivered in January payment is due by the end of February. Maxipod has considered this gives customers up to 60 days to pay if deliveries are at the beginning of a month—and rather less if they are at the end.

Sales revenues of Maxipod are £8 million per year and bad debts are some £50000 per year.

Receivables days have been averaging 70 days because the credit control department has been reduced to one part time person in the interest of 'efficiency savings.'

Maxipod management have come up with a scheme whereby customers are to be offered a 2 per cent discount for payment within 30 days. The accountants estimate that only 50 per cent of customers will take this up with the remainder—who are the slow payers, taking up to 80 days to pay. However, if the plan were to go ahead bad debts would be cut to £25000 per year and there would be administration savings of £5000 per year.

Maxipod is paying for an overdraft at an interest rate of 8 per cent per year.

Required

a) Should the new plan be implemented?

b) Suggest other ways Maxipod could improve its debt collection period and increase its internal funding.

Introduction to Management Accounting

PART II

1 What is management accounting and what is it used for?

In this module we will consider:

- What is the purpose of management accounting?
- Differences between management and financial accounting
- Information needs of managers
- Uses of management information
- IT and management accounting

What is the purpose of management accounting?

The key objective of management accounting is the provision of information that is essential to the successful management of an organization. At every level, management of an organization has to plan, control and make decisions in order to fulfil its function. Management accounting provides the information to help management manage and direct the organization.

It is used for:

- planning—budgets and forecasts
- control—costing and monitoring performance
- decision-making—pricing and scenario planning

which involve:

- keeping score
- identifying problem areas
- problem solving
- scenario building

Management accounting is part of the decision-making process and involves not only the past but the future in the form of budgets and forecasts. Consequently, it utilizes not only financial information but non-financial details such as quantities, hours, units, etc. in order to provide the right level of information for users. For example:

- Supervisory managers on the factory floor may need information on the usage of raw materials, the hours used in production, idle time, outputs and so forth.

- Managers planning production schedules will need information as to the availability of materials and labour.
- Pricing and costing decisions need to be made for products and services, which require production of detailed information, such as the cost of providing one hour of accountancy services, the cost of providing one bed per day in hospital or the cost of providing education to one pupil.
- Senior managers have to produce budgets and forecasts and monitor performance against them.

There is a distinction to be drawn between management accounting and cost accounting. Cost accountants prepare costings, budgets and management data allowing analysis of variances from plans. Management accountants will be more high level, making use of the cost accounting information to help, and participate in, the decision making process by managers. Management accountants will analyze data; cost accountants will collate data. However, we will not draw such a distinction, calling everyone who prepares or is responsible for management information a management accountant.

Figure 1.1 shows the information needs of the different levels of management. Information flows upwards through the organization, as different levels of management require different amounts of information. For example, a supervisory manager might need information about the usage of materials and hours taken to produce a given batch of output, so that manager needs a lot of information about quantities of individual materials and hours worked by staff. A director looking at strategic planning needs summaries and totals so as not to be buried under a wealth of detail he/she doesn't need.

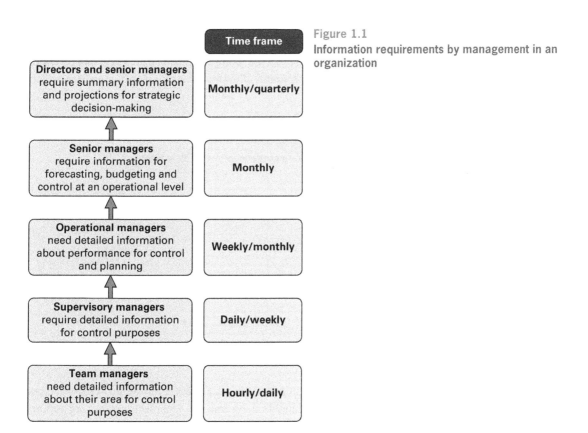

Figure 1.1
Information requirements by management in an organization

The overall objective is the provision of good information, which is:

- Relevant—this involves identifying the users of information and the reasons why they need it. Information can only ever be relevant if it has a purpose and a use.

- Reliable—reasonably accurate for its purpose. For example, it should be free from significant error and should not be taken from an unreliable source.
- Timely—provided in time for the purpose for which it is intended. Information has no value if it is provided too late. Some information, such as information provided for control purposes, may lose value with time.
- Clear and comprehensible—it must be presented in a format easy to understand by managers and staff who may not have accounting training and to whom presentation of financial reports may look daunting.
- Communicated appropriately—information will lose its value if it is not clearly communicated to the user in a suitable format and through a suitable medium. A large amount of management accounting information can, with the right software, be accessible to authorized managers immediately and online.
- Consistent—it must be produced on the same basis from period to period so that comparisons can be made.

Much of the information produced might be used once and discarded, but it is nevertheless important in management of the operational side of the business. Consequently, any management information system used by the organization has to be capable of preparing the right amount of information at the right time to the right people.

> **Stop and think**   Look at your own organization or an organization that you know. What information is required at each level in the organization? Are there any areas where information is needed but is not able to be produced? How important is this?

THE MANAGEMENT INFORMATION SYSTEM (MIS)   Managers make use of management information systems for budgeting and other planning functions. Budget reports can be created and compared with figures of actual revenues and expenses. Many budget-specific accounting software programs allow for creating 'what-if' scenarios, which can also be very complex.

Figure 1.2 shows the structure of a typical financial MIS.

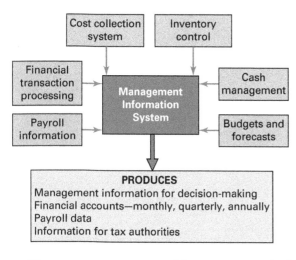

Figure 1.2
Management information system

The management structure of the organization also has important implications for the design of management accounting systems. For example, some organizations are highly decentralized, with decision-making authority delegated to relatively junior managers at lower levels in the organizational hierarchy. In this case, a major role of the organization's management accounting system will be to monitor outcomes and provide feedback to senior managers about the performance of those who have the decision-making authority. Such a role will not be necessary in a highly centralized organization, where senior managers make all the important decisions.

Differences between management and financial accounting

There are considerable differences between financial and management accounting; Figure 1.3 summarizes these.

Figure 1.3 Differences between management and financial accounting

	Financial accounts	Management accounts
Users	External stakeholders	Internal
Time frame	Past—(historical)	Past, present and future
Format	Set out by statute or international accounting standards	Any suitable as decided by users
Information	Financial (mainly)	Both financial and non-financial
Level of detail	Summarized grouping information into specific headings, often decided by accounting rules	Very detailed with analysis of results
Reporting interval	Usually annually, with some quarterly or half yearly reporting	As decided by management. Some information might be produced hourly, daily or weekly as needed by users
Focus	Generally on business as a whole	Report on individual business segments and the business as a whole
Information verification	Larger entities are audited. Financial information prepared and supported by objective evidence	Detailed information extracted and projected without objective evidence

Financial accounting is usually only used for reporting on past events (keeping score) and preparing financial reports to stakeholders including management; it is very much focused externally. Many organizations prepare monthly accounts for management, but these are, essentially, management accounts. They are designed to be used internally as part of management decision-making rather than being used externally by being sent to stakeholders. They are not widely shared.

Anyone looking at a set of monthly management accounts will see that they are not set out in a financial accounting format. For example, an income statement (formerly known as a profit and loss account) might look like this:

	20X8 $000's		20X7 $000's	
Revenues		X		X
Cost of sales		(X)		(X)
Gross profit		X		X
Less: expenses				
Administration costs	(X)		(X)	
Selling and distribution costs	(X)		(X)	
Property costs	(X)	(X)	(X)	(X)
Operating profit		X		X

Whilst this shows the financial position for an accounting period it provides very little detail and shows only a summarized position. There can be comparisons with a previous period but, essentially, because the detail is not reported the information available to managers for decision-making or control is very limited. Consequently, management accounts will show a much greater level of detail.

Compare the layout above with a suggested template shown in Figure 1.4.

Figure 1.4 Management accounts template

Management accounts for X Company Ltd for the month ended 30th June 20X8

Period No: 6

Financial year end date: 31/12/20X8

	Current period			Year to date					
	Actual	Budget	Variance	Actual	Budget	Variance	Annual budget	Projection	Notes on variances
Revenues									
Product A	0.00	0.00	0.00	0.00	0.00	0.00	0.00	0.00	
Product B	0.00	0.00	0.00	0.00	0.00	0.00	0.00	0.00	
Product C	0.00	0.00	0.00	0.00	0.00	0.00	0.00	0.00	
Other income	0.00	0.00	0.00	0.00	0.00	0.00	0.00	0.00	
Total income	**0.00**	**0.00**	**0.00**	**0.00**	**0.00**	**0.00**	**0.00**	**0.00**	
Expenditure									
Materials									
Material A	0.00	0.00	0.00	0.00	0.00	0.00	0.00	0.00	
Material B	0.00	0.00	0.00	0.00	0.00	0.00	0.00	0.00	
Material C	0.00	0.00	0.00	0.00	0.00	0.00	0.00	0.00	
Other	0.00	0.00	0.00	0.00	0.00	0.00	0.00	0.00	
Total materials cost	**0.00**	**0.00**	**0.00**	**0.00**	**0.00**	**0.00**	**0.00**	**0.00**	
Gross profit	0.00	0.00	0.00	0.00	0.00	0.00	0.00	0.00	
Gross profit %	0.00%	0.00%	0.00%	0.00%	0.00%	0.00%	0.00%	0.00%	
Staff Costs—Full-time									
Salaries	0.00	0.00	0.00	0.00	0.00	0.00	0.00	0.00	
Social Security costs	0.00	0.00	0.00	0.00	0.00	0.00	0.00	0.00	
Pension costs	0.00	0.00	0.00	0.00	0.00	0.00	0.00	0.00	
Temporary staff	0.00	0.00	0.00	0.00	0.00	0.00	0.00	0.00	

Staff costs—part-time and contract						
Salaries	0.00	0.00	0.00	0.00	0.00	0.00
Social Security costs	0.00	0.00	0.00	0.00	0.00	0.00
Pension costs	0.00	0.00	0.00	0.00	0.00	0.00
Temporary staff	0.00	0.00	0.00	0.00	0.00	0.00
Total staff costs	**0.00**	**0.00**	**0.00**	**0.00**	**0.00**	**0.00**
Staff costs as % of revenue	**0.00%**	**0.00%**	**0.00%**	**0.00%**	**0.00%**	**0.00%**
Overheads						
Rental costs	0.00	0.00	0.00	0.00	0.00	0.00
Property holding costs	0.00	0.00	0.00	0.00	0.00	0.00
Heat/light/water	0.00	0.00	0.00	0.00	0.00	0.00
Insurances	0.00	0.00	0.00	0.00	0.00	0.00
Telephone and internet	0.00	0.00	0.00	0.00	0.00	0.00
Cleaning	0.00	0.00	0.00	0.00	0.00	0.00
Print/post/stationery	0.00	0.00	0.00	0.00	0.00	0.00
Advertising and promotion	0.00	0.00	0.00	0.00	0.00	0.00
Travel and subsistence	0.00	0.00	0.00	0.00	0.00	0.00
Repairs and renewals—property	0.00	0.00	0.00	0.00	0.00	0.00
Repairs and renewals—equipment and vehicles	0.00	0.00	0.00	0.00	0.00	0.00
Vehicle costs—fuel	0.00	0.00	0.00	0.00	0.00	0.00
Vehicle costs—repairs	0.00	0.00	0.00	0.00	0.00	0.00
Marketing and advertising	0.00	0.00	0.00	0.00	0.00	0.00
General office expenses	0.00	0.00	0.00	0.00	0.00	0.00
Depreciation	0.00	0.00	0.00	0.00	0.00	0.00
Total overheads	**0.00**	**0.00**	**0.00**	**0.00**	**0.00**	**0.00**
Total overheads as % of revenue	**0.00%**	**0.00%**	**0.00%**	**0.00%**	**0.00%**	**0.00%**
Total expenditure	**£0.00**	**£0.00**	**£0.00**	**£0.00**	**£0.00**	**£0.00**
Operating surplus/(deficit)	**£0.00**	**£0.00**	**£0.00**	**£0.00**	**£0.00**	**£0.00**

The management accounts format is much more comprehensive and, as you can see, includes more information than the financial accounts do. In particular, the management accounts format includes:

- current month—actual and budget
- year to date—actual and budget
- budget for the year
- percentages of costs to revenues
- details of individual revenue receipts and cost centre expenditures

In short, management accounts include as much detail as the readers of those accounts need to review the situation to date and initiate any actions necessary once the financial position has been established.

Note that management accounts are prepared on exactly the same basis as financial accounts, including the use of prepayments and accruals. The only difference might be that, due to time constraints, management accounts may be more approximated (e.g. using estimated figures) than a set of properly prepared financial accounts. This is because management accounts are generally finalized within a week or so of the period end so that they are current and form a useful indicator of the financial position of the organization at that point in time.

Information needs of managers

Managers need up-to-date and relevant information to enable them to carry out their functions of planning and control.

This is to enable managers to implement a decision-making process in running the business. Managers, at whatever level in a business, have to make decisions: that is why they are managers. This could be:

- a supervisor allocating work tasks to a team
- a departmental manager deciding on inventory levels, dealing with staffing issues or local promotion and sales strategies
- a board of directors deciding the future course of the business and the resources needed—or not needed— to carry it out

At every level there is a decision-making process, which has to be informed by the information produced by the management accounts. This decision-making process is illustrated in Figure 1.5.

As can be seen from Figure 1.5, the process consists of two phases:

- the planning phase, in which objectives are identified and a plan of action formulated to achieve them
- the control phase where progress towards achieving those objectives is monitored—and this is where the management accounting process comes in

Figure 1.5 contains two feedback loops whereby the actual results inform the progress of the plan. If the actual results are deviating hugely from the plan, the whole plan might have to be changed and a new course of action implemented. If, however, the actual performance is within a tolerance of the planned objectives, it might mean that the plans need a little tweaking rather than a complete overhaul.

This is not a static process and is part of the day-to-day activities of managers at all levels in the organization. It is not confined to strategic decision-making but, for example, might be used by supervisors in a situation where progress towards a target level of achievement is slow, requiring them to reallocate staff so as to get back on track.

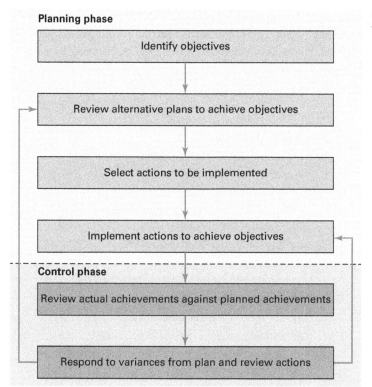

Figure 1.5
The decision-making process

> **Stop and think**
>
> This process of decision-making and feedback loops occurs in daily life as much as at work. Can you think of an occasion when this has applied? For example, a train is cancelled suddenly, causing a planned timetable to be thrown out of alignment. Examine the process of how you would tackle a situation where something like this happened. Will this make you late? Could you change your plans? What if it was a goods train? Where are the feedback loops and how were they applied?

Looking at the decision-making process in more detail provides an insight into the role of management accounting.

IDENTIFY OBJECTIVES This phase of planning can be broadly split into two parts:

- strategic objectives
- tactical or planning objectives

Dozens of management textbooks and courses have been written on strategic and operational planning and it is outside the remit of this module to go into the process in detail; we will look at it more closely in Module 10. Suffice to say, at this stage, that there might be broad strategic objectives such as:

- expanding the business into a new market
- increasing the product range by acquiring a business
- increasing profitability by reducing administration and other overhead costs by 15 per cent

These objectives are probably driven by the overriding objective of management, which is to maximize the return to shareholders by making the biggest profit possible. This might be the overriding objective in the minds of senior management, but is rarely stated; instead it becomes a context in which strategic planning happens.

The strategic objectives then have to be translated into practical action, so looking at the objectives identified above some actions might be as shown in Figure 1.6:

Figure 1.6 Objectives and actions

Strategic objective	Proposed tactical action
Expand the business into a new market	• Identify target market compatible with existing business • Research and identify barriers to entry • Quantify resources needed to enter market • Identify competitors and estimate their reaction
Increase the product range by acquiring a business	• Identify products compatible with existing business or that are suitable for inclusion in the product portfolio • Identify business controlling product • Identify method of acquisition—will any takeover be opposed? • Calculate time frame
Increase profitability by reducing administration and other overhead costs by 15 per cent	• Review all operations and associated costs • Identify suitable areas and consider outsourcing • Review how processes might be affected by cost reductions • Consider staff reaction to reduction in numbers

These broader objectives can be further broken down into specific targets for action, such as 'Increase the sales of Product Y in Region Z by 10 per cent' and so on.

REAL WORLD
Toshiba—it's not all about finance

Toshiba, the Japanese electronics conglomerate, have developed an Environmental Management Information System in order to collect and manage environmental data required to promote environmental management.

The Environmental Management Information System makes it possible to centrally manage and register not only performance data, such as energy consumption required for business activities and the amount of waste generated from these activities, but also environmental accounting information and the results of site environment audits. It covers all consolidated subsidiaries within the scope of management of Toshiba Group (445 companies in FY 2016) and is accessible from countries around the world.

With a view to promoting environmental management, Toshiba Group is working to introduce an environmental accounting approach aimed at collecting accurate data on investments and costs required for its environmental conservation initiatives and analyzing the collected data in order to reflect investment effects and cost benefits in managerial decision making.

Environmental costs are calculated in accordance with the Ministry of the Environment's Environmental Accounting Guidelines 2005. As for environmental conservation benefits, Toshiba Group's environmental accounting assumes four basic concepts:

• competitive advantages
• prevention of potential environmental risks
• external benefits
• internal benefits

Toshiba classifies benefits into four categories based on combinations of these concepts: customer benefits due to reduced power consumption of products; actual economic benefits resulting from reductions in the amount of energy consumed and waste processed; assumed economic benefits estimated to result from reductions in air pollutant emissions; and benefits resulting from preventing potential risks. To assess benefits, they show reductions in environmental impacts in physical amounts and also calculate benefits on a monetary basis.

Source: *Toshiba Group—2016–17*

Uses of management information

We have seen above how management accounting is important in providing information for decision making. We have also seen that differing levels of management within an organization require different quantities and types of information.

Let us recap: to be effective, information supplied to management has to be:

- relevant—to the needs of the user
- reliable/accurate—within a tolerance
- timely—speedily produced so it is not out of date
- clear and comprehensible—it must include all aspects of what is being reported on
- communicated appropriately—it must convey the right amount of information to the right readers
- consistent—it must be prepared on the same basis every time

It also has to be cost-effective to prepare; it mustn't require too much expenditure of time and resources to produce on a regular basis. If it does, then the system from which the date is prepared may have to be changed or upgraded. Modern systems allow easy collection and analysis of data. Supermarkets can track, in real time, things such as stock levels, spending patterns and customer favourites all through data collected at the tills. The relevant cost of this is minimal and the data collected can be changed easily at no extra cost.

Broadly, information within an organization can be analyzed into the three levels:

- strategic
- tactical
- operational information

STRATEGIC INFORMATION   Strategic information is used by senior managers to plan the objectives of their organization, and to assess whether the objectives they have established and defined are being met. Strategic information therefore has the following features:

- It is derived from both internal and external sources.
- It is summarized at a high level, and is directed at senior management.
- It is relevant to the longer term.
- It deals with the whole organization.
- It is both quantitative (i.e. it deals in numbers and facts) and qualitative (i.e. it deals with factors such as market conditions, consumer motivations, predicted reactions to events, etc.).
- It cannot provide complete certainty, given that the future cannot be predicted.

TACTICAL INFORMATION   Tactical information is used by middle management to decide how the resources of the business should be employed, and to monitor how they are being and have been employed. Such information includes:

- productivity measurements (output per direct labour hour or per machine hour)
- budgetary control or variance analysis reports
- cash flow forecasts

Tactical information has the following features:

- It is primarily generated internally.
- It is summarized at a lower level and is directed at middle management as well as more senior management.
- It is relevant to the short- and medium-term.
- It describes or analyzes activities or departments.
- It is prepared routinely and regularly.
- It is based largely on quantitative measures.

OPERATIONAL INFORMATION Operational information is used by frontline managers, such as foremen and supervisors, to ensure that specific tasks are planned and carried out properly. For example, in a manufacturing business the information might be related to quantities used, time spent, machine hours, etc. In some cases information might be required daily or weekly, but more urgent operational information may be required hourly or, in the case of automated production, second by second.

Operational information has the following features:

- It is derived almost entirely from internal sources.
- It is highly detailed, being the processing of raw data.
- It relates to the immediate term, and is prepared constantly, or very frequently.
- It is task-specific and quantitative.

Information is important for management because it provides awareness and understanding of an issue. By helping management to make better-informed decisions, information should contribute significantly to better-quality decision-making.

As we have seen, management accounting is mainly concerned with the provision of financial information to aid planning, control and decision-making. However, the management accountant cannot ignore non-financial influences and should include relevant non-financial information as appropriate.

Non-financial information may relate to matters such as:

- productivity
- quality
- health and safety
- customer satisfaction
- competitive advantage

Non-financial information could have financial consequences. Cost information will be linked to levels of productivity in that increased productivity means higher costs and vice versa. Therefore, non-financial information might include such reports as:

- output of finished product from quantities of raw material
- output for hours worked
- number of customer returns analyzed by type
- accident reports
- benchmark data from competitors

Not all of this will be produced by the MIS, but some might be held dependent on the system. The point is that the management accounting team are responsible for collating and reporting information and providing it to the management to assist them in running the business.

Poor or incomplete information can result in poor decision-making, with the consequent effect on the business. Whilst financial accounting will report what has happened to the business as a result of the decisions made by managers, the management accountants are actively involved in the decision-making process.

IT and management accounting

Management accounting systems are there to provide information that management can use in making decisions. For example:

- Manufacturing plants use these systems to help in costing, pricing and managing the manufacturing process.
- Hotels use such systems to monitor occupancy and look at the costing and profitability of services such as bars, restaurants and guest services.
- Wholesalers use systems to assist in inventory control, pricing, discounting and order tracking.

The main objective of a management accounting system is to capture valuable data that can be used to improve the management and control of a business. Since the internal needs of firms vary, so do their accounting systems, and they must be able to provide the information needed, which may not always be financial. For example, a manager in a factory making biscuits may want to know:

- the quantity of raw materials utilized for a certain product line of biscuits
- how many hours have been spent in manufacture of that line
- the consumption of heat and power
- how many biscuits have been produced
- how many packets of biscuits have been produced and sent to the warehouse for sale

Equally, a manager in a car service firm may want to know:

- average time taken to replace a set of tyres on a car
- cost of replacement tyres
- number of tyres sold

None of this information is financial, but it will eventually translate into accounting information as the production of those biscuits is costed. The management accounting or management information system (MIS) should be able to produce that information.

The impact of information technology has been considerable, and it has raised the potential of management accounting from basic costing and pricing activities to a much higher level. For example, the use of bar coding has made process and inventory control much simpler and quicker and the development of Enterprise Resource Planning Systems (ERPS) has had a huge impact on how information is processed and disseminated in an organization.

An ERPS is basically an integrated set of software applications that control all aspects of information flows within an organization. They are able to access information on all aspects of the business including the accounting function. Consequently, users of the system can gain a picture of what is happening in the organization in real time.

This has had an impact on the work of management accountants because it reduces the requirement for them to gather and collate information. Instead, managers can interrogate the ERPS and obtain the information for themselves. This has freed up the accountants to spend less time on routine information gathering and more time on scenario planning and reporting. Clearly much of this is applicable to larger companies who can afford the time and cost involved in implementing a full ERPS, but ever cheaper software is bringing this kind of application within the reach of smaller organizations.

Test yourself

1 Which of the following statements are true or false?   ✔   ✔

	True	False
Financial accounts are a good source of information for decision-making		
Strategic managers require concise and summarized information as a basis for decision-making		
Cost accountants are responsible for costing products and services and have no other function		

2 A production manager in a factory making moulded plastic toys requires a considerable amount of information. Which of the following might they NOT require?
a. Output of moulded toys by type per month
b. Quantity of plastic raw material used in a month
c. Machine hours used by moulding machines
d. Sales of moulded toys by product per month

3 Which of the following statements about management accounts is/are true?
   i. There is a legal requirement to prepare management accounts
   ii. The format of management accounts is largely determined by law
   iii. They serve as a future planning tool and are not used as a historical record
      A. i) and ii)
      B. ii) and iii)
      C. iii only
      D. none of the statements are correct

4 Managers receive a monthly performance report indicating that costs in the previous month were 15 per cent more than expected. Which one of the following would be the most appropriate response by management to this information?
a. Control action should be taken to deal with the problem and reduce costs by 15 per cent.
b. The reasons for the overspend may be controllable; therefore, they should be investigated with a view to reducing the overspend as much as possible.
c. The reasons for the overspend may be controllable or uncontrollable; therefore, they should be investigated with a view either to reducing the overspend as much as possible or revising forecasts or targets.
d. The overspend indicates that planning targets will not be met, and forecasts should be revised.

5 Management accounting information should be relevant to the user's needs, and should be reliable. It should also be timely, appropriately communicated and cost-effective. Which one of the following best describes the consequences if management accounting information does NOT have these qualities?
a. Management will be forced to rely more on external information.
b. Management will be forced to rely more on financial accounting statements.
c. None of the information will be used by management.
d. The quality of decision-making will be poor.

6 Which of the following is NOT an essential quality of good information?
   a. it should be timely
   b. it should be completely accurate
   c. it should be relevant for its purposes
   d. it should be communicated to the right person

7 Which of the following statements is NOT correct?
   a. Financial accounting information can be used for internal reporting purposes.
   b. Routine information can be used to make decisions regarding both the long term and the short term.
   c. Management accounting provides information relevant to decision-making, planning, control and evaluation of performances.
   d. Cost accounting can only be used to provide inventory valuations for internal reporting.

8 Which of the following statements is/are correct?
   i. A management information system is a term used to describe the hardware and software used to drive a system that produces information outputs that are used by management.
   ii. An objective is a course of action that an organization might pursue in order to achieve its strategy.
   iii. Information is data that has been processed into a form meaningful to the recipient.
      a. i), ii) and iii)
      b. iii) only
      c. ii) and iii)
      d. i) and iii)

9 An example of qualitative data is:
   a. product cost
   b. customer satisfaction response
   c. net income
   d. inventory cost

10 The sales manager has prepared a direct labour plan to ensure that sales targets for the year are achieved. This is an example of:
   a. tactical planning
   b. strategic planning
   c. corporate planning
   d. operational planning

In the next module we will start to look at costs and costing in more detail and how costing is applied to products and services. We will look at how costs are built up and what is included, or not included, in product or service costs.

Test yourself

1 Bikkiepax Ltd has expanded rapidly in recent years. It was started in 20X5 as a kitchen table operation by Dave and Marjorie Sparg making a range of biscuits to sell to local shops. Word spread and soon they had to rent a workshop and buy some industrial machinery to make biscuits in the quantities demanded by customers. In 20X7 they moved into a larger factory unit and started making cakes to add to the biscuit

range. Revenue increased from a few thousand pounds in 20X5 to over £10 million by the beginning of 20X8. They now employ twenty people, including four supervisors, a sales manager and a production manager.

Throughout this period of expansion, Marjorie, who keeps the books among other tasks, has managed with a proprietary accounting package designed for small businesses and a series of Excel spreadsheets for cost information on their biscuit and cake range.

Dave and Marjorie are always looking to innovate their product range and are now looking to add chocolate products to their portfolio. However, they have also realized that they are struggling to obtain information about their existing products, as Marjorie now has so many spreadsheets she's losing track of them. Something needs to be done.

Required

a) What are the dangers of not having good management accounting information in these circumstances?
b) What information might Dave and Marjorie need to make decisions?
c) What information might other managers or supervisors need and at what frequency?

2 Creaky Ltd is a long-established company making wooden furniture and outdoor buildings such as sheds and greenhouses for gardens. The buildings are made in the form of wooden walls and a roof to be erected by the purchaser. They have been making more or less the same products for some twenty years and are well established in the industry. They make a quality product and have never let customers down on delivery. They sell mostly to garden centres, by mail order and through some larger department stores.

They have used the same costing system for twenty years and have simply updated it as the prices of raw materials, mainly wood and preservative paints, go up. They don't analyze the payroll at all as the workforce can make all the products and work all the equipment in the factory to make whatever management decides needs making that week.

They keep a stock of finished product in a warehouse, which management like to have 'in case of a sudden order.' This has never happened in twenty years, as customers generally agree a supply contract during the winter when sales are slow and Creaky supplies them according to a pre-agreed schedule. They can make any extra product quite quickly if this were needed and the inventory in the warehouse had run out.

However, a Swedish company has now started to sell similar products in their market. These are cheaper, of lower quality and come packed flat and boxed with instructions to customers for self-assembly. At first Creaky derided these products and predicted customers would not buy them, but they featured in a well-known gardening programme on TV and are proving increasingly popular.

Creaky's management have decided to fight back. They have looked at their systems and have discovered that all they have is a system that records the build up of product costs and nothing else.

They want to specify a new system.

Required

a) Creaky already has a basic costing system—what else might they need to improve their management information?
b) What strategic decisions should Creaky's management be looking to make and what information might they need to help them with that process?
c) What additional information could be made available to managers and team leaders?

2 What are costs and how are they defined?

Cost behaviour: fixed and variable costs

Costs are, on the surface, simple things. You go to a shop, you buy something, and that is what it costs. So far so good—but what underlies that cost? For example, the cost of a coat is made up of the cost of:

- the material it is made from, including the outer visible material and any lining or filling
- buttons or zips
- badges, logos and labels
- the machine time to stitch it all together
- storing it and transporting it
- costs of the factory it was manufactured in

In other words, a much more complex build up of costs than we first thought.
Let us look more closely at the characteristics or behaviour of costs.

There are three categories of cost behaviour, which are:

- fixed costs
- variable costs
- semi-variable costs

We will look at each of these in turn, but first let us introduce some further terminology related to costing. Costs can be either direct or indirect. A direct cost can be directly attributable to a product or service. For example, the cost of the wood used to make one table can be directly attributed to that table; similarly the cost of the time of the table maker.

An indirect cost is one that is not direct. For example, the salary of a manager supervising table and chair makers cannot be directly attributed to just chairs or tables.

It is important to understand that an individual cost can have a mix of type (direct/indirect) and behaviour (fixed/variable): it could be a direct variable cost, an indirect fixed cost or a semi-variable direct cost, but it cannot be both direct and indirect or fixed and variable. It can be semi-variable, but that's a different thing, which we'll look at later.

FIXED AND VARIABLE COSTS

Fixed costs stay fixed—up to a point. They do not vary with the level of activity in the organization. The simplest example is rent. No matter what activity takes place in a building—whether it is a factory working at full capacity or empty—the cost of the rent stays the same.

We can express this as a graph. This is a graph of fixed cost behaviour.

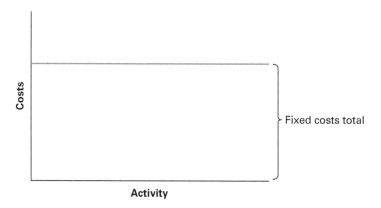

FIXED COST   Other examples of fixed costs might be:

- Salaries—tend to be the same each month when there are no bonus or commission payments
- Insurance—does not vary with output or activity
- Audit fees

There is a slight variation on this, which arises when a certain level of activity is reached. Taking our example of rent—suppose the factory is working at full capacity and the management decide to increase capacity by renting additional factory space. The total cost of rent suddenly goes up by a significant amount. The same point holds true as before: if management can only use part of the additional factory they will still be paying rent on all of it, so rent is still a fixed cost, but it has increased or, in costing terms, it has taken a step.

The graph will look like this:

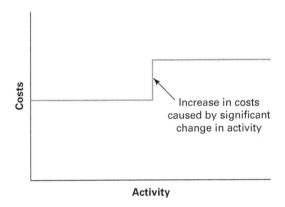

STEPPED FIXED COST We will not worry too much about this in these modules, but you need to be aware of the possibility of a step change in fixed costs.

Variable costs, on the other hand, do vary with the level of activity. The best example of this is raw materials. When a factory is working at full capacity it is buying raw materials for its production at that level. However, if production levels drop, the business does not need as much raw material so it buys less. The cost of raw material directly correlates with the activity/production level.

Looking at variable costs graphically:

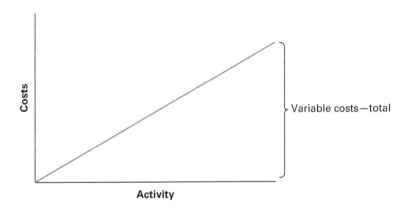

VARIABLE COST As you can see, the costs rise with the activity level—they are fully variable. The unit cost stays the same—it is just the activity level which causes the increase in total cost.

Semi-variable costs are a hybrid of the two. A good example of a semi-variable cost is telephone costs. Traditionally, a landline phone attracted a "line rental" charge which was the same regardless of the use of the phone. This would be the fixed element. As soon as the user made a call extra costs were incurred and would be higher as phone use went up. This is the variable element. Most phone packages still have some sort of fixed element, such as free evening calls, but have variable elements, such as calls to premium rate numbers or calls at peak times.

A graph would look like this:

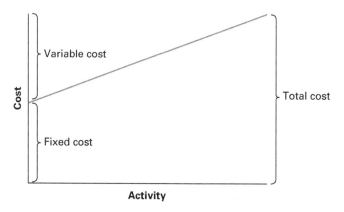

SEMI-VARIABLE COST   Note that the line starts partway up the cost axis of the graph. That is the fixed component and the line shows the variable part of the total cost.

Note two things which are quite important at this stage:

1 These graphs assume a linear relationship; i.e. for variable costs, the level changes in direct proportion to activity, so if one costs €10, two will cost €20, three €30 and so on. However, we know this is not necessarily true as, in some instances, the more that is produced the cheaper the cost of one more becomes, as either bulk discounts from suppliers reduce materials prices or people simply get better at making products—something called the 'learning curve effect.'

    This aspect of cost behaviour is outside the scope of this course but it explains why economists, for example, expect that variable cost lines are curved rather than straight.

2 Much of management accounting—and cost accounting in particular — derives from manufacturing, so it is usual to look at examples based on manufacturing scenarios. Clearly manufacturing, in some countries, is rather less important than it once was, but costing service-based activities is either extraordinarily difficult — how do we cost hospital services or what a university degree costs per student?—or very straightforward, as it is a simple and uncomplicated service, e.g. cleaning windows.

    We will consider costing services later in the course, but for now we will look at examples from manufacturing as this tests all aspects of costing and management accounting.

Stop and think	Consider your personal household expenditure. What part of these are fixed costs and which are variable? If you wished to reduce your cost base, which would be most easy to cut?

Direct and indirect costs

The distinction between direct and indirect costs is quite straightforward. Direct costs relate directly to the costs of providing the activity. So, in manufacturing for example, direct costs would be:

- raw materials or materials for resale
- wages cost of people engaged directly in the activity
- some other costs, such as direct power and heat costs applicable to a specific area

Indirect costs are those that are not direct costs—in other words they are costs not directly related to the activity, such as:

- administration costs
- storage and transport
- selling and marketing
- accounting and management costs

The category of indirect costs includes more cost headings than that of direct costs, so the majority of cost types will be indirect.

Cost centres

Costs tend to be allocated to specific areas known as cost centres. These are for accounting purposes and group together costs in order to calculate the costs of a particular department, activity or area. Each organization will be different but a cost centre could be a whole department (e.g. finance department), a person (e.g. chief exec), a team within a department (e.g. payroll within finance) or a business unit (e.g. a bar in a hotel). For example, inventory control might be a cost centre. Included in it would be:

- costs of individuals working in the area
- cost of machinery or equipment used in the storage area, e.g. forklift trucks
- provision of racking and storage facilities

In other words, everything to do with inventory control.

Having established the principles of cost behaviour, we need to look at how we cost an item and how we allocate costs to specific products or activities. There are two main ways of doing this:

- absorption costing
- marginal costing

Absorption costing principles

Costing a product or service involves two components:

- the direct costs of the product or service
- the indirect costs relevant to the product or service

Allocating direct costs is easy: the constituent components are identified and a cost ascertained from invoices, wages records or similar. It is allocating the indirect costs that is more problematic. These are costs that relate to the wider provision of the business which contribute to making a unit of the product or service. These costs include:

- the costs of the premises in which the product is made
- the costs of allied services such as:
  - administration
  - accounting
  - repairing premises and equipment
  - light, heat and power, except that applied directly to the manufacturing process
  - inventory storage and issue of materials
  - transport
  - depreciation
  - health and safety
  - security, etc.

In other words, costs that need to be incurred but that can't be allocated directly to a unit of product or service are known by various names such as **overheads**, indirect costs or expenses.

What would **not** be included in this cost calculation would be costs that relate entirely to a different part of the process from actual manufacturing, such as selling and distribution costs. It can always be argued that the indirect office costs at least have some bearing on production as they relate to the business as a whole, but selling costs and distribution of the finished product relate only to that; no part of them relates to manufacturing, so they really should not be included as part of the cost of a product. This would leave some costs excluded from the calculations so, in practice and exam questions, you will quite often see them included, but this is strictly not correct.

Accordingly, there has to be a mechanism whereby we can allocate these overhead costs to a unit of product or service, and this is the basis of absorption costing. We group the budget for all these costs together and then allocate them to a unit of the product or service on the basis of a budgeted direct cost—most commonly direct labour hours—using that as an arithmetical way of allocating costs. This is known as the **overhead recovery rate**.

It is called the overhead recovery rate on the basis that if all the overhead is allocated to products and all the products are sold, then the business will have covered all its relevant indirect costs (i.e. excluding selling costs, etc.) through product sales. This rarely works in practice, but is a nice theory.

The best way to illustrate this is by example.

EXAMPLE

Boggis Ltd makes escalators. Each escalator requires:

Direct materials	$60 000
Direct labour	1 000 hours at $25 per hour
Other direct costs	$5 000

Boggis has budgeted to make 150 escalators per year.
The indirect costs for Boggis are budgeted to be $1.5 million.
How do we allocate the indirect costs to the cost of an escalator?

ANSWER

Boggis has budgeted to make 150 escalators per year, each one taking 1000 direct hours.
The total direct hours are therefore $150 \times 1000 = 150000$ hours.
The budgeted overheads are $1.5 million. Consequently, the overheads per hour are
$1.5m \div 150000 = 10 per hour. This is the overhead recovery rate.
Each escalator takes 1000 hours, so the indirect overheads apportioned to each one are $1000 \times $10 - 10000
So the cost of an escalator is:

	$
Direct materials	60 000
Direct labour	25 000
Other direct costs	5 000
Prime cost	90 000
Indirect costs	10 000
Total cost	$100 000

There are three key things to note here:

1 We are using budgeted numbers to build up the cost of an escalator. Why is this? The reason is a practical one. The budget is prepared at the beginning of the financial year and is based on estimates of cost and production levels, etc. It is not practical to wait until partway through a year in order to discover the cost of a product from actual invoices—it has to be costed from day one. If actual costs diverge significantly from the budget, then the budget will have to be changed and the costings will also change but it is assumed that, at least at the outset, the budget will be reasonably accurate.

2 The allocation is made on the basis of labour hours, not labour cost. This is because the cost of labour can vary, not only because of wage rises or bonuses but primarily because of factors outside the business's control, such as tax rates, social insurance or pension contribution rates. Consequently, time spent is seen as a better basis.

   In modern manufacturing where machines or robotics are used as major part of the process, machine hours might be a better substitute for labour hours, but the principles are the same.

3 The total of all the direct costs has been given a name: that of prime cost. This is simply the total of direct costs before any overhead or indirect cost is added.

As we can see the calculations are fairly straightforward; the key to them is establishing the total of direct labour hours forecast and dividing that by the total of applicable budgeted indirect costs to give a cost rate per hour. Once this is done, it can be applied to each unit of the product or service produced.

Stop and think

If selling and distribution costs are to be excluded as they don't relate to production, are there any other costs which might be excluded on the same grounds? What about, for example, audit fees, the cost of receptionists, research and development costs? Are these relevant to the current activity?

ADVANTAGES OF ABSORPTION COSTING

Absorption costing recognizes the importance of including fixed costs in product cost determination and in establishing a suitable pricing policy. The argument is that fixed costs are just as much used in the production of goods and services as variable costs.

Consequently, pricing based on absorption costing ensures that all costs are covered. The argument runs that if pricing policy includes only variable costs this may, in the long run, result in the profit made on those goods failing to cover all the fixed costs. However, there is an important caveat here in that if actual sales of products don't reach budgeted levels, some proportion of costs will remain unrecovered because the overhead recovery rate is based on the budget. We will look at this a little later.

Absorption costing has been recognized under International Accounting Standards for the purpose of preparing external reports and for inventory valuation purposes.

There is no need to separate costs into fixed or variable, which makes accounting somewhat easier.

PROBLEMS WITH ABSORPTION COSTING

Over the years there has been some dispute over absorption costing principles among academics and among management accountants. There are some key points:

It could be argued that including lots of indirect costs, particularly fixed costs, can inflate the price of products or service if they are priced on a cost plus basis: cost of product plus profit equals selling price.

Where, say, labour hours are used to allocate costs, cost allocation is naturally weighted towards products with the highest number of labour hours. This can distort product pricing.

EXAMPLE

R ubble Ltd makes two products, A and B. The details of these products are:

	Product A £	Product B £
Materials	50	50
Labour hours	25	35
Cost per labour hour	10	10

Rubble has worked out that the overhead recovery rate is £15 per direct labour hour. The costs of each product will therefore be:

	Product A		Product B
Materials	50		50
Labour	250		350
Overhead (25 × £15)	375	(35 × £15)	525
	675		925

Thus Product B carries a much greater cost burden simply because it uses more labour than Product A. The cost of labour is exacerbated by the allocation of overhead. This can distort pricing such that Product B appears to be uneconomic if its cost plus price is too high for the market. If management reduce the price, it appears to be being produced at a loss.

Are labour hours the best basis of allocation? If the business uses a lot of robots and machines and very few people, which is becoming increasingly common in manufacturing, this is becoming obsolete. Let us look again at the example from above.

EXAMPLE

U sing the facts in Rubble Ltd from above, suppose Product A uses 30 hours of machine time and Product B uses 20 hours. Machine time is charged at £25 per hour.
The cost allocation is now:

	Product A		Product B
Materials	50		50
Labour	250		350
Overhead (30 × £25)	750	(20 × £25)	500
	1050		900

This now gives a completely different picture, as Product A is now more expensive to produce.

Another problem with absorption costing is the basis of allocation. Which costs to include and which to exclude? Should fixed costs be included, as they don't really relate to production activity, they stay the same whatever happens? Suppose we are costing a heart operation in a hospital. At what point do we stop including overheads?

Is it:

- The overhead costs of the operating theatre?
- The overhead costs of the operating theatre and all the ancillary services such as recovery rooms, intensive care units, etc.?
- The overhead costs of the wing of the hospital the theatre is situated in, which includes the general wards?
- The overhead costs of the hospital as a whole?

Clearly there has to be a consistent basis used and some precise rules, but it is easy to see how an absorption costing basis can, in a complex organization, be used to distort costs or include costs that may not be relevant to the process being costed.

Fixed costs relate to the period for which they are incurred, so should not be carried forwards as part of the inventory valuation. We will look at this in more detail later.

Absorption costing is of little value in decision-making, as it does not require the separation of fixed and variable costs. Accordingly, setting production levels, product mix calculations and make or buy-in decisions is more difficult using absorption costing.

A proportion of overhead costs may not be recovered if output does not meet budgeted levels, or may be over-recovered if output exceeds budgeted levels depending on the levels of actual costs incurred. We look at this in more detail later.

UNDER/OVER RECOVERY OF OVERHEADS   As mentioned above, if output doesn't reach budgeted levels, there may be a balance of overhead costs that is not recovered.

Remember that the overhead recovery rate is based on the budget, so is set at the beginning of the year based on budgeted numbers. If they are not achieved, or the actual costs are much higher than budget, there will be an under- or over-recovery of overhead.

EXAMPLE

Vogon Ltd has a machine shop for producing its goods. During the year the budget was set as:

| Overhead costs | $72 000 |
| Machine hours | 12 000 |

So the overhead recovery rate was $72 000 ÷ 12 000 = $6 per machine hour.
During Period 1, the actual hours were 1030 and the actual overhead was $6450.

	$
So the overhead absorbed by production was 1030 × $6 =	6180
The actual overhead was	6450
Under-recovered	270

This is made up of:
The actual overhead being more than budgeted:

$$\$6450 - (\$72000 \div 12)\, \$6000 = 450$$

Actual hours worked being more than budgeted:

$$1030 - (12000 \div 12)\, 1000 = 30 \times \$6 = \underline{(180)}$$
$$\underline{270}$$

The amount of $270 will have to be written off in the income account as unrecovered cost and represents a loss to the business. Conversely, if costs are lower than budgeted the output will over-recover costs, which represents a surplus, as more cost will be recovered from eventual sale of the product than will actually have been incurred.

So absorption costing, whilst relatively straightforward, does have some major drawbacks. This is why a variation on simple absorption costing known as activity based costing or ABC, was developed and we will look at this in a later module.

For now we will look at an alternative basis of costing that gets around the problem of the recovery of fixed costs in a different way altogether: marginal costing.

Marginal costing principles

Marginal costing principles are relatively straightforward. Instead of concentrating on allocating all overheads to products, marginal costing concentrates solely on variable costs and leaves fixed costs to be covered by what is known as contribution.

Variable cost includes direct costs such as materials and labour, etc., as these vary with production. So what are included are:

- direct costs
- indirect variable costs

but not indirect fixed costs.

Under marginal costing, the variable costs of a product or service are allocated to it and fixed costs are ignored. They are left in total to be covered by the contribution, which will then turn into a profit, so:

Sales value	X
Minus: Variable costs	(X)
Contribution	X
Minus: Fixed costs	(X)
Profit or loss	X

So

$$\text{Sales} - \text{Variable cost} = \text{Contribution}$$

is a formula you have to remember.

Let us look at an example that highlights the difference between marginal costing and absorption costing.

EXAMPLE

Wimpole produces a product with the following budget per unit:

	€
Sales value	12
Direct materials	6
Direct labour	2
Variable overhead	1
Fixed overhead	€12 000 per month
Estimated production volume per month	6 000 units

In Month 4, actual production was 5800 units. What does the costing statement look like under marginal costing and absorption costing principles?

MARGINAL COSTING

		€
Sales value	5 800 × €12	69 600
Variable costs	(€6 + €2 + €1) 5 800 × €9	(52 200)
Contribution		17 400
Fixed overhead		(12 000)
Operating profit		€5 400

ABSORPTION COSTING

		€
Sales value		69 600
Direct costs—materials	6	
—labour	2	
—variable overhead	1	
Overhead (€12 000 ÷ 6 000)	2	
	11 × 5 800	(63 800)
Operating profit		5 800

Under absorption costing, this profit appears to be greater than under marginal costing. However, Wimpole budgeted to make 6000 units and that was the budget and therefore what the overhead recovery rate was based on—but it only made 5800 units, so it has under-recovered overheads in the period.

So, we need to include that in the calculation:

			€
Operating profit			5 800
Under-absorbed overhead			
Fixed overhead budgeted		12 000	
Fixed overhead absorbed	(5 800 × 2)	11 600	(400)
Operating profit			€5 400

So both systems will provide the same bottom line operating profit if the over- or under-absorption of overhead under-absorption costing principles is taken into account.

Complications arise, however, when we have to consider the valuation of inventory, and this produces a different result under the two systems.

Valuation of inventory

As we have seen, the principles of absorption costing require us to include a proportion of fixed costs as part of the cost of a product or service. What this means is that we also have to include it as part of the valuation of inventory when we value that.

Those of you familiar with accounting principles will recall that inventory is valued at the lower of cost or net realizable value.

Cost, in this instance, is based either on variable cost under marginal costing or on both fixed and variable cost under absorption costing. Because the valuation of inventory is different under the two systems, it follows that the operating profit will also vary.

Let us look at an example and we will use the facts in Wimpole, above, except that the production for the month was 7000 units, so 5800 units were sold and 1200 left in inventory.

EXAMPLE

MARGINAL COSTING

			€
Sales value	5800 × €12		69600
Variable costs	(€6 +€2 +€1) 7000 × €9 =	63000	
Less: Inventory	1200 × €9 =	10800	(52200)
Contribution			17400
Fixed overhead			(12000)
Operating profit			€5400

The profit is the same as before as we have accounted for the sales value and the variable cost of the units actually sold. Everything is at variable cost so there is no element of overhead recovery. The inventory value of €10800 will be carried forward to the next period.

Using absorption costing principles the picture is a little different.

ABSORPTION COSTING

Sales value			69600
Direct costs—materials	6.0		
—labour	2.0		
—variable overhead	1.0		
Overhead (€12000 ÷ 6000)	2.0		
	11 × 7000	77000	
Less: Inventory	1200 × €11	13200	63800
Operating profit			5800
Over absorbed overhead			
Fixed overhead budgeted		12000	
Fixed overhead absorbed	(7000 × 2)	14000	2000
Operating profit			€7800

As we can see, the bottom line operating profit on the two bases is different.

	€
Under marginal costing principles it is	5400
Under absorption costing principles it is	7800
Difference	€2400

The profit using the absorption costing basis is higher because the inventory valuation includes an element of fixed costs. The difference between the two bases is:

$$1200 \text{ units} \times €2 \text{ per unit of fixed costs} = €2400$$

Some accountants argue that it is not correct to include an element of fixed overhead from one period in another following period. The counterargument is that these items are inventory; they are not sold until the following period, so that period should reflect the cost of what has been sold, which includes overheads.

Absorption costing is the only acceptable basis for valuing inventory under the formal international accounting rules for financial accounting but as this is management accounting we can value inventory for management purposes on whatever basis we like.

Product costing for decision making

One of the decisions management has to make is the basis of costing a product. Do they include only variable costs and hope for a big enough contribution to cover all the fixed costs, or do they include fixed costs in the product costs? If cost plus pricing is being used, they have to hope that this does not increase the costs significantly in the marketplace so that, when a suitable margin is added, the product is not overpriced.

Clearly, using marginal costing only will give a contribution, but will they sell enough product or service to generate enough contribution in total to cover fixed costs?

Let us look at a business that has three products and compare the results.

EXAMPLE

Nargle produces three components, conveniently named X, Y and Z.
Let us look at the results on both bases:

	Component X	Component Y	Component Z
Selling price per unit	5	6	8
Variable cost per unit	1	4	4
Production for the year	1000	1500	2000

Fixed overhead is £9000 and is apportioned to each product on the basis of production

ABSORPTION COSTING

	Component X	Component Y	Component Z	Total
Sales value	5000	9000	16000	30000
Variable costs	−1000	−6000	−8000	−15000
Fixed costs at £2 per unit (£9000/4500)	−2000	−3000	−4000	−9000
Operating profit	2000	0	4000	6000

(continued)

MARGINAL COSTING

	Component X	Component Y	Component Z	Total
Sales value	5 000	9 000	16 000	30 000
Variable costs	−1 000	−6 000	−8 000	(15 000)
Contribution	4 000	3 000	8 000	15 000
Fixed costs				−9 000
Operating profit				6 000

Whilst the operating profit is the same on both bases, there are two interesting points to be made:

1 What is the point of allocating fixed costs over products in this way using absorption costing? It does not really help with product decision-making, as the fixed costs are the same whatever the sales and production levels and whatever the product mix.
2 The addition of fixed costs has distorted the results for individual products. Under absorption costing principles, Component Y makes no money at all; should it be kept on? Under marginal costing rules, it is clear that it makes a contribution to fixed overhead of £3 000—costs which would have to be shared by the other two components it Component Y was discontinued.

Marginal costing is a much better tool for management decision-making as it highlights what contribution is being made by individual products or parts of the business.

Test yourself

1 Which of the following statements are true or false?   ✔   ✔

	True	False
When comparing profits reported under absorption costing and marginal costing principles, at a time when inventory levels are increasing, profits will be higher and inventory levels lower under absorption costing as opposed to marginal costing.		
When comparing profits reported under absorption costing and marginal costing principles, at a time when inventory levels are increasing, profits will be lower and inventory levels higher under absorption costing as opposed to marginal costing.		
When comparing profits reported under absorption costing and marginal costing principles, at a time when inventory levels are increasing, profits will be higher and inventory levels higher under absorption costing as opposed to marginal costing.		
When comparing profits reported under absorption costing and marginal costing principles, at a time when inventory levels are increasing, profits will be lower and inventory levels lower under absorption costing as opposed to marginal costing.		

2 Huble makes components. In Period 1 it made 17 500 at a cost of £16 each. Three-quarters of these costs are variable, and the remainder are fixed. 15 000 units were sold at £25 each. There was no opening inventory.

By how much would the operating profit based on absorption costing principles differ from the operating profit made under marginal costing principles?

Use the following information for questions 3 and 4

Maginot Ltd makes lawnmowers. One of its departments reports the following information:

Budgeted labour hours	12 500
Budgeted overheads	£118 750
Actual labour hours	11 850
Actual overhead	£121 946

3 What is the overhead recovery rate based on direct labour costs?
a) £10.02 per hour
b) £10.29 per hour
c) £9.50 per hour
d) £9.76 per hour

4 Based on the information above, what is the amount of overhead under- or over-absorbed?
a) £9371 under-absorbed
b) £6679 under-absorbed
c) £3304 over-absorbed
d) £6290 under-absorbed

5 Snaggle Ltd uses a robotic production line and an automated warehouse system, but also employs some 30 people in production and warehousing for its products.

Snaggle has the following information for Period 1:

	£
Budgeted fixed overhead	270 000
Labour hours	5 000
Machine hours	18 000
Units made	4 500
Actual fixed costs	288 000

Snaggle absorbs overheads on the most appropriate basis. What is the overhead recovery rate Snaggle should be using?
a) £54 per hour
b) £16 per hour
c) £60 per hour
d) £15 per hour

6 The following budgeted information relates to a manufacturing company for next period:

Units			$
Production	14 000	Fixed production costs	63 000
Sales	12 000	Fixed selling costs	12 000

The normal level of activity is 14 000 units per period. Using absorption costing, the profit for next period has been calculated as $36 000.

What would be the profit for the next period using marginal costing?

a) $25 000

b) $27 000

c) $45 000

d) $47 000

7 Which of the following statements are true or false?   ✔   ✔

	True	False
Marginal costing is more suitable for management to make operational decisions.		
Semi-variable costs vary directly with outputs.		
The International Accounting Standards accept both absorption and marginal costing as a basis for valuing inventory.		
An under- or over-absorption of overheads occurs under marginal costing when actual activity levels are not the same as budgeted activity levels.		

8 Woody Ltd uses absorption costing to cost its single product but is looking to use marginal costing in future.

The fixed overhead recovery rate is £68 per unit.

At the beginning of Period 3 there were 200 units in inventory and at the end of Period 3 there are 360. If marginal costing principles were applied the operating profit would be:

a) £6800 lower

b) £10 880 lower

c) £10 880 higher

d) £24 480 higher

9 Jonty Ltd absorbs overheads on the basis of units produced. In Period 4, 100 000 units were produced and the actual overheads were $500 000. Overheads were $50 000 over-absorbed in the period.

The overhead absorption rate was:

a) $4.00 per unit

b) $4.50 per unit

c) $5.00 per unit

d) $5.50 per unit

10 Which of the following statements is true or false?   ✔   ✔

	True	False
The overhead absorption rate is used to allocate fixed costs to units of production.		
Direct costs and variable costs are the same thing		
The accounting and finance department could be a cost centre		
The contribution made by an individual product is an indicator of whether it is viable or not		

In the next module we will be looking further at the question of contribution and how it can help management with strategic planning decisions. We will also look at decision-making and the costing of ad hoc and opportunity contracts.

Test yourself

1 Bakeries Ltd makes biscuits and cakes. For one of their best-selling products, a birthday cake, the costs are made up as follows based on a budget of 10 000 cakes per year.

	€ per cake
Ingredients and labour	5
Variable production overhead	3
Fixed production overhead	4
Variable selling costs	1
Fixed selling costs	2
Profit	5
Selling price	20

In Year 3, Bakeries made 11 000 cakes and sold 9000.

Required

i. What would be the profit on an absorption costing basis?
ii. What would be the profit on a marginal costing basis?
iii. Reconcile and explain the difference between the two

2 Pongo Ltd manufactures a specialized chromatograph machine. Because of overseas competition, Pongo has been operating at below full capacity for the last two years.

Pongo has provided the following information:

Budget

	Year 1	Year 2
Annual sales demand (units)	70	70
Annual production (units)	70	70
Selling price per machine	£50 000	£50 000
Direct costs for each machine	£20 000	£20 000
Variable production overheads per machine	£11 000	£12 000
Fixed production overhead	£525 000	£525 000

Actual

	Year 1	Year 2
Annual sales demand (units)	30	60
Annual production (units)	40	60
Selling price per machine	£50 000	£50 000
Direct costs for each machine	£20 000	£20 000
Variable production overheads per machine	£11 000	£12 000
Fixed production overhead	£500 000	£530 000

There was no opening inventory at the beginning of Year 1.

Required

Prepare the actual profit and loss statements for each of the two years using:
i. Absorption costing
ii. Marginal costing

3 Costing and decision-making

In this module we will consider:

- The use of contribution in decision-making
- Contribution to sales ratio or contribution margin
- Break-even
- Cost–volume–profit (CVP) chart
- Limiting factors
- Decision criteria
- Relevant costing

In Module 2 we introduced the concept of marginal costing and the idea of contribution. Contribution is critical to what we are about to look at so, as a reminder:

$$\text{Contribution} = \text{Sales} - \text{Variable costs}$$

There is no mention of fixed costs. What a business is looking to do is to make sufficient contribution from all the products and services it sells to cover all its fixed costs and, hopefully, make a profit.

One of the key aspects of management accounting is contribution analysis and we can use this to establish some key parameters in order to assist management in decision-making.

The use of contribution in decision-making

Let us look at a couple of scenarios to illustrate the use of contribution in decision-making. We will do this by example.

EXAMPLE

H orko makes a single product.

Budgeted production is 10000 units and fixed costs are $150000. The business can sell all it makes:

	$ per unit	$ per unit
Selling price		100
Costs		
Materials	15	
Labour	10	
Variable production costs	5	
Fixed costs	15*	45
Profit		55

Based on total fixed costs of $150000 over 10000 units

Budgeted sales are 10000 units.
The gross profit is clearly $10000 \times \$55 = \$550000$

DECISION SCENARIO 1

Suppose sales volume fell by 20% — what would be the effect on gross profit?
What it would NOT be is $20\% \times \$550000 = \$110000$. Why?
The reason is that the cost of the product includes fixed costs, which do not vary with the level of activity. So a fall in volume of 20% would not affect fixed costs at all. What we have to do is look at contribution.
The contribution is:

	$	$
Selling price		100
Variable costs		
Materials	15	
Labour	10	
Variable production costs	5	30
Contribution		70

So on sales of 10000 units, the total contribution will be $700000.
If there is a reduction of 20% in volume, the contribution will fall by 20%, assuming variable costs fall directly in line with activity levels. So, the reduction in contribution will be:

$$\$700000 \times 20\% = \$140000$$

The total contribution will now be $700000 − $140000 =	$560000
From which we can deduct total fixed costs of	$150000
Giving a revised profit of	$410000

(*continued*)

We can check this by reworking the figures:

	$ per unit	At 10000 units	At 8000 units
Selling price	100	1 000 000	800 000
Costs			
Materials	15	(150 000)	(120 000)
Labour	10	(100 000)	(80 000)
Variable production costs	5	(50 000)	(40 000)
Contribution		700 000	560 000
Fixed costs	15	150 000	150 000
Profit		$550 000	$410 000

So, sales have dropped by 20% resulting in a drop in contribution of 20%, but profit has fallen by 25%. This is because fixed costs are inflexible and consequently have a greater effect on falling profits.

DECISION SCENARIO 2

We can look at contribution in another way using the same figures as above.

Supposing we have the same contribution as before for our product:

	$	$
Selling price		100
Variable costs		
Materials	15	
Labour	10	
Variable production costs	5	30
Contribution		$70

Fixed costs are again $15 per unit based on budgeted fixed costs of $150 000.

Suppose we revise our target and we now want to make a gross profit of $760 000 instead of the $550 000 in our original forecast? How many units will we have to sell?

A revised contribution has to cover both the target profit and the fixed costs, so it will have to be:

Target profit	760 000
Fixed costs	150 000
Required contribution	$910 000

If each unit makes a contribution of $70, we will have to sell $910 000 ÷ $70 = 13 000 units

Management will have to decide if this is feasible and:

- whether or not they have the resources to make and sell 13 000 units
- whether the market is big enough for them to sell 13 000 units
- how the competition will react to the increased sales activity

By using contribution in this way, management can evaluate a range of scenarios without the complexity of trying to include fixed costs in the decision-making. For example, using the figures above, only if profits fell to below $150 000 would management have cause to be seriously concerned; at that point they would not be covering their fixed costs so the business would therefore be making a loss.

The key to this kind of financial modelling is to remember that profit is made up of costs, which behave in different ways. Where decision-making scenarios involve changes in activity levels, contribution is the best way to evaluate the effect of changes.

Contribution to sales ratio or contribution margin

This ratio, often abbreviated to the C/S ratio, and also sometimes referred to as contribution margin, represents the percentage of the selling price, which is represented by contribution. It is the contribution per unit expressed as a percentage of the unit sales price.

The formula is:

$$\text{Contribution/sales ratio} = \frac{\text{Contribution per unit}}{\text{Unit sales price}}$$

This can be expressed as either a ratio or a percentage. Why is this relevant? If we know what percentage contribution per unit is, we can go on to calculate the total turnover required to break even.

EXAMPLE

Janet sells a product for R1 000 (South African rand) each. The variable costs of each unit of product are R800. Janet's fixed costs are R90 000.

What is Janet's break-even turnover?

The contribution per unit is (1000 − 800) R200.

The selling price is R1000 which is a contribution/sales ratio of:

$$\frac{200}{1000} = 1{:}5, 0.20 \text{ or } 20\%$$

What does this mean? What it means is that for every R1 of turnover, 80% will go towards variable costs leaving 20% available to cover fixed costs and profit. So we can use the C/S ratio to calculate a target turnover in the same way as we used contribution in the example above.

Janet's break-even turnover is:

$$\frac{90\,000}{0.20} = R\,450\,000$$

We can check this is correct by calculating that, at R1000 each, she has to sell 450 units. As each one makes a contribution of R200, this is a total contribution of $450 \times R200 = R90\,000$, which equals Janet's fixed costs, so she will break even.

However, Janet is not making any profit to live on, so we can include that in our calculations. Let us look at another example.

EXAMPLE

Sound Monster Ltd presses and sells CDs for local acts at £5 each. Pressing and packaging costs £2 per CD. Sound Monster's fixed costs are £30 000 per year, but they make about £9000 per year from renting out space and contributions from the acts themselves.

How many CDs must Sound Monster sell to stay in business?

ANSWER

Sound Monster has to cover $£30\,000 − £9000 = £21\,000$ of fixed costs from its sales of CDs.

Each CD makes a contribution of £3, so they must sell $£21\,000/£3 = 7000$ each year.

We can expand this slightly to include a target profit so as to establish a sales target for the business.

(continued)

Suppose the owner of Sound Monster wants to make a target profit of £12000 as well as covering fixed costs. Again, we can use contribution to calculate the required sales volume.

Sound Monster has to raise a total contribution of:

Fixed costs	21 000
Target profit	12 000
Total contribution required	£33 000

On the basis of a contribution per unit of sales sold of £3 per CD, Sound Monster will have to sell 11 000 to cover all the fixed costs and make a £12 000 profit. The managers of the business then have to decide if this is possible.

Using the C/S ratio we can check this conclusion. Each CD has a C/S ratio of:

$$3 \div 5 = 0.6$$

To hit a target contribution of £33 000, Sound Monster must generate a turnover of:

$$\frac{33000}{0.6} = £55000$$

That is 11 000 CDs at £5 each. As they each have a contribution of £3, we know this is the correct answer.

The C/S ratio gives us a target of sales in terms of income to be earned, whereas the contribution per unit gives us the number of units required to break even or achieve a target profit.

This relationship between selling price, variable cost, contribution and fixed costs must be clearly understood. It can then be used to calculate a range of different values in different scenarios.

For example, it can be used to calculate an optimum selling price or a required sales level.

EXAMPLE

Joe has fixed costs of £20000. His variable product costs are £12 each and he thinks he can manufacture 2000 units. He wishes to make a profit of £10000 in the year. What should his selling price be?

Joe must cover fixed costs of £20000 and also a profit of £10000, a total of £30000.

He must therefore make a contribution of £30000/2000 = £15 per unit.

His selling price then should be:

Contribution	15
Variable costs	12
Selling price	£27

Joe can then decide if this is a feasible selling price given the market for his product.

Stop and think

This is a useful tool for decision-making. Consider if it could be used to look at a range of scenarios within set parameters.

Break-even

It is important for managers to know where their break-even position is in terms of units sold or total revenue.

The point is that once the break-even position is reached, everything else is profit, so the sooner that is achieved, the longer the business has to generate surpluses. What is the break-even position? Quite simply, it is the point at which:

$$\text{Revenues} = \text{Variable costs} + \text{Fixed costs}$$

In other words, there is no profit or loss, but total costs are covered by revenues.

This can be illustrated graphically. We can look at this in stages:

Firstly, the starting point is fixed costs. As we saw in Module 2, fixed costs are there whether the business sells no products or services or lots of products and services. It is the base cost from which the business operates and, as we saw in Module 2, these can be represented graphically thus:

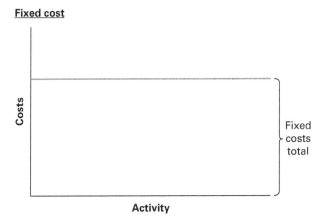

What we then need to do is to add a variable cost line to give us a graphical representation of total cost. The starting point is fixed cost, and variable costs rise with activity levels. We can add a variable cost line to the graph thus:

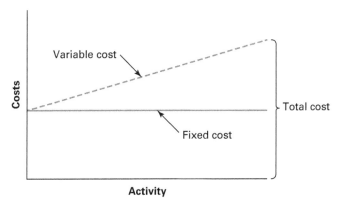

As we can see, the addition of the variable cost line starting from the level of fixed cost now gives us total cost.

Finally, we need to add the revenue line. This starts at zero, of course, as with no activity there is no income. The graph then looks like this:

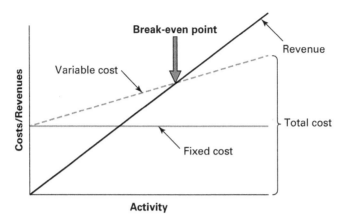

The break-even point is where the revenue line crosses the total costs line (i.e. the line representing variable costs, which starts at the level of fixed costs).

We can look at this way without using graphs and by using the concept of contribution.

At the break-even point:

$$\text{Total contribution} = \text{Total fixed costs}$$

so that there is neither a profit nor a loss.

If total contribution is:

$$\text{Volume} \times \text{Contribution per unit}$$

it follows that at the break-even point:

$$\text{Contribution per unit} \times \text{Volume} = \text{Total fixed costs}$$

So we can calculate a break-even volume by:

$$\text{Volume} = \frac{\text{Total fixed costs}}{\text{Contribution per unit}}$$

This little formula gives us a very useful number. The break-even volume of sales can be established relatively easily.

BREAK EVEN EXAMPLE

Forty Towers is a hotel in a popular tourist area, with 25 rooms available. It charges £50 per room per day to guests for a bed and breakfast service. It has the following costs:

	£
Fixed Costs (per day)	320
Room Cleaning (per room when used)	10
Laundry (per room when used)	15
Breakfast (per room when used)	5

How many rooms each day must be filled to break even?

$$\text{Break even volume is found at} = \frac{\text{Total fixed costs}}{\text{Contribution per unit}}$$

Total fixed costs are £320 and contribution is £50 − £30 = £20.
Thus, break even is £320/£20 = 16 units, ie rooms.

MARGIN OF SAFETY

The margin of safety is simply the difference between the break-even point and the budgeted level of activity. This indicates the problems a business might encounter if there is a fall in demand, and is usually shown as a percentage of budgeted sales.

EXAMPLE

Budgeted sales	120 000 units
Selling price	£12 per unit
Variable costs	£6 per unit
Fixed costs	£600 000

The break-even volume is thus:

$$\frac{\text{Fixed costs}}{\text{Contribution per unit}} = \frac{600\,000}{6} = 100\,000 \text{ units}$$

The margin of safety is thus 120 000 − 100 000 units = 20 000, or 20% of budgeted sales.

Consequently, if actual sales volumes fall below 20% of budgeted sales the business will not be covering its fixed costs and will be operating at a loss.

We can show this on a graph. It is the difference between the revenues at the break-even point A and the actual revenues at point B:

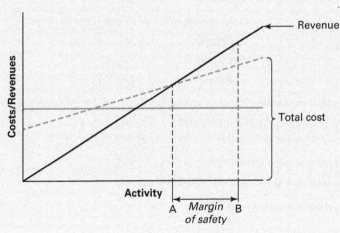

Stop and think   If actual turnover is approaching break-even turnover, what might management do in the short term to increase the margin of safety?

Cost–volume–profit (CVP) chart

The relationship between fixed costs, contribution and margin of safety can be best illustrated by a different kind of break-even chart called a cost–volume–profit or CVP chart. This is presented differently from the conventional graphs shown above, because it shows both profits and losses so it is prepared in the form of a horizontal T shape.

This shows the level of activity on the horizontal or X axis and the profit or loss on the Y axis thus:

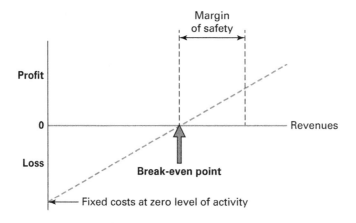

Here is an example.

The following cost information is given for Huge Productions:

	£
Sales	120 000
Variable costs	60 000
Contribution	60 000
Fixed costs	40 000
Profit	£20 000

We need to plot the graph in the form of a horizontal T. We do this by establishing the parameters.

The horizontal line is the revenues line on a scale of 0—120 000.

The vertical line, which shows profits and losses, has a scale which runs from:

- minus £40 000 (fixed costs at zero activity hence maximum loss) to
- profit of £20 000 (as calculated at revenues of £120 000)

We can now draw in the diagonal line, which links the maximum loss of £40 000 to the profit of £20 000 at revenues of £120 000.

If this information is reproduced on a CVP chart it looks like this:

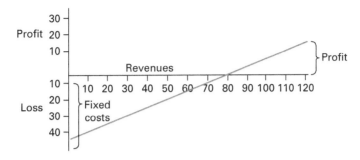

The chart shows that the break-even point is sales of £80 000.
This can be verified by calculation thus:

$$\text{Contribution to sales ratio} = £60\,000/£120\,000 = £0.50$$

$$\text{Fixed costs} = £40\,000$$

$$\text{Break-even point} = £40\,000/0.50 = £80\,000$$

Using this method we can create a graph which, at any given level of sales, will tell us on the basis of budget assumptions whether we are in profit or loss.

This graph can be amended for changes in cost levels as time progresses.

ASSUMPTIONS

All of the relationships outlined above hold true, providing certain conditions are fulfilled.

The relationship between revenues, contribution and profit is constant, provided that:

- volume is the only factor influencing the level of variable costs
- sales prices stay constant
- this is only true between certain parameters, known as the 'relevant range,' above or below which either cost structures or selling prices change. Recall fixed costs may actually be 'stepped', resulting in a jump in costs at a certain level of output. Looking at this is outside the scope of this module, but learners should be aware that the conditions as set out may only be true within certain parameters.

Limiting factors

What has been considered so far are examples of scenarios involving a single product and we have assumed the required numbers of product can be made and sold. However, most organizations have more than one product and, in reality, it is not always possible to make and sell unlimited quantities of product or service.

In most cases there is some form of limiting factor such as a limit on the amount of resources available or a limit to the amount of product that can be sold.

It may be, for example, that there are only a limited number of labour or machine hours available, or that the supply of raw materials is limited. In the case of a range of products, with differing contributions, the challenge to management is then to decide which product should have the biggest benefit of the limited resources.

Management must maximize the contribution earned by the organization as a whole. When there are limited resources, management must look to maximize the use of those resources. Consequently, what managers will try to do is to maximize the contribution earned from using that scarce resource.

Managers will not simply look at which product gives the most contribution per unit, but how much contribution is generated per unit of scarce resource; this is the key to this kind of decision-making.

Stop and think   If possible, look at the pricing policy in your organization. How are prices calculated? Is it always cost plus or are other factors in play? Is contribution a significant factor in pricing?

EXAMPLE

Big Spanner Ltd manufactures three products: A, B and C.

Product	A	B	C
Costs			
Materials at £2 per kilo	10	12	8
Labour at £7 per hour	7	14	10.50
Variable overhead at £4 per hour	4	8	6
Total variable cost	21	34	24.50
Selling price per unit	25	40	29.50
Contribution	4	6	5

Sales of each product are estimated to be 3000 units.
There are a maximum of 10 500 labour hours available.
How much of each product should Big Spanner make to maximize their contribution?

ANSWER

The first thing to establish is whether or not there is a limiting factor. In this case there is, because it isn't possible to make all products to their full sales potential, so:

Product A requires	3000 × 1 hr	=	3000 hrs
Product B requires	3000 × 2 hrs	=	6000 hrs
Product C requires	3000 × 1.5 hrs	=	4500 hrs
			13 500 hrs

There are only 10 500 hours available.

At first glance the obvious solution might be to make as much of product B as possible, as this shows the biggest bottom line contribution, followed by Product C and finally product A. This however ignores the fact that there is a limiting factor, i.e. the amount of labour hours available.

Looking at the issue of resources it is, in fact, possible to make two of Product A for each one of Product B so it would be more accurate to consider the level of contribution earned in relation to the amount of the limiting factor consumed by each product.

We can calculate this quite easily:
Contribution per unit of limiting factor

Product	A	B	C
Contribution	4	6	5
Labour hours required	1	2	1.5
Contribution per labour hour	4	3	3.33

In fact, to maximize contribution, Big Spanner should maximize production of Product A, followed by C, and then B. Production would therefore be:

		Hrs	Cumulative hours
Product A	3 000 × 1hr	3 000	3 000
Product C	3 000 × 1.5 hrs	4 500	7 500
			10 500

So Big Spanner's contribution is maximized by making as much as possible of Products A and C and none of Product B.

Decision criteria

Remember that all these decision-making techniques involving contribution analysis are a production solution. They are not market or sales focused but help managers consider costs at varying levels of production. There are several other factors that should be taken into account by management in their decision-making. For example:

- Cost plus pricing (cost + profit = selling price) may not be appropriate in the marketplace. Competitors who can manufacture or source more cheaply will force prices down until below a break-even position so the organization is selling at a loss. This cannot be sustained. Consequently, the market price of a product must also be a consideration in addition to the one calculated by the cost accountants.
- Marketing and sales issues may outweigh an optimum production decision. In the above example, Product B might be the most popular one, so not making it may affect the market for other products made by Big Spanner adversely.
- Sales of other products may follow sales of Product B, i.e. people might buy Product B and then buy additional products, in the same way as the purchaser of a razor subsequently buys blades to fit it.
- Suppliers might be annoyed if production patterns are altered and orders to them are affected.
- Competitors might react to an attempt to maximize sales of one particular product by reducing prices of rival products to Products A and C.
- Workers may react if work patterns are changed as a result of new production plans.

  All these factors would have to be considered before final decisions are made.

Relevant costing

In Modules 2 and 3 we looked at conventional costing approaches involving the use of absorption and marginal costing. We have looked at the use of contribution analysis in assisting management to decide on pricing, sales targets and best use of limited resources. However, there is another aspect to decision-making and that is looking at costs that are relevant only to the decision being made.

In many cases an opportunity presents itself for a business to take a sales opportunity, say a contract they have tendered for or an unsolicited enquiry. The question then becomes:

- Do we or do we not take up the opportunity?
- What sort of consideration should we give to this? What factors are involved?
- What costs would we incur?
- What is the alternative if we don't take it on?

In making the decision, management should consider certain key aspects that do not relate at all to conventional costing approaches. These are:

Sunk costs—this is money already spent on goods or services so that expenditure is irrelevant to any decision being made. For example, if a new contract opportunity is being considered and it involves use of a product that the company already owns, has no alternative use for and has no scrap value, then this is a sunk cost. Similarly use of assets that are already owned is a sunk cost; the cost is there whether or not the decision is made.

Incremental costs—these are new costs that will have to be included in the factors relating to the decision; they are relevant costs because they arise as a result of the decision. For example, if a contract means that an additional machine has to be hired in at a cost of $1 000, this is an incremental cost.

Opportunity cost—this is the cost of giving up a viable alternative course of action. For example, a product might be used in a contract that would bring in a contribution or it could be scrapped for £500. The use of the product in the contract means that the opportunity to scrap it is lost. The contract therefore involves a sacrifice of an opportunity cost, so this too is relevant to the decision-making process.

Fixed costs should be ignored in the calculations as they are the same whatever decision is made; they are therefore not relevant costs.

Let us look at an example illustrating these concepts.

EXAMPLE

Lettuce Ltd is considering a contract which requires the use of materials and labour. The contract value is £125 000. It requires the use of 1000 kg of material Z. Lettuce has 600 kg in inventory already at a cost of £5 per kg because material Z is used in the production of Lettuce's main product, the Snibber. The resale value of material Z is £4 per kg and its replacement price is £6 per kg. It is easy to obtain.

It also requires 200 kg of material Y. Lettuce has this in inventory. It has no other uses as it was used on a now discontinued product, so Lettuce was going to scrap it for £150.

In addition, the contract would require four skilled workers. They would be recruited on a one-year contract at a cost of £30 000 per employee. They would be supervised by one of Lettuce's existing managers, who costs £50 000 per year. This would involve about 20% of their time.

However, instead of recruiting new employees, Lettuce could retrain some existing employees who currently earn £30 000 per year. The retraining costs would be £15 000, and they would need to be replaced at a cost of £100 000.

Should Lettuce accept the contract?

ANSWER

MATERIALS

The relevant cost of the materials to be included in the contract is £6 150. The reason is that if Lettuce were to take up the contract, all it would have to do would be to buy the materials at the current price. Although Lettuce already has 600 kg in stock, this is used in the main product and would thus have to be replaced at a cost of £6 per kg, and the remaining 400 kg would have to be purchased on the open market also at £6 per kg.

The scrap value of product Y, £150, is an opportunity cost which is also relevant to the decision, as this is now not available if Lettuce takes the contract.

LABOUR

The relevant cost of labour is more complicated to work out as there are two possibilities.

a) Recruit

	£
4 employees at £30000 incremental cost	120000
Manager—not relevant—employed whether or not the contract goes ahead	–
Total cost	120000

b) Retrain

	£
Cost of retraining—incremental cost	15000
Replacement staff—incremental cost	100000
Total cost	£115000

So the total of relevant costs is:

Materials	6150
Labour	115000
	121150
Contract value	125000
Surplus	£3500

The result is a surplus, so Lettuce should accept the contract.

The key to this process is to remember that what is being costed is the decision, not the actual process.

Only factors relevant to the decision are included—anything other than those are unnecessary and should be excluded.

Clearly, again there are other factors which are relevant—for example, the workforce can't necessarily be moved around like pieces on a chessboard, there may be more problems with materials than anticipated, but overall the principle is a sound one—costing the decision rather than the contract.

Test yourself

1 Alia has a small workshop making tables. She has worked out that her personal living costs amount to £17000 per year. Her main product has a variable cost of £110 and sells for £250. The fixed costs in her shop are £25000. What is Alia's minimum sales level?
   a) 300 units
   b) 179 units
   c) 122 units
   d) 280 units

2 Binky is a manufacturer of paint. It makes four products—Red, Green, Blue and Yellow.
   The contribution from each product is:

Red	£7
Green	£10
Blue	£20
Yellow	£12

Each colour is in high demand, but some require more ingredient than others. All require Zorbo, a
colour enhancer in the following proportions:

Red	1 kg
Green	2 kg
Blue	2.5 kg
Yellow	3 kg

Zorbo is expensive and in limited supply, so the manufacturers don't want to buy more than they need.
Which product should have its production maximized?

a) Red
b) Green
c) Blue
d) Yellow

3 Wilmot Ltd makes three products. The details are

	Product A $	Product B $	Product C $
Selling price	25.00	15.00	30.00
Variable cost	10.00	8.00	15.00
Fixed cost	7.00	3.00	9.00
	17.00	11.00	24.00
Profit	8.00	4.00	6.00

Grummit offers to make products A, B and C for the following prices

Product A	$11.00
Product B	$ 7.50
Product C	$16.50

Should Wilmot accept Grummit's quote and buy all or some of the products in?

a) All of them
b) Product A only
c) Product B only
d) Product C only

4 Madelaine produces a product. The details are

	£
Variable production cost	8.00
Fixed production cost	5.20
Variable selling costs	2.50
Fixed selling costs	1.80
Profit	4.50
Selling price	22.00

She budgets to sell 1000 units.

How many units must she sell to break even?

a) 452

b) 609

c) 500

d) 427

5 Yellowstand has material which originally cost R450 000. It could be sold for scrap for R125 000. If it was reworked it could be sold for R175 000, the cost of the rework would be R75 000. What would be the incremental effect of reworking and selling the material?

a) A loss of R270 500

b) A loss of R25 000

c) A profit of R50 000

d) A profit of R100 000

6 Willow has fixed costs of £20 000 per year. Its single product sells for £20 per unit and its contribution to sales ratio (C/S ratio) is 40%.

What is Willow's break-even point in units?

7 Alan makes a product which he sells for €16 per unit. His fixed costs are €76 800 per month and the product has a C/S ratio of 40%.

In Period 2 actual sales were €224 000.

What was Alan's margin of safety in units?

a) 2000

b) 6000

c) 8000

d) 12 000

8 Beckett Ltd makes three different products. The details per unit are as follows:

	A12	A14	A21
Selling price	25	20	23
Variable cost	10	8	12
Weekly demand (units)	25	20	30
Machine time (hours)	4	3	4

Machine time is limited to 148 hours per week.

How should Beckett maximize its profit?

a) Make 30 units of A21 and 7 units of A12

b) Make 20 units of A14 and 22 units of A12

c) Make 25 units of A12 and 16 units of A14

d) Make 20 units of A14 and 11 units of A12

9 Poddlers sells shoes. It sells 25 000 pairs annually.

   The selling price per pair is £40 and they cost £25 to buy in.

   Poddlers has annual fixed costs of:

Salaries	100 000
Rent	40 000
Other administrative costs	100 000

   In order to boost sales, the manager has introduced a £2-per-pair sales commission.

   How many pairs of shoes would have to be sold to earn a net profit of £10 000?

   a) 16 000

   b) 18 462

   c) 19 231

   d) 16 667

10 Wimble is currently about to undertake a special contract. It requires 250 hours of skilled labour at £10 per hour and 750 hours of unskilled labour at £8 per hour.

   Skilled labour is in short supply and all the labour used on this contract will be at the expense of another contract, which generates £12 of contribution per hour after charging labour costs. There is plenty of unskilled labour and Wimble has calculated that it has 1200 hours of excess unskilled labour available with no work for them to do. However, it has a policy of no redundancies.

   What labour cost should Wimble take into account when reviewing this contract?

In the next module we will look at activity-based costing and understand how this contributes to a more accurate costing of products and services but also has some significant issues that have to be considered.

Test yourself

1 Polidor Ltd has been asked to tender for a contract for which it has production capacity due to a temporary downturn in demand for its products.

   The contract is to manufacture 20 000 electronic devices, which require quite an intricate assembly operation. The price of each device is €75.

   The specification is:

Assembly	4 hours
Component X	4 units
Component Y	3 units

   There would be the need to hire in a specialized assembler unit at a cost of €180 000 for the duration of the contract.

The assembly is a highly skilled operation and the workforce is currently under-utilized, hence the availability of Polidor's production capacity. The business is retaining its workforce on full pay in anticipation of an increase in demand for its products as a new product line is being developed. There is a sufficient number of skilled workers to undertake the project and Polidor pays them €15 per hour. A specialist assembler consultant will be hired in for the duration of the contract at a cost of €20 000.

Component X is used by Polidor for other products, so is readily available. 50 000 units are currently held in inventory. Component Y was bought in by mistake for a product line that never materialized. Polidor has 100 000 units in stock, which, if not utilized, will have to be sold off at a secondhand value.

Inventory control has supplied the following information about components X and Y:

	Component	
	X	Y
	€ per unit	€ per unit
Historic cost	4	10
Replacement cost	5	11
Net realisable value	3	8

Additional costs relating to completion of the contract are estimated to be €10 per item.

Required

You have been asked to evaluate the figures and advise the board of Polidor whether or not to accept the contract.

2 Becker Ltd is considering several proposals to improve its profitability.
A summarized profit and loss statement for the previous year is:

	$,000	$,000
Sales (50 000 units)		1000
Direct materials	350	
Direct wages	200	
Fixed production overhead	200	
Variable production overhead	50	
Administration overhead—fixed	180	
Selling and distribution overhead—fixed	120	(1100)
Loss		(100)

The board is considering three options:

1) Pay the sales team a commission of 10% and thus increase sales to reach a break-even point.

2) Reduce selling prices by 10%, which is estimated will increase sales volume by 30%.

3) Increase direct wages by 25% per hour as part of a productivity deal. It is hoped this will increase production and sales by 20%, but will necessitate an increase in advertising costs of £50 000.

Required

You have been asked to make the necessary calculations and comment on each of these three proposals.

4 Activity-based costing (ABC)

In this module we will consider:

- Approaches to ABC
- Cost pools and cost drivers
- ABC versus marginal costing
- ABC in service industries
- Benefits of ABC
- Disadvantages of ABC
- Decision-making using ABC

We saw in earlier modules that costing principles involve providing information to management so they can make decisions that will enable the business to recover all of its overheads and make a net profit.

In Module 2 we looked at the principles of absorption (or full) costing and an alternative approach involving marginal costing and the use of contribution. In Module 3, we saw how contribution can be used as part of decision-making.

In this module we are returning to the principles of absorption costing, but in a different way.

Approaches to ABC

Traditionally, a straightforward absorption costing system tended to throw all the indirect overheads, whether fixed or variable, into one big cost pool and then allocate them to products or services using some measure such as labour hours or machine hours. This was fine in a situation where:

- production was labour-intensive
- indirect costs were low relative to direct costs
- markets were less competitive so cost plus pricing was a reasonable approach

Nowadays the reverse of this tends to be true.

- production is becoming less labour-intensive and more mechanized
- indirect costs are much higher in proportion to direct costs
- markets are extremely competitive and are consumer-driven

Production is becoming increasingly mechanized with the introduction of robot machines, automated warehousing, etc. Increasingly the role of the workforce is to service the machines with labour, only carrying out activities which are too costly or difficult to mechanize.

From a company perspective this is a good thing, as machines only require servicing, not holidays; can work 24 hours a day without complaint and don't object to working in noisy, cramped or badly lit conditions. It has been noted that in some circumstances, machines can work in the dark and the cold, and a factory space only needs to be heated and lit when humans enter it, the Real Life example below illustrates.

This has increased power and servicing costs and, of course, increased depreciation and funding costs for organizations investing in machinery for production and servicing.

REAL LIFE
The rise of the machines

At one Fanuc manufacturing plant in Oshino, Japan, industrial robots produce industrial robots, supervised by a staff of only four workers per shift. In a Philips plant producing electric razors in the Netherlands, robots outnumber the nine production workers by more than 14 to 1. Camera maker Canon began phasing out human labour at several of its factories in 2013.

This 'lights out' production concept—where manufacturing activities and material flows are handled entirely automatically—is becoming an increasingly common attribute of modern manufacturing.

In part, the new wave of automation will be driven by the same things that first brought robotics and automation into the workplace: to free human workers from dirty, dull, or dangerous jobs; to improve quality by eliminating errors and reducing variability; and to cut manufacturing costs by replacing increasingly expensive people with ever-cheaper machines.

Today's most advanced automation systems have additional capabilities, however, enabling their use in environments that have not been suitable for automation up to now and allowing the capture of entirely new sources of value in manufacturing.

Source: *McKinsey & Company—'Automation, robotics and the factory of the future'. Sept 2017*

Indirect costs are increasingly a major proportion of overall costs as companies face:

- increasing administration costs
- higher staff welfare costs
- health and safety demands
- increasing power and serving costs

The increasing use of automation and the reduced involvement of direct labour in production are lowering direct costs, thus swinging the balance of total costs away from direct cost towards indirect costs, to a much greater extent than previously. Better quality control and less waste have ensured direct materials costs are as low as possible, and innovations such as just-in-time (JIT) production techniques have kept warehousing costs to a minimum for manufacturers.

Markets are increasingly becoming globalized and the ability of companies to source from many places in the world has meant that, for example, clothing retailers can source production in Vietnam or China where labour costs are low. It is no longer necessary for production facilities which service retail operations to be within driving distance. Modern communications have made international working much easier, so price competition is fierce.

This is as true of service-based industries as for manufacturers, and concern is building about the increasing use of Artificial Intelligence (AI) in service-based industries to replace expensive humans. Increasing investment in capital assets and high levels of indirect costs are an increasing feature of the activities of service providers. Consumers have the advantage of being able to compare prices and to buy online from overseas businesses, thus increasing competitive pressures.

Increasing choice has resulted in increasing pressure on margins and prices. This meant traditional absorption costing approaches became to be seen as inappropriate with too much emphasis on linking costs to production output and not considering what was causing the cost. Consequently, businesses have developed a much more sophisticated way of allocating overheads to products than simply using one cost pool and one basis of allocation but rather considering the activities undertaken to provide their goods or services—and this is activity-based costing (ABC).

We will look at costing services later but, for now, we will examine the principles of ABC using a straightforward manufacturing situation.

Consider a traditional absorption costing basis for two products A and B that we saw in Module 2, and which is worth repeating here.

EXAMPLE

Rubble Ltd makes two products A and B. The details of these products are

	Product A £	Product B £
Materials	50	50
Labour hours	25	35
Cost per labour hour	10	10

Rubble has worked out that the overhead recovery rate is £15 per direct labour hour. The costs of each product will therefore be:

		Product A		Product B
Materials		50		50
Labour		250		350
Overhead	(25 × £15)	375	(35 × £15)	525
		675		925

Thus Product B carries a much greater cost burden simply because it uses more labour than Product A. The cost of labour is exacerbated by the allocation of overhead. This can distort pricing such that Product B appears to be uneconomic if its cost plus price is too high for the market. If management reduce the price it appears to be being produced at a loss.

As we can see, the use of one driver for costs is crude and can distort the product costing. What is needed is a more accurate and sophisticated way of allocating overheads to products.

Cost pools and cost drivers

ABC is a step by step process as shown by Figure 4.1.

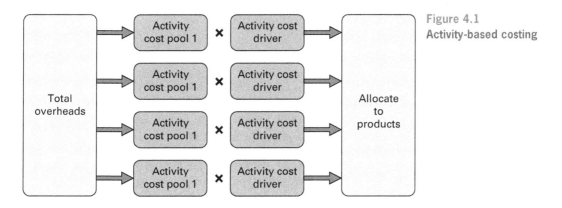

Figure 4.1
Activity-based costing

The basic idea is that, instead of seeing indirect overheads as one big pool and using one big driver (labour or machine hours), we break the overheads down into smaller pools and use a series of more relevant drivers to allocate them to products.

Note that we are still allocating the same pool of overheads—just doing it in a different way.

So a step-by-step approach is:

STEP 1   The first step on the road to an ABC system is to identify the activities being costed. How does the organization produce its products or services? What stages do they go through in order to be completed and sold to a customer?

This process enables the business to identify where costs originate and to group costs together by activity so that they can be allocated to product costs based on the usage of that activity by each product.

Included in the analysis may be a need to review all indirect costs for a direct cost component. For example, the business might decide that machine cleaning is an indirect cost. However the costs of cleaning can be attributed to specific machines so those costs might be reallocated to the costs of operating that machine and charged to the product accordingly.

STEP 2   The next step is to group costs of activities into activity cost pools. Consider the cost basis of a product. Looking at all the activities and costs associated with it, we might find they include a broad range of costs:

- Direct materials
- Direct labour
- Machine X
- Machine Y
- Assembly
- Materials purchasing costs
- Production and quality control costs
- Inventory control costs
- Transport and distribution costs
- Selling and marketing costs
- Administration costs

We can establish a series of activity cost pools so that all indirect overhead costs are allocated and included into a cost pool.

For example, materials purchasing costs may in fact be three activities:

- Purchase materials
- Receive materials into inventory
- Allocate materials to production

We establish the cost of these activities and that is the cost pool for materials purchasing activity.

This exercise can be carried out for each activity identified. Some will be very straightforward so that one activity equals one cost, but others may be a combination of costs as shown above.

STEP 3   Once we have the cost pools we need to allocate to them an activity cost driver. Now this can be a complicated process in real life, and the key to it is to look at the type of activity which generates all the cost. It will be necessary for the organization to have done a lot of basic work in identifying the precise nature of each cost driver. For example, it must know how many purchase orders it issues.

Let us look at the materials purchasing cost pool above.

Looking at what costs might be in there, we can see what has created that cost. So for materials purchasing the activity might be broken down further into separate cost pools as follows:

Activity	Cost driver
Purchase materials	Number of purchase orders
Receive materials into inventory	Number of purchase orders
Allocate materials to production	Number of production runs

Each cost pool has its own driver. The driver is related to the usage of that activity by the product. So, Product A might require 20 purchase orders, Product B 10 purchase orders and so on. The costs are allocated differently to each product on the basis of usage.

STEP 4   The next step is to allocate the costs to production on the basis of the cost driver. Once this has been established the costs allocated into the cost pool purchase materials can be divided by the number of purchase orders to give a cost per order, which can then be allocated to a product on the basis of the number of orders issued for that product.

Cost pool ÷ Number of units of cost driver × Number of orders issued = Cost allocated to product

The best way of illustrating this is by means of an example.

EXAMPLE

Megablast has identified the following activities and cost drivers as part of its production activities:

Activity cost pools Activity	Step 1 Activity cost $	Activity cost driver	Units of cost driver	Cost driver rate $
Materials purchasing				
Purchase materials	450 000	Number of purchase orders	5 000	90.00 per order
Receive materials into inventory	300 000	Number of purchase orders	5 000	60.00 per order
Allocate materials to production	200 000	Number of production runs	2 000	100.00 per run

General support

Production scheduling	50000	Number of production runs	2000	25.00 per run
Set up machines	600000	Number of production runs	2000	300.00 per run
Quality control	100000	Number of inspections	1000	100.00 per inspection

Megablast has identified:

- the various activities associated with production
- cost per activity—this is the cost pool
- how many units of each activity Megablast incurs, i.e. how many machine hours, purchase orders, inspections, etc.—this is the cost driver
- a cost per activity—this is the basis of allocation to the product

It now has to allocate these to products based on how much of each activity is used by each product.

		Step 2			
Activity	Cost driver rate	Quantity of each activity used by Product A	Quantity of each activity used by Product B	Cost to Product A $	Cost to Product B $
Materials purchasing					
Purchase materials	90.00 per order	250	400	22500	36000
Receive materials into inventory	60.00 per order	250	400	15000	24000
Allocate materials to production	100.00 per run	5	2	500	200
General support					
Production scheduling	25.00 per run	5	2	125	50
Set up machines	300.00 per run	5	2	1500	600
Quality control	100.00 per inspection	2	1	200	100
Total overhead costs				39825	60950
Units produced				75	25
Overhead cost per unit				$531	$2438

The overheads have been allocated to each product by multiplying the cost driver rate by the number of times it applies to each product.

Consequently, overheads are allocated to products on the basis of activity and not on an arbitrary basis that may bear no relation to the actual way the product is produced.

It is worth comparing the outcome of an ABC approach with that of a conventional absorption costing approach.

EXAMPLE

Brittle manufactures four products A, B, C and D.
Product information is as follows:

	Output units	Number of production runs	Materials cost per unit €	Direct labour hours/unit	Machine hours/unit	Total direct labor hours
A	20	4	40	2	2	40
B	20	4	160	6	6	120
C	200	10	40	2	2	400
D	200	10	160	6	6	1200
		28				1760

Direct labour cost per hour is £10

Overhead costs are:

Variable costs	7160
Set up costs	20840
Planning and scheduling	18200
Materials handling	15400
	61600

Let us look at the costing of each product using a conventional absorption costing approach.

Absorption costing approach

	A €	B €	C €	D €	Total
Direct materials	800	3200	8000	32000	
Direct labour	400	1200	4000	12000	
Overheads*	1400	4200	14000	42000	
	2600	8600	26000	86000	123200
Units produced	20	20	200	200	
Cost per unit	**130**	**430**	**130**	**430**	

Based on €61600 ÷ 1760 = €35 per labour hour

Let us now do the same exercise based on ABC principles
The cost drivers for the various cost pools are as follows:

Cost pool	Cost driver
Variable costs	Machine hours
Set up costs	Number of production runs
Planning and scheduling	Number of production runs
Materials handling	Number of production runs

Activity-based costing approach

Working out the costs based on the cost pools:

Variable costs	7160	÷	1760 = €4.07 per machine hour*
Set up costs	20840	÷	28 = €744.28 per run
Planning and scheduling	18200	÷	28 = €650 per run
Materials handling	15400	÷	28 = €550 per run

Note that the number of labour hours and the number of machine hours are the same.

So the costs on an ABC basis* are:

	A	B	C	D	
	€	€	€	€	Total
Direct materials	800	3200	8000	32000	
Direct labor	400	1200	4000	12000	
Variable costs*	162	488	1628	4884	
Set up costs*	2977	2977	7442	7442	
Planning and scheduling	2600	2600	6500	6500	
Materials handling	2200	2200	5500	5500	
	9139	12665	33070	68326	123200

(Some costs rounded down for presentation)

Units produced	20	20	200	200
Cost per unit	**457**	**633**	**165**	**342**

Difference in costs

Product	Absorption costing €	ABC cost per unit €	Difference €	Difference in total €
A	130	457	327	6540
B	430	633	203	4060
C	130	165	35	7000
D	430	342	(88)	(17600)

The results of this exercise suggest that there are problems with a conventional absorption costing approach. It tends to:

- Under-allocate overheads to low volume products (A and B) and over allocate overheads to high volume products (D in particular)
- It under-allocates overheads to smaller products, e.g. A and C with only 2 hours of direct labour each and over allocates them to larger products. e.g. C and particularly D.

ABC versus marginal costing

As we saw in Module 3, marginal costing techniques are very useful for short-term decision-making. However, marginal costing too has its problems when it comes to product costing.

Marginal costing techniques divide costs into fixed and variable, and they ignore fixed costs in favour of establishing a contribution from each product to offset against fixed costs.

However, a failure to consider fixed costs may be deceptive and lead to incorrect product pricing if fixed costs become variable according to another cost driver than production volume. For example, the cost of a supervisor would be a fixed cost when linked to production volume; but under activity-based costing the cost would vary based on the time spent in different production areas with more complex products requiring more of the supervisor's time.

If that is the case then there is an argument for including some element of these fixed costs as part of the ABC process.

ABC in service industries

ABC is probably more relevant in service industries than in manufacturing, as a large proportion of the costs of a service are likely to be made up of overheads. Direct materials costs, for example, are likely to be minuscule in service delivery, although direct labour costs may not be.

In a business where:

- overhead costs are high
- overheads are not just driven by output volume
- there is a wide variety in the product range
- the overhead component varies widely in the product range

The use of an ABC approach may well be able to contribute to an increase in the organization's profitability. Thorough analysis of costs and a clear identification of cost drivers will enhance efficiency and make operation of an ABC system relatively straightforward.

For example, let us look at the possible cost pools and cost drivers for a hotel.

Activity	Possible cost driver
Cleaning rooms	Number of rooms or number of guests
Maintenance of common areas	Area per square metre
Laundry costs	Number of beds occupied

The hotel can break its activities down into key areas and, within those some sub-areas; for example, guest accommodation involves reception staff, room servicing, laundry, etc. so cost pools can be developed along those lines and costs identified related to those activity pools.

As most of the costs for a hotel are fixed, this might give the hotel a much better allocation of costs between different areas and enable hotel management to understand and review the processes being carried out in those areas.

Benefits of ABC

The main benefit of ABC is that the more precise identification and allocation of costs enables managers to look at product and service pricing in a more accurate way. In a highly competitive marketplace, product pricing is critical and managers need to know whether or not a product is profitable at a given price point. For example, if the market decides that a reasonable price for a product is, say, £100, managers have to know whether or not this price point will give them a profit on sale after apportionment of overheads. ABC gives managers a good idea of what is driving overhead costs.

If the company is using a cost plus pricing model and the product is labour or machine intensive, a traditional absorption costing system may well allocate a high level of fixed overheads to it, so pricing it at £110. On that basis managers would either try and cut the profit margin or, possibly, withdraw the product from the market. However, under an ABC system the product cost may be better allocated over products, resulting in a product price of £90 so making it more competitive.

One of the key features of ABC is that it looks at processes not just costs. Consequently, this forces managers to review processes in order to establish activity cost pools and cost drivers, and this can enhance productivity and improve the flow of processes in the workplace. Unnecessary tasks and duplicated processes can be identified and dealt with before any cost decisions are made. Questions to be asked might be:

- Why are we carrying out this activity?
- What benefit does it bring to the organization?
- How can we reduce the costs of engaging in this activity?

The use of an ABC system forces the management to look at its operations, its activities and its costings in a great deal of detail so that they inevitably carry out a thorough overhaul of their cost structures. This is likely to promote efficiency and careful cost control, again leading to improved productivity.

Changes in levels of activity can be identified. For example, a more efficient purchasing system might lead to a reduction in purchase ordering and materials processing, so staff savings could be identified.

Identifying the supporting activities which indirect costs represent can assist in forward planning. Managers will be able to cost new products more accurately and will be able to calculate the effect of new products on prices and costs.

Disadvantages of ABC

The fundamental criticism of ABC is that analyzing activities and allocating overheads is a very time-consuming and costly process.

The costs of setting up an ABC system can be high and so are the costs of maintaining it. Cost drivers have to be amended if processes change, cost pools have to be revisited regularly and the allocation rates of overhead to product changed if costs change significantly.

Where there are many products, all of which are quite similar, the need for an ABC system may not be apparent as there may be little difference between allocating overheads on an ABC basis and a traditional approach. However, supporters of ABC argue that the review of costs and activities is worthwhile doing, even if a full ABC system is not, ultimately, installed.

There are other problem issues such as:

- Some quite arbitrary cost apportionments might still have to be made for overheads which don't really fit into any cost pool such as rent, building depreciation, etc.
- These may not be hugely significant in the context of overheads as a whole.
- Can one cost driver represent the behaviour of all the items in a cost pool?
- There cannot be too many cost pools and cost drivers, otherwise the system becomes complex, expensive and unmanageable; there have to be compromises.
- Unless costs can be related to some form of output, it is difficult to establish a cost driver. What drives professional fees costs, e.g. audit fees?

So whilst ABC is seen as a more sophisticated and accurate way of apportioning costs than simple absorption costing, there are still problem areas where management will have to exercise judgement in order to achieve a form of apportionment.

Decision-making using ABC

Both ABC and absorption costing share the same criticism when it comes to their use in decision-making and that is that they are both based on past costs. As we have seen, absorption costing is based on a budget that is, undoubtedly, rooted in the past; ABC uses historic data to establish its cost drivers.

Accordingly, critics say, this negates the ability to make predictions. However, promoters of traditional costing approaches consider that the past is a guide to the future, so analysis of costs and volumes from the past is likely to provide a good indication of future trends.

However, perhaps the biggest problem with these traditional absorption costing-type approaches is that they are quite cumbersome to deal with and far from flexible when it comes to scenario building. However, the information database gathered through the review of operations and the establishment of cost drivers can be used in planning scenarios.

For example, management will set a budgeted production level or activity level. From this, the cost pools can be budgeted, the cost drivers estimated and the relevant staffing and activity levels predicted. A financial budget can be prepared based on ABC principles using the information gained from past activities.

The problem with this is that, whilst that remains a valid process assuming one year is to be the same as the next, it does not help with scenario building or where processes and activities undergo a significant change from one year to the next.

For example, suppose management has adopted an ABC approach and has gathered information about a particular process applied to a product that required ten staff to carry it out. The business then buys a machine which replaces eight staff. All of the previous information is redundant and new information has to be calculated and costs prepared. This can be quite a cumbersome process.

Marginal costing, which does away with the need to allocate fixed overheads, is considered to be a much more user-friendly approach to scenario planning as there is no need to consider a proper allocation basis for fixed overhead. Whilst the use of marginal costing may lack some precision because of the lack of full cost allocation to products, it is a much more commonly-used tool in planning and forecasting than ABC or, indeed, simple absorption costing.

Test yourself

Use the following information for questions 1–4

Lollipop Manufacturing has the following information:

Activity	Overhead costs €	Cost driver €	Product Poppo €	Product Lillo €
Machining department				
Set up costs	200 000	Number of setups	200	50
Machining	700 000	Machine hours	20 000	15 000
Packaging department				
Assembly	300 000	Direct labour hours	40 000	60 000
Inspection	180 000	Number of inspections	120	60

1 Using an absorption costing basis with labour hours as a cost driver, what is product Poppo's share of total overhead?
   a) €324 000
   b) €416 000
   c) €638 000
   d) €552 000

2 Using ABC principles, what is the overhead rate for the machining department with machine hours as the cost driver?
   a) €39.43 per machine hour
   b) €25.71 per machine hour
   c) €13.71 per machine hour
   d) €20.00 per machine hour

3 Using ABC principles, what is product Lillo's share of the packaging department overhead?
   a) €270 000
   b) €580 000
   c) €240 000
   d) €380 000

4 Using ABC principles, how much overhead cost is allocated to product Poppo?
   a) €580 000
   b) €800 000
   c) €950 000
   d) €670 000

5 Which of the following are true or false?   ✔   ✔

	True	False
There has to be a cost driver for every item in a cost pool.		
The cost driver for a cost pool for payment processing in a bank is likely to be the number of payments processed.		
A cost driver is a cost which varies with production levels.		
Absorption costing allocates costs in an arbitrary way which can produce distorted costings.		

6 Zoom produces products for the aircraft industry. Details of its three main components are:

	A £ per unit	B £ per unit	C £ per unit
Selling price	200	185	170
Direct materials	50	40	35
Direct labour	30	35	30
Units produced and sold	10 000	15 000	18 000
Number of purchase requisitions	1 200	1 800	2 000
Number of machine hours	240	260	300
Costs			
Materials cost pool	£1 500 000		
Machine operation cost pool	£1 200 000		

Using ABC principles, calculate the profitability of each product.

The most profitable product is:

a) A

b) B

c) C

7 Which of the following are true or false?   ✔   ✔

	True	False
ABC can be expensive and time-consuming to implement.		
ABC would be no use if the business only produced a single product.		
ABC is only of use in a manufacturing environment.		
ABC generally produces the same result as absorption costing but is much more elaborate.		

8 Tutu produces two products: the Twizzle and the Bendo.
The following information is available about them:

	Twizzle	Bendo
Budgeted production (units)	800	000
Machine hours per unit	8	12
Number of production runs required	10	15
Number of quality inspections	3	1
Total production set up costs	R300 000	
Total inspection costs	R120 000	
Other overhead costs	R220 000	

Other overheads are absorbed on a machine hour basis.

Using ABC, what is the cost of one Bendo?

a) R373.40

b) R353.40

c) R323.40

d) R355.55

Use the following information for questions 9 and 10

Big Music manufactures three types of keyboard: Beginner, Standard and Advanced. The company, which uses ABC, has identified five activities (and related cost drivers).

Each activity, its budgeted cost, and related cost driver is identified below:

Activity	Cost £	Cost driver
Material handling	225 000	Number of parts
Material insertion	2 475 000	Number of parts
Automated machinery	840 000	Machine hours
Finishing	170 000	Direct labour hours
Packaging	170 000	Orders shipped
Total	£3 880 000	

The following information pertains to each product line for next year:

	Beginner	Standard	Advanced
Units to be produced	10 000	5 000	2 000
Orders to be shipped	1 000	500	200
Number of parts per unit	10	15	25
Machine hours per unit	1	3	5
Labour hours per unit	2	2	2

9 Using ABC principles, what is the per unit cost of the Standard model keyboard?

10 Using ABC principles, what is the per unit cost of the Advanced model keyboard?

In the next module we will look at another costing system, that of standard costing. This takes a rather different approach to costing than both absorption and marginal costing and is closely allied with budgeting and forecasting.

Test yourself

1 Baggie and Dim Ltd is a company that specializes in the design and installation of clinical waste disposal systems, mainly for the health sector. The pricing policy of the company is long established and was developed by the previous financial controller of the company. It involves the inclusion of all direct costs (equipment and labour installation costs) with an added mark up of 50 per cent of total direct cost to establish the selling price. This allows an adequate amount of money to be generated to cover company overheads and contribute to net profit.

The company has been approached to bid for two contracts for NHS Trusts in the region. These are Keltie NHS Trust and Farflung NHS Trust.

The sales director has expressed concerns that the current method of pricing may be leading to cross subsidization between contracts and uncompetitive pricing. She has recently attended a finance conference and is particularly interested in ABC.

She has asked you to investigate a proposal to replace the current 50 per cent markup with overhead costs that have been determined using ABC. She is keen to maintain a net profit margin of 20 per cent.

You have the following information about the two potential contracts:

Contract:	Keltie	Farflung
Direct costs:		
Direct materials	£262 500 (975 items)	£180 000 (615 items)
Direct labour	15 000 hours at £19.50 per hour	9 000 hours at £16.50 per hour

Other information:
- The Keltie contract will take 1920 design hours in total from the design team. The Farflung contract will take 930 design hours.
- Each contract will need a number of supervisor visits to the site and these will amount to 45 visits for Keltie and 15 visits for Farflung.
- Keltie NHS Trust is 80 miles from the main factory and offices and Farflung NHS Trust is 45 miles.

You have done some initial work on ABC systems and have ascertained the following information in relation to overhead costs:

Activity	Cost pool cost per annum £	Cost driver	Cost driver units per annum
Site management	1125000	Direct labour hours	450000
Design offices	1012500	Design hours	37500
Site supervisors	555000	Miles travelled	277500
Post installation			
Equipment inspection	120000	Items purchased	30000
Purchasing department	157500	Items purchased	22500
Payroll function	112500	Direct labour hours	450000

Required

a) Calculate the prices to be quoted for each of the two jobs based on the current method of pricing.
b) Calculate the amount of overheads that should be allocated to each contract using ABC.
c) Assuming that the net profit margin of 20 per cent is maintained, calculate and comment on the revised price for each contract.

2 Brickies Ltd manufactures a range of products used in the building industry. It uses two processes: Heavy 1 and Press. All the products are manufactured in batches and the current pricing policy is to allocate direct costs plus overheads based on a labour hour rate then add a markup of 35 per cent. Recent overhead costs are:

	Cost per month £	Monthly volume
Heavy 1 process cost	96000	480 hours
Press process cost	44800	1280 hours
Set up costs	42900	260 set ups
Handling costs	45600	380 movements
Other overheads	50700	
	£280000	

The top two products actually manufactured by Brickies, as opposed to being bought in for resale, are concrete beams of different lengths. The smallest, the Minibeam, is produced using the Heavy 1 process and the second, the Maxibeam, is made using the Press process.
Details for the products are:

	Minibeam	Maxibeam
Monthly volume	1000 metres	500 metres
Batch size	1000 metres	50 metres
Processing time per batch		
Heavy 1	100 hours	
Press		25 hours
Set ups per batch	1	2
Handling charges per batch	1 movement	5 movements
Materials cost per metre	£16	£15
Direct labour per metre	½ hour	½ hour

Direct labour is paid at £16 per hour

Other overheads are allocated using direct labour hours.

Required

- Calculate the price per metre for the Maxibeam and the Minibeam using conventional absorption costing methods.
- Calculate the price per metre of the Maxibeam and the Minibeam using ABC methods.
- Comment on the results and the implications for Brickie's management.

5 Standard costing

Standard costing is somewhat misleadingly named, as it is essentially a control technique rather than a method of costing in the way that, say, absorption or marginal costing is. It is, in reality, a part of budgetary control. We'll look at budgets in more detail in Module 7 but, for now, the key point to remember is that standard costing is designed to aid management in discovering why things did not turn out the way they had forecast they would in the budget—which could be either better or worse.

So standard costing relates the actual performance of an organization to the one the management forecast when it set its budget at the beginning of a financial period. The differences between the actual results and what those results should have been, had the standards been achieved, are known as variances. In this module we will look at how variances relating to materials, labour costs and fixed overheads are calculated.

This module considers the basic variances. Other variances can be calculated but they are beyond the scope of this text.

REAL LIFE
The view from the experts
In February 2010, The Chartered Institute of Management Accountants (CIMA) in cooperation with accounting mega-firm KPMG produced a report called 'Standard costing—insights from leading companies.'

They acknowledged that standard costing is an important financial tool that often is used to determine dimensional profitability, e.g. the profit by customer, by product and by channel.

They commented that standard costing needs to be considered in a wider framework of business intelligence where companies are seeking to improve performance and competitiveness. Ensuring that the right information is delivered to the right people at the right time and focusing on how strategies and operations are connected can improve strategic competitiveness.

However, they also acknowledged that research has shown that as much as 50 per cent of management do not trust the information presented to them. Addressing the relevance, timeliness and consistency of standard cost information is a first step on the pathway to enhancing business intelligence.

Source: 'Standard costing—insights from leading companies'. *CIMA and KPMG Feb 2010*

Principles of standard costing

Standard costing was developed by manufacturing industries as a way of monitoring actual performance against a range of standards or benchmarks for the cost of the business's product.

There is an important note which we should mention immediately: standard costing is of use only where there are repetitive processes for which times or quantities can be accurately measured. It is of no value in costing situations involving:

- a single product, for example building a ship or a building
- a situation where the business consists of a series of small, distinct tasks, for example a freelance writer

Consequently, it was developed for manufacturers producing large quantities of virtually identical products, e.g. biscuits or pens. For this reason, it is little used in service or non-manufacturing industries, although there are certain applications where it could be used.

In principle, standard costing works by allocating a set of standard costs, quantities, prices, times and rates to build up a cost structure for an individual product. When the business forecasts its production level it can, by simple multiplication, arrive at a standard cost budget for its product.

An example of a standard cost budget for a product is:

Product: Smasher Mark 3

Costs per unit		$
Materials	2 kgs at $4 per kilo	8
Labour	1.5 hrs at $16 per hour	24
Machine time	30 mins at $12 per hour	6
Variable overhead	$8 per labour hour	12
Fixed overhead	£10 per labour hour	15
		$65
Budgeted selling price		$90
Budgeted profit per unit		$25

Once the standards have been established for each product, it is straightforward enough to forecast the total cost of the production of the Smasher Mark 3 once the production level has been decided.

From there, the standard costs and revenues for all products can be amalgamated to form the budget for the financial period.

Stop and think	Think of four products you use every day whose production costs might be measured using standard costing techniques.

Setting the standard

One of the overriding assumptions that has to be made is the level at which standards should be set. There are several fundamental bases for assumptions as shown in Figure 5.1.

Figure 5.1 **Bases of setting standards**

Basis of standard setting	Key features
Basic	• Standards set many years ago and do not change
	• Business is dynamic and constantly changing so this basis is little used
Ideal	• Maximum output
	• All resources available when required
	• No or little idle or non-productive time
	• No allowance for unforeseen delays
	• Production and sales are maximized with little or no rework or quality problems
Attainable	• Output will never be maximized
	• Allowances made for idle or non-productive time based on budgeted targets
	• Allowance made for possibility of delays based on previous experience but also in line with management objectives
	• Allowance made for wastages and breakdowns, etc. based on budgeted target
Current	• Based on current levels of efficiency for scrap, breakdowns, losses, etc.
	• Does not encourage improvement as standards based on what has been achieved not what might be achieved
	• Past anomalies or inefficiencies built in to current standards
	• Tends to lower standards over time as inefficiencies become built-in
	• Not recommended for use

It may look obvious that an ideal standard will never be achieved but there is an argument for saying that what should be measured is the variance from the best possible situation. In practice, however, management accountants are aware that this will always give adverse or negative variances as the ideal standard will never be achieved. Setting an ideal standard can also be quite demotivating as it can never be realized. Staff therefore may tend to feel that any attempt to achieve it is doomed to failure so may become demotivated—the opposite of what the standard setters want to achieve.

The basic standard and the current standard bases for standard setting are intrinsically flawed and are, in practice, almost never used.

In budgeting, improvements on previous performance are invariably being sought as a key management objective is invariably growing the business and making more profit. Consequently, standards are set making allowances for non-productive time and a certain amount of scrap and wastage based on a level of previous experience but also in line with management objectives.

Managers will attempt to forecast what they expect to happen during the coming financial period on the basis of reasonable assumptions about what might be achievable. This is true of production levels, sales and the availability of resources.

For this reason the basis is nearly always set on the attainable standard.

Establishing a standard cost

In order to arrive at a cost buildup, like the one shown above for the Smasher Mark 3, there has to be some research. This is carried out as part of the budgeting process before the financial year begins.

Some costs, such as materials, are fairly easy to estimate. Costs can be established from:

- suppliers' price lists
- agreed by contract in the case of a long-term agreement

For example, firms involved in making cars will enter into supply agreements with component suppliers some time before the components are actually delivered. The cost of the components per the agreement becomes the standard cost.

Labour costs are more difficult to establish:

- rates can be agreed by negotiation with the workforce prior to the financial period
- times can be established through work study techniques, through testing production under factory conditions, or by experience
- non-productive time can be estimated through experience or by using work study techniques

Overheads are estimated through the budgeting process. Standard costing can be computed on either a marginal cost or absorption costing basis (Module 2). On a marginal cost basis, fixed overheads are not included in product costing and the standard computes only variable overhead. Using an absorption costing approach, overheads are costed into products on the basis of labour or machine hours.

Consequently:

- a budget for all the overheads has to be calculated
- the total of direct labour hours or machine hours can be established based on standard costs and forecast production levels
- the total of budgeted overheads is divided by the appropriate hours to give an absorption rate per hour for either labour or machinery used
- the rate can be applied to each product based on the hours used in producing the product

Stop and think   Are there any service industries where standard costing principles could be applied? What about hotels or airlines?

Here is an example of a standard cost buildup for a product:

EXAMPLE

Buffalo Ltd makes a product Alpha.
The standard cost buildup is:

Materials	
A	5 kg
B	8 kg
Labour	2 hrs
Machine time	½ hr

(continued)

With Material B there is a loss of 20 per cent during processing.
Costs are anticipated to be:

Material A	£3 per kg
Material B	£2 per kg
Labour	£15 per hour
Machine time	£30 per hour
Cost buildup	
Material A – 5 kg @ £3 per kg	15
Material B – (8 kg ÷ 0.8) = 10 kg @ £2 per kg	20
Labour 2 hrs at £15 per hour	30
Machine time ½ hr at £30 per hour	15
Standard cost	£80

Variance analysis

Budgets are set at the beginning of a financial period so in reality costs vary from planned levels for many reasons. For example:

- suppliers have to raise prices due to unanticipated changes in their marketplace
- materials specifications may have to be changed during production
- output takes a longer or shorter time than predicted
- budgeted overhead levels aren't met or are exceeded

All of these factors cause a difference between the standard cost of the output produced and the actual costs incurred during the financial period.

These are called variances and the process of analyzing them is variance analysis.

Variance analysis is used to measure the difference between the costs actually incurred for the actual level of output and what they should have been had the standard costs, quantities and times been adhered to.

There is another important point to bear in mind: It is of no value to measure what actually happened against the original budget. What needs to be measured is the variance from the actual output—at standard cost. The original budget should be adjusted from:

the forecast level of output

to

the actual level of output

At that point the differences, variances, between what costs should have been at standard cost and what they actually were can be measured. Let us look at variances for materials and labour costs.

Materials and labour variances

The basic concept is not difficult. Costs are made up of two components—quantity and price—so total costs are calculated using the formula:

$$\text{Cost} = \text{Price} \times \text{Quantity}$$

Clearly if the actual costs of production vary from the standard cost of production, we can break the difference down between:

- variances attributable to quantities
- variances attributable to prices

Consequently, both materials and labour variances have two components, one attributable to price variances and one attributable to quantity variances, which combine to make the total variance.

One further point: standard costing, in common with many other topics in accounting, has its own terminology, so:

- materials quantity is known as 'usage', i.e. how much material was used
- labour quantities in hours are known as 'efficiency', i.e. how much time was spent, so how efficient the workforce was

Variances are either:

- adverse—if the actual cost is greater than the standard or
- favourable—if the actual cost is less than the standard

MATERIALS VARIANCES

Materials variances comprise:

- a total cost variance which can be subdivided into:
  - price and
  - quantity (known as usage) variances

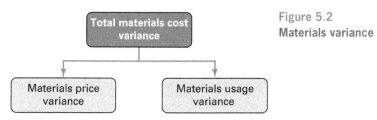

Figure 5.2
Materials variance

The total materials cost variance is calculated using the formula:

The standard cost of the materials used for the actual production

minus

The actual cost of the materials used

EXAMPLE

Paint Makers Ltd makes paint in 1 litre tins.
Each litre tin of paint takes 1.5 kgs of ingredient. The standard cost of each kilo of ingredient is £5.
During Month 1 production was planned to make 1500 tins. Actual production was 1560 tins and ingredients used amounted to 2450 kgs at a cost of £12 375.

REQUIRED

Calculate the total materials variance.   (continued)

ANSWER

The total materials variance can be calculated as follows:
The standard materials cost of the actual production was:

1560 tins at 1.5 kgs per tin × £5 =	£11 700
The actual cost of materials was	£12 375
The total cost variance is therefore	£675 Adverse

The variance is described as being adverse because the actual costs are greater than the standard cost for the actual production.

Management has now established that it has spent £675 more than planned for the actual production. But what was the reason for the overspend—was it price or quantity?

So the total materials variance, as shown in Figure 5. 2, can be subdivided into a price variance and a quantity or usage variance.

MATERIALS PRICE VARIANCE   One of the reasons for the total materials cost variance might be that the materials could not be bought at the standard price, i.e. the price at which the materials were costed when the budgets were being set.

This might have occurred because:

- a different supplier had to be used
- discounts which had been assumed didn't materialize
- materials of a different specification had been purchased

It is necessary therefore to calculate that part of the total materials variance which related to price changes. The formula for this is:

$$\text{Actual quantity at standard price} - \text{Actual quantity} \times \text{Actual price}$$

EXAMPLE

In the Paint Makers example above, the actual quantity of ingredients purchased was 2450 kgs at a cost of £12 375. The standard cost per kilo is £5.
So the materials price variance is calculated as:

	£
2450 kilos of material should have cost 2450 × £5 at standard price =	12 250
but actually cost	12 375
The variance attributable to the price of materials is	£125 A

The variance is adverse because the actual cost of material was greater than the standard cost. The second part of the total materials variance relates to quantities and is known as the materials usage variance.

MATERIALS USAGE VARIANCE   Another reason for a variation in total materials cost is that quantities used varied from planned levels.

This could be because:

- the quality of materials purchased was better or worse than planned thus affecting wastage levels
- gains or losses arising during the manufacturing processes in the factory

It is necessary therefore to calculate the proportion of the total materials variance, which is caused by using higher or lower quantities of material in the actual production than planned.

The difference in quantities is valued at the standard price of materials because price changes are accounted for in the price variance, as shown above.

So the formula here is:

$$(\text{Actual quantity used at standard usage} - \text{Actual quantity used}) \times \text{Standard price}$$

EXAMPLE

In the Paint Makers example above, the actual production was 1560 tins. Each tin was budgeted to contain 1.5 kilos of ingredient at £5 per kilo. The actual quantity of ingredients used was 2450 kilos

So the materials usage variance is:

The actual production should have used 1560 × 1.5 =	2340 kilos
But instead used	2450 kilos
A difference of	110 kilos
Which, at the standard cost of £5 per kilo, gives a variance of	£550 (A)

This variance is adverse because the actual quantity used was greater than the quantity which should have been used for the actual production.

The price and usage variances can now be totalled to agree to the total variance

Thus:

Materials price variance	125 (A)
Materials usage variance	550 (A)
Total materials cost variance	675 (A)

This gives management the whole story. The materials cost more than they should by £125, but the main problem was that they used much more than planned, with the result that they spent an extra £550 on paint.

This then gives production management an area to review and find out why they used more than planned. Was it wastage due to inefficiency or simply that the plan was wrong? Either way management can now act on the situation in a much more focused way than if they simply had a total difference in costs.

We can bring all the aspects of materials variances together to show a composite example:

EXAMPLE

Raven has the following production materials figures for period 4.

	Budget	Actual
Production level (units)	3000	3200
Material quantity (kgs)	6000	6750
Cost	$15000	$15800

(continued)

What are the total cost, price and usage variances for materials?

The first thing to do is to work out the standard costs for each component of materials involved in production.

Based on the budget figures the standard quantity of materials used in each unit of production is (6000 kgs/3000 units) = 2 kgs of material.

The standard cost of that material is ($15 000/6000 kgs) = $2.50 per kilo

The variances can now be calculated for the actual production.

TOTAL MATERIALS COST VARIANCE

The actual production of units was 3200 units, which should have cost:

3200 × 2 kgs × $2.50 =	16 000
but actually cost	15 800
The total variance is	200 F

The variance is favourable because the cost of the actual materials used is less than the standard cost of materials for that level of production.

MATERIALS PRICE VARIANCE

The actual quantity of material used was 6750 kgs, which should have cost:

6750 × £2.50 =	16 875
but actually cost	15 800
giving a variance of	$1075 F

MATERIALS USAGE VARIANCE

The actual production should have used:

3200 units × 2 kgs =	6400 kgs
but actually used	6750 kgs
a difference of	350 kgs
which at the standard price of	
$2.50 per kilo gives a variance of	$875 (A)

The variances can be summarized as:

Materials price variance	1075 F
Materials usage variance	875 (A)
Total materials variance	$200 F

The price variance is favourable, but the usage variance is adverse. This could mean that cheaper quality materials were used than planned but that wastage levels were higher as a consequence.

Stop and think

Management needs a lot of information to make decisions, but the information from the costing system is past information, i.e. the variances are divergences from a plan that have already happened. Does analyzing these variances in this much detail add anything to management's ability to make future changes?

LABOUR VARIANCES

These variances are calculated in the same way as variances for materials, in fact the formulas are exactly the same. The only difference is that for labour we talk about efficiency rather than usage for quantities of time, and rate rather than cost for units of time.

The total labour cost variance is subdivided into:

- Labour rate variance—the variance in the price of labour used for the actual quantity of labour expended, eg hourly rate higher than budgeted.
- Labour efficiency variance—the variance in the amount of labour used in the actual production against what it should have been for the actual production, costed at standard cost, eg fewer labour hours taken than the standard expected.

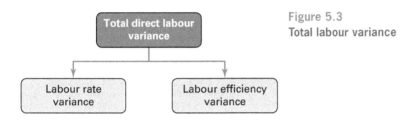

Figure 5.3
Total labour variance

The total direct cost labour variance is:

The standard cost of the labour hours used for the actual production

minus

The actual cost of direct labour hours used

EXAMPLE

Acme Fertilisers Ltd makes fertiliser in 50 kg bags. Each bag requires 1.5 hrs of labour to process the ingredients and to fill it. The standard cost per labour hour is £7.
During Month 1:

- Production was planned to make 5000 bags.
- Actual production was 5400 bags.
- Direct labour hours amounted to 9200
- Cost of labour amounted to £59875.

The total direct labour variance can be calculated as follows:
The standard direct labour cost of the actual production was

5400 bags at 1.5 hrs per bag × £7 =	£56 700
The actual cost of direct labour was	£59 875
The total direct labour cost variance is therefore	£3 175 Adverse

Again the variance is described as being adverse, because the actual costs are greater than the flexed budgeted costs. But why was the variance so big? What caused the excess cost?
We can, as we did with materials, divide the total variance into price and quantity components and look at the variances attributable to both of them.

DIRECT LABOUR RATE VARIANCE   One reason for a variance in total direct labour costs might be that the actual labour used cost more or less than planned. This might have occurred because:

- different grades of worker were used than planned
- increases in pay rates were more or less than forecast

It is necessary therefore to calculate that part of the total labour variance which relates to rate changes. To do this we take the actual amount of labour hours used and value it at both actual price and standard price.

EXAMPLE

In the Acme example above, the actual quantity of labour hours used was 9200 at a cost of £59 875. The standard rate per hour is £7.
So the labour rate variance is:

	£
9,200 hours of labour should have cost 9200 × £7 =	64 400
but actually cost	59 875
the variance attributable to the labour rate is	£4 525 F

The variance is favourable because the actual cost of labour was less than the standard cost.

DIRECT LABOUR EFFICIENCY VARIANCE   Another reason for a variation in total direct labour cost is that the total hours incurred varied from planned levels. This could be because work was completed more quickly or more slowly than planned.

It is necessary therefore to calculate the proportion of the total direct labour variance, which is caused by using higher or lower quantities of labour used in the actual production than planned.

The difference in quantities is valued at the standard price of labour because price changes are accounted for in the price variance, as shown above.

EXAMPLE

In the Acme example above, the actual production was 5400 bags. Each bag was budgeted to take 1.5 hours at £7 per hour. The actual quantity of labour used was 9200 hours.
So the labour efficiency variance is:

The actual production should have used 5400 × 1.5 =	8100 hours
But instead used	9200 hours
A difference of	1100 hours
Which, at the standard cost of £7 per hour gives a variance of	£7700 A

This variance is adverse because the actual quantity of labour used was more than the quantity which should have been used for the actual production.
The rate and efficiency variances can now be totalled to agree to the total variance thus:

Labour rate variance	4525 F
Materials usage variance	7700 A
Total labour cost variance	3175 A

So management has saved money on what was actually paid for labour against what the standard anticipated, but the hours taken were longer. This indicates that perhaps more unskilled labour was used than originally planned or that there were holdups or problems with production, which caused it to take longer than it should have at standard.

Management can now investigate why that level of production took longer than it should have and take appropriate action.

We can bring all aspects of the calculation of labour variances together in a composite example.

EXAMPLE

Raven has the following direct labour figures for Period 4:

	Budget	**Actual**
Production level (units)	3000	3200
Labour hours	1500	1750
Cost	$13500	$14000

Calculate the total, rate and efficiency variances for labour.

The first thing to do is to work out the standard costs for each component of labour involved in production.

1 Based on the budget figures the standard amount of labour used in each unit of production is (1500 hrs/3000 units) = 0.5 hr
2 The standard cost of labour is ($13500/1500 hrs) = $9 per hour

The variances can now be calculated for the actual production.

TOTAL LABOUR COST VARIANCE

The actual production of units was 3200 units, which should have cost:

3200×0.5 hrs $\times$ $9 =$	14400
but actually cost	14000
so the total variance is	400 F

Splitting the total variance into rate and efficiency variances gives us:

LABOUR RATE VARIANCE

The actual quantity of labour used was 1750 hrs, which should have cost:

$1750 \times $9 =$	15750
but actually cost	14000
giving a variance of	$1750 F

The variance is favourable because the actual cost was less than the standard cost for that level of production.

LABOUR EFFICIENCY VARIANCE

The actual production should have used:

3200 units $\times$ 0.5hrs $=$	1600 hrs
but actually used	1750 hrs
a difference of	150 hrs
which at the standard price of $9 per hour gives a variance of $(150 \times $9) =$	$1350 (A)

(continued)

The variance is adverse because the actual cost was more than the standard cost for that level of production. The variances can be summarized as:

Labour rate variance	1750 F
Labour efficiency variance	1350 (A)
Total labour cost variance	400 F

So the report to management will say that although the cost of labour was favourable, the number of hours used was adverse, indicating that production took longer than it should have done. This indicates that there were either unforeseen production delays or less well-trained or experienced staff were used than planned.

Stop and think   Modern manufacturing uses a lot of part time or contract labour. Does this invalidate the calculation of these labour variances?

Overhead variances

Whilst materials and labour variances are relatively straightforward, looking only at prices and quantities, there is also the question of overhead variances. Overhead variances tend to be linked to labour hours and, as such, will follow labour efficiency, ie if labour efficiency is adverse, so too will overhead efficiency.

Overhead variances can be split into variable overhead variances and fixed overhead variances for the purposes of analysis.

VARIABLE OVERHEAD VARIANCES

Variable overheads vary with production in the same way as direct materials and direct labour so can be calculated in the same way.

The variable overhead variances are relatively easy to deal with as they use exactly the same formulae as the materials and labour variances we looked at above, except that instead of an hourly labour rate, the standard cost to be used is the variable overhead recovery rate. This is normally based on labour or machine hours and is simply:

Total variable cost ÷ labour (or machine) hours = variable overhead recovery rate

Again, the variable overhead variance can be split into the two components of price and quantity as shown in Figure 5.4.

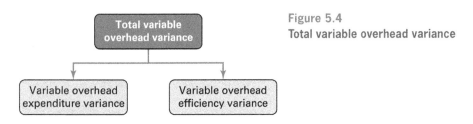

Figure 5.4
Total variable overhead variance

We can use a simple example to illustrate these variances.

EXAMPLE

P enny Ltd has budgeted total variable overhead of £90 000. Budgeted production is 20 000 units and the company budgeted 30 000 labour hours, i.e. 1.5 hours per unit.

During Period 3 the actual production was 22 000 units and variable overhead amounted to £100 000. Actual hours worked were 38 000.

The variable overhead recovery rate based on the budget is therefore:

$$\frac{\text{Budgeted overhead}}{\text{Budgeted labour hours}} = \frac{90\,000}{30\,000} = £3.00 \text{ per labour hour}$$

So we can now work out the variances:

Total variable overhead variance	
The recovery of variable cost at standard amounted to 33 000 hrs × £3.00 =	99 000
The actual variable overhead was	100 000
Variance	£1 000 A

The variance is adverse because the actual cost of variable overhead is £1000 more than the recovery at standard, i.e. 22 000 units actually produced at 1.5 hours per unit—this is an under-recovery of overhead.

We can subdivide the total variable overhead cost variance into cost and quantity variances.

VARIABLE OVERHEAD EXPENDITURE VARIANCE

This calculates the variable overhead that should have been recovered based on actual hours worked against what the actual overhead was.

Actual hours worked	38 000 × £3	= 114 000
Actual variable overhead		100 000
Variance		14 000 F

This represents an over recovery of overhead based on actual hours.

VARIABLE OVERHEAD EFFICIENCY VARIANCE

This represents the actual hours worked against what should have been worked for the actual production to give an indication if there had been a shortfall in hours available for overhead recovery.

Hours for actual production at standard 22 000 units at 1.5 hours	33 000
Actual hours worked	38 000
Variance in hours	5 000
At standard recovery rate £3	£15 000 A

The variance is adverse because the actual hours exceeded the standard hours for that level of production.

So putting this together we have:

Variable overhead expenditure variance	14 000 F
Variable overhead efficiency variance	15 000 A
Variable overhead total variance	1 000 A

So whilst the number of hours worked represented an over-recovery of the cost of variable overhead, that number of hours should have produced far more product for the cost to be recovered against. Effectively, one balanced out the other so the net effect was a small under-recovery which would be charged against profit.

FIXED OVERHEAD TOTAL VARIANCE

There are several subdivisions of the fixed overhead total variance but these are outside the scope of this module. We will just look at the total cost variance and not attempt to subdivide it any further. That is the subject of a more advanced course.

Fixed overheads do not vary with production, and whether or not a variance matters depends on whether a marginal or absorption costing system is being used. We will assume an absorption costing system is being used.

So, the total fixed overhead variance is based on the total amount of overhead absorbed by the actual production against the actual fixed overhead incurred. The best way to illustrate this is with an example.

EXAMPLE

A lberto Ltd has the following data regarding fixed overheads.

Budgeted cost	€44000
Budgeted production	8000 units
Budgeted labour hours	16000
Actual overhead cost	€47500
Actual production	8450 units
Actual labour hours	16600

Calculate the total fixed overhead variance.
Firstly, we need to calculate the standard absorption rate:

This is
$$\frac{€44000}{16000} = €2.75 \text{ per hour}$$

Next we need the standard hours for production, which is 16000 hours ÷ 8000 units = 2 hours per unit.
Now we can calculate the variance for the actual production:

8450 units × 2 hours × €2.75 per hour =	46475
Actual overhead	47500
	1025 A

The variance is adverse because the actual production at standard hours and standard recovery rate did not produce enough to recover the actual overhead incurred. Remember that the overhead recovery rate is based on the budget so it is a standard cost, which does not change.

Investigating the reasons for variances

As we have noted above a variance from budget can be attributed to these basic causes:

- Price variations
- Quantity variations created by variations in the level of output

Clearly these can arise in the normal course of trading. Businesses try and achieve budgeted levels of output, but maybe fall short because of problems in production or lack of demand or, alternatively, produce more than planned because things are going well. Either way it is extremely rare for production or output to exactly achieve the budgeted levels and for prices to stay as originally budgeted. As such, management should consider when to investigate variances. Small variances may not be of concern and time would be wasted in investigating. It may be only variances above, say, 5% of budget, either favourable or adverse, are investigated.

The nature of variance such as material price or labour efficiency would indicate where the issue lies. Consequently, variances can arise and generally fall into the following categories:

FAVOURABLE PRICE VARIANCE BUT ADVERSE EFFICIENCY OR USAGE VARIANCE   This generally is an indication that:

- cheaper labour was used than planned but
- they took longer to achieve the production level or
- cheaper materials were used than planned but
- the materials were poorer quality, so the business used more than anticipated

ADVERSE PRICE VARIANCE BUT FAVOURABLE EFFICIENCY OR USAGE VARIANCE   This is the opposite situation:

- more expensive labour was used than planned and
- they were quicker to achieve the production level because they could work faster and were more skilled or
- more expensive materials were used than planned but
- the materials were better quality so the business used less than anticipated, e.g. there was less wastage

Fundamentally reporting to management on variance analysis will be likely to highlight these points in some way.

Advantages and disadvantages of standard costing

The main advantages of using standard costing techniques are:

- it assists in the process of setting prices for outputs
- it raises awareness of cost issues
- it assists in planning resource requirements for the required level of output
- it is a mechanism for controlling costs through the process of variance analysis
- it can highlight inefficiencies in the production process

However, standard costing has some disadvantages that you should also be aware of:

- it requires a considerable amount of data collection for cost monitoring
- it can be complex and expensive to operate
- it is only suitable for repetitive processes with standardized component parts

One of the main problems with standard costing is that it is primarily manufacturing based. Because it relies on the costing of identical products to create the standard against which actual costs are measured it has limited applicability in the service sector. It has been used to a limited extent in the hotel and catering industry but there are problems with standard setting and applying standards to a diverse range of products with variations. It can become very complex and there are better ways of cost monitoring.

Consequently, most of the applications are confined to a particular type of manufacturing.

Test yourself

1 Bozo Ltd makes product Boz. In Period 2, the budget for materials to manufacture 2500 units of Boz was £25 000. Each Boz unit uses 2 kg of materials at £5 per kg.

In Period 2, Bozo actually used 450 kgs of material at £4.50 per kg.

So the materials variances are:

	Price	Usage
a)	1250 F	2375 F
b)	2375 F	1250 F
c)	3625 F	1250 A
d)	1250 F	3625 F

2 Bozo makes another product, the Ozo. In Period 2, Boz made 2450 Ozos at a labour cost of £96 125. The actual hours were 14 125. The budgeted production for that period was 2450 units at 5.5 hours per unit at £7 per hour. The labour variances were:

	Rate	Efficiency
a)	1800 A	2750 F
b)	4550 F	2750 A
c)	2750 A	1800 F
d)	2750 F	4550 A

3 A business purchased materials costing £43 250. The standard cost of the materials was £2.00 per kilo and there was an adverse price variance of £3250.

How many kilos were purchased?
a) 40 000
b) 21 625
c) 20 000
d) 23 250

4 Hugo Ltd has the following information regarding fixed overheads:

Budget cost	€60 000
Budgeted production	12 000 units
Budgeted labour hours	15 000
Actual cost	€62 348
Actual production	13 500 units
Actual labour hours	15 800

The fixed overhead total variance is:
a) 5152 F
b) 7500 F
c) 5152 A
d) 22 027 F

5 During Period 3, 17 500 labour hours were worked at a standard cost of $6.50 per hour. The labour efficiency variance was $7800 favourable.

How many standard hours were produced?
a) 1200
b) 16 300
c) 17 500
d) 18 700

6 For material Z used by Beetle Ltd, the material price variance for Period 4 was £1000 F and the usage variance was £300 A.

The standard material usage is 3 kg and the standard price is £2 per kg. 500 units were produced in the period.

How much material was purchased in the period?
a) 1500 kg
b) 1800 kg
c) 1650 kg
d) 1300 kg

7 Jacopo makes a product J034 which uses 4 hours of direct labour at £12 per hour.
During Period 3, Jacopo made 3350 J034s, which was 150 units less than budgeted. The labour cost incurred was $159 786 and the number of direct hours was 13 450.

The direct labour variances for the month were:

	Labour rate variance	Labour efficiency variance
a)	1614 F	600 F
b)	600 F	1614 A
c)	1614 F	600 A
d)	600 A	1614 A

8 In Period 4, 6500 units were made and there was an adverse labour efficiency variance of €26 000. Workers were paid €8 per hour, total wage cost was €182 000 and the labour rate variance was nil. The number of standard labour hours per unit was:
a) 3.0 hours
b) 3.5 hours
c) 4.0 hours
d) 4.5 hours

9 During Period 5, 223 tonnes of material Podd costing $6913 were purchased to make 500 units of Product 07/31. The standard usage of material Podd is 0.4 tonnes and the standard price is $30/tonne. The price and usage variances were:

	Price	Usage
a)	223 F	690 F
b)	913 A	690 A
c)	223 A	913 A
d)	223 A	690 A

10 Beetle Ltd uses standard costing to monitor its activities and absorbs overhead on the basis of standard machine hours. Details of budget and actual figures for Period 10 are:

	Budget	Actual
Overheads	€1 250 000	€1 005 000
Output	250 000 units	220 000 units
Machine hours	500 000 hours	450 000 hours

Which of the following statements is correct?
a) Overheads were €95 000 over-absorbed
b) Overheads were €95 000 under-absorbed
c) Overheads were €120 000 over-absorbed
d) Overheads were €120 000 under-absorbed

In the next module we are going to look at three different forms of costing. These are process costing—how to allocate costs to continuous processes, batch costing and job costing. These use basic costing methods and incorporate some of the principles already studied and relate them to every day manufacturing situations.

Test yourself

1 Bobbies is a medium-sized business that manufactures and distributes a range of garden building materials and accessories. One of the newest product lines is fencing. The fencing is produced in panels and sold in packs to the customer. To produce the fencing, untreated wood is cut to size and then treated manually in order to protect it from the weather.

Standard costing and budget data for the four-week period ended 31 May 20X8 is shown below.

The planned production for the period was 3500 packs. The budgeted standard cost of planned production was £527 450. The standard costs are shown below.

	Quantity per pack	Unit price £	Cost per pack £
Untreated wood (kg)	9	9.50	85.50
Labour (hours)	4	8.70	34.80
Fixed overhead (hours)	4	7.60	30.40
Standard cost per pack			150.70

Although the standards were useful to the company in planning their budgets for the period, the actual production and expenditure differed from that expected:

● The actual number of packs produced was 3100.
● 29 450 kilograms of wood were used at a total cost of £262 105.
● 12 175 hours of labour were used at a cost of £112 500.
● Expenditure on fixed overheads that was directly attributable to the decking was £105 800.

Required

a) Calculate the materials, labour and total fixed overhead variances.
b) Briefly explain the possible reasons for significant variances.

2 You are the management accountant in a large manufacturing company that operates a system of four-weekly reporting. The company makes an industrial form of plastic resin blocks and because of its toxic nature, no stocks are kept of the product in the form of work in progress.

Your colleague has recently gone on annual leave for one week and was in the process of preparing the next set of management accounts for the product. He has asked that you finish them for the managing director. His workings are shown below:

Standard costing and budget data for the four-week period ended 31 October 20X8.

	Quantity	Unit price	Cost per batch
Materials (litres)	6	£8.00	£48.00
Labour (hours)	9	£10.60	£95.40
Fixed overhead (hours)	9	£7.20	£64.80
Standard cost per unit			£208.20

Standard cost of budgeted production was £2 498 400.
Budgeted production for the period was 12 000 units.
Actual production and expenditure information was:

11 200 units produced.

71 000 litres of materials were used at a total cost of £488 000.

99 350 hours of labour were worked at a total cost of £1 142 000.

Expenditure on fixed overheads was £885 000.

Required

Prepare a report for the managing director that:

a) Details all the materials, labour and total fixed overhead variances.

b) Briefly explains possible reasons for significant variances.

6 Job, batch and process costing

In this module we will consider:

- Job costing

- Margin or markup?

- Charge-out rates

- The effect of overhead on costing and pricing

- Job costing in service industries

- Batch costing

- Process costing

- Losses in production

In previous modules we have looked at various types of approach to costing of products and services. We have examined the principles of:

- Absorption and marginal costing—Module 2
- Relevant costing—Module 3
- Activity based costing—Module 4
- Standard costing—Module 5

Now it is time to look at some of the applications of some of these and to consider a situation we have not previously looked at—the costing of continuous processes.

We will look at the costing of individual one-off jobs or services and the cost of producing goods in batches. We will also look at process costing where a production line or a process doesn't stop and takes the form of a continuous flow of output.

In previous modules we have considered concepts like the cost per unit as merely being a sum of materials and labour with added overhead and we've used the resultant total in other calculations.

What we need to do is look at the concept of cost in a little more detail and see how we arrive at a cost for a product or activity. So we will look at:

- Costing specific orders—job, contract and batches
- Continuous operation—process and service costing

Job costing

Job costing is what it says it is. It is a cost buildup for a specific order and is used for costing one-off or unique jobs.

The costing is triggered when an order is received for a single product or, in the case of a service-based operation, a single task. We will look at its applicability to service industries later—for now we will concentrate on the cost buildup in a manufacturing setting.

A job may be required to be produced to a high standard. It might be a complex task requiring the use of:

- skilled labour
- various machines for specific operations
- high specification materials

Businesses that engage in this kind of work are producing individual items. These could be such items as:

- specialized tools for machines
- specialized parts or high specification parts for vehicles or equipment
- replacement parts manufactured specifically as the originals are no longer available

They tend to make items of a much higher standard than mass-produced items, or in such small quantities that it is not economically feasible for larger factories to make them.

Often such firms act as subcontractors for larger firms, which do not have the tools or skills to make specific items.

Occasionally such businesses do produce short runs of identical items, but this is not their normal business unless they are producing very specific items with a wide applicability for sale.

The principles behind job costing can be applied to the service sector. For example, a painter and decorator will cost out decorating a room in terms of the materials needed and the time it will take. They will then cost a completely different job on the same basis.

The important aspect of job costing is pricing. The buildup of costs is there to enable management to calculate a price, on a cost-plus basis, for the work to be undertaken so the buildup of cost elements is fairly critical. Key to successful pricing is twofold:

1 Successful estimating of what the job entails, what resources will be needed and how long it will take, thus enabling a good estimate of labour and machine costs.
2 A sound basis for overhead apportionment. This requires good budgeting in order to establish the level of overhead to be recovered. Management could adopt marginal costing and simply cost in direct and variable costs in order to arrive at a contribution instead of the more conventional absorption costing approach, but either way the indirect overhead still has to be covered and a profit made.

The principles underlying job costing are quite straightforward. Normally the business will estimate costs based on:

- Materials costs—based on price lists from suppliers if they have to be bought in or materials drawn from stock at original cost
- Other direct expenses—e.g. equipment hire, vehicle leasing, consumables
- Machinery costs—based on a machine hour rate
- Labour costs based on actual costs calculated from the payroll or, more usually, a charge-out rate (see later).
- Overheads allocated on a per-hour basis.

Margin or markup?

There is often confusion between a profit margin and a profit markup. Profit margin is a percentage of the price; profit markup is a percentage of costs.

A profit margin is the amount of profit included in a price or an amount of revenue—it is the relationship between the profit and the selling price. So an item sold at £100 with a 20 per cent profit margin is made up of:

Costs	80
Profit	20
Price	100

A markup is generally meant to indicate an amount added to costs. So with a 20 per cent markup in this case the price would be:

Costs	80
20% markup	16
Price	96

In the first case where the price is £100, the markup is actually 25 per cent: £80 + (25% × £80) = £100.

So there is a considerable difference between the two things and care has to be taken in describing whether a price includes a margin or a markup.

Charge-out rates

This is common in many trades and professions. The basis of it is quite straightforward and is a multi-step process:

1 Estimate the annual overheads for the business that need to be recovered
2 Estimate the number of working hours available for all employees
3 Divide the overheads by the annual hours to give an overhead recovery rate per hour
4 Estimate the cost of the individual employee including any employer's portion of social insurance or pension contributions
5 Estimate the number of working hours available for the individual employee
6 Divide the cost of the employee by the working hours to give an hourly rate
7 Add the overhead recovery rate and the employees cost to give a charged-out rate per employee

EXAMPLE

Dobbin owns a garage with four mechanics and an apprentice. Each mechanic works 44 weeks × 35 hours. The apprentice works fewer hours as she is at college.

The total hours available are:

Mechanics 4 × 35 × 44		6160
Apprentice		840
		7000

The overhead costs of the garage are £91 000 so the overhead recovery per hour is:

$$\frac{91\,000}{7\,000} = £13 \text{ per hour}$$

Each mechanic costs, including employer's proportion of pension and social insurance, £30 000 per year and the apprentice costs £12 000 per year so the total wages cost per hour is:

Mechanics 4 × 30 000		= 120 000
Apprentice		12 000
		132 000

so the rate per hour for labour is:

$$\frac{132\,000}{7\,000} = £19 \text{ hr (rounded up)}$$

There is also a profit margin to add on so let us assume a required profit of £35 000 requires an additional £5 per hour, so the total charge out rate is:

Overheads	13
Labour	19
Profit	5
	£37 per hour

Clearly this is a simple example and there are problems with it such as the fact that, if activity levels decline not all the workforce will work a productive 35-hour week; there will be time between jobs or when they are waiting for materials or components. This is known as idle time. The charge out rate will, effectively, have to take account of this as if it were an overhead.

Stop and think	If you were running your own business from home and it was your only source of income how much would you have to charge per hour to maintain your lifestyle?

The key to it is a specific document known as a job sheet or job card. Nowadays these are most likely electronic, but were originally literally paper or card. The job sheet records the cost buildup for the particular job. It will include:

- A reference number
- The customer details
- Dates of estimated and actual delivery
- Materials costs
- Labour costs
- Machine costs
- Other items costs
- An overhead recovery based on labour or machine hours

Note that job costing is almost invariably absorption costing-based. There will be a multiple of labour or machine hours to cover overhead.

This will be based on a budget of variable and fixed overhead and available hours.

A job card could look as shown in Figure 6.1.

Figure 6.1 Job card example

	Budget	Rate	$		Actual	$	Diff
Job number	**Customer details—Invoice to:**					**Date**	
Job description						**Completed (date)**	
Special instructions							
Materials							
TOTAL MATERIALS	A						
Labour skilled (hours)							
Labour unskilled (hrs)							
TOTAL LABOUR	B						
DIRECT COST	A + B						
Overhead—rate per hour							
TOTAL COST							
Profit margin		30%					
PRICE to customer							
Despatch date							
Invoice number							

As you can see, the job card contains all the information relating to the job including invoicing details. In reality, this information would now be stored by computer with the costing produced by software using this information and any inputs required.

One of the key factors in recording costs in this way is to record the original estimated cost or budget for the job and the actual finished result. This will provide managers with two pieces of information:

- the accuracy of initial estimating and budgeting
- the profit or loss on the job analyzed between any original profit margin or markup and any additional surplus arising from costs being less than estimated.

The job card actual costs can be matched to the estimate to examine any differences which may arise from:

- Errors in initial pricing of components
- Under-/over-estimation of labour hours
- Items missed off the card such as parts, consumables (welding rods, sandpaper, bolts, etc.)

If the work is unfinished at any accounting period end, the costs incurred to date can be calculated and the total included as work in progress in the financial statements.

Let us look at an example.

EXAMPLE

Doggety Ltd is an engineering company which has recently received an order to construct a machine. The price agreed for the order was $4000.

Doggety had budgeted as follows for the construction of the machine:

	$	$
Materials		
Component 1	130	
Component 2	180	
Component 3	95	
Steel	225	630
Labour		
Skilled worker: 36 hours @ $45	1620	
Unskilled worker: 20 hours @ $20	400	2020
Overhead allocation		
56 hours @ $8 per hour		448
		$3098
Profit mark up 30%		902
Quoted price		$4000

In the event the following actual costs were incurred, and the job card looked something like this:

Job number D08/18/4	Grimping machine for BossyCo					
	Budget	$		Actual	$	Diff
Component 1	130			135		
Component 1	180			180		
Component 1	95			100		
Steel	225	630		275	690	(60)
Labour skilled (hours) @ $45	36	1620		51	2295	(675)
Labour unskilled @ $20	20	400		32	640	(240)
Overhead @ $8	56	448		83	664	(216)
TOTAL COST		3098			4289	(1191)
Add 30%		902			(289)	
PRICE		4000			4000	

As can be seen something went wrong during the manufacturing process with the result that costs exceeded budget by $1191. Not only did the company not make its mark up of $902, it actually lost $289 on the job.

(continued)

What happened was that the labour hours were almost 1½ times the estimate at 83 hours instead of 56. What this then meant was that the overhead absorption was calculated based on 83 hours, which further increased costs so the company lost money on the arrangement. The company might have been guilty of under-pricing if the estimation of time to be taken was overly optimistic.

The absorption rate was calculated at $8 per hour. This is a key figure in job costing as it does increase costs considerably where there are a significant number of labour hours involved. Consequently, management should review the actual overhead costs being incurred against the budget to ensure the rate remains applicable throughout the year.

Stop and think   Have you used a garage for car repairs or employed a tradesperson for domestic household functions such as plumbing, building or decorating? What do they base their job estimate on? How important are materials in the calculation? Do they use an hourly rate?

The effect of overhead on costing and pricing

An overhead estimate might be calculated quite simply.

Suppose the workforce comprises ten individuals who each work a basic 35 hour week:

- They work 44 weeks of the year allowing for holidays, public holidays and sickness.
- This gives $35 \times 44 \times 10 = 15\,400$ hours of direct labour to absorb overheads.
- Suppose overheads—administration costs, rent, property, taxes, light, heat and power etc for the business come to £231 000, then the job card will include

$$\frac{£231\,000}{15\,400} = £15 \text{ for every hour of direct labour charged.}$$

Management has to consider the volume of labour hours included in the initial budget when the rate was set. If, for example it was based on 100 000 labour hours being incurred and the overhead recovery rate was therefore set at, say, £12 per labour hour, a significant shortfall in labour hours charged would mean an under-recovery of overhead and a loss to the business.

EXAMPLE

Overhead recovery in Dodo Ltd is charged at the rate of €7.50 per labour hour based on budgeted overhead of €750 000 and an estimate of direct labour hours of 100 000.

Analysis showed that the actual direct labour hours were only 75 per cent of budget. Overheads fell but not by the same amount, as many of them were fixed so overheads fell to €600 000. The amount recovered was 100 000 × 75% × €7.50 = €562 500—an under-absorption of €37 500, which represents a loss to the business in under-recovered overhead.

Remember that if activity levels fall, overheads may not fall by a similar amount if a high proportion of them are fixed.

Management would have to review the job in the light of the final result and see if lessons could be learned or if this was just a one-off unfortunate occurrence.

Another problem area would be to use one overriding absorption rate when there are different resources in the business that cost different amounts to operate.

Here is a business with two different cost centres which calculates an overall absorption rate.

EXAMPLE

	Overhead cost	Labour hours
Cost centre A	90 000	5 000
Cost centre B	45 000	5 000
	£135 000	£10 000

The overhead absorption rate would be calculated as:

$$\frac{135\,000}{10\,000} = £13.50 \text{ per labour hour}$$

A job that takes one hour in Cost centre A will be charged the same as a job that takes one hour in Cost centre B, even though Cost centre A costs twice as much to operate.

This could lead to a failure to accurately price in the use of resources and lead to under- or over-pricing.

Job costing is, to some extent, an art not a science, and relies a good deal on the experience of the estimators and the ability of the workforce to work to a plan. Some jobs will be very profitable and some may go horribly wrong—but such is the nature of contract work.

Job costing in service industries

Job costing is particularly relevant to service industries. As already mentioned, tradespeople such as electricians, plumbers, joiners and builders work very much on a job costing basis, as they carry out a series of discrete tasks which vary from week to week.

Job costing, though, is not confined to trades such as this but is also used by professions such as lawyers and accountants. They also tend to work purely on a task-by-task basis.

The principles which apply to a manufacturing business apply also to professions. The main difference is that there is a very low, if not non-existent, level of direct cost in most cases. Clearly where there are direct costs such as travel, accommodation, etc., these can be charged to the job as direct costs. In professions, as with most trades, the vast majority of costs are indirect and fixed.

These include:

- office rents and property costs
- salaries of non-professional staff not involved with clients
- insurance
- utilities—largely with some variable element

Consequently the business has to estimate the totality of overheads and the total of professional staff hours available to be charged to clients.

EXAMPLE

A firm of lawyers consists of six lawyers who deal directly with the clients. These include partners who do not receive a salary but a profit share.

- Indirect costs both fixed and variable amount to £942 480
- Professional chargeable hours can be calculated based on, say, 44 weeks at 35 hours per week × 6 lawyers

However, not all the lawyers will work every hour for every week so there has to be an allowance for what in manufacturing is called idle time, but in a service-based industry is non-chargeable time. This could be 15 per cent. Combining this information provides a charge out rate per hour as to:

Chargeable hours	$44 \times 35 \times 6 = 9240$
Less: allowance for non-chargeable time (15%)	(1386)
Hours available	7854

So the charge out rate is:

$$\frac{\text{Costs}}{\text{Hours}} \quad \frac{942\,480}{7\,854} = \underline{\textbf{£120.00}} \text{ per hour}$$

Clearly not every lawyer will be charged out at this rate—some may be more and some less but, providing the chargeable hours target is achieved and the average rate is £120, overheads will be recovered in full. A profit will be made if the rate is increased and if more chargeable hours are sold to clients than forecast.

Batch costing

Batch costing is what it says it is: collecting the costs of a batch of products. Businesses that manufacture short runs of identical products may use batch costing. For example, businesses making hairdryers or washing machines may make a batch of identical machines made to a certain specification, then re-tool and make a batch of machines to a different specification.

Consequently, batch costing is very similar to job costing. A batch is given a unique identifier—a batch number—and costs relevant to that batch are charged against that number.

Individual items in the batch can be costed as:

$$\frac{\text{Total cost of batch}}{\text{Number of items in batch}}$$

The process can be shown as:

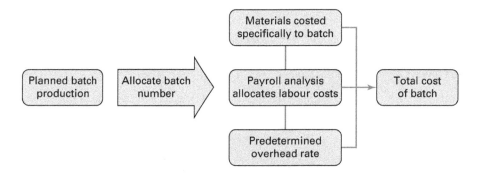

Job costing combines cost allocations to a particular cost code with a sales value for the job to arrive at a profit for the job. Batch costing, whilst sharing some of the same characteristics as job costing, is essentially a purely costing exercise rather than a small profit and loss account. Batches of products obviously do have a sales value but generally this is not applied.

Batch costing is not usually used in a service industry environment as it involves the production of a number of identical items, so would be difficult to apply to a non-production situation. However, it could be used in some circumstances, such as a payroll provider running a batch of payslips for one customer and then a batch for a different customer.

Stop and think	If a service business produced an identical number of activities, could they use a form of batch costing? For example, cafes and restaurants offering a fixed menu. Can you think of examples where this might work, or are there better methods?

Process costing

So far we have looked at various ways of costing products and services which are produced individually, i.e. one after another. They may be identical products, e.g. the production of a series of identical caravans but the production of them is not continuous; they are, after all, discrete products even if they are identical one to the other. Complications arise when we are considering non-discrete products, such as drinks. Beer is brewed in one big vat, going through a number of processes, before being separated into individual bottles. For pricing, we need the cost per bottle but we may also want to see the cost and efficiency of each process or the cost of the product at a certain stage of production. Splitting the total cost of production across the bottles would not provide such information.

REAL WORLD
Process costing—the real thing
The Coca-Cola Company is one of the world's largest producers of non-alcoholic beverages. According to the company, more than 11 000 of its soft drinks are consumed every second of every day.

In the first stage of production, Coca-Cola mixes direct materials—water, refined sugar and secret ingredients—to make the liquid for its beverages. The second stage includes filling cleaned and sanitized bottles before placing a cap on each bottle. In the third stage, filled bottles are inspected, labelled, and packaged.

Work in process begins with the first stage of production (mixing and blending), continues with the second stage (bottling), and ends with the third stage (inspecting, labelling, and packaging). When products have gone through all three stages of production, they are shipped to a warehouse, and the costs are entered into finished goods inventory. Once products are delivered to retail stores, product costs are transferred from finished goods inventory to cost of goods sold.

Source: Coca-Cola Company, 'Home Page,' www2.coca-cola.com/ourcompany/bottlingtoday

Imagine, for example, making paint. This is made in a continuous stream, so the difficulty arises that, if it is made in this way how do we cost a tin of paint? A lot of products are made in this way: think of fertilizer and chemical producers, steel foundries, paper mills, sweet factories, biscuit and cake manufacturers, etc.—anything where there is a continuous process. The products are, of course, homogenous; they are all the same, so the assumption is that one unit of product costs the same as any other—so one tonne of output costs the same as the next tonne.

The simple answer is of course, to measure the resources put in to the process and divide them by the output.

EXAMPLE

Brighty makes paint in a continuous process. During Period 1, costs amounting to £1 250 000 were incurred and the output was 250 000 litres.

Consequently, the cost per litre is:

$$\frac{1\,250\,000}{250\,000} = £5 \text{ per litre}$$

If only it were so simple.

The point of a continuous process is that materials continue to be added to the process to keep the flow going, labour costs continue to be incurred and, quite frequently, the product passes through a series of stages of production before emerging as a finished item. What if, at the end of period 1, we had some unfinished paint – can we cost it at £5 per litre the same as finished goods? Process costing allows us to see the cost of the product at the end of each process.

So we have to expand our example above to take account of different stages of a process. Consequently, determining the costs of production involves:

- Working out the costs—both direct and indirect—associated with each stage in the production process.
- Calculating an average cost for the process by dividing these costs by the output from the process.
- The costs of output from the first process become the cost of input to the second process and so on.
- Any product that hasn't completed a process becomes work in progress which can be valued at unit cost of the processes it has been through and partially completed for the financial statements.

The problem is not so simple for one good reason, and that is that during the process there are invariably losses of materials, so that the quantity of output does not equal the quantity of input.

Losses in production

There are two types of losses identified in the production process:

- normal losses
- abnormal losses

We will look at both in turn.

NORMAL LOSSES   For example, where the process involves heating fluids there may be losses due to evaporation or spillage, and the production costings will make an estimate of what they consider this normal loss to be. The loss is part of the cost of the input and must be borne by the amount actually produced as output.

EXAMPLE

A process requires the input of 10 000 litres of material costing €140 000.

Labour cost in the process was €30 000.

Direct overheads were €10 000.

A normal loss of 10 per cent of the input volume is expected during the process. Actual output was 9000 litres.

Total costs were €180 000.

So the cost per unit is $\dfrac{180\,000}{9\,000} = €20 \text{ per litre}$

This can be written up into the costing system in a process cost account.

Process account

	Kg	€		Kg	€ per Kg	€
Material input	10000	140000	Normal loss	1000		
Labour		30000	Output	9000	20	180000
Overhead	_____	10000		_____		_____
	10000	180000		10000		180000

As can be seen from the above example:

- The account includes columns for both quantities and amount—both of which are balanced off.
- No value is given to the loss.

However, it may be that the loss has a value, i.e. it could be sold for scrap or as a by-product at a low value. The amount for which the 'lost' materials could be sold for will reduce the overall costs of the process. So using the example above assumes the materials represented by the normal loss could be sold for scrap at €4.50 per litre.

The process cost then becomes $€180\,000 - (1000 \times €4.50) = €175\,500$

So the cost per litre is now $\dfrac{175\,500}{9\,000} = €19.50$

and the process account now looks like this:

Process account

	Kg	€		Kg	€ per Kg	€
Material input	10000	140000	Normal loss	1000	4.50	4500
Labour		30000	Output	9000	19.50	175500
Overhead	_____	10000		_____		_____
	10000	180000		10000		180000

Scrap sales

	Kg	€		Kg	€
Process account	1000	4500	Cash book	1000	4500

In the above example, we can see that the process cost has been reduced by the scrap value and we have opened a separate scrap account to keep track of scrap sales.

ABNORMAL LOSSES   Life being what it is, processes very rarely conform to the budget ideal. Losses are not likely to hit the forecast figure every time, so we have to deal with losses or gains outside the budgeted parameters, which we call abnormal losses or gains. This is the most likely scenario, so we will look at it in detail.

An abnormal loss is the amount by which the actual loss exceeds the normal loss. The loss is, by definition, not what was planned for, consequently management would take the view that the reason for the loss is some form of error or fault, which could be rectified or controlled.

Therefore, management will be anxious to monitor abnormal losses, so will treat them differently to the way normal losses are treated, as we saw above.

The main difference is that abnormal losses have a value, because they represent a loss of output and potential income. Normal losses, as we have seen, do not have a value—they are, as it were, built in to the costings—but abnormal losses are unexpected losses, so have a value.

Accordingly, the accounting is to value them at the same rate as output and charge the loss to the income account by means of an abnormal loss account. In this way management can keep a total of accumulated abnormal losses.

EXAMPLE

Bee Ltd produced concrete bars in Period 3 and had the following information:

Input materials 12000 kg at a cost of $2.50 per kilo	$30000
Input labour cost	$94800
Overheads	$48000

Normal loss is set at 10 per cent
The actual output was 9800 kg
The waste materials have no value
The steps to take towards preparing the process cost account are:

- The normal loss is $12000 \text{ kg} \times 10\% = 1200 \text{ Kg}$
- The actual output is less than the budgeted output
$$12000 - 1200 = 10800 - 9800 = \underline{1000 \text{ kg}}. \text{ This is the abnormal loss.}$$
- The cost per kg of output is

$$\frac{\$172\,800}{10\,800} = \$16 \text{ per kg}$$

So the process cost account looks like this:

Process account

	Kg	$		Kg	$ per Kg	$
Material input	12000	30000	Normal loss	1200		–
Labour		94800	Output	9800	16	156800
Overhead		48000	Abnormal loss	1000	16	16000
	12000	172800		12000		172800

Abnormal loss

	Kg	$		$
Process account	1000	16000	Income account	16000

As can be seen, the process cost account balances as the abnormal loss and the actual output are valued at full cost ÷ (output—normal loss). As with Example 2, if the scrap had a value this would have been deducted from the total cost before arriving at a cost per unit of output.

If the loss can be sold for scrap, we need to account for this and this involves creating a scrap sales account.

There is one key thing to remember, and that is that as far as scrap sales are concerned there is no difference between scrap from a normal loss and that from an abnormal loss: it is all just scrap.

EXAMPLE

U se the figures for Bee Ltd above except that they have been able to sell the waste concrete for rubble at $4.50 per kg.

- The cost per kg of output is thus:

$$\$172\,800 - (1200 \text{ kg} \times \$4.50) = \frac{\$167\,400}{10\,800} = \$15.50 \text{ per kg}$$

Remember, we work out the cost per kg based on the normal loss, because we are going to value both the output and the abnormal loss at the same amount, i.e. the full cost per kg.

So the process cost account now looks like this, with the abnormal loss and scrap sales accounts.

Process account

	Kg	$		Kg	$ per Kg	$
Material input	12000	30000	Normal loss	1200	4.50	5400
Labour		94800	Output	9800	15.50	151900
Overhead		48000	Abnormal loss	1000	15.50	15500
	12000	172800		12000		172800

Abnormal loss

	Kg	$		Kg	$
Process account	1000	15500	Scrap account	1000	4.50	4500
			Income account			11000
		15500				15500

Scrap sales

	Kg	€		Kg	€
Process account	1200	5400	Cash book	2200	9900
Abnormal loss	1000	4500			
		9900			9900

As we can see from the example above:

- The abnormal loss account includes the loss as valued by the process. This is lessened by the value generated by selling the waste material as scrap, so the net loss $11 000 is what ends up as a cost in the income account.
- As far as the scrap sales account is concerned, the whole of the waste materials—abnormal or normal—is valued at the same rate, so generates $9900 of cash to reduce the impact of the losses.

So far we have only dealt with losses—but what about gains?

ABNORMAL GAINS   An abnormal gain is created when the actual loss is less than the forecast normal loss. Obviously the word 'gain' is slightly misleading here, as it can't be a surplus as such—the output cannot be more than the input!

What it is, is less loss.

Let us look at the example of Bee Ltd above; this time we have an abnormal gain.

EXAMPLE

Input materials 12 000 kg at a cost of $2.50 per kilo—$30 000

Input labour cost	$94 800
Overheads	$48 000

Normal loss is set at 10 per cent
The actual output was 11 000 kg
The waste materials are sold for scrap at $4.50 per kg
The steps to take towards preparing the process cost account are:

- The normal loss is 12 000 kg × 10% = 1 200 kg

- The cost per kg of output is

$$\frac{\$172\,800 - (1\,200 \times 4.50)}{10\,800} = \$15.50 \text{ per kg}$$

So the process cost account, abnormal gain account and scrap sales account look like this:

Process account

	Kg	$ per Kg	$		Kg	$ per Kg	$
Material input	12 000		30 000	Normal loss	1 200	4.50	5 400
Labour			94 800	Output	11 000	15.50	170 500
Overhead			48 000				
Abnormal gain	200	15.50	3 100				
	12 200		175 900		12 200		175 900

Abnormal gain

	Kg	$		Kg	$
Normal loss	1 200	5 400	Process account	200.00	3 100
			Income account		2 300
		5 400			5 400

Scrap sales

	Kg	€		Kg	€
Process account	1 000	4 500	Cash book	800	3 600
			Abnormal gain account	200	900
		4 500			4 500

Note that the abnormal gain reduces the charge to the income account from $5400 to $2300 and scrap sales are lower than in the previous Example 2 as there is less waste; only 800 kg of waste instead of 1000 kg so scrap sales are reduced by 200 kg × $4.50 = $900 .

This is an introduction to the principles of process costing. We are not going to look at the valuation of uncompleted units as part of work in progress, nor will we look at the question of joint products or by-products. These are topics for another module.

Test yourself

Use this information for Questions 1 and 2

Bogle Ltd had three jobs which had costs as follows:

	Job 1 £	Job 2 £	Job 3 £
Opening costs	35 829	22 471	–
Materials in period	123 765	67 046	19 842
Labour in period	87 532	91 283	21 185

The overheads for the period were as budgeted at £400 000.

Jobs 1 and 2 were not completed at the period end. Job 3 was completed and billed with a 20 per cent mark up.

1 What is the value of work in progress at the period end?
   a) £427 926
   b) £468 953
   c) £785 556
   d) £606 741

2 How much was Job 3 billed for? What was the selling price?
   a) £100 076
   b) £104 246
   c) £74 654
   d) £49 232

3 Dobbin produces oils in a continuous process. Normally 10 per cent of output is lost during operation. In Period 2, costs were:

Materials—17 000 litres at $5 per litre
Labour—2000 hours at £11 per hour
Overhead—£18 000
   In the period 15 400 litres were produced.

What is the cost of the abnormal loss?
   a) $4987
   b) $4800
   c) $3000
   d) $4897

4 Betty Fabricators are quoting for a job. They aim for a profit margin of 20 per cent on sales. The estimated direct materials cost for the job is £125.
   Fixed overheads for the company are estimated at £250 000. The budgeted total labour hours are 12 500 and this job is expected to take three hours. Selling and distribution costs are recovered on the basis of £15 per job.

What price should Betty Fabricators quote?
   a) £240
   b) £222
   c) £231
   d) £250

5 Doris, a lawyer, has set up her own practice. She expects to work a 35-hour week and takes four weeks holiday per year. She anticipates that 80 per cent of her time will be chargeable to clients. Office general expenses amount to €25 000 per annum and she is aiming for a profit of €35 000.

How much should she charge a client for a job that is expected to take 40 hours?

a) €1428

b) €1648

c) €1488

d) €1786

6 Which of the following statements are true?

In a process account, abnormal losses are valued at:

a) scrap value

b) raw materials cost

c) the same rate as good production

d) good production cost less scrap value

7 Hulot is pricing a job for a customer.

The relevant details are as follows:

	Dept A	Dept B
Materials	£20 000	£16 000
Labour hours	4 000	2 000
Rate per hour	£12	£10
Production overhead per direct labour hour	£8	£15

Administration and general overhead—15 per cent of production cost

Profit markup—20 per cent of sales price

What is the selling price for the customer?

a) £238 625

b) £229 080

c) £207 500

d) £227 000

The following information is used for Questions 8 and 9

Bogles Ltd operates a process costing system to make paint. The paint passes through two processes. Details in Period 5 for Process 1 are:

Materials	40 000 kg @ $4 per litre
Direct labour	$12 500
Production overhead	$18 000

Normal losses are 15 per cent in Process 1 and waste material can be sold on for $2 per litre. The actual output in Period 5 from Process 1 was 36 000 litres.

8 What is the value in Period 5 of the normal loss?

a) $28 500

b) $25 800

c) $12 000

d) $6000

9 What is the value of the abnormal loss or gain in Period 5?
   a) $10 555
   b) $10 500
   c) $9917
   d) $11 205

10 A firm of chartered accountants, Puce Watermelon, charges out time on the basis of €100 per senior chargeable hour and €55 per junior chargeable hour.
   Its total budgeted chargeable hours were 15 000.
   Office overhead costs for administration and property costs were €660 000.
   The firm added a 20 per cent profit margin on cost.
   One assignment involved 10 senior hours and 30 junior hours.

   How much should Puce Watermelon bill the client?
   a) $4410
   b) $3180
   c) $5512
   d) $5292

In the next module we will look at the principles behind budgeting. This is one of the most important management processes and is inextricably linked to the objectives and processes for managing the businesses. We will consider the various approaches to budgeting and how budgets are used in a dynamic way to monitor the progress of the business and how management can use budgets as part of their control function in the organization.

Test yourself

1 Megachem makes a chemical compound called Baldycure which is used as an ingredient in shampoo for men. It is made by processing the raw material through two processes: mixing and compounding. The output from mixing is included in the costs of compounding.
   The details of each process cost for Period 7 are as follows:

Mixing	
Direct material	2000 litres @ $5 per litre
Direct labour	$7200
Machine time for process	140 hours at $60 per hour
Compounding	
Direct material	1400 litres @ $12 per litre
Direct labour	$4200
Machine time for process	80 hours at $72.50 per hour

The departmental overhead for Period 7 was $6840, and is absorbed into the costs of each process on the basis of direct labour hours.

Outputs were:		
	Mixing	Compounding
Expected output	80% of input	90% of input
Actual output	1400 litres	2620 litres

There is no finished stock or work in progress for the period.

The output from each process can be used by other manufacturers. The waste output from mixing is sold for $0.50 per litre and the waste output from compounding is sold for $1.825 per litre.

Required

1 Prepare the process accounts for Period 7 including the normal loss, abnormal losses or gains and the scrap accounts.

2 Calculate the loss or gain shown in the income account for Period 7.

3 Printfast is a small jobbing printing company specializing in jobs which require a quick turnaround. It has received an order from one of its regular customers for 4000 diaries and 2300 calendars. Printfast has worked out the following costs:

Direct material	
Diaries	$40 per 100 diaries
Calendars	$20 per 100 calendars
Machine printing time	
Diaries	30 minutes per 100
Calendars	15 minutes per 100
Direct labour	$12 per machine hour
Production overheads	$16 per machine hour
Setup costs	
Diaries	$1000
Calendars	$500

Required

a) Compute the total costs of the printing job and the unit cost per diary and per calendar.

b) Compute the unit cost for diaries if the order is for 6000 diaries.

7 Budgeting

Budgeting is one of the most critical management processes any organization can undertake. Without any form of budget, an organization, particularly a business, is really operating in the dark because, whilst financial and management accounts may tell managers where the operation is financially, they have no idea of where it should be.

Financial accounts are historical, looking back at the period ended, and any issues will be identified after the fact. Budgets allow organizations to look forward and provide figures against which to measure actual performance and provide a route map to tell managers what actions they may have to take to get to where they want to be. Of course, budgets may be imperfect, inaccurate and incomplete; actual performance may demonstrate that the budget is woefully pessimistic or optimistic and may not have considered all the problems which the business may face. So merely preparing a budget will not make a better manager, but it will give a manager some incentive and some help in making the business perform.

Budgets can be used to:

- incentivize staff and management
- act as instruments of control
- act as an indicator of performance

They serve many purposes and should not be treated lightly. In many organizations, budget preparation is seen as an annual chore that must be got through as quickly and painlessly as possible, but the importance of the budget lies in thorough preparation, so managers must ensure that their attitude to budgeting is a positive one.

Budgets serve two key functions. These are:

- planning – what we would like to spend
- control – monitoring what we've spent against that plan.

Having a budget does not equate to having to spend all of it but rather having an approved amount available if required. We will come on to issues of control later in the module; for now let us look at the issues around planning.

Strategic issues in budgeting

All managers make plans for their organizations. Wise managers generally have some long-term objectives for their organization, some goals which they recognize may take years to achieve but which, nevertheless, they are working towards. These objectives may be expressed in quite broad terms and may not be refined to the extent that they constitute a plan. However, they should always be:

- realistic
- achievable
- capable of being measured

They may take the form of a generalized statement such as:

'To become the market leader in pet accessories in Scotland'
'To increase turnover to $10 000 000 within the next two years'
'To open ten new profitable outlets within the next five years'
'Survive this downturn and be here next year'

All of these are goals, but they are measurable. Whether they are realistic and achievable depends on the management's ability to turn a goal into a workable plan. There will always be outside factors to be considered. No business is fully in charge of its own destiny and there will certainly be problems and pitfalls along the way such as:

- Unforeseen disasters: fires, floods, etc.
- Sudden loss of key personnel
- Unforeseen reactions by competitors
- Changes in fashion
- Technological change
- New competitors entering the market
- Changes in legislation, new rules and requirements

There may be some factors that are predictable, but which the business may be powerless to do anything about. These long-term, broad aims are what might be described as strategic objectives: they are a goal towards which the senior management is directing the business. They may, of course, change. They may become unattainable for whatever reason, they may be achieved and have to be replaced by new ones—the point is that there should be some form of strategic, long-term planning aimed at achieving specific objectives, however broadly they are described. We look at this in more detail in Module 10.

Once the strategic goals are clarified the path towards achieving them can be established and translated into a series of short-term steps or objectives. For example, if the objective is to expand the number of outlets so as to achieve regional or national coverage, this might translate into a step-by-step plan detailing the locations, types of property, timing, etc., which can be implemented year by year until the objective is achieved.

Strategic objectives and the budget process

Budgeting is an essential part of the process of long-term and short-term planning built around business objectives. The first and most important thing to understand about the budget process is that it represents corporate goals for the budget period, expressed in financial terms.

The process of creating a budget should be inextricably linked with business objectives. So it must reflect the strategic and tactical issues which will be important to the business in the coming financial period.

The budget process has many functions:

- it compels a business to plan its activities
- it assists in coordinating the activities of each part of the business towards a single plan
- it communicates targets to the managers responsible for achieving them
- it establishes a system of control by matching actual achievement against forecasts

> **Stop and think**   Do you prepare a household budget? How do you go about doing this? Can the same process be applied to preparing a budget for a business?

Budgets are a very powerful tool in the management's toolbox. The reason for this is that the budgeting process is not something that can be done in isolation. Inevitably all of the people in the organization who have responsibility for a profit centre or cost centre should be involved in the process.

It is thus an opportunity for senior management to:

- communicate their objectives
- receive feedback from operational departments
- discuss key issues with line or operational management
- consider resource requirements

It is an opportunity to involve all the key members of the organization in a common cause. This can be a valuable process providing communication is a two-way process. Unfortunately, not all organizations make use of this opportunity, simply allowing the budgeting process to be one where senior managers simply transmit their instructions and decide on the outcomes, risking the budget process becoming futile and, ultimately, fail.

If senior management simply impose targets on operational centres without any consultation, the targets, however reasonable they may be, are likely to be met with, at best, a certain amount of detachment and at worst outright resentment. If managers are not involved in the budget process they not feel part of the drive to achieve the objective, they will not be able to pass any motivation on to their staff and they will have no incentive to improve or change the way the business operates.

Involving all the cost and profit centre management in the process:

- allows them to buy into it
- allows them feel part of the team
- makes them more likely to be motivated to achieve challenging targets
- the budget process is more likely to be accorded the significance it deserves in the annual financial cycle rather than to be seen to be a form filling exercise for head office

Senior management's role in the process is to pull all the strands together and to moderate centre managers' instinctive reaction to maximize the benefits for their own area of responsibility.

REAL LIFE
Budgeting as a management tool in freight

The British International Freight Association, in issuing guidance to its members, had this to say about the budget process:

'Suppose the sales budget has been prepared for an airfreight forwarder. From available data, and knowing the amount of traffic moving on a particular route, capacity requirements by day and airline could be built up. This might involve talking to carriers about availability and pricing. There are further "knock-on" effects: first there is the question of the availability of operations and, for instance transport, and the correct mix of skills. This may in turn lead to decisions about recruitment/training or even changes in working practices. Then there is the question of shift patterns, support staff availability, etc.

'A realistic budget will motivate action. A sales budget is a target that must be achieved. This will motivate the sales managers and their teams to get out there and get the business.

'Budgets often fail because of accountants who think of budgets as being a preview of what the accounting reports will look like if everyone does as they are told. The produce them once a year for a year, failing to see the much bigger picture of a closed loop control system playing a dynamic role in the decision-making process.'

Accountants are often criticized for spending more time establishing controls than understanding the true nature of control within the enterprise. In the dynamic environment currently faced by most businesses, the budget is still an important information source.

Source: British International Freight Association: 'The advantages and disadvantages of budgeting'.

Responsibility accounting

A significant part of the underlying purpose of budgeting is to involve management in the budgeting process to enable them to 'buy in' to corporate objectives. If managers are responsible for the day-to-day operation of profit or cost centres, then they should also be involved in the process of budget setting for the areas for which they have responsibility.

It is important that clear lines of budget setting responsibility are set from the outset by senior management and these should be in line with operational responsibilities.

Examples of such areas of budget responsibility for a manufacturing business could be:

- Sales manager—set sales budget
- Production manager—set production cost budget
- Factory manager—set labour cost budget
- Purchasing manager—set materials purchasing budget
- Office manager—set administration costs budget

Again, line managers may well have to consult with members of their team to get their input on the feasibility of achieving particular objectives or targets. It is of little use setting a sales target or production target if the resources are not available to achieve them, which is why managers should not set budgets in isolation.

EXAMPLE

Senior management in Boldercorp plc have decided that their strategic objectives for 20X8 should include:

- Increasing the turnover of their best-selling product the Bolder by 50 per cent
- Bringing in a new product, the Mini-Bolder, with a sales target of 1 million units by the end of the year
- Reducing overheads and streamlining production by closing a factory in North and moving production to South

The sales manager says:

- Their existing customers will not increase their orders for the Bolder by 50 per cent or tolerate a price rise of that size, so this will involve getting new customers who are already buying from competitors. This means incentivizing them to move with discounts and promotions which may trigger a price war and antagonize existing customers if new ones are getting a better deal.
- The market for the Mini-Bolder is already saturated with similar products so the sales target looks unrealistic.

The production manager says:

- Closing a factory and moving production will delay production whilst the move is underway and the production resumes in the new factory. Most of the staff in North won't move, so will have to be made redundant. This will have implications for staff morale. It will also mean hiring and training new staff.
- Once all the facilities are relocated in South, there will be no room to increase production of the Bolder to meet an increased sales demand of 50 per cent.
- To manufacture the Mini-Bolder in the quantities forecast will mean new equipment and additional staff will be needed—is there a budget for this?

The office manager says:

- Closing North has HR implications which must be dealt with; there will be a significant cost.
- North office has its own payroll and purchasing staff so presumably these functions will relocate to South. This will mean increasing admin staff in South.

Consequently the budgeting process is not one where management can simply decide a list of objectives and mould the business around them: it is an holistic and iterative process. Everyone has to be involved and the process involves amending and updating the budgets until an optimum solution presents itself.

By involving managers who have operational responsibilities in the budget setting process, senior management can devolve the responsibility for meeting budget targets down to those managers. They can then become accountable for the actual results of their area against the budget. This enables senior management to achieve both of the key functions of the budgeting process: those of both planning and control.

Stop and think   What would be the best process for resolving budget issues such as these? How is it handled in an organization you know of? Does it involve an endless series of emails and meetings or does a decision-maker simply make a choice as to what goes in to the budget?

The budget process

The whole process of preparing the budget should be planned and coordinated so that everyone involved knows what to do.

This might involve, as a minimum:

- explaining the purpose of the budget process and what the budgets will be used for
- outlining the organizational objectives for the financial period
- listing individuals with budget responsibilities
- setting deadlines and milestones
- providing standard forms
- explanations from the finance department of how to prepare key budget numbers if there is likely to be any difficulty

Most organizations combine all this information into a budget pack, combining:

- instructions for preparation
- how to deal with difficult matters
- a list of contacts
- a set of pro forma budget schedules

This last point, issuing a set of pro forma schedules, is important when the budget for the organization has to be prepared by several different people for several departments of subsidiaries. The point is that the formats need to be identical so that when all the budgets are combined the information is presented in a coherent way and is easy to follow.

The overriding objective is to produce a master budget for the organization, supported by detailed budgets for each operational area or activity, such as sales budgets, production budgets and even budgeted financial statements. Clearly this is unlikely to happen at the first attempt, so there may have to be many meetings and discussions before all the issues are resolved and decisions made.

The budget process can be summarized as shown in Figure 7.1.

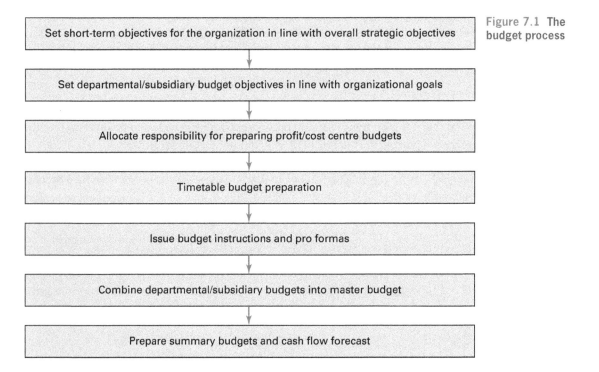

Figure 7.1 **The budget process**

Key budget factors

As we have seen, budgets for different parts of the organization cannot be prepared in isolation. For example:

- The production budget cannot be prepared unless sales and required finished goods inventory levels are known.
- The materials budget cannot be finalized until the production budget and required raw materials stock levels are known.
- The sales budget cannot be set unless production capacity is established.

The key to a successful budget process is to identify the **key budget factor**, which sets the limit on the level of activity the organization is capable of achieving.

This is a limit to what an organization can achieve in one budget area. For example, there might be a limit to the amount of product that can be produced. The equation is quite a simple one: if the organization can sell all the product the business can make, production becomes the key budget factor. If market share is limited, sales or revenues is likely to become the key budget factor.

Once the key budget factor is identified and quantified all the other budgets can be developed based on quantities and costs devolved from it.

EXAMPLE

Toby plc is in the process of setting its budgets. The sales manager estimates that the maximum sales of its main product, the Hopper, are 25 000 units per year. The factory can produce 20 000 Hoppers per year due to limitations in the production process. Hoppers cannot be sourced elsewhere as they are a unique product.

How does this affect the budget process?

ANSWER

It would be of little use setting budgets based on sales of 25 000 units. Instead budgets should be set based on maximum achievable production of 20 000 units.

As a consequence, the key budget factor sets a hierarchy of budgets. In the example of Toby shown below the budgets are dependent on the level of production as Toby can sell all it makes, so the hierarchy is:

Of course the hierarchy is not fixed. If Toby expands its production capacity then sales may become the key budget factor, but the expansion of capacity will have to be factored into a budget. If the expansion is part way through a financial period, the budget hierarchy may change part way through the period.

The important thing is that such changes are planned and factored in to the budget process.

Once the budget is established and finalized it becomes fixed. At this point:

- it becomes the yardstick by which actual activity is measured.
- if the business is using absorption costing it is used to set the overhead absorption rate (Module 2)

However a fixed and immutable budget can only tell management certain things—principally by how far actual performance is deviating from planned performance. What it is not telling management is whether or not, at the actual activity level, they are controlling their costs and margins so as to maximize their return.

So during the financial period the initial budget may be flexed to reflect the actual activity level.

Fixed and flexible budgets

The budget set at the beginning of the financial period is the fixed budget for that period. It, hopefully, represents the collective wisdom of all the management team and is their best estimate of the likely outcome for the financial period.

As each month goes by management will measure their actual result against this budget and seek to explain why there are variations from the forecast figures.

However, this is of limited value. Unless the actual level of output is very close to the original budget figures, this basis of comparison is of little use for management purposes.

The reason is simple: suppose the original budget forecast an output of 1500 units and the actual output is 1800 units. The reason for every variation in the amounts of cost and revenue between the budget figures and the actual figures will be attributed to the difference in the level of output. In Module 2, we saw how costs behave differently (fixed or variable) and we can make use of this behaviour to compare costs at different levels of output.

EXAMPLE

Bolo Ltd has set its budget based on 1500 units of output and at the end of the financial year actually achieved sales of 1800 units. The summarized results were as follows.

	Budget 1 500 units £000's	Actual 1 800 units £000's
Sales	20 000	23 000
Direct costs	8 000	9 250
Indirect production costs	5 000	5 500
Fixed overheads	2 000	2 000
	15 000	16 750
Profit	5 000	6 250

Bolo is congratulating itself on having put in a really good performance and beating its targets. But how well has it done really?

ANSWER

It is difficult to tell if Bolo has done well or badly through a simple comparison of the actual result with the original budget.

In order for management to find out if the business has performed well or badly compared with its budget it is necessary to amend, or flex, the original budget up or down to the actual level of output.

Using the budget data for Bolo above we can flex the original budget figures to reflect the actual level of output. For this purpose, we will assume all revenues and costs are variable, so we can simply flex the original budget by:

$$\text{Original budget} \times \frac{1800}{1500}$$

	Budget 1 500 units £000's	Flexed budget 1 800 units £000's	Actual 1 800 units £000's
Revenues	20 000	24 000	23 000
Direct costs	8 000	9 600	9 250
Indirect production costs	5 000	6 000	5 500
Fixed overheads	2 000	2 000	2 000
	15 000	17 600	16 750
Profit	5 000	6 400	6 250

Because the budget has been adjusted to the actual level of output, a direct comparison can be made between the actual result and what it should have been had the revenue and cost levels been achieved based on the flexed budget. So, we can now see that:

- turnover was below the level it should have been at that level of output
- there were savings in direct costs
- because some of the overhead was fixed, this did not change with activity

So, in fact, Bolo narrowly missed its flexed budget target because of the shortfall in revenues, although this was partly outweighed by cost savings.

In practice this budget flexing will be done as the financial period progresses, thus enabling managers to take action as required.

It is clear that comparison between the actual figures and the flexed budget figures gives management a much greater insight into what actually happened in the financial period. It enables them to achieve the second objective of budgeting, that of control.

Managers using flexible budgets can detect variations in performance and raise questions or take action to enable budget objectives to be achieved.

Approaches to budget preparation

There are two approaches to actually preparing the figures to go into the budgets. These are:

- zero base budgeting
- incremental budgeting

INCREMENTAL BUDGETING   Using an incremental budgeting approach the individual who has to draft a budget, say for the next financial year, will take this year's budget and amend it for:

- inflation
- known price increases
- known or likely changes in operations

It is generally known as *'last year plus x per cent'* and, fundamentally, all that is required is to adjust for:

- known changes since the last financial period or forecast to be in the budgeting period
- the percentage level of change

On this basis organizations produce a budget that is basically little changed from what went on before. This approach has advantages:

- it is simple to prepare
- it is quick and inexpensive
- it takes all known factors into account
- it is relatively simple to explain

However, it has one major drawback: It doesn't encourage anything to change. Inefficiencies that are in the system stay in the system because they don't have to be questioned, merely budgeted for.

It is very popular in larger organizations because it can, generally, be prepared quite quickly so a complex budgeting process is avoided. Public sector organizations which are government-funded use this method almost exclusively.

ZERO BASE BUDGETING   Zero base budgeting does not refer to previous accounting periods. Instead all budget headings start from a zero base and have to be built up from there. Thus, no assumptions are made about previous levels of revenue or expense.

This method has the advantage that, carried out properly, all budget headings are considered afresh every year and all assumptions are challenged. Thus, wastages and inefficiencies in the organization are tackled, and steps taken to improve processes and results.

This approach has several disadvantages:

- it is only often fully implemented in organizations with a commitment to change
- it is time-consuming
- it can be expensive in terms of time
- it can be difficult to explain the approach to non-financial managers

It is popular among organizations with quite flat management structures where there is much more of a team approach to management, commitment to organizational goals is more apparent and the business is able to react and absorb change quickly.

Preparation of a budget

The best way to illustrate the budget process is to show by example the process of preparation. This obviously necessitates preparation of a good deal of information and detail.

EXAMPLE

Tumbledown Ltd makes two products: X42 and the Z31. Managers have prepared forecasts of potential sales for the next financial period of:

X42 – 12 000 units at £95 each
Z31 – 8000 units at £75 each

It has inventory levels of:

	Opening inventory	Required closing inventory
X42	500 units	1000 units
Z31	250 units	300 units

Cost details are as follows:

Raw materials	Price per unit	X42	Z31
Component 1	£3.50	4 per unit	3 per unit
Component 2	£2.00	3 per unit	4 per unit
Direct labour hours	£12.00 per hour	4 per unit	3 per unit
Machine time (hours)	£5.00 per hour	2 per unit	1 per unit

Component inventory required:

	Opening inventory	Required closing inventory
Component 1	2000	1500
Component 2	700	400

Production overheads are recovered based on labour hours and are:

Variable	1.60 per hour
Fixed	0.80 per hour
	£2.40 per hour

So we can now begin to prepare the budgets. There are no constraints on production as the key budget factor in this case is sales, so we prepare the sales budget first.

SALES BUDGET

	Total	X42	Z31
Unit sales	20000	12000	8000
Price		£95	£75
Sales value	£1 740 000	£1 140 000	£600 000

In reality, there would be more than two products and sales forecasts would come from all departments involved in direct selling.

Now we can prepare a production budget of units to be made. Notice that we have to build into the production budget the closing inventory, but we don't need to make the whole of the forecast sales units + the closing inventory, as we already have some in our opening inventory.

PRODUCTION BUDGET (UNITS)

	Total	X42	Z31
Opening inventory	(750)	(500)	(250)
Forecast sales	20000	12000	8000
Closing inventory	1 300	1 000	300
Production required	20 550	12 500	8 050

(continued)

Once we have the production requirements we can use these to prepare budgets for materials, labour and machine hours.

MATERIALS BUDGET

	Total	Component 1 (units)		Component 2 (units)
Production X42				
12,500 units × 4	87 500	50 000	12 500 × 3	37 500
Production Z31				
8050 units × 3	56 350	24 150	8050 × 4	32 200
Opening inventory	(2 700)	(2 000)		(700)
Closing inventory	1 900	1 500		400
Units required	143 050	73 650		69 400
Price per unit		£3.50		£2.00
Purchases	£396 575	£257 775		£138 800

Again we have to take account of opening and closing inventory to give the full level of purchasing of components required.

DIRECT LABOUR BUDGET

X42	12 500 units @ 4 hrs per unit x £12	=		600 000
Z31	8050 @ 3 hrs per unit x £12		289 800	
Total				£889 800

MACHINE HOURS BUDGET

X42	12 500 units @ 2 hrs per unit × £5	=	125 000
Z31	8050 @ 1 hrs per unit × £5		40 250
Total			£165 250

PRODUCTION OVERHEAD

Labour hours	
X42	12 500 × 4 = 50 000
Z31	8050 × 3 = 24 150
	74 150

So the budget for overhead is:

		X42	Z31
Fixed	74 150 × 0.80 = £59 320	40 000	19 320
Variable	74 150 × £1.60 = £118 640	80 000	38 640

We now have all the components with which to formulate a budget. We can look at it in total for the organization.

Operating budget for Tumbledown

	£
Sales	1 740 000
Materials	396 575
Labour	889 800
Machine time	165 250
Variable overhead	118 640
Fixed overhead	59 320
Total costs	1 629 585
Budgeted profit	£110 415

This is an operating budget and can be broken down by product, providing the inventory is allocated so materials costs can be shown by product; this has not been done for convenience.

Note that it is not strictly a profit and loss or income account in the full accounting sense, as it does not deal with opening and closing inventory valuations. Those with knowledge of financial accounting will have noticed that in the production budget and the materials budget we deduct the opening inventory and add the closing inventory in order to arrive at the required quantities.

This is the opposite of what is done in financial accounting, where we add opening inventory to purchases and deduct closing inventories. However, we are preparing an operating budget, not an income account, so we have missed this step in order to illustrate the preparation of a budget.

Obviously in the real-world budgeting is more complex than this, as it involves many more products and lots of variables but the point is made that this is the methodology to adopt, no matter how complex the information which is going to go into a budget.

In particular, an operating budget will be prepared on a monthly basis so that it can be matched against the actual revenues and costs from monthly management accounts. At this point the original budget can be flexed, as shown above, to facilitate comparison with actual output levels rather than those anticipated at the beginning of the financial period.

Cash budgets

Cash flow is the most important aspect of the financial management of an organization. It is quite acceptable to prepare budgets and forecasts and to anticipate sales volumes and costs, but the key to survival and prosperity is cash flow.

A business can survive making losses—at least for a while—it cannot manage without cash. Even the biggest businesses fail if the cash flow dries up, so it is imperative that, once the budget process is complete in terms of an operating budget, this is translated into a cash flow statement.

The key to preparation of the cash budget is time. As most businesses of any size operate on credit, both for buying and for selling, this means that:

- customers take time to pay in accordance with credit terms
- suppliers are not paid straightaway but also on credit terms

so that the actual movement of cash does not follow the accounting.

In addition, there are various items classified as costs, but which do not represent actual cash outflows. Principal among these is depreciation, which is merely an accounting construct, but it would also include such items as provisions for doubtful debts, general provisions for unquantified costs, etc. In short, if it isn't represented by cash it doesn't go in.

As we know financial or management accounts are prepared on an accruals basis: this is the convention that revenues, costs and other expenditures that relate to a particular accounting period are included in that period whether cash has changed hands or not.

EXAMPLE

Happyco Ltd must pay for insurance for its assets and public liability. The insurance company bills Happyco R2400 every six months (one bill in January, the next in July). If each bill is for six months of coverage, then under cash accounting, Happyco would record a R2400 expense in January and a R2400 expense in July.

However this would not be correct, as each month should carry its own share of insurance cost, therefore Happyco would include a R200 charge for insurance in each of its monthly accounts for the accounting year.

When we are preparing a cash budget or cash flow statement we are looking to establish when cash actually moves through the organization's bank account, not when invoices are processed through its system.

So the information needed is:

- Budgeted sales
- Time taken for customers to pay sales invoices
- Forecast purchasing requirements
- Time taken to pay suppliers
- Other cash movements such as capital equipment purchases, tax payments, interest receipts, etc.
- Normally wages and salary costs are assumed to be paid monthly

This information is then collated into a management information system.

The schedules and workings for these statements tend to be long and complicated as each item of revenue or cost must be calculated separately.

The best way to illustrate this is by an example.

EXAMPLE

Happyco is preparing its cash budget for the year ended 31 December 20X8.

It has set its budget for 20X8. Key information extracted from that budget and other relevant information is:

1 The following are estimates of sales for the first four months of the financial year.

20X8	$
January	280000
February	420000
March	490000
April	560000

2 Sales for the last three months of the previous year were:

20X7	$
October	420000
November	350000
December	420000

3 Sales are expected to be paid as to:

- 1st month after invoice—70%
- 2nd month after invoice—20%
- 3rd month after invoice—10%

4 Purchases of materials are 50% of selling price.
5 The inventory at 1 January 20X8 is £90000. The company wishes to maintain an inventory level based on one month's sales as shown by the forecast.
Purchases are paid for 100% in the following month.
6 Opening payables at 1 January 20X8 were $120000.
7 Payments for wages and salaries were:

20X8	$
January	95000
February	98000
March	96000

8 Other payments for overheads in each month were forecast to be:

20X8	$
January	35000
February	40000
March	38000

These are paid 100 per cent the month following invoice.
Opening payables for overheads were $32000.

9 During the year the company aims to launch an advertising campaign. The costs will be paid equally in February and June. The full cost of the campaign is $80000.
10 Replacements for machinery will have to be made. This will involve an acquisition of equipment in January, which will be paid for in equal instalments over six months starting in February. The full cost of the equipment is $120000.
11 The opening bank balance at 1 January 20X8 is $81000.

We are required to work out the cash budget for the first three months of the year 20X8.
So, we have to deal with each of these separately and bring them all together at the end to form a summary cash budget.

Stop and think

Is there an easy way to work out how quickly customers pay? Would an aged receivables report help?

Firstly let us deal with revenues. We know that customers don't pay straight away, and we have been given the company's estimate of the proportion of customers who pay after the first month, the second month and so on. That is why we are given the sales figures from months prior to the start of the period because some of the money from those invoices will come in during the period for which we are preparing the statement.

So the cash inflow from sales invoices looks like this:

Step 1 Sales and revenues

	Invoiced sales	October	November	December	January	February	March
20X7							
October	420 000		294 000	84 000	42 000		
November	350 000			245 000	70 000	35 000	
December	420 000				294 000	84 000	42 000
20X8							
January	280 000					196 000	56 000
February	420 000						294 000
March	490 000						
					406 000	**315 000**	**392 000**

We are only looking for the cash receipts for three months. Notice that no receipts for March 20X8 are included but there are receipts from invoices issued before the start of the year.

The next step is to deal with purchases and payments to suppliers. There are two things to bear in mind here.

Purchases are described as being 50 per cent of selling price—that is, 50 per cent of invoiced value not of cash received.

The company wishes to maintain inventory levels, so this means we have to buy for inventory as well as for sale. We have an opening inventory, so that is our starting point:

Step 2 Purchases and payments to suppliers
First of all, we have to work out what liability is going to be incurred to supplier each month.
To do this, we have to work out the value of materials purchases each month.

	Invoiced sales	Purchases @ 50%	Opening inventory	Closing inventory	Net payment
December	420 000	210 000			
20X8					
January	280 000	140 000	(190 000)	210 000	160 000
February	420 000	210 000	(210 000)	245 000	245 000
March	490 000	245 000	(245 000)	280 000	280 000
April	560 000	280 000			

Remember that we subtract the opening inventory because we already have it, so do not have to buy it.
The opening inventory for January is given in the question.
We are also given the opening amount for payables at 1 January, which will be paid in January.
January's purchases will be paid in February and so on.

So the cash budget for purchases for the three months will look like this:

	January	February	March
Opening payables	120 000		
Purchases		160 000	245 000
	120 000	**160 000**	**245 000**

Looking at the question, none of the other features of the cash budget appear to need to be reallocated for time so we can proceed to put together a total budget.

Step 3 Cash budget

	January $	February $	March $	Total $
Revenues	406 000	315 000	392 000	1 113 000
Purchases	120 000	160 000	245 000	525 000
Wages and salaries	95 000	98 000	96 000	289 000
Overheads	32 000	35 000	40 000	107 000
Advertising campaign		40 000		40 000
Equipment purchases		20 000	20 000	40 000
	247 000	353 000	401 000	1 001 000
Cash movement	159 000	(38 000)	(9 000)	112 000
Opening balance	81 000	240 000	202 000	81 000
Closing balance	**240 000**	**202 000**	**193 000**	**193 000**

As can be seen, the final balance in the Total column is the same as the closing balance in March 20X8, which indicates that the schedule is arithmetically correct. We can see from the forecast that the company has generated cash of $112 000 from operations mainly due to the fact that November and December of the previous year were very good. January sales were weak, so February and March showed a cash outflow, which would no doubt be remedied later in the year as March and April sales were quite strong.

This is quite a straightforward example designed to illustrate the key points of preparing a cash budget. The key to preparing the budget is to work carefully through each item and schedule them all separately so that they can be brought together as a summary.

Clearly, in practice, such budgets would be prepared for a year and would form part of an integrated whole with the main budget for sales, costs and expenses. This then provides management with a mechanism for both planning and control.

As the year progresses, the budgets will be revised and amended as part of management control but the original budget, prepared at the start of the financial period, will remain fixed as a yardstick to measure the ultimate performance of the organization in the period.

Test yourself

1 The following information has been extracted from the payables records of Teddy Ltd:

Invoices paid in the month of purchase	25%
Invoices paid in the month after purchase	70%
Invoices paid in the second month after purchase	5%

Purchases for March to May are budgeted as:

March	€250 000
April	€300 000
May	€280 000

For supplier paid in the month of purchase there is a 5 per cent prompt settlement discount.

The payments budgeted for suppliers in May is:

a) €227 000

b) €240 000

c) €289 000

d) €292 500

The following information relates to questions 2 and 3

Bilto is preparing a production budget for the next financial period.

The estimated sales in units for the first four periods in the financial year are:

Month 1	6000 units
Month 2	7000 units
Month 3	5500 units
Month 4	6000 units

40 per cent of each month's sales are to be produced in the month of sale and the remainder in the previous month.

50 per cent of the direct materials required for each month will be purchased in the month of production and the remainder in the previous month.

Direct materials cost is £5 per unit.

2 The production budget in units for Month 1 is:

a) 2400 units

b) 5200 units

c) 6000 units

d) 6600 units

3 The materials cost budget for Month 2 is:

a) 29 750

b) 30 500

c) 31 750

d) 35 000

4 Which of the following statements are true or false?

	True	False
A flexible budget is a budget that is prepared for a year, reviewed monthly and each time actual results are reported a further forecast period is added and previous forecast periods deleted.		
Depreciation would not be included in a cash budget.		
Objectives can be expressed in broad terms as they represent aspirations rather than actual targets.		
The key budget factor sets the limitations on how the budget should be structured.		

The following information relates to questions 5 and 6

Twinkle Plc is preparing a production budget for one of its products, the Nord. Each Nord requires 5 kg of a material called Seaspod.

Twinkle has 5000 units of the Nord already in inventory at the beginning of the period and, due to anticipated demand, the company wants to increase this by 30 per cent by the end of the period.

Twinkle has 50 000 kg of Seaspod in its warehouse but, again, feels that an inventory level of 60 000 kg would be better to avoid production delays.

The anticipated sales of the Nord for the period are expected to be 70 000 units.

5 How many units of the Nord are forecast to be produced in the period?
   a) 68 500 units
   b) 71 500 units
   c) 76 500 units
   d) 80 000 units

6 What will be the materials purchases budget for Seaspod?
   a) 347 500 kg
   b) 350 000 kg
   c) 357 500 kg
   d) 367 500 kg

7 Humble Ltd has the following sales forecast:

	Jan £000's	Feb £000's	March £000's	April £000's
Sales	700	900	500	750

All sales are on credit. Customers pay 10 per cent in month of sale, 40 per cent one month after and 45 per cent two months after sale.

The company makes a provision of 5 per cent for doubtful debts.
What are the budgeted receipts from customers in April?
   a) £750 000
   b) £656 000
   c) £680 000
   d) £390 000

8 Able has the following extract from its budget preparation:

	Jan	Feb	Mar
Opening inventory in units	200	300	240
Closing inventory in units	300	240	360
Sales in units	800	900	840

Materials cost is $10 per unit. 40 per cent of purchases are for cash and 60 per cent on credit paid two months after purchase.

There are no changes to inventory levels.

What is the purchases cash budget for March?

a) $9240

b) $8880

c) $7080

d) $8160

9 Which of the following statements are true or false?

	True	False
Incremental budgeting is simply taking the previous budget and adjusting it for inflation and known changes.		
Establish a materials purchasing budget by taking purchases + opening inventory − closing inventory.		
The key budget factor is always sales.		
Companies could use zero base budgeting if they wished to totally review their operations.		

10 Bolington plc has the following overhead budget in one of its departments:

Period 1   £98000

Period 2   £82000

One quarter of the budget is for fixed costs including depreciation of £4000 per month.

Payments for variable overhead are made as to 50 per cent in the current month and 50 per cent in the month following.

Payments for fixed overhead are made 100 per cent in the month following them being incurred.

What will be the payment for fixed and variable overheads for Period 2?

a) £67 500

b) £88 000

c) £92 000

d) £84 000

In the next module we are moving away from costing and budgeting to look at investment appraisal. Companies commit large amounts of money towards purchasing major assets—but how can they predict whether or not the investment will pay off over time? We look at the time value of money and how it affects investment decision-making.

Test yourself

1 Abalone plc is a manufacturing company, which makes a product Able.

The budgeted monthly production and sales are 200 000 units. The selling price is £18 per unit.

A standard cost has been estimated on the basis of direct costs of £7.00 for materials (2 kg @ £3.50 per kg) and £6.00 for wages (half an hour @ £12 per hour). In addition, variable overheads have been determined as £2.00 per unit and monthly fixed overheads are £200 000.

Monthly sales for the first five months of 20X8 have been estimated as:

	Units
January	210000
February	180000
March	210000
April	220000
May	200000

Actual sales at the end of 20X7 were 190000 in November and 220000 in December. Cash received from sales is based on previous experience and is expected to be received:

- 60 per cent in the month of sale
- 25 per cent in the following month
- 10 per cent two months after the sale

Creditors for raw materials are paid at the end of the month of purchase.

Direct wages are paid in the month in which they are incurred.

Variable overheads are paid 60 per cent in the month in which they are incurred, and 40 per cent in the following month.

Fixed overheads include £25000 of depreciation and are paid one month after the costs are incurred.

At 1 January 20X8 payables for variable and fixed overheads are estimated as £92000 and £150000 respectively.

The company intends to have finished inventory at the end of each month equivalent to 15 per cent of the following month's budgeted sales. For raw materials inventory, the policy is to have 25 per cent of the following month's production requirements.

Stocks at 1 January 20X8 are estimated as 22000 units of finished goods and 104000 kg of raw materials.

The cash balance at 1 January 20X8 is estimated as £31000.

Produce for the months of January, February and March 20X8:

a) A production budget in units
b) A materials purchases budget
c) A cash budget

2 Last year Bigboy College of Further Education contracted out its catering function to a private company Noshers Catering Services, During the next week there is to be a meeting of the management board of the college to review the success of this policy from a financial perspective.

You are employed in the college finance department and have been asked to prepare a report showing the performance of Noshers in running the catering function for the last college term. The manager of Noshers has provided you with an operating statement and, in accordance with the original agreement, he has also provided an analysis of the costs incurred during the first year.

The statement is shown below:

Noshers Catering Services

Operating statement for the 12-week period—Spring term 20X8 Bigboy College of Further Education

	Fixed budget	Actual results	Variance	
Number of meals provided per week	700	620	80	
	£	£	£	
Variable costs				
Food	37800	36450	1350	(F)
Catering consumables	10500	9872	628	(F)
Domestic supplies	2100	2070	30	(F)
Semi-variable costs				
Menu printing	1122	1145	23	(A)
Stepped costs				
Cooks	16800	16800	nil	
Catering assistants	12000	12000	nil	
Fixed costs				
Rent and rates	7000	7200	200	(A)
Catering manager's salary	8200	8200	nil	
Equipment maintenance contract	750	730	20	(F)
Insurance costs	300	305	5	(A)
Total cost	96572	94772	1800	(F)

Additional information provided by Noshers:
- Food costs are £4.50 per meal.
- Catering consumables cost £1.25 per meal served.
- Domestic materials are £0.25 per meal served.
- Menus are produced by an external printing contractor and Noshers are charged £450 at the start of each term for this service. They are charged an additional cost of £12 for each batch of menus produced. Each batch is sufficient to cover 150 meals.
- One cook is required for every 4000 meals produced. This limit cannot be exceeded. Cooks are paid £5600 per term. All cooks are employed on a full-time basis. Catering assistants are paid £200 per week. One catering assistant is required for every 2000 meals. This limit cannot be exceeded, and all catering assistants are also paid on a full-time basis.
- Fixed costs are charged by the term.

Rachel Waters is the college manager responsible for the provision of catering services and is pleased with the results from the first year. She believes that the policy with regards to the contracting out of the service has been a great success.

Requirement for question

(a) Prepare a revised operating statement for Bigboy College that will more accurately represent the performance of Noshers Catering Services over the spring term.

(b) With reference to cost behaviour, explain for the benefit of Rachel Waters why your operating statement is of more use to management than the one prepared by Noshers.

8 Capital investment appraisal

So far, we have looked at costing and at budgeting techniques that relate to individual financial periods, and how managers budget for the business over a relatively short period. However, as part of the resource planning for the business as a whole, it is also necessary to consider longer-term factors. These include capital expenditure decisions, which can affect the business over several years.

Capital expenditure is expenditure to buy, maintain or improve an organization's assets, such as buildings and machinery, that are required to produce its goods or services. There is little point forecasting production levels if there is no machinery with which to make things. So, managers will review their resources each budgeting period and decide whether or not they need to spend money on buying capital assets.

Clearly it is important that this expenditure is properly planned and controlled. A decision to invest in a major expansion of the factory can involve the business in a major spending programme, often financed by borrowings, so the impact on all aspects of the business can be considerable.

Why appraisal?

The purpose of capital expenditure is to increase the capability of the business to make profits. This can range from the purchase of a car for a sales representative to enable them to visit customers, to a huge new piece of equipment designed to replace outdated machinery and reduce production costs.

It is important to recognize that, from a budgeting point of view, capital expenditure should meet the same criteria as any other expenditure: and thus be included in the budgeting process outlined in Module 7.

- it should be in line with business objectives
- it should be made with a view to increasing profits
- there should be control and monitoring at all levels

Major investment programmes should be subject to a lot of scrutiny and analysis before being started, but it is important to remember that a lot of capital expenditure does not always consist of huge projects. Smaller items of capital expenditure that, individually, seem insignificant, can accumulate into a considerable amount of money over time.

| **Stop and think** | Could you justify capital expenditure on installing a fish tank and expensive lighting into a reception area? |

Capital expenditure decisions must meet overall budget objectives, as discussed in Module 7.

In addition, there must be clearly-defined procedures in place for not only authorizing the expenditure but also monitoring the level of expenditure over time.

Capital projects should be monitored on an ongoing basis during their life and, at the end of the project or at the end of the build phase, there should be a full project review where managers are accountable for:

- what went right
- what went wrong
- any overruns of cost or time
- what lessons can be learned

This is important as senior management must be in control of the project from start to finish, and line managers must be aware that they will be subject to a performance review. There is a long history of capital projects running away with costs and time, with potentially serious problems for the business.

REAL LIFE
Computer meltdown at TSB

A rift has emerged between TSB in the UK and its parent company in Spain, Banco de Sabadell. The IT project, involving the transfer of 1.3 billion customer records from TSB's previous owner, Lloyds, was managed from Spain.

The project led to a complete meltdown of the TSB online banking service.

TSB had claimed before the botched transfer that switching customer records would save more than £100 million a year. 'A new, state-of-the-art platform designed and built with Sabadell … will reduce TSB's costs considerably,' the bank claimed but it now faces a ballooning compensation bill.

TSB customers have spent their seventh successive day battling to access their accounts as the bank admitted the crisis could run into the following week. The bank's boss, Paul Pester, said TSB will waive £10 million in overdraft fees and pay extra interest on current accounts. He has hired a new team of IT experts from IBM, who have been told the problems must be fixed within a few days.

'We are on our knees,' Pester admitted in a BBC interview, adding: 'We will get up and come back fighting.'

More than a day after Pester declared: 'Our internet banking and mobile app are back up and running,' around 50 per cent of TSB online customers were still struggling to access their accounts.

Many reported hour-long waits to speak to TSB staff on the phone, while some of those able to get through online said passwords failed and they remained unable to complete transactions. Customers heading into TSB branches were told by some staff that it could be another five working days to completely clear all the technical faults.

The cause of the IT problems remains unclear. A spokeswoman for TSB said: 'It's really a bandwidth issue that we're facing. On the mobile app, nine in 10 customers are getting through to us. On internet banking, one in two customers are getting through to us. The phones are certainly busier than usual, but people are getting through.'

In a bid to prevent a mass exodus of customers, TSB said: 'We will be waiving all overdraft fees and interest charges for all of our retail and small business customers for April. As a way of saying thank you to our customers for sticking with us, we'll be increasing the interest rate on our Classic Plus account to 5% AER.'

Source: *Guardian Online: 26/04/2018* 'We're on our knees…' *and* 'What does the TSB fiasco tell us about banking in Britain' *27/04/2018*

Capital budgeting

There are two main aspects to creating a capital budget:

- How do we justify the expenditure?
- How is it to be financed?

Clearly the first criterion is whether or not the overall business objectives require the expenditure. If the objectives are expansion or modernization this is going to involve cost, and capital expenditure will be a significant part of that cost. In order to ensure that projects meet the necessary criteria there should be a procedure for dealing with capital projects such as:

- evaluation of the projects
- consideration of any non-financial more qualitative factors
- approval of the project if appropriate
- monitoring the progress of the project
- carrying out a post-completion review for any lesson learned

Let us look at these briefly:

EVALUATE THE PROJECT   Several key questions need to be asked and answered before the project can be approved. These might include:

- What is the project for?
- How does it fit with the organization's objectives?
- Is it something we have to do, i.e. for health and safety reasons or a change of regulations?
- Is there any form of risk evaluation we need to consider?
- Is there another way of achieving the same objective?
- How much will it cost?
- Has a financial evaluation been carried out? What does it show?
- What other resources are needed, e.g. project management?
- Can these be provided in-house or will we need to contract out the whole project?
- How long will it last?
- What are the success criteria?

A financial evaluation of the project is a key part of any system of project approval. In essence, the basic premise is quite simple: how long will the project take to pay for itself?

There is no point is spending money if it isn't going to bring in a return in some way. This might be a cost reduction, e.g. we will spend £1 million on installing robots in our paint line, which means we can replace twenty staff and work more quickly, thus eliminating a bottleneck in the factory.

Clearly there are often lots of financial implications and we will look at these later in the module. There may also be an element of risk involved: for example, the capital expenditure might involve new and untried processes, or equipment that may be prone to breakdown, or increased wastage of materials until it is under control. This risk element will also have to be factored in to the evaluation.

NON-FINANCIAL FACTORS   There may be some non-financial factors relevant to the decision that have to be considered. For example, a decision to buy robot equipment and dispense with people may have a knock-on effect on staff morale elsewhere. This may have to be factored into the decision and a way of dealing with the people affected may have to be found, and any cost attached to that factored in to the project evaluation.

Considerations might include:

- What are the consequences of not undertaking the project? Is it needed expenditure that, if not carried out, would have an adverse affect on staff morale, lead to limitation on product development, possible loss of market share, etc.?
- What is the effect on the business's reputation or image of carrying out the project, if any?
- If we start this investment will we have to continue with more investment in the future—i.e. have we started a whole modernization programme?
- Will it improve our speed of response to market forces and make us better able to develop and produce new products, or distance us from our competitors?

PROJECT APPROVAL   This is usually a formal process whereby a document is produced to the decision-making body, e.g. the board of directors or a subcommittee of the board, for formal approval. Once this is received and recorded the project can proceed.

MONITOR THE PROJECT   The monitoring function will be trying to ensure:

- The capital expenditure limit is not exceeded
- The project is not delayed
- The benefits of the project will be achieved

Large capital expenditure projects have a nasty way of exceeding their budgets, for example, the recent construction of Crossrail in London went over budget by £900 m. This causes problems for the business as it requires additional resources over and above those forecast and the business may find itself in a situation where it cannot stop or pull out of the project because it is so far advanced. Consequently, it has to commit more and more resources.

This will, usually, require further submissions to the authorizing body, which will require detailed explanations of what is happening. Clearly there may be some discretion in the original authorization of expenditure—say a 5 per cent limit on cost exceeding budget—but when that limit is exceeded more resources might have to be committed, so further financial evaluations will be needed.

POST COMPLETION REVIEW   Once the project is completed there should be some form of review or audit to consider:

- What went right and what went wrong?
- Did we meet our budgeted targets?
- Was it completed on time? If not why not?
- How effective was the project management?

- Was there anywhere where costs could have been saved now we have the benefit of hindsight?
- Were there any factors outside our control which affected the project, e.g. weather, failure of suppliers, etc.?
- Will the anticipated benefits still emerge?
- What could we do better next time?

Clearly, even relatively small projects would benefit from such a review and larger projects may well require quite a comprehensive analysis in order to identify the costs and future implications of the project. It may not be possible precisely to identify cause and effect in the case of complex projects. A problem in one area may well lead to cost implications in another area and there is probably a limit as to how far a post-completion review should go.

There will be main themes that could be identified, and these will form the basis of experience for handling future projects, but despite the willingness of cost accountants to analyze all cost variances in detail, much of that sort of work may be a futile exercise if the project or something like it is not going to be repeated.

However valuable lessons may have been learned about:

- poor project planning
- bad design requiring rework
- inadequate scheduling of materials and equipment causing delays
- weak project management
- the unreliability of certain suppliers
- issues with the workforce
- the time of year to undertake or not undertake such projects

and so on.

Or, alternatively, all may have gone wonderfully well, so the review will be full of praise for expert management, wonderful suppliers and a diligent workforce who brought in the project ahead of time and under budget.

The outcome of the review should take the form of a formal report, which is circulated for information and considered for the benefit of future projects.

Stop and think	Before committing funds for a big purchase, i.e. a new car, new computer system, training course, what factors would you take into consideration? How would you evaluate the benefits? Can they all be translated into financial terms?

Capital project appraisal

Each project is unique—although there may be some common factors between projects—but most have to be evaluated on their own merits. Clearly there will be specific financial factors unique to each project, but at some point these have to be collated and summarized to identify:

- the costs of the project
- the benefits in terms of improved profits or better cash flow

Once this is done, a further exercise has to be carried out to look at the viability of the project over time.

The cost of the project will be an outflow of resources in, say Year 1 or Years 1 and 2. The benefits from the project will, hopefully, last for much longer. However, there is the question of the effect of time on these benefits. To put it simply, €100 now is worth a lot more than €100 in five years' time, partly because having the money now allows you to use it to earn a return. By waiting for the money in five years' time you go without that opportunity. So how can the project be justified in terms of the benefits exceeding its cost?

There are several techniques which can be used to evaluate this. These are:

- payback period
- accounting rate of return
- net present value

The objective of all these techniques is to relate the return, or payback, to the level of the expenditure. In most cases, the return is the cash flow arising from the project, except the accounting rate of return method which is based on increased profit generation. The main difference is that profit is stated *after* depreciation and cash flow is stated *before* depreciation.

As with all budgeting processes, investment appraisal looks forward into the future so there is always an element of uncertainty involved. The longer the period involved the greater the level of uncertainty and the greater the chance of unquantifiable factors appearing to affect carefully laid plans.

Whilst evaluating projects can look quite straightforward in textbook examples, in real life matters are not so clear cut. There are particular problems:

- How do we identify the returns from the investment? How do we isolate increased profits or cash flows caused by the investment and nothing else? Unless the investment is for a completely new venture where the results can be clearly identified, there has to be a certain amount of judgement and arbitrary decision-making in deciding what inflows to use as paybacks for the investment.
- How do we decide what discount rate is suitable? The basis has to be the rate at which the business can borrow money. The discount rate has to be better than this, otherwise the project becomes difficult to justify.

These two factors mean that carrying out this exercise in reality is neither simple nor straightforward, but nevertheless has to be carried out to create a case for the initial investment. Without any form of calculation, funds can be committed without any evaluation of a return.

Consequently the process of evaluation of the project is as important as as the calculations themselves.

REAL LIFE
IT and investment appraisal

For many businesses, IT is one of the biggest areas of investment today. However, it is also one of the most difficult. While IT projects can promise high returns, they can be particularly risky. It is commonly observed, for example, that the anticipated benefits from IT investments are not fully achieved and the media continues to report high profile failures.

Many businesses also struggle to articulate and quantify the benefits of IT systems, reducing the usefulness of the appraisal and investment management process. What makes IT investment so difficult in practice is isolating the impact of IT from other influences and attributing changes in cash flow to IT systems. The benefits from IT projects, in many cases, are integrally linked with process changes, creating new customer services or providing more data to support decision-making. This makes the benefits often unpredictable, dependent on many other factors and impossible to separate.

As a result, the usefulness of established techniques, such as return on investment (ROI), can be reduced in practice. This also leads onto complex implementation projects which need to go far beyond technology and consider factors such as process change and competitive strategy.

Source: Investment Appraisal. Finance & Management—Special Report. *Institute of Chartered Accountants in England and Wales,* December 2009

Payback period

When deciding between several projects this method can give a quick decision as to which one might be the most favourable.

Broadly it considers the time it takes for the inflows from the project to equal the initial outflow—or in other words, to pay it back. Under this method, the inflows are the profits before depreciation because the appraisal is based on a cash return to match a cash outflow.

EXAMPLE

H ere are the figures for two projects:

	Project A	Project B
	£	£
Capital expenditure	100 000	100 000
Profits before depreciation		
Year 1	20 000	55 000
Year 2	25 000	40 000
Year 3	30 000	35 000
Year 4	30 000	5 000
Year 5	35 000	5 000
Year 6	40 000	5 000
Year 7	35 000	5 000

REQUIRED

Using the payback method, which project would be preferred?

ANSWER

One of the ways we can do this is by looking at the cumulative cash flow from each project:

	Project A	Cumulative cash flow	Project B	Cumulative cash flow
Expenditure	(100 000)	(100 000)	(100 000)	(100 000)
Year 1	20 000	(80 000)	55 000	(45 000)
Year 2	25 000	(55 000)	40 000	(5 000)
Year 3	30 000	(25 000)	35 000	30 000
Year 4	30 000	5 000	5 000	35 000
Year 5	35 000	40 000	5 000	40 000
Year 6	40 000	80 000	5 000	45 000
Year 7	35 000	115 000	5 000	50 000

Project A will payback £100 000 shortly towards the end of Year 4 whereas Project B will payback £100 000 at the beginning of Year 3. Consequently, Project B might be preferred.

DISADVANTAGES AND ADVANTAGES OF THE PAYBACK METHOD   The example shown above illustrates the major problem with this method. Project A will pay back £215 000 over seven years for the £100 000 investment. Project B on the other hand will pay back £150 000 over that same period, and yet, under the payback method, this could be the preferred project. The business will have to decide which of these factors is the most important.

This method has several other disadvantages:

- it ignores the time value of money
- it cannot distinguish between two projects with the same payback period, even if the timing of the cash flows is different
- it ignores the timing of cash flows
- it can lead to over emphasis on short-term projects.

However it has its advantages:

- it is simple to operate and understand
- it avoids projects where capital is tied up for long periods
- it maximizes projects which give quick returns.

The payback method should not be used as the only method of appraising projects but it can provide an initial indication of which projects might be worth considering in more detail.

Accounting rate of return (ARR)

The accounting rate of return method uses the rate of return, in terms of profit, a project should yield as a measure of its viability. If the project exceeds a target rate of return set by the business, the project is considered viable and may go ahead. It is basically the same as a ratio used in financial accounting called the return on capital employed (ROCE).

Remember that this is the only appraisal method that uses profit, which includes depreciation. All other methods use cash flow, which excludes depreciation, as the measure of return.

The level of investment, the capital expenditure, is usually fairly clear. The problem is often to decide what constitutes the level of return. There are two alternatives:

- estimated total profits
- estimated average profits

Most authorities seem to favour the first approach, using total profits estimated from the project, but it doesn't really matter which is used providing it is used consistently.

The calculation is based on a formula:

$$\frac{\text{Estimated total profits} \times 100}{\text{Estimated capital investment}}$$

or:

$$\frac{\text{Estimated average profits} \times 100}{\text{Estimated capital investment}}$$

In practice the profits after depreciation need to be calculated as a proportion of the average capital outlay over the period.

EXAMPLE

A company uses a rate of return of 15 per cent to justify capital projects. A project has the following proposal:

Capital expenditure	£100000
Useful life of asset	4 years

Profits before depreciation arising from project are estimated to be:

Year 1	30000
Year 2	32000
Year 3	35000
Year 4	30000

The asset will be depreciated over the four years and will have no residual value. Should the project be undertaken?

ANSWER

The total profit over the four years will be £127000, and after depreciating the asset to nil, the profit is reduced to £27000 for the four years. The average annual profit after depreciation is:

$$£27000/4 = £6750$$

The original cost of the investment is £100000. Its average net book value over four years is:

$$\frac{£100000 + 0\ (\text{residual value})}{2} = £50000$$

The project gives a return of:

$$\frac{6750 \times 100}{50000} = 13.5\%$$

This falls below the required return so the project should not be undertaken.

AVERAGE INVESTMENT VALUE   There is one point not included in the example above. Suppose the asset had a residual value of, say £20000.

When we are looking at the value of the investment we would need to **add** that residual value to the cost of the investment. This seems counterintuitive, but remember that we are working on the average value of the investment. It never falls below £20000, so the average is £100000 plus £20000 = £120000 ÷ 2 = £60000.

In that case the calculation will be:

$$\frac{6750 \times 100}{60000} = 11.25\%$$

Again the return is below the required return.

ADVANTAGES AND DISADVANTAGES OF ARR   The accounting rate of return method has both advantages and disadvantages.

Its advantages are:

- it is quick and simple to use
- it uses a common measure—a percentage return
- profits can be calculated relatively easily
- it looks at the whole project from start to end
- it is relatively easily understood

However it has some major drawbacks as a method of investment appraisal.

Its biggest disadvantage is that it doesn't take into account the timing effect of returns. It would give the same answer if all the return came in the last year or the first. As money tied up in a project cannot be used elsewhere, this is a serious drawback to using this method, except perhaps for relatively short-term projects.

Other disadvantages are:

- It is based on accounting profits, which are subject to a range of accounting treatments including estimates and constructs such as depreciation
- It takes no account of the size of the initial investment; it is simply a relative measure working out a percentage return, so it takes no account of cash flows
- It takes no account of the length of the project
- It ignores the time value of money

Net present value (NPV)

As we have seen, one of the problems with the two previous methods is that neither of them takes account of the time value of money. This concept is that £10 today is worth more to us than £10 in three years' time. If we get it now, we can invest, spend it or put it in the bank. In any event we can derive a benefit from it in some way. If we have to wait three years we cannot derive that benefit. This is an important consideration in evaluating larger scale projects, which might only bring benefits over an extended time scale.

NPV adjusts cashflows to allow for the time value of money. We start with a future value and convert it to a present-day value, using a discount rate. In other words, it estimates what the value of £10 in three years' time is worth today, based on a rate of return. The rate of return is the amount you would have to invest now, in your chosen method of investment, to achieve £10 in three years' time. This is called discounting.

DISCOUNTING   If a business has £10,000 to invest and can earn a return of 10 per cent, its investment will grow as follows:

After 1 year	10 000 x 1.10	= £11 000
After 2 years	10 000 x 1.10 x 1.10	= £12 100
After 3 years	10 000 x 1.10 x 1.10 x 1.10	= £13 310

This will be familiar to anyone who has seen compound interest calculations. Discounting works in precisely the same way but converts the future value back to the value of the original investment.

In other words, the net present value of an amount of £13 310 earned over three years at a discount rate of 10 per cent is £10 000. This is the basis of the net present value method.

The net present value method compares the present-day values of all the future inflows against the present-day value of all the future outflows.

If the net present values are positive, then the project can go ahead as the inflows exceed the outflows. If the NPV is zero the two flows are equal, and if it is negative the project is not worth undertaking as the outflows exceed the inflows.

Stop and think	Consider a job offer: you could have a 3 per cent increase in salary now, or a 5 per cent increase in eighteen months' time. Which would you prefer? What factors influence your decision?

Fortunately you don't have to work out the mathematics for all the different discount rates and years as this has already been done. The calculations are contained in net present value tables. All you have to do is to look up the discount rate and the year and the tables will give you a multiplier per £1.

This methodology is known as discounted cash flow (DCF).

EXAMPLE

Bigli plc is considering a capital project with the following cash flows. It uses a discount rate of 10 per cent. By convention, the year of investment is always Year 0.

Year	Cash flow
0 (now)	(100 000)
1	50 000
2	45 000
3	30 000
4	30 000

We need to calculate the NPV of the project and ascertain if it should be undertaken. We extract the discount factors from net present value tables. These have been included at the end of this module as an Appendix.

The calculation is carried out as follows. By convention, outflows are shown in brackets:

Year	Cashflow	Discount factor	Cash flow
0	(100 000)	1.000	(100 000)
1	50 000	0.909	45 450
2	45 000	0.826	37 170
3	30 000	0.751	22 530
4	30 000	0.683	20 490
			25 640

The NPV is positive so the project is worth undertaking. This is because it produces a DCF yield in excess of 10 per cent, which is what the company requires.

CONVENTIONS It is important to have a clear understanding of the conventions used in DCF calculations such as these:

- The cash outlay at the beginning of the project is now £100 000 and has a year value of zero. The present value of £1 now is £1.

- Cash flows that occur over a time period are assumed to occur at the end of the period all at once. So cash flows for Year 1 are assumed to occur at the end of Year 1.
- A cash outflow which occurs at the beginning of a time period is assumed to occur at the end of the previous time period. For example, a cash outflow at the beginning of Year 3 is assumed to take place at the end of Year 2.

These conventions make the calculations easier.

NET PRESENT VALUE—ADVANTAGES AND DISADVANTAGES   NPV has certain advantages as a method of project appraisal:

- it takes account of the time value of money
- it takes all cash flows into account
- it is useful for comparing projects as it gives an absolute value, i.e. an amount rather than a percentage return or a period of time as with the other two methods

Its major disadvantage is that it can be difficult to explain to individuals with no financial background.

The DCF calculations can, in reality, become more complex when additional factors are taken into account. For example, businesses receive tax allowances for capital investment, which can be factored into the calculations. Similarly, investment in stages can make the calculations more difficult but, providing the discounting principles shown above are followed the NPV method produces a reliable and reasonable appraisal method, particularly where there are competing projects.

In many cases, two or more projects might be competing for the same investment. Of the methods shown here the payback method will give a quick and easy decision based on a sort of return on investment calculation, but it is slightly flawed for the reasons outlined above.

The accounting rate of return method is more arbitrary, as it relies on accounting profits which may be subject to adjustments unconnected with the project.

Only the NPV approach gives a balanced view of the return and takes account of the effect of time. However the comments made above about the difficulties of applying these methods in real life should not be forgotten.

Test yourself

1 The following statements about the drawbacks of the accounting rate of return (ARR) were made at a recent meeting:

1. ARR is based on accounting profits and not cash flows, and can change because profits are subject to different possible treatments.
2. ARR only considers cash flows within a given time period, and ignores cash flows after that time period.
3. With the ARR method, $1 receivable today is worth the same as a $1 in five years. Therefore, it ignores the time value of money.

Which combination of the above statements is true?
   a) 1, 2 and 3
   b) 1 and 2 only
   c) 1 and 3 only
   d) 2 and 3 only

The following information relates to questions 2–4

Boggis Ltd has three projects under consideration. Each has an initial investment of $400 000
The projects are estimated to bring in the following cash flows:

	A	B	C
Year 1	80 000	160 000	100 000
Year 2	160 000	240 000	150 000
Year 3	240 000	200 000	250 000
Year 4	160 000	80 000	120 000
Year 5	100 000	20 000	100 000

2 Using the payback method, which project would be the one chosen? A, B or C?

3 The equipment purchased will have a useful life of five years and will be depreciated on a straight line
basis of 20 per cent per annum. After five years it will be scrapped with no residual value. Using the ARR
method, which project will be chosen: A, B or C?

4 The company is applying a discount factor of 8 per cent to the outflows. Under the NPV method, which
project will be chosen: A, B or C?
    The relevant discount factors are:

Year 1	0.926
Year 2	0.857
Year 3	0.794
Year 4	0.735
Year 5	0.681

5 Twingo Ltd wants to buy a new item of equipment. There are two choices: firstly, a basic machine, which
will cost less than the more advanced model but cost more to operate so the returns will be lower; or
secondly, a more advanced model which requires a greater initial outlay but provides a better return. Both
have a useful life of five years.
    The details are:

	Basic	Advanced
	€	€
Capital cost	80 000	150 000
Profits before depreciation		
Year 1	50 000	50 000
Year 2	50 000	50 000
Year 3	30 000	60 000
Year 4	20 000	60 000
Year 5	10 000	60 000

Using the ARR method, what would be the rate of return for the advanced model?
a) 74.6%
b) 18.6%
c) 34.7%

6 Balti is considering a project with the following cash flows:

Outflow	
Year 1	(250 000)
Year 2	95 000
Year 3	80 000
Year 4	70 000
Year 5	65 000

Balti is looking at a cost of capital at 12 per cent.
What would be the NPV of the project?
The discount factors are:

Year 1	0.893
Year 2	0.797
Year 3	0.712
Year 4	0.636
Year 5	0.567

7 Which of the following statements are true or false?

	True	False
All capital expenditure projects should have a post-completion audit irrespective of size.		
Capital projects that are not in line with objectives shouldn't have funds committed to them.		
Projects should be subject to a review one week after completion.		
Managers should be aware that a project could be subject to a post-completion review.		

The following information relates to questions 8 and 9

Vulcan is considering investing in a grommeting machine. The initial cost would be $900 000 and it would have a useful life of four years. Annual running costs will amount to $828 000, including annual straight line depreciation of $210 000. The estimated disposal value at the end of Year 4 will be its net book value.

The output from the machine will be 6 million grommets per annum for the first two years and 5 million for the next two. It will sell all it produces. Profit from the sale of the grommets before running costs will be $180 per 1000 grommets.

8 What is the payback period for the machine, assuming all costs occur evenly?
a) The machine will never earn enough to pay for the investment
b) 1.95 years
c) 0.833 years
d) 2 years
e) 3.16 years

9 What will be the average accounting rate of return based on the average net book value?

a) 36.9%

b) 77.5%

c) 36.0%

d) 16.9%

e) 33.8%

10 Hugo Ltd is proposing to buy a machine with a cost of £900 000, which it estimates will save labour costs of £250 000 per year over the next two years and then £200 000 for the next three years. Hugo's CEO has worked out the payback period as being at the end of Year 4, which is good enough for him so he's all for it. However, you have your doubts about the return in real terms over that period. Hugo's cost of capital is 9 per cent.

Using a NPV technique, what advice would you give to Hugo Ltd's CEO?

The discount rates are:

Year 1	0.917
Year 2	0.842
Year 3	0.772
Year 4	0.708
Year 5	0.650

a) You're quite right, the project is viable as the NPV is positive.

b) Payback is all very well but the NPV is negative so over four years it will not make a return.

c) It's quite neutral—the NPV balances out to zero so let's go with a payback period.

In the next module we will be looking at management performance and looking at some ways of measuring how effective management's efforts have been. We will examine some techniques which can be used as a measure of management performance and which can be used to evaluate the success or otherwise of their policies. These include the balanced scorecard and economic value added.

Test yourself

1 A company is considering an investment in new machinery. The annual incremental profits/ (losses) relating to the investment are estimated to be:

	£000
Year 1	(11)
Year 2	3
Year 3	34
Year 4	47
Year 5	8

Investment at the start of the project would be £175 000. The investment sum, assuming nil disposal value after five years, would be written off using the straight line method. Depreciation has been included in the profit estimates above, which should be assumed to arise at each year end.

Required

a) Calculate the net present value (NPV) of the investment at a discount rate of 10 per cent per annum (the company's required rate of return). Discount factors at 10 per cent are:

Year 1	0.909
Year 2	0.826
Year 3	0.751
Year 4	0.683
Year 5	0.621

b) State, on the basis of your calculations, whether the investment is worthwhile. Justify your statement.

2 Winterhalter is looking at three projects. It has raised $350 000 for corporate expansion and the three projects will all contribute to that, but only one of them can be undertaken.

The details of the returns from each project are as follows:

	Cash flows ($000)		
Project	X	Y	Z
Year 1	100	40	200
Year 2	110	100	150
Year 3	104	210	240
Year 4	112	260	40
Year 5	138	160	–
Year 6	160	–	–
Year 7	180	–	–

The board has requested a comprehensive review, as they don't want to make any mistakes.

You have been asked to evaluate the three projects. You discover that the expenditure will be written off on a straight line basis over the life of the project with no residual value.

The company has a cost of capital of 20 per cent.

The discount rates are:

Year 1	0.833
Year 2	0.694
Year 3	0.579
Year 4	0.482
Year 5	0.402
Year 6	0.335
Year 7	0.279

Required

Evaluate the three projects using:
- payback
- accounting rate of return
- net present value

Rank them in order of preference and make a report to the board.

NET PRESENT VALUE TABLES

PRESENT VALUE OF $1

n	1%	1.5%	2.0%	2.5%	3.0%	3.5%	4.0%	4.5%	5.0%	6.0%	7.0%	8.0%	9.0%	10.0%	12.0%	14.0%
1	0.990	0.985	0.980	0.976	0.971	0.966	0.962	0.957	0.952	0.943	0.935	0.926	0.917	0.909	0.893	0.877
2	0.980	0.971	0.961	0.952	0.943	0.934	0.925	0.916	0.907	0.890	0.873	0.857	0.842	0.826	0.797	0.769
3	0.971	0.956	0.942	0.929	0.915	0.902	0.889	0.876	0.864	0.840	0.816	0.794	0.772	0.751	0.712	0.675
4	0.961	0.942	0.924	0.906	0.888	0.871	0.855	0.839	0.823	0.792	0.763	0.735	0.708	0.683	0.636	0.592
5	0.951	0.928	0.906	0.884	0.863	0.842	0.822	0.802	0.784	0.747	0.713	0.681	0.650	0.621	0.567	0.519
6	0.942	0.915	0.888	0.862	0.837	0.814	0.790	0.768	0.746	0.705	0.666	0.630	0.596	0.564	0.507	0.456
7	0.933	0.901	0.871	0.841	0.813	0.786	0.760	0.735	0.711	0.665	0.623	0.583	0.547	0.513	0.452	0.400
8	0.923	0.888	0.853	0.821	0.789	0.759	0.731	0.703	0.677	0.627	0.582	0.540	0.502	0.467	0.404	0.351
9	0.914	0.875	0.837	0.801	0.766	0.734	0.703	0.673	0.645	0.592	0.544	0.500	0.460	0.424	0.361	0.308
10	0.905	0.862	0.820	0.781	0.744	0.709	0.676	0.644	0.614	0.558	0.508	0.463	0.422	0.386	0.322	0.270
11	0.896	0.849	0.804	0.762	0.722	0.685	0.650	0.616	0.585	0.527	0.475	0.429	0.388	0.350	0.287	0.237
12	0.887	0.836	0.788	0.744	0.701	0.662	0.625	0.590	0.557	0.497	0.444	0.397	0.356	0.319	0.257	0.208
13	0.879	0.824	0.773	0.725	0.681	0.639	0.601	0.564	0.530	0.469	0.415	0.368	0.326	0.290	0.229	0.182
14	0.870	0.812	0.758	0.708	0.661	0.618	0.577	0.540	0.505	0.442	0.388	0.340	0.299	0.263	0.205	0.160
15	0.861	0.800	0.743	0.690	0.642	0.597	0.555	0.517	0.481	0.417	0.362	0.315	0.275	0.239	0.183	0.140
16	0.853	0.788	0.728	0.674	0.623	0.577	0.534	0.494	0.458	0.394	0.339	0.292	0.252	0.218	0.163	0.123
17	0.844	0.776	0.714	0.657	0.605	0.557	0.513	0.473	0.436	0.371	0.317	0.270	0.231	0.198	0.146	0.108
18	0.836	0.765	0.700	0.641	0.587	0.538	0.494	0.453	0.416	0.350	0.296	0.250	0.212	0.180	0.130	0.095
19	0.828	0.754	0.686	0.626	0.570	0.520	0.475	0.433	0.396	0.331	0.277	0.232	0.194	0.164	0.116	0.083
20	0.820	0.742	0.673	0.610	0.554	0.503	0.456	0.415	0.377	0.312	0.258	0.215	0.178	0.149	0.104	0.073

(continued)

NET PRESENT VALUE TABLES (continued)

PRESENT VALUE OF $1

n	1%	1.5%	2.0%	2.5%	3.0%	3.5%	4.0%	4.5%	5.0%	6.0%	7.0%	8.0%	9.0%	10.0%	12.0%	14.0%
21	0.811	0.731	0.660	0.595	0.538	0.486	0.439	0.397	0.359	0.294	0.242	0.199	0.164	0.135	0.093	0.064
22	0.803	0.721	0.647	0.581	0.522	0.469	0.422	0.380	0.342	0.278	0.226	0.184	0.150	0.123	0.083	0.056
23	0.795	0.710	0.634	0.567	0.507	0.453	0.406	0.363	0.326	0.262	0.211	0.170	0.138	0.112	0.074	0.049
24	0.788	0.700	0.622	0.553	0.492	0.438	0.390	0.348	0.310	0.247	0.197	0.158	0.126	0.102	0.066	0.043
25	0.780	0.689	0.610	0.539	0.478	0.423	0.375	0.333	0.295	0.233	0.184	0.146	0.116	0.092	0.059	0.038
26	0.772	0.679	0.598	0.526	0.464	0.409	0.361	0.318	0.281	0.220	0.172	0.135	0.106	0.084	0.053	0.033
27	0.764	0.669	0.586	0.513	0.450	0.395	0.347	0.305	0.268	0.207	0.161	0.125	0.098	0.076	0.047	0.029
28	0.757	0.659	0.574	0.501	0.437	0.382	0.333	0.292	0.255	0.196	0.150	0.116	0.090	0.069	0.042	0.026
29	0.749	0.649	0.563	0.489	0.424	0.369	0.321	0.279	0.243	0.185	0.141	0.107	0.082	0.063	0.037	0.022
30	0.742	0.640	0.552	0.477	0.412	0.356	0.308	0.267	0.231	0.174	0.131	0.099	0.075	0.057	0.033	0.020
31	0.735	0.630	0.541	0.465	0.400	0.344	0.296	0.256	0.220	0.164	0.123	0.092	0.069	0.052	0.030	0.017
32	0.727	0.621	0.531	0.454	0.388	0.333	0.285	0.244	0.210	0.155	0.115	0.085	0.063	0.047	0.027	0.015
33	0.720	0.612	0.520	0.443	0.377	0.321	0.274	0.234	0.200	0.146	0.107	0.079	0.058	0.043	0.024	0.013
34	0.713	0.603	0.510	0.432	0.366	0.310	0.264	0.224	0.190	0.138	0.100	0.073	0.053	0.039	0.021	0.012
35	0.706	0.594	0.500	0.421	0.355	0.300	0.253	0.214	0.181	0.130	0.094	0.068	0.049	0.036	0.019	0.010
36	0.699	0.585	0.490	0.411	0.345	0.290	0.244	0.205	0.173	0.123	0.088	0.063	0.045	0.032	0.017	0.009
37	0.692	0.576	0.481	0.401	0.335	0.280	0.234	0.196	0.164	0.116	0.082	0.058	0.041	0.029	0.015	0.008
38	0.685	0.568	0.471	0.391	0.325	0.271	0.225	0.188	0.157	0.109	0.076	0.054	0.038	0.027	0.013	0.007
39	0.678	0.560	0.462	0.382	0.316	0.261	0.217	0.180	0.149	0.103	0.071	0.050	0.035	0.024	0.012	0.006
40	0.672	0.551	0.453	0.372	0.307	0.253	0.208	0.172	0.142	0.097	0.067	0.046	0.032	0.022	0.011	0.005

9 Performance measurement

In this module we will consider:

- Responsibility centres—divisionalization

- Transfer pricing

- Financial performance indicators (FPIs)

- Non-financial performance indicators (NFPIs)

- The balanced scorecard

- Residual income (RI)

- Economic value added (EVA)

In previous modules we have been looking at methodologies: the how-to of costing, budgeting and capital investment appraisal. These are all valuable techniques and are a key part of the management accountant's toolbox. Many of these techniques have within them ways of measuring performance—actual against budget, actual against standard, and so on—and of identifying areas where performance has slipped or been better than forecast.

What we are going to look at in this module are some techniques that examine parts of the organization at a more macro level.

In previous modules we have introduced the concept of the ratio return on capital employed (ROCE), a ratio that is calculated with the formula:

$$\frac{\text{Profit or Return}}{\text{Capital employed}} \times 100$$

There is no ideal answer—each business sets their own required level—but this is a measure often used to assess the performance of individual segments of a large organization.

Responsibility centres—divisionalization

One of the features of large organizations is that they are often separated into separate areas of responsibility, which are often described as divisions. Note that these can be companies in their own right or groups of companies, which are created into a subgroup. These subsidiary companies remain accountable at a divisional level to divisional management and at a group level to senior management of the group as a whole. So a business with several differing types of business may well be divided up into divisions with management and staff engaged in the business of selling particular types of product or service.

Figure 9.1 shows how such an organization can have various levels of management and accountability. Each of the divisions may well be a company. The finance and management function sits outside the direct line management, relates to the whole organization and is often part of the head office function. Divisions and subsidiaries will also have their own finance and administrative functions reporting to the head office—ideally through an interconnected MIS.

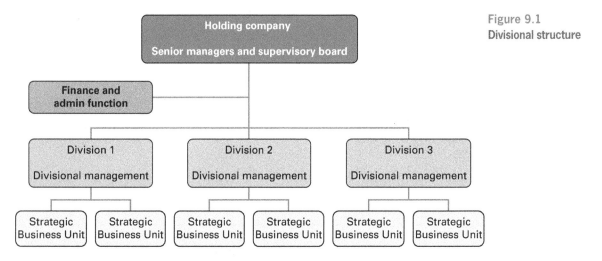

Figure 9.1
Divisional structure

Figure 9.2 shows the overall structure of worldwide life sciences firm Bayer.

This shows that the worldwide structure is divided into three main product divisions dealing with pharmaceuticals, consumer health and crop science; agriculture with a subdivision of animal health dealing with veterinary medicines, animal food supplements, etc.

Each division has its own management board responsible to the main board of management.

Corporate functions such as accounting and finance are group wide.

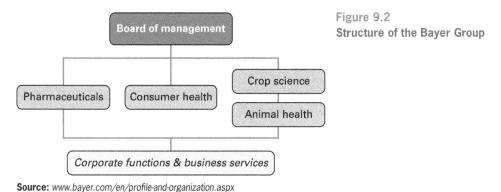

Figure 9.2
Structure of the Bayer Group

Source: www.bayer.com/en/profile-and-organization.aspx

Divisions are normally profit centres and are treated as strategic business units for planning and control purposes by the main board. Although they are part of the global business they operate as autonomous units within the ethos and objectives of the main board.

Consequently, with a company like Bayer, although the crop science division may develop new products, compete in the market place with other suppliers and generally act as an independent business unit, everything it sells will have the Bayer brand and it will ultimately come under the control and management of the main board to which the divisional management is accountable.

There are advantages and disadvantages to such a divisionalized structure.

ADVANTAGES OF DIVISIONALIZATION

- If an organization wants to grow and diversify, a functional structure, i.e. one divided by task (sales, production, finance, etc.) is less flexible. A divisional structure can be adopted to develop business in specific areas either geographical or by product type. Should the company want to diversify further, it is easy to 'bolt on' another division.
- Centralized management of large organizations can become too distant to manage a wide range of products or a large geographical spread of operations effectively. This almost forces large organizations to adopt a divisionalized structure.
- It encourages growth and diversity of products, e.g. by adding additional brands or products to capture other segments of the market. This in turn promotes the use of specialized equipment and facilities.
- Due to the breakdown of the company's activities into divisions, divisional managers can concentrate on their area of responsibility. They should have good knowledge of local market conditions and detailed product knowledge. This lets senior management focus on strategic matters rather than getting involved in the day-to-day operations of each division.
- Divisional managers can be incentivized with bonuses to improve divisional performance, thus benefiting the business as a whole.
- Divisional management provides a training route to future top management positions.
- The focus of attention is on product performance and profitability. By placing responsibility for product profitability at division level, then divisions are able to react quickly. Decision-making processes are shortened and response times improved.
- Where the divisions are geographic, this enables geographic growth, e.g. the business can add a new division if it expands into a new country. Examples of business divisionalized on these lines are McDonald's and Coca-Cola. This gives clear line management responsibility for geographical sales areas.

DISADVANTAGES OF DIVISIONALIZATION

- With divisional management given a wide degree of autonomy to manage their divisions in their market, there can be a danger of lack of what has become known as goal congruence. This is where divisional structures can begin to drift away from the rest of the organization and act with too much independence so that they, effectively, develop their own strategic goals.

   Consequently, the main board management have to ensure that whilst divisions can act within their own best interests they must also act within the best interests of the organization and its goals.
- Coordination—there can be difficulties in coordinating different divisions to achieve overall corporate objectives.
- Transfer prices—how transfer prices should be set? These effectively move profit from one division to another. This is where one division produces product for another—at what price should the product be charged between divisions—cost or with a markup?

- Controllability—divisional managers should only be held accountable for those factors that they can control. The performance of a division's manager must be appraised separately to the performance of the division. It may be difficult to determine exactly what is and what is not controllable.
- Interdependence of divisions—the performance of one division may depend to some extent on others, making it difficult to measure performance levels.
- In most divisionalized companies, some functions, e.g. accounting or human resources, will be provided centrally. If this is the case, the cost of the centralized function could be recharged to those divisions using measures such as turnover or numbers of employees. There are different ways of calculating the recharge and this is often a source of complaint from divisional managers at the perceived size/unfairness of the recharges from head office.

EXAMPLE

Suppose Division A makes components that are subsequently used in Division B to make the finished item that is then sold to customers. The following are examples of areas where the performance of B will be affected by problems in A.

- Productivity—suppose some staff in Division A have low productivity, slowing down the supply of components to Division B. This will slow down Division B as well, unless adequate inventories are held.
- Quality—poor-quality work in Division A will ultimately compromise the quality of the finished product.
- Service levels—customer queries to B could involve A's component in which case they need to be redirected. Division A may not be as customer-focused as B, compromising customer goodwill.

Stop and think

For a multinational company does divisionalization help with tax planning? Suppose all the operations were carried out in Country A but all the invoicing was from low-tax Country B? Is this a desirable way to structure a business? Does it have ramifications for the countries in which the business operates? Is there a business case to be made or is it simply tax planning with no commercial justification?

REAL LIFE
Pearson—the shape of things to come

In May 2013, the global education group Pearson announced a reorganization into six new business units as the company looked to position itself for growth in emerging markets and digital services.

Pearson's five existing units, which include international education, Penguin and the FT Group, would be reorganized around six new divisions, each with their own business heads. Alongside three new global business units of School, Higher Education and Professional, the company would also operate three geographic business units of North America, Growth and Core.

The CEO reported that the reorganization was a significant change in the way the company was run and would take time and sustained commitment to complete, but it is one that must be made to be able to accelerate the execution of their global education strategy. Analysts said the move to a 'product line' structure resembled that adopted by companies in the fast-moving consumer goods sector, where products are created with global markets in mind.

After the reorganization, analysts stated that Pearson's future will look quite different from its past, with emphasis shifting geographically (to emerging markets), in terms of format (from print to digital/services) and also, critically, in terms of customer (from government to consumers).

Source: *Financial Times*, 'Pearson to reorganize into six business divisions,' Budden R., 23.05.2013

Transfer pricing

This is a complicated area and one which can have a profound influence on divisional results. For example, Division A makes product for Division B. If Division A transfers the product at cost, it will make no profit—so how can it be properly monitored financially except through cost control? There is no real incentive for Division A to improve productivity or seek cost reductions.

Conversely, if Division A adds a markup to its product, it will make a profit but it will also increase Division B's costs for the product which it will sell to customers. This may force up retail prices and make the product uncompetitive if Division B is also adding a markup.

The answer lies in compromise. Division B must share some of its profit with Division A by accepting a transfer price which includes a profit for Division A. That way both sets of managers can be assessed on their performance and both will be encouraged into seeking cost savings and economies to produce results. However, this too is fraught with difficulty. Here is an example to illustrate the point:

EXAMPLE

A company has two divisions, A and B. Division A produces mostly for Division B and sells at full cost plus a mark up of 25 per cent. Division B sells at a similar mark-up. The key information is:

TRANSFER PRICING

	Division A £		Division B £
Variable cost per unit	30	Transfer price from Division A	50
Fixed cost per unit	10	Variable costs per unit	20
Total cost per unit	40	Fixed costs per unit	10
Markup—25%	10		80
Transfer price to Division B	50	Markup—25%	20
		Selling price	100

Division A sells to Division B at full cost and makes a markup. Division B also has added its own overheads and markup so the final price to the customer is £100. If this is more than the market price, then Division B may well look to sell at a lower price. It still has to cover its variable costs, so it might sell at £90. However, as far as the company is concerned, this is not advantageous as Division A is still covering all its overheads and making a markup.

So what the firm might do is set the transfer price to cover variable costs only with no mark up so that A transfers to B at £30 and B can sell at £30 + £20 + £12.50 (25 per cent) ignoring fixed costs. So its lowest selling price will be around £62.50. This, again, is unsatisfactory as it does not give Division A any markup nor does it cover fixed costs—if fixed costs of £20 for the company as a whole are taken into account, the company is selling at a loss of £7.50 if it sells at £62.50, so the lowest selling price consistent with breaking even is £70. At that there is no markup for either division.

The only real answer is for the two divisions to negotiate a transfer price which gives both of them a return. This incentivizes Division A to reduce costs, given that it now has a guaranteed price so it can make an additional margin and gives B a fixed price so that it can calculate a competitive selling price.

The transfer prices could, alternatively, be set by the finance section independent of both divisions, although they should be involved in the decision-making process, so that budgets and targets can be set for each division.

The only time these arrangements are not followed is when profits are deliberately moved into low-tax jurisdictions by multinational companies. By amending the transfer price, profits can, effectively, be moved from one country to another. Public authorities frown on such arrangements but find, in practice, they are difficult to counteract.

Financial performance indicators (FPIs)

Divisions have to be accountable for their contribution to overall group financial performance. Clearly a failing division may well be put under pressure to improve or be closed and management is incentivized to improve results throughout the group.

Stop and think	Is incentivizing management based on financial results the best way to promote efficiencies and profitability, or could it lead to short-term decision-making by managers and wasteful competition at divisional or subsidiary level?

Here is an example of three divisions.

RETURN ON INVESTMENT

	Division 1	Division 2	Division 3
	$m	$m	$m
Sales	1200	1400	1700
Variable costs	500	700	1150
Fixed costs	300	200	300
Head office costs	200	100	100
	1000	1000	1550
Profit	200	400	150
Capital investment	1200	2000	300
Contribution* % of sales	**58%**	**50%**	**32%**
ROCE	**17%**	**20%**	**50%**

*Contribution = Sales − Variable costs

As can be seen from the example, Division 1 makes a good profit but its ROCE is the lowest at 17 per cent, because it requires a high level of capital investment to do what it does. Division 2 makes the biggest profit and a reasonable ROCE. The best ROCE is Division 3 because it requires a relatively low level of capital commitment, but it makes a relatively low profit compared with the other two divisions.

If the group is looking to expand and invest more money into one of its divisions which one should it choose?

- the one that gives the highest return on its investment (Division 3)
- the one that generates the biggest contribution to fixed costs and head office costs (Division 1)
- the best all around (Division 2)

Clearly, at this level, decision-making is not so simple, but this serves as an illustration that financial measures may not be the only criteria for decision-making. They are important but should not be used exclusively as the basis for either decision-making or evaluation of performance.

There are a number of problems associated with the exclusive use of financial performance indicators to monitor performance. The main one is short-termism—linking rewards to financial performance may tempt managers to make decisions that will improve short-term financial performance, but which may have a negative impact on long-term profitability. For example, a manager may decide to delay investment in order to boost the short-term profits of their division because of lower depreciation. This will also improve their ROCE measure as ageing assets are shown at a lower value in the calculation but may not be in the best interests of the business in the longer term.

- Focus—financial performance measures tend to have an internal focus, i.e. they relate to the organization's results and take no account of what might be happening outside the organization. In order to compete successfully it is important that external factors such as customer satisfaction and the actions of competitors are also considered.
- Manipulation of results—in order to achieve target financial performance, particularly if it is linked to a bonus, managers may be tempted to manipulate results. For example, inventory valuations may be adjusted to inflate closing inventories and thus improve profits. This kind of management fraud does have repercussions as the results for the following year will also be affected but managers may have moved on or have found more creative ways to manipulate the figures by then. This kind of management fraud is distressingly common.
- Does not convey the whole picture—the use of financial performance indicators has limited benefit to the company since they do not convey the full picture regarding the more intangible factors that can drive long-term success and maximization of shareholder wealth such as customer satisfaction, quality of product, new product design, etc.
- Financial performance measures are traditionally backward-looking, so the activities of the division or branch have already happened by the time the results are prepared and there may be little time or opportunity for action.

The solution is to use both financial and non-financial performance indicators.

Non-financial performance indicators (NFPIs)

There are a number of areas that are particularly important for ensuring the success of a business and where the use of NFPIs plays a key role. These include:

- human resources
- product and service quality
- brand awareness and company profile

HUMAN RESOURCES   Staff are expensive, and businesses have recognized that they can be a major asset. Many businesses operate a mixture of staffing involving:

- a permanent staff of skilled or experienced employees who carry out key roles and act as supervisors and trainers
- temporary staff brought in a peak periods to carry out specific tasks. They are employed for a fixed period and then their employment ceases
- staff on contracts such as 'zero hours' where they are given no guarantee of work but are brought in as needed and paid only for the hours they work

Many businesses recognize that it is important to attract, motivate and retain highly qualified and experienced staff but are less concerned with temporary or zero hours contract staff who, they feel, can be easily replaced.

As a result, NFPIs are now also used to monitor and control permanent staff. These can include the following:

- staff turnover
- absentee rates/sick days
- percentage of job offers accepted
- results of job satisfaction surveys
- competence surveys

Overall staff costs are a major expense for organizations so financial indicators are also a key part of cost control.

PRODUCT AND SERVICE QUALITY   Problems with product or service quality can have a long-term impact on the business and can lead to customer dissatisfaction and loss of future sales. A product or service and its components should be critically and objectively compared both with those of the competition and with customer expectation and needs.

Considerations will include:

- Is ours good value compared with the competitor's offer?
- Does it deliver on what was promised by the marketing?
- How will it compare with competitor offerings in the future given competitive innovations?

Product and service quality are usually based on several critical factors that should be identified and measured over time. Performance on all these factors should be combined to give a complete picture. For example:

- a car manufacturer can have reliability, fuel performance, emissions control, measures of defects, durability and ability to repair as key factors
- a bank might be concerned with waiting time, accuracy of transactions and making the customer experience friendly and positive
- a computer manufacturer can examine relative performance specifications and innovation as key drivers of sales

BRAND AWARENESS AND COMPANY PROFILE   Developing and maintaining a brand and/or a company profile can be expensive. However, it can also enhance performance. The value of a brand/company profile is based on the extent to which it has:

- high loyalty
- name awareness
- perceived quality
- other attributes such as patents or trademarks

NFPIs may focus on areas such as customer awareness and consumer opinions.

DIFFICULTIES IN USING AND INTERPRETING QUALITATIVE INFORMATION

Particularly at higher levels of management, non-financial information is often not in numerical terms, but qualitative, or soft, rather than quantitative. Qualitative information is generally based on opinions of individuals and focus groups. There are some problematic issues related to its use:

- Information in the form of opinions is difficult to measure and interpret. It also requires analysis around motivations and trends.
- Qualitative information may be incomplete.
- In both decision-making and control, managers should be aware that an information system may provide a limited or distorted picture of what is actually happening. Financial information may have to be placed in the context of more qualitative factors such as lack of brand awareness, low staff morale, adverse publicity, etc.
- Qualitative aspects are often interdependent, and it can be difficult to separate the impact of different factors.
- Evaluating qualitative information is subjective. There are no objective formulae as there are with financial measures.

- The cost of collecting and improving qualitative information may be very high.
- Difficulties in measurement and interpretation mean that qualitative factors are often ignored.
- Conventional management information systems are designed to carry quantitative information and are less able to convey qualitative issues.

The balanced scorecard

The balanced scorecard was developed, by Kaplan and Norton, to provide a more rounded basis of assessment of management performance, so includes both financial measures and non-financial measures. It will take into account both external as well as internal information.

The balanced scorecard allows managers to look at the business from four perspectives (see Figure 9.3). These are:

- Financial perspective—how do we look to our shareholders?
- Customer perspective—how do customers see us?
- Internal business perspective—what must we excel at?
- Learning and growth perspective—can we continue to improve and create value?

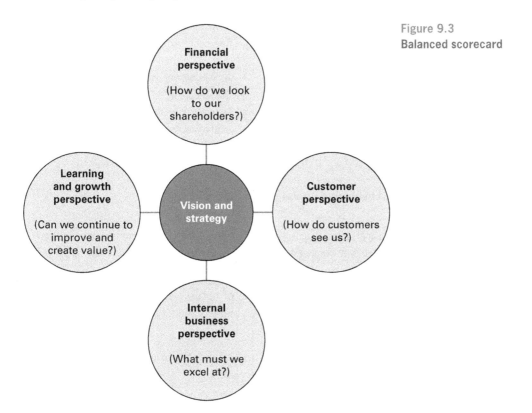

Figure 9.3
Balanced scorecard

Within each of these perspectives the organization business should seek to identify a series of goals in the form of critical success factors (CSFs) and measures indicating progress towards achieving those goals known as key performance indicators (KPIs). These should be in line with the overall strategic objectives and vision of the organization(see Figure 9.4).

Figure 9.4 Examples of goals and measures

	Goal or CSF	KPI or measure
Financial perspective	• Revenue growth • Cost reduction • Improved asset utilization	• Percentage revenue from new products • Percentage revenue from new customers • Sales growth from target market segments • Reduction in cost per unit • Costs percentage of total revenues • ROCE
Customer perspective	• Increase customer retention • Increase customer satisfaction • Increase market share • Improve product quality • Shorten delivery times • Fewer defects	• Percentage growth in business from existing customers • Customer satisfaction surveys • Percentage market share • Measure of customer returns/complaints • Percentage on time deliveries • Customer returns
Internal business perspective	• Develop new markets • Develop new products • Improve process efficiencies • Improve product quality • Develop new products/services • Improve customer relations and response times	• Percentage sales from new markets • Number of new products and sales from them • Reduce time from prototype to full product • Response time in handling customer queries • Reduce unit costs
Learning and growth perspective	• Improve employee training • Expand and improve MIS • Improve employee satisfaction	• Achievement of employees in training • Output from MIS and effectiveness • Employee satisfaction surveys • Staff turnover • Illness and sickness percentage • Employee suggestion scheme

Goals and measures can be prioritized in order of importance to the organization.

Stop and think Can you apply this to your place of study or employer? What information would you need to gather to create a set of metrics to use as a benchmark for future periods?

IMPLEMENTING THE BALANCED SCORECARD The balanced scorecard is only of any use if it is implemented successfully in an organization. It needs to link back to organizational objectives, budgets and targets. To do so requires four main approaches (see Figure 9.5):

1 Explain the strategy and approach. Ensure everyone involved understands the principles
2 Choose the right measures—these will form the basis for the scorecard
3 Develop the MIS so it will provide the information needed
4 Reward and incentivize based on the scorecard. Deal with issues arising in the process

Clearly the key here is communication and preparation. Ensuring that everyone involved understands the process and what it is designed to achieve will go a long way towards making it a success. Reinforcement of achievement through bonus incentives will help to cement the process in place.

The starting point in producing a balanced scorecard is identifying the strategic requirements for success. Those strategic requirements will relate to products, markets, growth and resources (human, intellectual and capital).

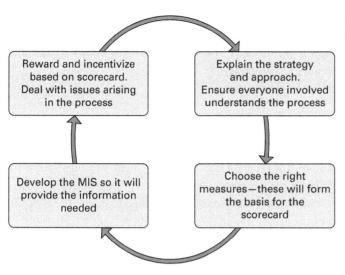

Figure 9.5
Implementing the balanced scorecard

Performance measures have to be selected that clearly relate to the achievement of the business strategies, so the selection of appropriate indicators and measures is critical. These goals are what management and staff will be working to achieve. If the wrong goals are selected, the firm will expend time and money pursuing something that is unattainable.

One major problem that has to be addressed is that performance measures that relate to limited parts of the business can be prone to inducing dysfunctional behaviour in line management. For example, a subsidiary or division might minimize its receivables days in order to meet some cash generation target, but at the expense of relationships with customers.

The MIS will have to be set up to track and report the measures regularly. This involves all the issues relating to the processing of data and the reporting of information. This should normally be carried out by the finance function independently of any division or subsidiary. It will be necessary to draw down or track information from various sources so there may have to be some form of limited periodic internal audit of information.

The balanced scorecard is an exercise in modifying human behaviour. It is its interaction with people that determines whether or not it will work. If it is badly set up, it can easily become a confusing mass of measures, which may actually start to demotivate staff and managers. There may be too many measures and action to achieve some of them may contribute to failure to achieve others. The measures may not always be prioritized.

To be effective, the measures contained in the scorecard should be:

- limited in number
- reasonably consistent
- ranked in some order of priority

Further, performance measures should be aligned with the management structure. Career progression and remuneration should be appropriately linked to scorecard measures related to performance. Organizations which adopt a balanced scorecard but continue to reward managers on the basis of traditional simple financial measures, e.g. hitting a profit target, will devalue all the other measures in the scorecard as managers concentrate on the one that brings them the bonus.

The balanced scorecard is an all round methodology which enables businesses to assess and improve their all round performance.

Residual income (RI)

Residual income is a measure used as part of divisional performance management for divisions with substantial investment in non-current assets or income generating investments.

It is based on a calculation which uses a relatively simple measure.

Profits before interest and tax	X
Capital employed (total assets − current liabilities) × cost of capital	(X)
Residual income	X

The capital employed is usually based on book values or carrying values in the financial statements.

The cost of capital can be the cost of borrowing or the weighted average cost of capital (WACC). The weighted average cost of capital is based on the interest or finance cost, which different components of the financing of the businesses are charged, adjusted by the proportion that each component bears to the whole.

EXAMPLE

WACC = (proportion of equity × cost of equity) + (proportion of debt × post tax cost of debt)

Don't forget that interest on loans is tax deductible, so the calculation takes account of that by deducting a notional value based on the tax rate from the interest cost charged to the income account. Similarly, the cost of equity shares is any dividend paid to the shareholders.

For example, suppose that a company is 60 per cent financed by equity, which has a cost of 10 per cent pa and 40 per cent financed by debt, which has an after-tax cost of 6 per cent. The calculation is therefore:

WACC = (0.60 × 0.10) + (0.40 × 0.06) = 0.084 therefore 8.4 per cent to give a weighted average between 6 per cent and 10 per cent.

Providing the resultant figure of the calculation shows the entity is generating a result with an economic benefit, i.e. the profits exceed the cost of borrowing. If it is a negative, there are problems to be dealt with as the business is not generating any form of economic profit.

One of the problems with using ROCE as a measure of performance is that, if managers are being incentivized by maximizing ROCE, they will be reluctant to invest in new assets as this will reduce their ROCE and thus, potentially, a bonus.

Using RI, providing the return from the investment is greater than the cost of the capital to finance it, the RI will go up so the managers will be encouraged to invest for the future.

EXAMPLE

A division has operating profits of $40 000 based on assets of $160 000 with a cost of capital of 12 per cent on borrowed money.

An investment of $10 000 is planned, which will increase profits by £1600.

Before Investment

	Profit	Asset value
	$	$
	40 000	160 000
Cost of capital (12% × $160 000)	(19 200)	
ROCE (40 000/160 000)		25%
Residual income	$20 800	

After investment

	Profit	Asset value
	$	$
	41 600	170 000
Cost of capital (12% × $170 000)	(20 400)	
ROCE (41 600/170 000)		24.5%
	$21 200	

As can be seen from this small example, the ROCE has reduced as a result of the new investment, whereas the residual income has increased. This is a much more positive view of investment.

Compared to using ROCE as a measure of performance, RI has advantages and disadvantages:

ADVANTAGES

- It encourages investment centre managers to make new investments if they add to RI. A new investment might add to RI but reduce ROCE. In such a situation, measuring performance by RI would not result in dysfunctional behaviour, i.e. the best decision will be made for the business as a whole.
- Making a specific charge for interest helps to make investment centre managers more aware of the cost of the assets under their control.

DISADVANTAGES

- It does not facilitate comparisons between divisions, since the RI is driven by the size of divisions and of their investments.
- It is based on accounting measures of profit and capital employed, which may be subject to manipulation, e.g. in order to obtain a bonus payment.

Directors have a duty to maximize shareholder value so a more specific measure of performance was developed measuring this particular aspect of performance, known as economic value added. This is similar to residual income, but is more complex and brings in additional factors relevant to the future performance of the business.

Economic value added (EVA)

EVA was developed by consultants Stern Stewart & Co and is copyrighted to them.

It is a calculation that comprises three components:

- The net operating profit after tax (NOPAT)
- A capital charge
- The weighted average cost of capital

The EVA calculation uses what is described as the economic profit, which is calculated by adjusting the accounting profit.

The capital charge is based on the replacement value of the assets rather than any book value. This is multiplied by the weighted average cost of capital to create a notional 'interest' charge for the use of the capital in generating NOPAT.

Remember that the weighted average cost of capital is based on the interest or finance cost that different components of the financing of the businesses are charged, weighted by the proportion which each component bears to the whole.

The fundamental rationale for the EVA calculation is that a business is not contributing to the economy unless it is making a real profit (as opposed to an accounting profit), which is greater than its cost of capital.

> **Stop and think**   This technique creates a distinction between accounting profits and economic profits. Ensure you grasp the distinction. Is economic profit a subjective measurement? If so does it have any real validity as a measure of performance in the real world?

NET OPERATING PROFIT AFTER TAX (NOPAT)

To calculate NOPAT, the accounting profit has to be amended. The amendments take out any non-cash items to bring the profit closer to a figure for cash generation rather than accounts profit. This is because cash is more closely correlated to shareholder benefits than accounts profit.

In addition the adjustments seek to adjust for the future potential of the business by capitalizing such costs as product development and special marketing costs, which are considered to be investments for the future rather than costs to be written off against profits.

The calculation is based on the true cost of financing, including equity financing, which has a dividend cost rather than an interest charge.

The adjustments are to add back to the profit after tax as shown by the income account:

- depreciation
- non-cash costs, e.g. provision for doubtful debts
- interest payments net of tax—as these are taken account of in another part of the calculation
- any accounting amortization (depreciation) of goodwill—an intangible asset
- costs that add value such as research and development, and advertising and marketing. These are considered investments for the future.
- costs of operating leases—these are leases for the hire of equipment, vehicles, etc.
- economic depreciation—based on the fall in asset value due to wear and tear and obsolescence rather than an annual write-off under accounting rules
- any impairment to the value of goodwill rather than an accounting write-off
- amortization of development and advertising costs, as these are classed as investments in the future they are not treated as costs but as assets, so have to be written off over their effective life, e.g. costs of a marketing campaign expected to have an effect on sales for three years are written off over the three years.

The calculation looks like this:

Profit after tax per income account	X
Add	
Non-cash costs	
Depreciation per income account (accounting depreciation)	X
Non-cash costs, e.g. provision for doubtful debts	X
Interest—as this is used in another part of the calculation	X

Costs which add value	
Development and advertising costs	X
Costs of operating leases for vehicles and equipment	X
Any write down of goodwill such as amortization	<u>X</u>
	X
Deduct	
Economic depreciation—based on any fall in asset values	(X)
Impairment to the value of goodwill	(X)
Amortization of development and advertising costs	<u>(X)</u>
NOPAT	<u>X</u>

The best way to illustrate this is with an example.

EXAMPLE

A business has reported an operating profit of R16 million. Included in the profit are the development and launch costs amounting to R5 million of a new product, which is expected to generate profits for five years. Tax is charged at 25 per cent.

The company has a weighted cost of capital of 12 per cent and is paying interest at 8 per cent on a long-term loan.

The non-current assets are valued at R40 million with a replacement cost of R60 million. Net current assets are R12 million.

The first thing to do is to calculate NOPAT:

	R m
Operating profit	16
Add: Development costs	5
Less—One year's amortization of development cost	<u>(1)</u>
	20
Tax at 25%	<u>(5)</u>
NOPAT	15

Next we need to look at the economic value of assets:

Replacement cost of non-current assets	60
Net current assets	12
Development costs—investment in the future (net)	<u>4</u>
	<u>76</u>

The weighted average cost of capital is 12 per cent, which includes what is being paid on the loan so the interest rate to be used is 12 per cent.

So the EVA is:

	R m
NOPAT	15.0
Capital charge R76 m × 12%	<u>(9.12)</u>
EVA	<u>5.88</u>

The calculation shows that the EVA is positive, so the company is performing well as it is generating an economic profit greater than its cost of capital.

As with most forms of measurement there are advantages and disadvantages.

These can be summarized as shown in Figure 9.6.

Figure 9.6 EVA advantages and disadvantages

Advantages	Disadvantages
Adjustments take out accounting constructs so are closer to cash flows than accounting profits.	Requires a lot of adjustments to the accounting profit and assumptions about the adjustments.
It treats expenditure such as marketing and development as investments in the future, so managers try to keep costs down by not spending in these areas so they don't reduce the EVA.	Based on historical data, which may not be a guide to the future.
It measures an absolute value, which can be easily understood in principle.	Does not facilitate comparison between different divisions as it is an absolute measure.
It records the true cost of financing.	

Consequently, whilst EVA is a measure of performance, it is not an easy calculation and is possibly prone to some element of manipulation or adjustment when working out the various add-backs and replacement cost numbers.

Test yourself

The following information relates to Questions 1 and 2

A division with a capital employed of $800 000 currently earns a ROCE of 22 per cent. It can make an additional investment of $100 000 with a five-year life and no residual value. The average net profit from the investment will be $24 000 after depreciation. The cost of capital is 14 per cent.

1 What are the residual incomes before investment?
   a) $288 000
   b) $56 000
   c) $64 000
   d) 14 per cent

2 What are the residual incomes after investment?
   a) $326 000
   b) $74 000
   c) $72 000
   d) 22 per cent

3 Bamalam Ltd has non-current assets amounting to £176 000, which have a replacement cost of £196 000. Working capital amounts to £38 000.

   Profits for the last financial year were £37 000 after charging depreciation of £16 200. The economic depreciation charge would be £24 600. The profits were also stated after charging the costs of a special marketing campaign of £12 000. This is expected to boost revenue for the next two years.

   The weighted average cost of capital is 11 per cent.

   What is the EVA for Bamalam?
   a) £8200
   b) £8260
   c) £14 860
   d) £11 780

4 Which of the elements of the balanced scorecard is the objective 'Reduce staff turnover' likely to relate to?
 a) Finance perspective
 b) Internal business perspective
 c) Customer perspective
 d) Learning and growth perspective

5 Which of the following answers is true?   ✔

Economic value added is:	
How much value is added by the economy	
How much value is added by operations	
How much a business affects the economy	
How much wealth a company is creating compared to its cost of capital	

6 Megablast transfers raw materials from its production from its manufacturing division in the USA to its retail division in the UK.

In Period 1 it transferred 4000 units. Each unit cost $350 to manufacture. The variable cost component is 75 per cent. The product was sold for £400. The UK division incurred sales and marketing costs of £8 per unit.
The exchange rate is $1.50 to £1.

If the transfers were at variable cost what are the retail division's profits?
 a) $768 000
 b) $868 000
 c) $168 000
 d) $518 000

7 A division of Supertools Ltd has the following results:

	€000's
Net profit	1440
Non-current assets	6000
Net current assets	400

The division is considering a project that will increase annual net profit by €100 000 but will also require average inventory levels to increase by €120 000 and non-current assets to increase by €400 000. Supertools imposes a 16 per cent capital charge for funding each division.

Supertools requires every project to be positive both for ROCE and RI. Using that criteria will the project be accepted?

		ROCE	RI
a)		Yes	Yes
b)		Yes	No
c)		No	No
d)		No	Yes

8 Which of the following statements are true or false?   ✔   ✔

	True	False
A divisionalized structure makes expanding the business more flexible.		
Divisionalization can lead to a breakdown in goal congruence.		
Loss of customers can be a measure for the customer perspective.		
Qualitative information can be more valuable than quantitative information because it is based on fact not opinions.		

9 Willowbrae Ltd uses residual income as a measure of divisional performance. It uses a cost of capital of 10 per cent.

Managers of divisions have considerable autonomy, although the cash and bank control remains with head office.

The stores division has the following details extracted from its management accounts at the end of Period 4:

	£000's
Net profit after tax	94
Profit before interest and tax	138
Divisional net assets	208
Bank overdraft	(42)

What is the RI for this division based on controllable profit and net assets?
a) £73 200
b) £117 200
c) £113 000
d) £121 400

10 Which of the following statements are true or false?

	True	False
Increasing control over credit granted to customers would be an objective under the customer perspective.		
Customer surveys are a way of measuring performance.		
Divisional management provides a training route for future senior managers.		
Transfer pricing ensures that all divisions get a fair share of any profits from the sale of goods and services.		

In the next module we will look at financial management and financial modelling. It will consider how managers use financial information to achieve the best results for the business and also how they can avoid future problems through scenario modelling.

Test yourself

1 Bogle plc has two divisions called the Makin and Sellin divisions. The Makin division makes one product which it sells to the Sellin division. It also sells to organizations outside Bogle.

The following information is relevant to both divisions:

	Makin division sales to Sellin	Makin division external sales
Sales at $140 per unit		1 400 000
Sales at $120 per unit	600 000	
Variable costs at $72 per unit	360 000	720 000
Contribution	240 000	680 000
Fixed costs	200 000	480 000
Profit	40 000	200 000

The Bogle group profit is $1 100 000

A supplier offers to supply 3000 units at $100 each to division R.

As managers are evaluated on divisional results, they are given full autonomy to make buying decisions.

Required

a) What will be the profit for the Makin division if it cannot match the lower price from the competitor and cannot increase external sales?

b) What will be the effect on the group profit of Bogle?

c) Comment on whether this is advisable from a group strategy perspective.

2 Megachem is a manufacturer and supplier of agricultural fertilizers and industrial chemicals.

It has two divisions, Agricultural and Industrial. Each division is autonomous having control over its own non-current and current assets, including cash and bank balances and managers are free to make the most advantageous deals they can to maximize results.

Each divisional manager is paid £150 000 per year plus a bonus based on performance. This is based on the ROCE achieved by the division; each manager has to achieve an ROCE in excess of 10 per cent.

The bonus scheme provides that for each percentage point above 10 per cent ROCE the manager receives a bonus equivalent to 1 per cent of annual salary subject to a maximum bonus of 20 per cent of annual salary.

At the end of the financial year to 31 December 20X8 the two divisions reported the following:

	Agricultural	Industrial
	£000's	£000's
Sales	29 000	17 400
Profit	5 290	3 940
Less head office costs	(2 530)	(1 368)
Net profit	2 760	2 572
Non-current assets	19 520	29 960
Current assets	4 960	6 520
Trade payables	5 920	2 800

During the year Industrial invested £13.6 million in new equipment, which will, it is hoped, increase productivity by 8 per cent per year. Agricultural made no new investment in assets although some of its equipment is now quite old and prone to breakdown. The manager of Agricultural has claimed cash shortages as a reason for taking extended credit from suppliers, even though the cash balance is quite satisfactory. He has also stated that he believes in 'sweating' the assets until they are no longer useful before replacing them.

Required

a) Calculate the ROCE on which managers bonuses will be paid.

b) Based on the answer to a), calculate the bonuses for each manager in accordance with the bonus scheme.

c) Comment on whether or not this is the most appropriate method for calculating a bonus and the points arising from its use in Megachem for the year. Is the approach taken by both managers in the best interests of the group?

10 Using financial information to manage the organization

In this module we will consider:

- Principles of financial management

- Strategic objectives and targets

- Setting financial targets

- Sensitivity analysis and fixed costs

- Stakeholders

- Non-profit-making bodies

So far, we have looked at the practicalities of costing and budgeting and the use of several techniques to assess divisional performance—but what about the organization as a whole?

In this module we will look at strategic financial management—the view from the boardroom.

What decisions need to be made as to the future of the organization and how are they to be informed? Of course a lot of information can be supplied to aid decision making at this level—a lot of which we have already looked at in previous modules—but there are some aspects to strategic management we need to consider which directly affect the management accountant.

In the context of this module we are using the term 'financial information' to mean information from whatever source—so that will include financial accounts. However, these are of little use in decision-making as they are:

- historical
- generally out of date by the time they are finalized

Whilst historical financial accounts may have some value in informing management of where the organization has been, they are of little use in telling them where it is going. Consequently, most of the information used in strategic decision-making is generated by the management accountants and derives from the MIS and from forecasts and projections prepared by the management accounting team.

Principles of financial management

Strategic financial management is the identification of possible financial strategies to assist in:

- maximizing shareholder value
- allocating scarce resources among competing opportunities
- the implementation and monitoring of the chosen strategy so as to achieve the stated objectives

We might also include in that definition:

- the management of any risk involved in the chosen strategies
- the financing of operations, and
- dealing with any unforeseen obstacles that may suddenly appear to prevent the organization achieving its objectives

Senior management need to have a clear view of corporate objectives and devise approaches towards achieving them. Objectives can vary depending on the nature of the organization. Figure 10.1 illustrates the differing values of organizations whose financial management approaches may be very different.

Figure 10.1 Organizational values

Organization type	Organizational objectives
Commercial	• Maximizing shareholder wealth
	• Meeting the expectations of other stakeholders
	• Maintaining market share
	• Survival
Non-profit-making	• Maximizing use of resources to achieve objectives
	• Investing scarce resources directly where required
	• Eliminating waste and duplication of effort
	• Fundraising to preserve the organization
Government or quasi-government body	• Use of public money for the purpose intended
	• Maximizing efficient use of funds in order to achieve political or social objectives
	• Being accountable to public for outgoing funds
	• Avoiding corruption and fraud

> **Stop and think**
>
> Have you been told what the organizational objectives are for your college or university? Where might you find them stated? If you are not working have you any personal objectives to aim for? Have you written these down?

As can be seen from Figure 10.1, the objectives are very different but, surprisingly, many of the financial objectives are not. There are commonalities such as:

- using funds efficiently
- avoiding waste
- maintaining funding to preserve the organization, whether this be from commercial operations or fund raising

Financial managers in different types of organization still have a lot in common!

Clearly though they will use different techniques to measure success. For example, in a commercial organization the measure might be earnings per share (EPS).

EARNINGS PER SHARE   This relates to the amount of a company's earnings available to ordinary shareholders. So the measure is of the profit after taxation, minus any preference dividend, divided by the number of ordinary shares.

$$\frac{\text{Profit after taxation, interest and preference dividend}}{\text{Number of ordinary shares in issue}}$$

Here is an example of the calculation.

EXAMPLE

Biggasplash has the following share structure:

Ordinary shares	1 000 000 ordinary shares of £1 each	1 000 000
8% preference shares of £1 each		500 000
		£1 500 000

Biggasplash has made a profit for the year of £900 000 on which tax is payable of £160 000. The EPS calculation is thus:

Profit for the year	900 000
Less: Tax payable	(160 000)
Preference dividend	(40 000)
Profit available to ordinary shareholders	£700 000
Number of ordinary shares	1 000 000
Earnings per share	0.70 pence

This measure is often seen as a fundamental measure of the performance of an ordinary share in the company. Note that this is not what a shareholder might receive—that would be a dividend on the ordinary shares—but it is a measure of the value of an ordinary share. Again the trend is significant—an investor would be looking to see this increasing year on year, hopefully, and this would be a guide to potential investors of the investment value of ordinary shares in the business.

Stop and think   If maximizing earnings per share is a key management objective, how might this influence management decision-making in the short- and the long-term?

There is an analogy between EPS and ROCE (Module 9) which is a similar measure. Company managers can focus on increasing EPS without giving significant consideration to the needs of the company as a whole. Increasing the ordinary share capital with a new issue might be good for the business if it replaces interest-bearing debt with equity funding. It would, however, dilute the EPS (more shares in issue) so managers might be reluctant to do this if it was likely to deter potential investors by affecting the share price.

If the business is expanding the answer is likely to be borrowing more money. EPS might continue to increase, but the ROCE may start to fall as this ratio includes all forms of capital including borrowings, and this is a warning sign for the business.

Shareholders will be conscious of:

- the dividends they receive on their shares
- any potential capital gain they will make if the market price of the shares increases

The management of the company will be looking to pay a suitable dividend: not too much to drain cash out of the business, but not too little to depress the shareholders and thus the share price. If the company is listed on a stock exchange, they will be looking to increase the value of the business by reporting growth and expansion of the business.

Strategic objectives and targets

Financial management at a strategic level includes:

- Investment decisions—whether to invest in new assets, new projects, research and development or marketing campaigns
- External investment decisions—whether to attempt to acquire another business or become involved in a joint venture
- Divestment decisions—whether to close down part of the operation, sell off assets

Financial managers are responsible not only for investment decisions and the financing of non-current assets, but also ensuring the availability of working capital to finance current assets. They will be looking to manage working capital (inventories, receivables and cash minus payables) in order to create free cash for investment. We will look at this later in the module.

At a strategic level, management will be looking to set a series of strategic objectives based on where the organization is presently. They will consider such factors as:

- Financial results
- Market share for key products
- Competitors
- Productive capacity
- Ability to deliver products and services
- Staffing and structure of the organization

In Module 9 we looked at the question of divisionalization and how the performance of divisional management is measured and much the same considerations will persist across the whole organization. Management will be looking at strategic objectives such as:

- Gearing or leverage position
- Maximizing free cash flow
- New product or service development
- Expanding market share
- Overseas investment
- Improving margins on key products

They might set some financial targets such as reducing dependence on borrowings, retaining more profit to cover interest payments or achieving a target ROCE for the organization.

The capital structure of the organization is one which may trouble management if they feel they have too much dependence on funds carrying a fixed interest component. This obviously includes long term loans but also includes preference shares and debentures. The simple reason is that this form of fixed interest finance is less flexible than other forms of finance and acts like a fixed cost—the interest payments have to be met no matter what the economic situation of the business.

So when economic times are hard, an organization that is heavily financed by borrowed money can find life difficult.

BORROWING AND THE EFFECTS OF GEARING   The ratio of borrowed money to equity finance is known as gearing, or alternatively leverage, which is a US term coming into more common use.

When times are hard, borrowed money can work against the organization simply because it has to pay interest on the money. Businesses do not fail because they make accounting losses; they fail because they run out of money and cannot pay their bills. If loan repayments cannot be met and the bank calls in the loan, the company will fail unless it is able to refinance in some way.

Let us consider the capital structure of two companies of the same size.

Suppose two companies have the following capital structure:		
	Co A	Co B
Capital structure		
Share capital	1000	2000
Loans	1000	—
	2000	2000

Loan carries interest at 5 per cent p.a.

Dividends paid at 3 per cent

In a normal trading year their results look like this:		
	Co A	Co B
Revenues	150	150
Cost of sales and expenses	(55)	(55)
Operating profit	95	95
Finance costs	(50)	—
Operating profit	45	95
Dividend	(30)	(60)
	15	35

When things go wrong in times of depression results drop

Income and COS drop by 10 per cent

	Co A	Co B
Revenues	135	135
Cost of sales and expenses	(50)	(50)
Operating profit	85	85
Finance costs	(50)	—
Operating profit	35	85
Dividend	(30)	(60)
	5	25

Clearly Company B has a much more flexible capital structure. Not only are its financing costs lower, which protects its profits when business turns down in a depression, it does not have to pay a dividend at all, or at least only a very small one, so its financing costs are much reduced.

Having said that, not paying a dividend will affect the share price as nervous investors may take it as a sign the company is in trouble so, in most cases, companies often will pay a dividend even when they are in trouble financially.

The problem is that loan finance is considerably easier to obtain than raising capital from investors. Banks will lend in a considerably more generous way than investors who require lots of information and may need to be cajoled into parting with yet more money. From an investors' point of view, the level of gearing is an indicator of the level of risk. A high level of gearing means that interest payments must be met before a dividend is paid so, in difficult times, there may not be sufficient profit available for a dividend.

Managers will thus be looking to manage their free cash flow; that is, cash generated by controlling working capital.

FREE CASH FLOW   Free cash flow is defined as:

$$\text{Operating cash flow} - \text{gross capital investment}$$

What it measures is the ability of the business to fund expansion or the addition of new assets through cash generation from operations, i.e. through maximizing the cash able to be generated from managing current assets and current liabilities: inventory levels, receivables and payables effectively.

If that number is negative, and the business still wishes to expand, the most obvious route is to borrow money, and this can have significant effects on the ability of the business to service its debt and also to generate a sufficiently good return to ordinary shareholders.

Consider this: A business that has inventory of £150 000 is funding that amount for the length of time it takes the inventory to be turned into cash. If the inventory is held for 30 days before being sold and the customer takes 45 days to pay, the company is funding 75 days of holding that potential cash in another form. Clearly some of that funding is by taking credit from suppliers, but there is a limit to how far that can go before suppliers start to protest—but the rest has to be found from borrowings or capital.

Shortening the period of stockholding and collecting debts more quickly can speed up the amount of free cash available to the business and cut the requirement for borrowing significantly.

REAL LIFE
Airbus strategic approach
Extract from strategic planning document provided to shareholders at their meeting October 2017

By their nature, forward-looking statements involve risk and uncertainty because they relate to future events and circumstances and there are many factors that could cause actual results and developments to differ materially from those expressed or implied by these forward-looking statements.

These factors include but are not limited to:

- Changes in general economic, political or market conditions, including the cyclical nature of some of Airbus' businesses
- Significant disruptions in air travel (including as a result of terrorist attacks)
- Currency exchange rate fluctuations, in particular between the Euro and the US dollar
- The successful execution of internal performance plans, including cost reduction and productivity efforts
- Product performance risks, as well as programme development and management risks
- Customer, supplier and subcontractor performance or contract negotiations, including financing issues
- Competition and consolidation in the aerospace and defence industry
- Significant collective bargaining labour disputes
- The outcome of political and legal processes including the availability of government financing for certain programmes and the size of defence and space
- Procurement budgets

(continued)

- Research and development costs in connection with new products
- Legal, financial and governmental risks related to international transactions
- Legal and investigatory proceedings and other economic, political and technological risks and uncertainties

As a result, Airbus' actual results may differ materially from the plans, goals and expectations set forth in such forward-looking statements.

As the basis for its 2017 guidance, Airbus expects the world economy and air traffic to grow in line with prevailing independent forecasts, which assume no major disruptions

- Airbus expects to deliver more than 700 commercial aircraft which depends on engine manufacturers meeting commitments
- Free Cash Flow is expected to be similar to 2016

Objectives

- Focus on key programmes
- Drive innovation and digitalization for the longer term to secure our future
- Work to secure EPS as platform to deliver 2018/2019 growth

Source: *Airbus Member state shareholders meeting Toulouse October 2017*

Setting financial targets

The process of setting financial targets is simple in theory but more complicated in practice. Clearly a simple statement such as 'Increase revenues by 5 per cent' is easy to set as a target or objective but there may be all sorts of issues affected by that simple ambition such as:

- Will the market stand an increase in output or supply? If the market is saturated, i.e. it is already well served by suppliers to it, an increase in output of 5 per cent by one supplier to the market may mean a reduction in supply for other suppliers. Company A may increase its market share, but Companies B, C and D are not going to sit idly by and let them do it—they may start price discounting or introduce special offers to retain their customer base. Company A may then fail to achieve its target and, worse, may lose some of its existing market share to rivals
- Does the business have the resources to make or deliver such an increase? If it is already working at capacity or near capacity it may require investment in new resources. The cost implications of that have to be thought through and planned. If new facilities have to be built, this will take time before they come on stream.
- To outsource or make in-house? One way of increasing resources is to outsource so that other businesses are involved in producing the product. This may result in efficiencies as the contractors will presumably be specialists, but they will want a profit margin on what they produce.
- What is the current situation with the workforce? Can we get more from them to meet increased output targets? Are any of the processes capable of being automated? This may require additional investment, but may also speed up delivery and assist in achieving quality targets. Should the full-time workforce be down-sized and replaced with more part-time casual workers brought in as needed—or do we need more skilled workers, in which case do we start a training programme?

There may be additional considerations, but this quick overview indicates the scale of the problem—all the factors involved in strategic decision-making are interconnected.

MAKE OR BUY DECISIONS   As part of a strategic review the senior management may well be looking to revise how their products are produced—in other words, whether or not to outsource part of their production, particularly where there are limitations on internal resources. We looked at this in Module 3.

Many companies now outsource much of their production and merely act as assemblers. This enables a range of suppliers to become dedicated to making specific components which has advantages and disadvantages for both as shown in Figure 10.2.

Figure 10.2 **Outsourcing production—advantages or disadvantages**

Advantages	Disadvantages
Suppliers can become very proficient in manufacturing specific components	Supplier is vulnerable to being delisted by main customer, but main customer is also dependent on supplier
Adoption of just-in-time deliveries reduces Inventory holding costs	Failure to deliver by supplier can prejudice production schedules for main customer
Supplier is tied to its customer who may take most of its business	Suppliers may grow complacent and relationship can become comfortable, so efficiencies are lost

There may be financial savings to be had but prices have to be carefully negotiated. Here is an example:

EXAMPLE

Drillers (the company) makes oil rigs and, at present, all of the production is in-house except for specialized equipment such as engines, winches, etc. The management of Drillers is looking to outsource production of some of the components, principally accommodation modules, helicopter platforms and anchors.

Labour hours are limited to 4000 hours and there is no immediate availability of skilled labour.
The management accountants have produced the following information:

	Accommodation $m	Platforms $m	Anchors $m
Variable cost	2.4	1.6	0.8
Outsource price	3.1	2.2	0.6
Difference	(0.7)	(0.6)	0.2
Labour hours per unit	2500	3000	1100

Looking at the financial aspects of the decision, given that there is a limitation on the number of labour hours available, there are two considerations.

The outsource price of anchors is cheaper than the variable cost of manufacture so these should be outsourced.

This will free up some labour hours to use on the other components. If consideration is to be given to these, the next consideration is the use of the scarce resource, e.g. labour hours. The two remaining components use this resource to this extent:

	Accommodation	Platforms
Excess cost	$700 000	$600 000
Labour hours	2 500	3 000
Cost per labour hour	$280	$200

Platforms have the lowest excess cost per labour hour and could then also be outsourced.

(continued)

Drillers thus now has a plan. It can outsource the production of anchors and also platforms. Consequently, it could either reduce its workforce and streamline its operations putting all the responsibility for making and delivering those components to its suppliers, or contribute to making some element of the platforms leaving most of the construction to external contractors.

However there are non-financial considerations to be borne in mind and management must consider a number of other issues before a final decision is made. These include:

- Can the external supplier be relied upon to meet the requirements in terms of:
  - quantity required
  - quality required
  - delivering on time
  - price stability?
- The external supplier may possess some specialist skills that are not available in-house. An alternative perspective is that outsourcing may result in the loss of in-house skills and competencies.
- Outsourcing will free up resources, which may be used in another part of the business.
- Will outsourcing result in a reduction of the workforce? Redundancy costs and the effect on the local community should be considered.
- Will outsourcing affect contractual obligations with existing suppliers or employees?
- Is there a risk of loss of confidentiality, especially if the external supplier performs similar work for rival companies?
- Do customers attach importance to the products being made in-house?

If alternative use can be made for the workforce by switching them onto making new or additional products then part of the problem disappears. Many organizations have found that trying to close unprofitable manufacturing units or moving production in order to consolidate resources is met by a wave of protest, not simply from the workforce but from the local community, politicians and the press, so great care has to be taken with this kind of decision-making.

Stop and think

Where you live, has a decision been made to close any factories or businesses and consolidate production or delivery in a different place? Has your area benefited from business activities transferred from another area? What has been the effect on the local community? Is there any way a business could reduce the effect on the community of the loss of jobs? Is it their responsibility to do so?

FINANCIAL PLANNING FOR THE FUTURE   Any business of any size is likely to want to budget for the future and we looked at budgeting in Module 7. Looking ahead from a strategic perspective involves a much more 'broad brush' approach involving less detail and considering themes and trends rather than absolute values.

For example we can look at the case of WoodyCo.

EXAMPLE

The board of WoodyCo is considering long-range plans.

At present, revenues are forecast to be R20 000 000 per year for the current year with revenues for the next five years forecast at R21 200 000, R22 800 000, R24 800 000, R27 200 000 and R30 000 000 respectively.

Net profit after tax averages 10 per cent of revenues and this is not expected to change. Total assets less current liabilities will remain at about 125 per cent of revenues.

The board have made further suggestions.

- If profits rise, dividends to ordinary shareholders should rise by the same percentage
- The business should attempt to retain 50 per cent of profits to build up its reserves
- The current gearing level of the company is 30 per cent and the board would not like to see this go any higher.

As a result of this, the management accounting team put together a draft financial plan which looks like this:

WoodyCo—Long-term planning

	Current					
	Year	Year 1	Year 2	Year 3	Year 4	Year 5
	Rm	Rm	Rm	Rm	Rm	Rm
Revenues	20.00	21.20	22.80	24.80	27.20	30.00
Net profit after tax	2.00	2.12	2.28	2.48	2.72	3.00
Dividend (50 per cent of after tax profit)	1.00	1.06	1.14	1.24	1.36	1.50
Total assets less current liabilities	25.00	26.50	28.50	31.00	34.00	37.50
Equity + retained earnings	17.50	18.56	19.70	20.94	22.30	23.80
Long-term debt (30 per cent)	7.50	7.94	8.44	8.97	9.56	10.20
	25.00	26.50	28.14	29.91	31.86	34.00
Shortfall			0.36	1.09	2.14	3.50

As can be seen from the forecast, sticking to the board's parameters results in a future cash shortfall in Year 2 onwards. This can be addressed by either:

- increasing borrowings—which the board are reluctant to do, or
- issuing more shares—this would involve a rights issue. There is no guarantee of existing shareholders taking up their rights to buy ordinary shares at a discount to market price, and those that did not participate would see their shareholding diluted.

Other actions the board could take include:

- reducing the dividend, which could have detrimental effect on the market price of the shares, and in Years 4 and 5 eliminating the dividend entirely would not solve the problem
- creating more business by using their assets more efficiently. Net assets are only 125% of turnover which is quite low. This could mean they are carrying a lot of liabilities in the form of payables or that the non-current asset base is old and heavily depreciated
- improving the profit margin and generating more income would be a partial solution
- if the directors decide to issue more shares this will increase the dividend payout

Clearly the decision is far from straightforward and will probably involve more detailed analysis and a combination of approaches to dealing with the issue. The board is aware of the problem in good time and should be able to devote effort and time into properly planning a strategy to deal with the shortfall.

Sensitivity analysis and fixed costs

Strategic planning requires evaluation of a range of options and consequently a series of evaluations will be prepared using different projections of revenues and costs so as to arrive at what looks like a realistic and achievable estimate of future performance.

However management approach this they have to consider two key aspects of forecasting:

- The margin generated by their range of products and services
- The level of fixed costs which have to be met

It is possible, using Excel, to carry out a basic sensitivity analysis to look at a range of options and possibilities. Here is an example of a company selling a product that, on their probable outcome budget estimate gives them a net profit after fixed costs of £32 000. However, management want to look at a range of what-if? scenarios at different prices and different levels of sales.

Using the data table function in Excel, a table of values can be prepared.

USING A DATA TABLE

The company has prepared a budget based on its probable outcome for the next financial period.
The basic information on which the budget was prepared is as follows:

Original budget—basic data

Sales (units)	5 000
Price per unit (£)	100
Variable cost per unit (£)	55
Rent	80 000
Salaries	100 000
Other fixed costs	13 000

So, in summary, the budget looks like this:

Income statement based on original budget

	£
Revenues	500 000
Variable costs	275 000
Gross margin	225 000
Rent	(80 000)
Salaries	(100 000)
Other fixed costs	(13 000)
Net profit	32 000

However, what would be the outcome based on a range of values?
Use Excel to create a data table.

Sensitivity analysis using a data table

Estimated sales (units)		3500	4000	5000	5500	6000
Suggested price range per unit	75	(123 000)	(113 000)	(93 000)	(83 000)	(73 000)
	90	(70 500)	(53 000)	(18 000)	(500)	17 000
	100	(35 500)	(13 000)	32 000	54 500	77 000
	110	(500)	27 000	82 000	109 500	137 000
	120	34 500	67 000	132 000	164 500	197 000
	130	69 500	107 000	182 000	219 500	257 000

This shows, as highlighted, that at lower price and/or volume levels the product makes a loss.

The reason for the loss is the £193 000 of fixed costs the business is carrying (salaries plus other fixed costs). At the lowest level of pricing and volume the company makes a loss of £123 000—so is not really covering fixed costs at all. Even if sales increased to 6000 units from 3500 units at a price of £75 per unit, the company still doesn't make a profit.

This form of sensitivity analysis has made several positions clear to management:

- The level of fixed costs is forcing them to sell at particular prices and particular quantities in order to make a profit
- If the pricing per unit is flexible and they can sell at a higher price, the number they have to sell to make a reasonable profit is reduced
- If the price of £100 per unit is considered reasonable, the effect on profit of selling an additional 500 or 1000 units is considerable. It may be worth spending money on a promotional campaign

Even with this relatively simple example, it is easy to see the value of this technique and the way that it can influence strategic decision-making.

For example, management will have to consider:

- Reducing fixed costs in order to increase their flexibility on pricing
- Increasing the margin by either price increases or reducing variable costs
- Considering the market, what is a realistic market price? Could they sell, for example, 5000 units at £110 instead of £100 which would increase the margin by £10 per unit and so bring them an additional £50 000 profit? Conversely, if the market was very competitive and they had to reduce the price to £90 with no additional increase in sales above 5000 units, they would be plunged into a loss.

Each situation is different and managers must make judgements according to the prevailing conditions, and be prepared to adapt to new situations if the market or the economic circumstances change.

Stakeholders

Stakeholder is the term used to describe those who have an interest in an organization. It used to be that management's primary duty was to make money for the shareholders in a commercial enterprise but, whilst that is still true, modern management has to have regard to many more interested parties.

The two most obvious classes of stakeholder are the people or entities which own the business and those who work for it. However there are, of course, many more and management has to have regard to them also these days. Thinking about who is involved in the business soon reveals that suppliers and customers are involved, the bank that lends money to the business have also got a vested interest in it.

Figure 10.3 illustrates the stakeholders in a typical commercial business.

All these stakeholders require information. Most of them have access to no more than the annual financial statements but some, principally the government and the tax authorities, often require a great deal more.

Others require specific information. For example, employees want their wages and salaries correctly calculated and paid to them on time with a payslip, but they also have an interest in the financial health of their employer, so would be interested in the annual financial accounts.

Requirements can be summarized as shown in Figure 10.4.

The accounting information system or management information system (MIS) must be able to produce all this information.

Note that not all information has to be financial. It could be quantitative information, giving details of units of output, numbers employed, delivery times, etc.

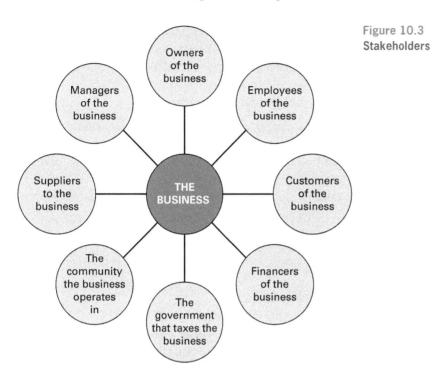

Figure 10.3
Stakeholders

Figure 10.4 Information needs of different stakeholders

Stakeholder	Relevant information
Staff	Wages information, bonus and overtime. Annual accounts
Owners/shareholders	Information to monitor their investment such as profit statements, annual accounts, etc.
Suppliers	Invoice processing and cheque payments. Information about ability to pay sums owed
Customers	Sales invoicing, banking of monies and debt collection
Lenders	Information to enable them to assess the ability of the business to repay and the value of any security for borrowings
Management	Budgets and management accounting information about how the business is performing
Government	Taxes, economic statistics
Community	Effect on local community, e.g. sponsorship information, employment statistics, etc.

Stop and think   Review the information available to different stakeholders in an organization you know about. Is the information enough for what they need? Would they benefit from additional information? Is any information deliberately concealed from them?

STRATEGIC OBJECTIVES TOWARDS STAKEHOLDERS   Management will have some strategic objectives towards stakeholders. These might include provision of safe working conditions and fair pay for employees, commitments to customers to deliver what was promised, commitments to suppliers to pay on time and so on.

Figure 10.5 summarizes some basic objectives towards stakeholders in the organization.

Figure 10.5 **Stakeholder objectives**

Stakeholders	Objectives
Staff	• Fair levels of remuneration for work done
	• Comfortable and safe working conditions
	• Career development opportunities
	• Pension scheme
	• Training
Owners/shareholders	• Survival of the organization
	• Maximize returns
	• Maintain share price
	• Expand business
Suppliers	• Maintain good trading relationship
	• Pay on time
	• Not to abuse buying power if in a dominant position
Customers	• Deliver product promised on time
	• Deliver quality promised
	• Deal honestly and fairly
	• Provide reliable supply
	• Provide after-care arrangements if required
Environment	• No pollution or toxic waste
	• Develop energy and water saving initiatives
	• Develop and deliver environmental policies
Government/society	• Comply with laws and regulations
	• Pay taxes due
Community	• Support local initiatives
	• Support local ventures wherever possible, e.g. local suppliers

Management may look to achieve all of these objectives as part of their operation of the organization. Many of them are non-financial and some of them may cost money to achieve but overall, in the modern world, all organizations are seen to have responsibilities wider than the self-interest of managers and shareholders.

Non-profit-making bodies

The management of non-profit-making bodies is rather different from that of a commercial enterprise insofar as the objectives are very different.

There are key differences:

● Objectives—the key objectives of a non-profit-making organization is to deliver a service. Charities are non-profit-making; their function is to deliver the objectives of the charity, be that saving lives at sea or feeding starving people.

- Financing—non-profit-making organizations are financed by grants, donations, legacies, subscriptions and a limited amount of commercial enterprise purely focused on fundraising.
- Cost structures—the main objectives of any non-profit-making organization are to keep administration and running costs to an absolute minimum. Their funds are devoted to delivering their objectives, so costs not directly related to that are at a minimum. Salaries tend to be lower, there are no additional benefits for staff and often they occupy premises which are either subsidized or are of relatively poor quality compared to richer commercial enterprises.

Many non-profit-making organizations use the principles of value for money (VFM).

THE THREE ES   VFM is often described and assessed in terms of the three Es of Economy, Efficiency and Effectiveness; sometimes a fourth E (for equity) is included:

- Economy—careful use of resources to minimize expense, time or effort
- Efficiency—delivering the same level of service for minimum input of cost, time or effort; or obtaining maximum benefit from a given level of input
- Effectiveness—delivering a successful outcome and meeting objectives as fully as possible
  The fourth E is:
- Equity—delivering services and using resources in a way that is fair to all

The objectives are not designed to save money. They are designed to eliminate waste and to deliver a service in the most efficient way consistent with the lowest cost for the level of quality required. Consequently, an organization adopting those principles will try to:

- reduce costs to the lowest compatible with level of service quality required
- keep waste to a minimum
- use efficient processes to deliver services
- measure the outputs and review processes used to achieve those outputs
- measure impact of programmes to determine whether or not they are effective

In certain areas, such as government and quasi-government bodies, indicators have been developed to measure the impact of VFM initiatives. These can be used to:

- pinpoint the strengths and weaknesses in the organization
- identify areas of efficiency and improve the use of resources
- compare financial performance with your similar or benchmark organizations
- demonstrate the commitment to improving efficiency

The management of a non-profit-making organization is, as we have outlined, different from managing a commercial entity but there are similarities. Both types of organization strive to maximize income and perform efficiently, they have responsibilities to staff and customers or service users and they have to use the financial information they generate to manage the organization in the best way they can.

Management of any organization at any level is far from easy and, as we have seen in these modules, requires a lot of the right kind of information delivered in the right way to the right people. It is the role of management accounting to deliver that information.

Test yourself

1 Jumble plc has the following issued share capital throughout 20X8:
   200 000 ordinary shares of €1 and 50 000 10 per cent preference shares of €1.

   Jumble's financial statements for the year ended 31st December 20X8 showed the following:

	€	€
Net profit before taxation		80 000
Taxation		(20 000)
Net profit after taxation		60 000
Preference dividend	5 000	
Ordinary dividend	12 000	
		(17 000)
Retained profit for the year		€43 000

Jumble's EPS for 20X8 is:
a) 27.5 c
b) 21.5 c
c) 30.0 c
d) 24 c

2 Within a heart disease research charity match the following three elements of the value for money maxim with the appropriate measure.

Element	Measure
A Economy	(i) The number of new treatments available for heart disease patients
B Efficiency	(ii) The cost savings made due to economies of scale
C Effectiveness	(iii) The number of heart attack sufferers helped for every pound spent

a) A iii, B ii, C i
b) A iii, B i, C ii
c) A ii, B iii, C i
d) A i, B ii, C iii

3 Polly's Cakes has to make decisions about which cakes to make and which to buy-in from third party cake bakers. The transport costs to customers are a fixed charge if Polly makes the cakes itself. Which cakes should Polly make?

	Carrot cake	Fruit cake	Jam sponge
Estimated sales	5000	2000	4000
Variable cost of ingredients per cake	0.40	0.80	0.40
Variable cost of wages per cake	0.10	0.12	0.25
Fixed overhead per cake	0.30	0.30	0.30
Transport costs to customers	$2500	$800	$2000
Costs to buy in from external bakers	$1.40	$1.60	$1.00

a) Buy in fruit and jam
b) Make all in house
c) Buy in jam only
d) Buy in all three

4 Which of the following statements are True or False?   ✔   ✔

	True	False
One of the key objectives of a quasi-government organization is to use the funds it has for the purpose for which they were intended.		
Earnings per share is a measure of the ability of management.		
Free cash flow is the amount of profit generated after tax minus depreciation		
Non-profit-making organizations will always try to keep administration costs to a minimum.		

5 Bigly Parts makes a component for the aircraft industry. At the moment it uses a specific machine to make the parts. The costs of using the machine are €10 per unit, of which €1 is fixed machine lease cost. Bigly makes 10 000 components per year on the machine.

   Bigly can buy in the same component for €9.50 from another manufacturer. It can rent the machine out to a car parts manufacturer for €6000.

   Bigly's management consider renting out the machine and buying in the components. If they do so how will this affect the results?
   a) Increase costs by €1000
   b) Increase profits by €1000
   c) Increase costs by €5000
   d) Increase profits by €5000

6 Which of the following is the generally accepted primary strategic objective of a commercial company?
   a) The maximization of a company's profit
   b) The maximization of shareholders wealth
   c) The pursuit of new opportunities
   d) The sustained employment of the workforce

7 A firm has the following extract from its income account:

	£m
Revenues	100
Variable costs	(20)
Fixed costs	(50)
Operating profit	30
Interest payable	(20)
Profit before tax	£10

What would be the effect of a 10 per cent drop in revenues?
   a) 10 per cent drop in profits
   b) 26.7 per cent drop in profits
   c) 30 per cent drop in profits
   d) 80 per cent drop in profits

8 The Department for Kingly Affairs in Ruritania has been reviewing its operations. On average its members work an eight-hour day and spend about six hours on Kingly Affairs and two hours on general administrative work. A new head of the department has just been appointed and has set out some new objectives. These are:

1. Cut departmental spend by 10 per cent
2. Increase the number of hours spent on Kingly Affairs to seven hours per day for each staff member
3. Obtain a score of 5 or above on a customer satisfaction survey

Which of the following options allocates these objectives to the correct VFM category?

Economy	Efficiency	Effectiveness
a) 1	2	3
b) 1	3	2
c) 2	1	3
d) 2	3	1

9 Which of the following statements are True or False?

	True	False
It is often easier to raise funds by borrowing than from shareholders.		
Earnings per share is based on the profit for the year after preference dividend divided by the amount of the share capital.		
Sensitivity analysis enables management to consider a range of options.		
ROCE is a measure of the efficient use of assets in the business.		

10 Billybob is reviewing a possible capital project. The initial outlay for the machinery will be £1 600 000 and at the end of seven years it can be sold for £200 000. The equipment will be depreciated on a straight line basis.

It is expected that the project will generate inflows as to:

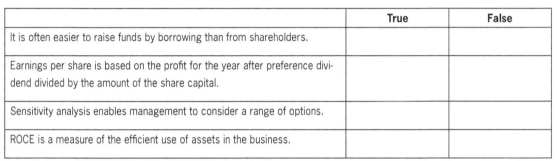

Year	1	2	3	4	5	6	7
Inflow	200	400	800	800	600	400	300

What is the ROCE of the project over the seven-year period?

a) 71.4 per cent
b) 42.8 per cent
c) 33.3 per cent
d) 37.5 per cent

This is the end of the course. We hope that it has been enjoyable and instructive and that the content has provided a good grounding into the fundamentals of management accounting.

Clearly there is a lot more to learn in more advanced courses as accounting is a wide and varied subject. However, if the basics are learned thoroughly more advanced topics should hold no terrors for the student as much can be worked out from first principles.

We trust that you have enjoyed working through these modules.

Test yourself

1 The following financial information relates to MFZ Co, a listed company:

Year	20X8	20X7	20X6
Profit before interest and tax ($m)	18.3	17.7	17.1
Profit after tax ($m)	12.8	12.4	12.0
Dividends ($m)	5.1	5.1	4.8
Equity market value ($m)	56.4	55.2	54.0

MFZ Co has 12 million ordinary shares in issue and has not issued any new shares in the period under review. The company is financed entirely by equity.

The annual report of MFZ Co states that the company has three financial objectives:

Objective 1: To achieve growth in profit before interest and tax of 4 per cent per year

Objective 2: To achieve growth in earnings per share of 3.5 per cent per year

Objective 3: To achieve total shareholder return of 5 per cent per year. Total shareholder return in this case is calculated as growth in market value plus dividends.

Required

Analyse and discuss the extent to which MFZ Co has achieved each of its stated objectives.

(ACCA)

2 DonkeySave is a charity devoted to the rescue of abandoned donkeys worldwide. It is funded by a mixture of grants, subscriptions from members and the sale of donkey-related items.

It is currently reviewing its financial position for the next five years. The management accountants have estimated the income for those years to be:

	£000's
Current Year	140
Year 1	156
Year 2	174
Year 3	196
Year 4	216
Year 5	253

The charity must retain a surplus of 10 per cent of its income to increase the capital base of the charity. Total assets less current liabilities (net assets) are estimated at 120 per cent of income.

The charity is allowed to borrow to the extent that its long-term borrowings amount to no more than 10 per cent of its net assets.

At the start of the current year, the statement of financial position showed that the capital account comprising all the retained surpluses of the charity was £151 000 and borrowings were £17 000.

Required

a) Prepare a forecast that shows the position of the charity for the years under review starting with the current year.

b) Comment on the results and any actions the board of management of the charity should take in view of the results of the forecast.

Glossary

'Above the line' items in an Income Statement shown as part of pre tax profit.

Accounting concepts not to be confused with accounting policies. These are four fundamental concepts, accruals, consistency, prudence and going concern, which form the framework for and underlie the principle of preparing a set of financial statements.

Accounting policies the rules relating to accounting for certain types of transaction adopted by the company. These may be determined by international accounting standards.

Accounting ratios a series of ratios which show the financial health or otherwise of the business. Includes ratios such as Gross Profit %, Inventory turnover, Receivables Days etc.

Accruals the accounts an organization prepares cover a fixed amount of time.

Activity cost driver the activity which drives the total costs within an Activity Cost Pool.

Activity cost pool indirect cost grouped by a particular activity e.g. materials purchasing.

Agency theory when the business is owned, effectively, by strangers. The managers or directors are agents for the investors or shareholders.

Amortisation amount written off the value of an intangible asset.

Annual General Meeting a meeting of shareholders to approve, or otherwise, the annual financial statements and to transact other business of the company such as the (re) appointment of directors and auditors.

'Below the line' items in an Income Statement shown after the pre tax profit e.g. taxation, dividends.

Capital an amount of cash or other assets contributed by the individuals invested in a business.

Charge out rate the rate at which an employee is charged to a job to recover the costs of that employee, overheads and a profit component.

Companies legal entities including limited liability partnerships.

Contribution the difference between the sales value and the variable costs of a product or service.

Control objectives what the system is designed to achieve in terms of the control over transactions.

Cost centre an activity or area where costs are collated to ascertain the cost of that activity or area.

Cost plus a basis for setting prices for a product or service based on the cost of producing the product or service plus a profit margin or mark up.

Credit note document used to cancel or amend an invoice requiring a refund or cancellation due to a failure to supply goods or services of the appropriate quality.

Critical success factors (CSF) objectives necessary to achieve in order to achieve the organization's goals. Conversely, failing to achieve one CSF means failing to achieve the goal, thus the name 'Critical'.

Economic life the useful life of an asset to a business.

Feedback loop a process whereby the actual results arising from a planned course of action are fed back so as to assist management in revising their activities in order to achieve planned objectives.

Financial accounts accounts prepared reporting the results for an accounting period.

Fixed cost cost which does not change with level of activity.

Goal congruence all of the separate parts or divisions of an organisation should work towards the same goals or within the same strategic framework to promote the best interests of the organisation.

Historical cost convention the convention that financial accounts always record the results of a financial period just ended.

Idle time a period during which an employee is not working productively but is still being paid.

Impairment loss of value of tangible assets due to obsolescence, damage or other reason.

Income statement the income statement shows the results of the organization's activities for the period.

Incremental costs these are new costs which will have to be included in the factors relating to a decision to take on a contract or not.

Intangible asset an asset with value but no physical presence e.g. a patent or trade mark.

Internal controls controls within an accounting system to ensure that the system objectives are achieved.

International Accounting Standards a series of standards developed by the International Accounting Standards

Boards and designed to ensure consistency of presentation and reliability of financial information in company accounts.

Job sheet or job card document on which the cost build up of materials and labour etc is recorded and summarised.

Joint and several liability if one partner in a partnership is unable to pay the debts of an entity, all the other partners are liable for their share of any debts in addition to their own.

Key budget factor the limiting factor in an organisation which sets a restriction on the capacity of the organisation. It could be production capacity, staff numbers, size of a market etc.

Key Performance Indicators (KPIs) a measurable value that demonstrates how effectively a company is achieving key business objectives or CSFs.

Lodgements old fashioned word for payments into a bank account i.e. banking cash or cheques.

Management accounts management accounts are designed to report information to be used as an aid to managing the business. They include budgets and forecasts and also analyses of actual performance against those budgets.

Management Information System (MIS) a system designed to record, collate and report financial information in a format required by managers.

Material an item that is significant enough to affect the economic decisions of a user of the financial statements.

Net Book Value original cost or revalued amount less accumulated depreciation.

Nominal value the amount each shareholder has to pay for each share.

NOPAT – Net Operating Profit After Tax a calculated profit used in EVA calculations which excludes non cash items such as depreciation and adds back costs which add value such as marketing costs.

Opportunity cost the cost of giving up a viable alternative course of action.

Overhead recovery rate the amount to be added to the cost of a product using absorption costing principles to cover the cost of indirect overheads.

Overheads indirect costs—generally the general running expenses of an organisation not directly related to the costs of a product or service.

Partnerships a group of sole traders working together in a common business, generally governed by a partnership agreement.

PBIT Profit before Interest and Tax—a figure used in financial analysis broadly equivalent to operating profit.

Posting entering a transaction in accounting records.

Present value the present value of a stream of income or expense is the sums involved expressed at today's value.

Money loses value over time i.e.$100 in two year's time is worth less than $100 today simply because having $100 today can mean that the money can be invested and used to earn a return. The value is calculated using Present Value Tables which give a discount factor to be applied to the future sums of money.

Prime cost the direct cost of a product or service before the allocation of any indirect costs or overhead.

Process costing a method of costing used mainly in manufacturing where units are continuously mass-produced through one or more processes.

Profit centre a part of an organization which incurs and reports both revenues and costs and consequently profitability.

Provision an estimated amount included in the financial statements based on information available.

Purchase Returns Day Book day book for recording the receipt of credit notes from suppliers.

Quantitative information information which is expressed in units. These can be financial e.g. £'s or $'s or non financial such as kilos or hours.

Reserves the remaining profits after paying the dividend.

Residual Value scrap or resale value of an asset after it has been fully depreciated.

Share capital the amount subscribed to fund the business in the long term. This is put into the company by the shareholders.

Sole Traders small businesses that work for themselves and keep all their profits and pay tax based on their financial result at the year's end.

Stakeholder a person or organisation with a financial interest in a business.

Sunk costs money already expended on goods or services so they are irrelevant costs in decision making.

Transactions on credit sales of purchases of goods and services where no payment or receipt is made at the time of a transaction but is made at a later date.

Unit cost cost of one unit of provision i.e. 1 kg of material or 1 hour of labour.

Value for Money (VFM) the optimal use of resources to achieve intended outcomes. This usually involves programmes to maximise the use of resources using the principles of economy, efficiency and effectiveness.

Variable cost cost which varies according to the level of activity.

Variance divergence from a budgeted standard.

Variance analysis analysing a variance to establish its cause. This can either be usage or volume or cost changes for the actual level of output.

Index